GW00786296

Penguin Books Australia Ltd
487 Maroondah Highway, PO Box 257
Ringwood, Victoria 3134, Australia
Penguin Books Ltd
Harmondsworth, Middlesex, England
Penguin Putnam Inc.
375 Hudson Street, New York, New York 10014, USA
Penguin Books Canada Limited
10 Alcorn Avenue, Toronto, Ontario, Canada M4V 3B2
Penguin Books (NZ) Ltd
Cnr Rosedale and Airborne Roads, Albany, Auckland, New Zealand
Penguin Books (South Africa)(Pty) Ltd
5 Watkins Street, Denver Ext 4, 2094, South Africa
Penguin Books India (P) Ltd
11, Community Centre, Panchsheel Park, New Delhi, 110 017, India

First published by Penguin Books Australia Ltd 2000

10 9 8 7 6 5 4 3 2

Copyright © Penguin Books Australia Ltd 2000

Cover photograph by Hans and Judy Beste/Lochman Transparencies
Digital imaging by Paul Fenton, Xelle Design
Text design by Lynn Twelftree
Typeset in 11pt Adobe Garamond by Midland Typesetters
Made and printed in Australia by Australian Print Group

National Library of Australia
Cataloguing-in-Publication data:

    The little book of Australia
    ISBN 0 14 029691 3
    1. Australia – Social life and customs – 1990–.
    2. Australia – Statistics. 3. Australia – Description and travel.

994.07

www.penguin.com.au

THE LITTLE BOOK OF
AUSTRALIA

PENGUIN BOOKS

AUSTRALIA

Introduction

What distinguishes Australia from other nations? 'Australia Fair', 'God's own country', 'A land of sweeping plains'. These are the epithets that have been used to describe Australia's assets, its natural wealth, and its easy-going, prosperous lifestyle. Australia is a sparsely populated country of immense natural resources. The flora and fauna is incredibly diverse, and many species are unique to this country.

It has some of the best beaches in the world, and one of the longest coastlines.

Australia is one of the world's longest-inhabited countries, and the Australian Aborigines have one of the world's oldest cultures. Australia was the last great landmass to be 'discovered' by Europeans. Since these settlers arrived two hundred years ago, Australia has become one of the world's most multicultural countries. One of the country's greatest strengths has been its ability to become the home for so many different cultures.

So, what does it mean to be Australian? Australians pride themselves on concepts such as an appreciation of mateship, egalitarianism and fair play. They have a keen sense of humour, and love to send themselves up. Australia is also peopled by millions of fanatical sports lovers.

In this book you'll find a range of interesting quotations, facts and trivia about Australia, and – who knows? – you may even discover what makes this country really tick . . .

"

It will take a century to work this miscellaneous gathering of rude people out of the scum. As they get money, they will, however, as in America, in time give their children some education; but out of them will grow, as is plain to see, a go-ahead, self-confident, Yankee sort of people.

William Howitt

"

MYSTERY RECIPE

Sift together 2 cups of self-raising flour
with ½ teaspoon salt. Mix in 1 cup of
milk to make a dough. Knead lightly, pat
into a round shape, place into a tin and
bake in a hot oven for 20 minutes.
Turn out and eat.
You've just devoured a Swagman's
Damper!

An Australian farmer's lament:
'First the drought killed some of the sheep, then the flood drowned some more, and now the grass has grown so high, I can't find what's left of 'em!'

I'm an Australian born and bred
Long in the leg
And thick in the head.

Anon

Australians have a love affair with 'big things'. One cynic has called this the 'edifice complex'! We have 'big things' all over the country – the Big Pineapple, Big Guitar, Big Banana, Big Cow, Big Prawn and even the Big Ned Kelly. These monuments are certainly popular tourist attractions, but some people say they're just examples of monumental bad taste!

"This is the most democratic place I have ever been in. And the more I see of democracy the more I dislike it. It just brings everything down to the mere vulgar level of wages and prices, electric light and water closets, and nothing else. You never knew anything so nothing, nichts, nullus, niente, as the life here . . . I feel if I lived in Australia for ever I should never open my mouth once to say one word that meant anything.

D. H. Lawrence

The platypus is said to be a danger to itself. This strange duck-billed and beaver-tailed creature is so aggressive that many males of the species have killed each other fighting for limited territory. This sort of behaviour makes the work of animal protectionists even more difficult. How do you protect an animal hell-bent on destroying itself?

Once a jolly swagman camped
by a billabong,
Under the shade of a coolibah tree,
And he sang as he watched and waited
till his billy boiled,
'Who'll come a-waltzing Matilda with me?'

A. B. ('Banjo') Paterson

Waltzing Matilda
Boo for St Kilda
Up with Fitzroy
And down with Geelong!

Anon

In Australia the word 'Matilda' was commonly used to mean a swag or a bedroll, which 'swaggies' had to cuddle instead of a real 'Matilda' while out in the bush. (In Germany the word 'Matilda' was a common name for 'girlfriend'!)

The very first day we landed
All on that fatal shore
The planters they came round us
About three score or more
So they harnessed us up like horses
And they fit us out of hand
And they yoked us up to the plough
my boys
To plough Van Dieman's Land.

Anon

Australians all let us rejoice,
For we are young and free,
We've golden soil and wealth for toil;
Out home is girt by sea;

Peter Dodds McCormick wrote these words
in 1878; they are now part of Australia's national
anthem, 'Advance Australia Fair'.

Question: What was Ben Lexcen
(1936–88) renowned for?

Answer: He was a marine designer who created the *Australia II*, a yacht known for its 'winged keel'. In 1983 it won the America's Cup, the first time in 132 years that America had lost the cup.

OBITUARY NOTICE

In affectionate remembrance of English cricket, which died at The Oval on 29th August, 1882. Deeply lamented by a large circle of sorrowing friends and acquaintances. RIP. The body will be cremated and the ashes taken to Australia.

Sporting Times (1882)

Lindy Chamberlain's trial is one of the most puzzling (and some say shameful) legal cases in Australia's history. Her conviction for murdering her baby Azaria was later overturned, though not before she had served several years in prison. She always swore that the baby was taken by a dingo while she and her family were camping near Ayers Rock. The body has never been found, and the disappearance remains unsolved.

Australia's population in June 1999 was 18 918 400. But five of the capital cities – Sydney, Melbourne, Brisbane, Adelaide and Perth – account for 60% of that population, with 11 951 945 residents. Of those, 3 986 723 live in Sydney. There are vast tracts of the inland that are completely unpopulated.

RECIPE

BANANA FRITTERS

Make up a standard batter recipe, and then add chopped slices of banana. Cook the fritter on each side until the mixture bubbles, turning when you are sure both sides are browned. Drain on absorbent paper and lightly dust with sugar before serving with ice-cream or cream.

Question: How many times have the Olympics been held in Australia, and when and where?

Answer: Twice – Melbourne in 1956, and Sydney in 2000.

John 'Jackie' Howe was a legendary shearer. In 1892 Jackie sheared 321 merino sheep at Queensland's Alice Downs Station in 8 hours and 40 minutes! This is believed to be a record, not only in Australia, but worldwide.

Cane toads were introduced to Australia in 1935 when 102 of them were released in Gordonvale. They were supposed to eat the Brayback beetle, which was threatening the sugar cane crops in North Queensland. Unfortunately they ate everything but the beetle, and their numbers have multiplied astronomically. They have been sighted as far south as Port Macquarie in NSW and in the NT. Scientists didn't reckon on the toad becoming a complete pest!

Question: Sir Donald Bradman is one of Australia's most famous figures. In what field did he become famous?

Answer: Cricket. Sir Donald Bradman turned 90 in 1998. He scored his first century at the age of twelve and was the first living Australian to have his portrait on a postage stamp.

Did you know that there are fifteen nations that gave women the vote before the US did so in 1920? New Zealand was first, in 1893. Australia gave women the vote in 1902.

> The country looks as though a great ash-heap has been spread out there, and mulga and firewood planted – and neglected. The country looks just as bad for a hundred miles round Hungerford, and beyond that it gets worse – a blasted, barren wilderness that doesn't even howl. If it howled it would be a relief.

Henry Lawson

Question: Australia has only one truly
national daily newspaper.
What is it called?

A

Answer: The *Australian.*

66

No mistake, it was a real wilderness –
nothing but trees, goannas, dead timber
and bears, and the nearest house – Dwyers
– was three miles away. I often wonder
how the women stood it for the first few
years; and I can remember mother, when
she was alone, used to sit on a log, where
the lane is now, and cry for hours. Lonely!
It *was* lonely!

Arthur Hoey Davis ('Steele Rudd') 99

Paul Hogan (1940–) is one of Australia's best-known overseas personalities. He began his television career as a guest on a news program, when he was a rigger on the Sydney Harbour Bridge. He has since become a multi-millionaire through enterprises such as his *Crocodile Dundee* movies. He is the 'larrikin' comedian who typifies the humour best loved by Australian audiences.

Question: Name the field in which the following successful indigenous Australians work. Deborah Mailman; Aden Ridgeway; Noel Pearson; Cathy Freeman.

Answer: Deborah Mailman – acting;
Aden Ridgeway – politics;
Noel Pearson – Aboriginal activism and
native title legislation;
Cathy Freeman – athletics.

Australia has the world's largest rock, Uluru (Ayers Rock), which is 348 metres high. It also has the world's largest reef. The Great Barrier Reef is more than 2000 kilometres long, and stretches from an area out from Bundaberg or Gladstone in Queensland and up the coast to the Torres Strait. Most of it is 2 million years old, but some sections are 18 million years old. It consists of over 400 types of coral and is home to 1500 species of fish.

Lamingtons are an Australian delicacy. They consist of squares of sponge cake carefully 'rolled' in chocolate icing and then in coconut. Children are fond of them as lunchtime treats, and adults have also been known to pack a lamington in their lunchboxes. Delicious!

Question: Name the current and the previous three Prime Ministers of Australia.

Answer: John Howard, Paul Keating, Bob Hawke and Malcolm Fraser.

The Tasmanian Tiger (or thylacine),
sometimes known as the Tasmanian Wolf,
is a large marsupial native to Tasmania.
Most believe it is extinct. The last tiger in
captivity was photographed in 1935,
though each year there are several
unconfirmed sightings of the animal.
Its jaws are said to open wider than those
of any other mammal.

Many Australian words have been inaccurately described as 'Aboriginal' words. The early European settlers did not understand that there were many hundreds of groups of native peoples and that each group spoke a different language. For example, Captain James Cook recorded that the word 'kangaroo' was used around the Endeavour River, but it was not recognised elsewhere or, indeed, years later by Aborigines in the area itself, when spoken there by subsequent visitors.

Edna Everage is perhaps the most famous
Australian lady of all. A character invented
by comedian Barry Humphries (1934–),
she has been included in his repertoire
now for decades. And she doesn't look a
day over thirty (?!).

Bush tucker has recently become widely fashionable in Australia. Foods such as witchetty grubs, emu and kangaroo are now served in the best restaurants, often in recipes that employ an Asian influence. Chillied Crocodile with Mango Salsa? Tempting?

Question: What do Australians celebrate on Anzac Day, 25 April, every year?

Answer: The ill-fated landing of Australian and New Zealand Army Corps troops at Gallipoli in Turkey in 1915. The battle was a disaster, but the bravery of our soldiers has become emblematic of concepts such as mateship and fair play.

I also made acquaintance . . . with the flesh of the iguana and that especial delicacy, the eggs of the black snake. I learned, too, to plait dilly-bags, to chop sugar-bags . . . out of trees, to make drinking vessels from gourds . . . but English life is not adapted to the display of such accomplishments.

Rosa Campbell Praed

Australia's first miniskirt was sighted at
Flemington during the 1965 Melbourne
Cup. Model Jean Shrimpton ('the
Shrimp') made world headlines for daring
to show so much leg in the conservative
members' enclosure. The rest of Australia
was pretty shocked too!

Question: The legendary and notorious film actor Errol Flynn (1909–59) was born in which city in Australia?

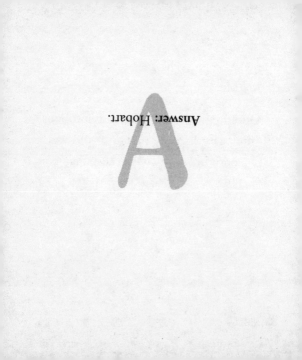

Answer: Hobart.

The very first all-Australian car produced by mass-production methods was the model 48-215, popularly known as the FX Holden. It was created in 1948 at Fishermans Bend, Victoria.

Earth is here so kind that just tickle her
with a hoe and she laughs with a harvest.

Douglas William Jerrold

Though Australia is said not to have a definitive cuisine, there are some favourite Aussie foods which have become uniquely identified with the country: a pie and peas; snags (sausages) on the barbie (barbecue); beer and prawns; pumpkin scones; and damper.

Peach Melba and Melba Toast are both named after Dame Nellie Melba (1861–1931). Dame Nellie was born Helen Porter Mitchell, the daughter of a Melbourne builder, and became an internationally famous opera singer. Peach Melba is a dessert made of peaches, ice-cream, whipped cream and raspberry syrup. Melba Toast is thinly sliced bread baked in the oven until crisp, and is also known as fairy toast.

Australia has several creatures that are in danger of extinction and that scientists are trying to save. The bilby, quokka and the numbat are three of them. Do you know what any of these animals look like?

> Palmerston . . . is filled with the boilings over of the great cauldron of Oriental humanity . . . Here are gathered together Canton coolies, Japanese pearl divers, Malays, Manilamen, Portuguese from adjacent Timor, Cingalese . . . Kipling tells what befell the man who 'tried to hustle the East', but the man who tried to hustle Palmerston would get a knife in him quick and lively.

A. B. ('Banjo') Paterson

Bunyips are mythical creatures that have provided poets and artists with inspiration for centuries. The word is said to derive from Aboriginal culture, and refers to a creature that inhabits swamps and billabongs. Australians who consider themselves upper class are called the 'bunyip aristocracy'.

Folk called the Bunyip cruel and wicked, and make the children tremble at its name . . . But it is only the lost soul of the ancient forest, that wanders abroad when the evening shadows deepen . . . At the coming of the white man to the South-Land where the gum trees grow, the Bunyip vanished, never more to be seen . . . But sometimes mystic guiding brings little lost ones safe home again.

Annie Rentoul

Question: What are the three most popular football codes in Australia, and when did they begin?

Answer: Rugby Union in 1864, National Rugby League (NRL) in 1908–9, and Australian Rules in 1858. (Soccer has also been played here since 1880.)

Cannibalism was a gruesome outcome of
the desperation experienced by many
convicts in the nineteenth-century
Australian colony. Some who escaped
from prisons such as Port Arthur were
forced to have recourse to this 'last resort'.
This human tragedy was well-documented
in Marcus Clarke's classic novel
For the Term of His Natural Life.

The eccentric Leonard Casley was so disillusioned with the government that in 1970 he 'created' his own state in WA; a principality called the Hutt River Province. Though it prints its own currency it is not recognised by any government and is populated by a handful of people.

Kalgoorlie in Western Australia boasts
being the world's largest electorate as it
extends over 2 255 278 square kilometres.

Stiffy and Mo were a famous Australian vaudeville team who shocked audiences with their bawdy humour in the 1920s. Mo went on to become a popular radio personality, famous for such memorable expressions as 'strike me lucky', 'you little trimmer', 'cheeky possum' and 'suck it and see'.

Australia has some unusual place names
that are tortuously difficult to say!
Oodnadatta, Wangaratta, Woolloomooloo
and Coolangatta are just a few. Which
have you found difficult to pronounce?

Illawarra, Mittagong,
Parramatta, Wollongong,
If you wouldn't become an orang-outang,
Don't go to the wilds of Australia.

Anon

Ken Done (1940–) is one Australian artist whose works are widely known. His distinctive use of primary colours coupled with his familiar subjects, which are often recognisable Australian landmarks, have made his work very popular overseas.

Australians love their golf. It is said that Australia has more public golf courses than any other nation in the world.

Question: Who is the most famous expatriate Australian golfer?

A

Answer: Greg Norman.

Australia's pop stars have been achieving a lot on the world stage. Artists like Natalie Imbruglia, Kylie Minogue and Tina Arena, and bands such as Savage Garden, Yothu Yindi and INXS are some of the big successes in recent decades.

Australia's governor-general has only once exercised his right to dismiss a government. Sir John Kerr dismissed the Whitlam Labor government in 1975, and the Liberal–Country Party coalition government was returned to power under Malcolm Fraser.

Australia's population has always been a multicultural one. Since federation the number of residents born overseas slumped between the 1930s and 40s, and has remained fairly static for the last two decades. However, the overall percentage of Australian residents not born here is now approximately 22% – as it was in 1900!

The highest recorded temperature in Australia, taken at Cloncurry, Queensland, in January 1899, was 53.1°C, and the lowest was −23°C, taken at Charlotte Pass, NSW, in June 1994.

Bananas in Pyjamas are amongst Australia's most marketable exports. The loveable B1 and B2 first appeared on the ABC's *Playschool* program, before branching out to become stars of their own children's program, which has been translated and aired in 69 countries. They have spawned merchandise, books and videos. Not bad for two bananas who started out as a nursery rhyme way back in 1972!

I have a holy horror of babies, to whatever nationality they may belong; but for general objectionableness I believe there are none to compare to the Australian baby . . . He has breathed the free air of Australian independence too early to have much regard for the fifth commandment . . . The child has no restrictions put on his superabundant animal spirits, and he runs wild in the most extraordinary, and often to elders, unpleasant freaks.

R.E.N. Twopenny

Australians love a challenge. The longest debate ever held here was conducted by the Melbourne University Debating Society, between 20 February and 6 March 1989, on the topic of 'Should Melbourne host the 1996 Olympics'. Apparently 350 people spoke during this marathon event!

Kookaburra sits on the old gum tree,
Merry, merry king of the bush is he,
Laugh! Kookaburra, laugh! Kookaburra,
Gay your life must be.

Anon. These lines are from a popular song about
the laughing bird, native to Australia.

The Melbourne Cup is Australia's premier racing event and carries the largest prize of all. It began in 1861, apparently because of the vast wealth being made on the gold fields at the time.

Question: Which horse won the first cup, the 1930 cup, and the 1999 cup?

Answer: The first cup winner was Archer. The 1930 cup winner was the famous Phar Lap. The 1999 cup winner was Rogan Josh.

The first Aboriginal person to be elected
to parliament was Neville Thomas
Bonner, who was selected to take
a senate seat in 1971.

There is only one known bushranger who was said to be of Asian descent. Sam Poo, a Chinese highway robber, was eventually hanged for his trouble.

Question: What have Ern Malley, Helen Demidenko and Wanda Koolmatrie got in common?

Answer: They are all false names used in three of Australia's most famous literary hoaxes.

The Miss Australia competition has been a long-lived tradition until recently, when the charity-sponsoring competition officially ended. The first Miss Australia was selected in 1926; she was Miss Beryl Mills of Geraldton, WA, and she was only nineteen. Judges described her as a 'splendid stamp of glorious womanhood'.

The oldest criminal on record ever to be charged in Australia was Thomas Wright, who in 1839, at age 102, was convicted for forging. He had been transported here in 1801, and later died in jail at the age of 105.

The first solo flight from England to Australia was made by a boy from Bundaberg, Queensland. Bert Hinkler left London in February 1928 and took sixteen days to reach Australia where he was greeted ecstatically by a crowd of well-wishers. He died when his plane crashed in Italy in 1933.

The Cricketers' Arms in Surry Hills, Sydney, was the first gay men's hotel in Australia when it opened in 1972. It remains one of the most popular gay venues in Sydney.

Question: Slim Dusty, Troy Cassar-Daley and John Williamson – these three famous Australians all work in the same industry. What is it?

Answer: Country music.

Australians love their Vegemite! This strong-flavoured vegetable extract is used as a spread on bread, toast and biscuits. In 1910, Marmite, a yeast extract, was registered in Australia, and enterprising Fred Walker produced a competing vegetable product. He called it Parwill (Marmite – mother might; Parwill – Father will). The name didn't take off, so Walker conducted a public competition to rename the product – and Vegemite was born!

Aussie blokes (and sheilas!) love a cool ale. Henry Lawson, who was fond of a tipple, was said to have delivered the memorable quote, 'Beer makes you feel as you ought to feel without a beer'.

Incredibly, Mt Isa, despite its relatively small population, is said to be the biggest city in the world in terms of size, for it has an area of 41 225 square kilometres.

"

I love a sunburnt country,
A land of sweeping plains,
Of ragged mountain ranges,
Of droughts and flooding rains.

Dorothea Mackellar

"

Question: What distinction does Evonne Goolagong-Cawley have as a sporting star?

Answer: She was the first Aboriginal woman to win the women's singles at Wimbledon. She won in 1971.

Mt Kosciuszko in the NSW Snowy Mountains is the highest mountain in Australia, at 2229 metres. The first people to climb it were Sir Paul de Strzelecki and James Macarthur, in 1840.

Australia's on the wallaby
Just listen to the coo-ee;
There's shadeless trees and sun-scorched
plains,
All asking us to toil;
But Australia's sons are weary
And the billy's on the boil.

Anon

The 1930 penny is a collectors' item in Australia. No such coins were officially struck that year, as the country was in the depths of Depression. They say that some coins were 'unofficially' struck at the mint purely as 'souvenirs' for visitors, and these days they are worth a small fortune!

The Eureka Stockade, an outbreak led by
Peter Lalor, was a revolt by miners at
Ballarat against the licence fee which
virtually made it impossible for them to
mine for gold. The Eureka flag was raised
in 1854, and led to success for the miners
in their claim. It has been remembered
ever since for its iconic significance.

"

The hot wind, born amid the burning
sand of the interior of the vast Australian
continent, sweeps over the scorched and
cracking plains, to lick up their streams
and wither herbage in its path, until it
meets the waters of the great south bay;
but in its passage across the straits it is reft
of its fire, and sinks, exhausted with its
journey, at the feet of the terraced slopes
of Launceston.

Marcus Clarke

"

Ned Kelly's final shoot-out was a real event – a thousand people gathered outside Jones' Hotel at Glenrowan in 1880 to watch the infamous Kelly Gang's last hurrah. Kelly's armour was one of the things which set him apart in the public memory, making him such a legendary figure. After his capture at Glenrowan, he was sentenced to hang, and gruesome legend has it that they made a death mask of his face, and a tobacco pouch from his skin!

Question: One of Australia's most widely recognised landmarks was designed by an architect who has never seen the finished building. What building is it?

Answer: The Sydney Opera House was designed by Danish architect Jørn Utzon (1918–), who left Australia in 1966, before the project's completion in 1973.

The *Bulletin* was the magazine that made many of Australia's best-loved writers famous. The renowned J.F. Archibald and John Haynes began the paper in 1880. Dubbed the 'Bushman's Bible', it published works by Henry Lawson and 'Banjo' Paterson amongst many others, and still exists today (albeit with a much-changed format, style and content).

"

Another peculiarity of this country is the incessant galloping that all the horses keep up. You never see anyone ride at a trot or walk; it is always a hard gallop uphill and downhill, all the same. I should think it must wear out the horses very soon, and you do see a lot of skeletons lying about in the bush and by the waterholes and creeks. Some of them are bullocks, but the greater number are horses . . . (whose) bones are bleached white by the Australian sun.

Rachel Henning (1862)

"

Australia's vegetation has experienced a long period of uninterrupted evolution in isolation. About 55 million years ago the country broke from the supercontinent of Gondwanaland. For all that time the unique species of Australian fauna and flora have been able to develop without interference – that is, until the arrival of European settlers about 200 years ago.

Our Andy's gone with cattle now –
Our hearts are out of order –
With drought he's gone to battle now
Across the Queensland border.

Henry Lawson

Upon arriving with the First Fleet at Botany Bay, Captain Arthur Phillip wrote to Lord Sydney, that when he saw a group of natives wading into the water, 'their confidence and manly behaviour made me give the name Manly Cove to this place'. This 'place', in Sydney, New South Wales, is still called Manly to this day.

Called the Never-Never, the Maluka loved
to say, because they who have lived in it
and loved it, Never-Never voluntarily
leave it . . . Others – the unfitted – will
tell you that it is so called because they
who succeed in getting out of it swear
they will Never-Never return to it. But we
who have lived in it, and loved it, and left
it, know that our hearts can Never-Never
rest away from it.

Mrs Aeneas (Jeannie) Gunn

In Queensland it is still constitutional law that all hotels/bars ('pubs') are required to have a railing outside to tie up a horse.

The largest state in the world is Western Australia. It covers over 2.5 million square kilometres (1 million square miles).

Question: Try these favourite Aussie expressions – what do they mean? Don't come the raw prawn with me, mate! As sharp as a tack. Like a possum up a gum tree. Like a hornet in a bottle.

Answer: Don't try to pull the wool over my eyes. As clever as can be. Moving quickly. Extremely angry.

Many enormous early-Australian properties still survive today. For example, Alexandria Station on the Barkly Tableland, Northern Territory, was 11 250 square miles in area. That made it one-eighth the size of the entire state of Victoria! To travel from the southern boundary to the homestead you had to cover 103 miles. That's a long way to travel if you just want a nice hot cup of tea!

Australia's land area covers 7 682 320 square kilometres, making it almost the same size as the US and 50% greater in landmass than Europe.

"

Why, do you know, in order to curry
favour with the voters, the government
puts down a road wherever anybody wants
it – anybody that owns two sheep and a
dog; and by consequence we've got, in the
colony of Victoria, 800 railway stations,
and the business done at eighty of them
doesn't foot up twenty shillings a week.'

Mark Twain (1897)

"

Australia boasts the fastest insect in the world! The Australian dragonfly has a top speed of approximately 57kph.

Question: Who was Sydney named after?

Answer: Thomas Townshend, 1st Viscount Sydney, the British home secretary at the time the original settlement was founded.

The 'Jackeroo' is traditionally a 'gentlemanly rouseabout' employed by graziers on their stations. The word is said to have come from Jack Carew, the name of one of the earliest 'Jackeroos', though others say it derives from the slang 'Johnny Raw' which was slang for a 'new chum' i.e. one not used to such outdoor work. It evolved into 'Jack Raw', then 'Jackeroo'. Wherever the term came from it has survived. So where does the term 'Jillaroo' come from?

Click go the shears boys, click, click, click,
Wide as his blow and his hands
move quick,
The ringer looks around and is beaten
by a blow,
And curses the old snagger with the
blue-bellied 'joe'.

Anon

Australians are said to be 'prodigious' readers of magazines, and spend $23 million each month on their purchase. One of the most popular is the *Australian Women's Weekly*, which was established by Frank Packer, and has been going since 1933. It's the only *monthly* magazine to be called a *weekly*!

The 'Dump' was a strange form of currency used in the early days of the Australian colony. Since there was no colonial currency then, Macquarie, Governor of New South Wales, ordered that a small piece be cut from the centre of Spanish dollars, the outer ring being worth five shillings and the cut-out, or 'dump', to be worth one shilling and three pence.

Question: What sport is Susie Maroney known for?

Answer: Marathon swimming.

"

Sydney, in spite of its exquisite harbour
and lovely Botanical gardens, is a crude
chaotic place. It is seemingly inhabited by
a lower-middle class population suddenly
enriched; aggressive in manners and
blatant in dress . . . In this city there is
neither homeliness nor splendour; only
bad taste and cold indifference.

Beatrice Webb

"

The lady featured on the Australian $5 note, Caroline Chisholm, arrived in Australia in 1838. Chisholm was the first person to compile a cookery book for Australian women, entitled *The Bush Cookbook*. She began a campaign in 1838 to help young girls arriving in New South Wales by offering them refuge. Though not officially recognised, she was unofficially known as 'the emigrant's friend'.

Of all the birds I'd like to be
I'd like to be a sparra,
So I could sit on Princes Bridge
And help to fill the Yarra.

Anon

Melbourne is in reality pagan, but a sort
of worldly Presbyterianism has inflicted
itself upon its official presentment as the
social counterpart of the political
stagnation.

Francis Adams

Question: What was the name of the first Prime Minister of Australia?

Answer: Sir Edmund Barton.

Australia is the only English-speaking
country that has compulsory voting for
federal and state governments.

"

In point of beauty Port Darwin has few
equals; only two other harbours were ever
named, when a comparison with this one
was sought for – those of Sydney and Rio
de Janeiro. Having made the entrance of
this magnificent haven, we found
ourselves sailing into an immense space of
perfectly smooth water, where . . . the
whole British fleet might lie at anchor.

Harriet Douglas

A Mother's Offering to her Children by 'A Lady Long Resident in New South Wales' was the first children's book published in Australia. Published in 1841, it is a very teacherly text, and is full of dire warnings such as, 'dear children, endeavour to profit by the frequent warnings we have, of the uncertainty of life.' Children today would find it very hard going!

RECIPE

POTATO ROLLS

Boil and mash two pounds of potatoes, working an ounce of butter and some milk through them. Mix half a pint of yeast and a quarter of a pint of lukewarm water. Pour the whole on the two pounds of flour, knead it well, let it stand before the fire to rise and make it into rolls. Toast and butter after baking.

The Colonial Cook Book

'Tis of a wild Colonial boy, Jack Doolan
was his name,
Of poor but honest parents he was born
in Castlemaine.
He was his father's only hope, his mother's
only joy,
And dearly did his parents love the wild
Colonial boy.

Anon

Governor: Rebel? ha! ha! surely in joke;
Rebellion here – a mere puff of smoke.
What would the people of England say
A rebellion! how queer! in Botany Bay!

William Forster

Question: Dawn Fraser, Kieren Perkins and Shane Gould are all famous in Australia for what?

▶▶▶

Answer: They are all champion swimmers.

66

Let me slumber in the hollow where the
wattle blossoms wave,
With never stone or rail to fence my bed:
Should the sturdy station children pull the
bush flowers on my grave,
I may chance to hear them romping
overhead.

Adam Lindsay Gordon

99

International Test cricket and one-day matches are played in all state capitals in Australia every summer. In Melbourne, they are played at the famous Melbourne Cricket Ground (MCG), which is the world's largest cricket venue.

One of Australia's worst natural disasters was Cyclone Tracy which struck Darwin on early Christmas morning in 1974. 50–60% of houses in Darwin were destroyed, and of 11 200 houses, only about 400 were left intact. Winds were said to have reached 280kph at the cyclone's peak. Darwin has been largely rebuilt and residents hope that new building regulations will better protect them should such a disaster strike again.

European settlers in Australia have a long theatrical history. The first recorded live performance was in Sydney Cove in 1789, and was held in a hut prepared for this purpose. The oldest surviving theatre in Australia is the Theatre Royal in Hobart, which opened in 1837.

Question: Australians are renowned for their colourful use of slang. They describe each other using words like bonzer; bludger; cobber; cocky; galah; ocker. What do these words mean?

Answer: Bonzer – excellent; bludger – someone who imposes on others; cobber – friend or mate; cocky – can mean a cockatoo, a farmer or someone who's conceited; galah – a small cockatoo or a fool; ocker – boorish Australian or something distinctively Australian (as in humour).

Australia's horse population reached its peak in 1918 with 2 527 000 horses in the outback. Thereafter, things began to change, and these days there are less than a million horses in the country. Four-wheel drives, motor-bikes, trucks, helicopters and small aircraft have changed the way graziers manage their properties, and such technology, together with new forms of communication, has decreased the need for horses to be used.

> In any city, except Paris, Rome or some other great metropolis with innumerable attractions, a visitor with no great business to attend to cannot fail to be bored after quite a short time. Brisbane is quite a pretty town, it is true, but it bores you to death.

Edmond Marie Marin La Meslée

Skiing was established as a sport in Australia, twenty years before it started in Switzerland. The Kiandra Snow Shoe Club was formed in 1878 at Kiandra, New South Wales, and is one of the oldest ski clubs in the world. Early members of that club included A. B. ('Banjo') Paterson. The sport really caught on in the 1920s when Australians brought their enthusiasm for the sport home from their overseas travels.

The blossoming of the waratah, the song of the lyrebird, typify the spirit of primitive loveliness in our continent; but the wail of the dingo, the gauntness of our tall trees by silent moonlight, can provide a shiver of terror to a newcomer. Against a background of strangeness, of strange beasts and birds and plants, in a human emptiness of three million square miles . . . A new nation, a new human type, is being formed in Australia.

P. R. ('Inky') Stephensen

Question: Australians often give affectionate nicknames to famous cricketers, for example, The Don, Thommo and Warnie. What are the real names of these three men?

Answer: Donald Bradman, Jeff Thompson and Shane Warne.

"

This country possesses numerous
advantages . . . We enjoy here one of the
finest climates in the world. The
necessaries of life are abundant, & a
fruitful soil affords us many luxuries.
Nothing induces me to wish for
change . . .

Elizabeth Macarthur

"

The colony's first architect was an ex-convict named Francis Greenway (1777–1837), who designed more than 40 Georgian-style buildings. Eventually his style 'went out of vogue', and he died penniless.

Question: Who is the only Australian ever to win the Nobel Prize for literature, and in what year?

Answer: Patrick White (1912–1990) in 1973.

James Fisher,

QUOTATIONS

THE WIT AND WISDOM OF 700 AUTHORS

This edition published 1993 by
Diamond Books
77-85 Fulham Palace Road
Hammersmith
London W6 8JB

© William Collins Sons & Co. Ltd. 1961

Printed and bound in Great Britain

CONTENTS

	Page
FOREWORD	7

DICTIONARY OF QUOTATIONS:

Accius–Austen	13– 31
Bacon–Byron	31–101
Cæsar–Curran	101–147
Dana–Dyer	147–177
Ecclesiastes–Ezekiel	177–194
Faraday–Fyleman	194–206
Galileo–Guinan	206–219
Haig–Huxley	219–240
Ibsen–Isaiah	241–244
James I–Juvenal	244–255
Karr–Knox	255–266
Lamb–Luther	267–281
Macaulay–Munro	281–315
Nash–Nursery Rhymes	315–321
O'Casey–Owen	321–323
Page–Putnam	324–342
Quesnay–Quiller-Couch	342
Rabelais–Ruth	343–352
Saikaku–Syrus	352–411
Tacitus–Twain	411–424
Ustinov	424–425
Vanbrugh–Voltaire	425–429
Wallace–Wyntoun	429–453
Yeats–Young	453–458
Zangwill–Zola	458

SUPPLEMENT OF SONGS	459
SUPPLEMENT OF HYMNS	463
INDEX TO ENGLISH QUOTATIONS	468
INDEX TO FOREIGN QUOTATIONS	601

FOREWORD

THIS book has three main purposes: to verify half-remembered quotations; to give the source of common sayings whose origins are forgotten; and to suggest apposite quotations on particular subjects. It will be useful to authors, journalists, clergymen, schoolchildren, cross-word puzzle addicts, politicians, students, speechifiers and all those with imperfect memories. It slips as easily into the pocket of the dinner-jacket as on to the library shelf.

Many methods of selecting quotations were considered in the planning stages and all were eventually rejected in favour of the criterion of sheer usefulness. Inevitably, then, the choice was governed mainly by tradition and established taste. On the other hand, we left out several trite moralisings which have often passed for quotations. Modern writers are well represented.

The limitations of space are obvious, and it is remarkable that this little book contains nearly 4000 quotations, drawn from about 700 authors, and in particular that it has been possible to accommodate so detailed an index.

The Bible and Shakespeare were, of course,

the most fruitful sources of material for this book. Hundreds of biblical sayings and phrases are part of our everday speech and, to quote Jane Austen, " We all talk Shakespeare, use his similes, and describe with his descriptions." It was not possible to quote the whole of each famous Shakespearian soliloquy or speech but the first few lines are given for all such passages.

All the great writers of English literature are included and also many American writers, and the famous orators of the English-speaking world appear in strength. It must be remembered, however, that an author's status in literary history is not to be measured by the number of quotations appearing below his name in this or any other reference book. Quotability depends, it is true, on the importance of the thought or idea conveyed, but it depends even more on the form in which it is presented. Thus Oscar Wilde, with his witty epigrams and paradoxes, secures 74 entries in this book, whereas Sir Walter Scott, the bulk of whose output consisted of narration and description in a comparatively leisurely style, is given only 28.

Modern and contemporary writers presented a special problem since no one can say which of their utterances will pass into the currency of speech. From the moderns such as Churchill,

Eliot, Osborne, Camus and Behan, therefore, we have made a purely personal selection of quotations which we think might be perpetuated, and such entries will have to be reviewed with each new edition of the dictionary.

With the earliest writers, on the other hand, the problem was mainly one of language. Sometimes we felt it desirable to modernise the spelling, realising however that some readers may object to any tampering with the original text. We hope they will accept this as being for the convenience of the majority. Medieval and modern Scottish poetry has been retained in its original form, as we felt it would lose much of its character if "translated."

We should have liked to include more foreign quotations, but Voltaire, Molière, Confucius, Dante, Virgil, Goethe and Horace have been given ample space and many others are represented. Sometimes, when the idea itself is more important than the manner of expressing it, we have, to save space, given only the English translation.

There are no quotations from songs, but a supplement lists titles of popular songs and the writers associated with them. There is also a supplement of hymns.

Some notes on the arrangement of the material may help the reader. The authors appear alphabetically, and under each author

9

verse quotations precede prose, except where the writer is better known for his prose. The quotations are then arranged either alphabetically according to the title of the source, or chronologically in the case of speeches.

Peers, and authors with pseudonyms, appear under the name by which they are usually known, e.g. *Disraeli, Benjamin, Earl of Beaconsfield* and *Montrose, James Graham, Marquis of.* With saints the personal name is given first, e.g. *Ambrose, St.* Bible quotations are grouped under the name of the Book from which they come, e.g. *Corinthians, The First Epistle of Paul to the*, and all are taken from the King James Authorised Version unless otherwise stated.

References to the sources of quotations are brief but easily understood. With plays, the act is given but not the scene. If several quotations from the same act are included they are arranged in the correct order. Quotations from books usually have chapter references, and if the work is divided into parts a reference to the part comes first. Numbers after the titles of poems refer to parts, and those following Bible quotations give chapter and verse.

The index is an extremely important part of this dictionary. Each quotation is indexed under several different key words to ensure that the reader can quickly find a vaguely remembered line or phrase. If, on the other hand, he requires a suitable quotation on some particular theme, he need only turn to the appropriate subject heading in the index and can choose from the quotations listed there the one best suited to his purpose. Foreign quotations in the original are indexed separately but their translations are included in the main index.

We are grateful for the assistance of Andrew Hood, Neil S. Hooper and Donald A. Lightwood, who contributed quotations from some of the less familiar byways of English literature, and Louise G. Storrie, R. Butchart and the Reverend D. Kyles who helped with the formidable task of assembling the index. The main task of compilation was undertaken by the editorial staff of the Collins Reference Book Department, and in particular by James Dow, Sheila Ross and Angela Leech, who have spared no effort to make this a useful and completely reliable work.

Accius, Lucius   **170-90 B.C**

Oderint dum metuant. Let them hate so long as they fear. *Atreus*

Acton, First Baron   **1834-1902**

Power tends to corrupt and absolute power corrupts absolutely. *Letter* in *Life of Mandell Creighton*

The Acts of the Apostles

It is hard for thee to kick against the pricks. 9, 5

God is no respecter of persons. 10, 34

For in him we live, and move, and have our being. 17, 28

It is more blessed to give than to receive. 20, 35

Adams, Henry   **1838-1918**

Every one carries his own inch-rule of taste, and amuses himself by applying it, triumphantly, wherever he travels. *Education of Henry Adams*

They know enough who know how to learn. *Ib.*

Addison, Joseph   **1672-1719**

And, pleas'd th' Almighty's orders to perform,
Rides in the whirlwind, and directs the storm.
           The Campaign

'Tis not in mortals to command success,
But we'll do more, Sempronius; we'll deserve it.
           Cato, 1

A day, an hour of virtuous liberty
Is worth a whole eternity in bondage. *Ib.* 2

Music, the greatest good that mortals know,
And all of heaven we have below.
                    Song for St. Cecilia's Day

Themistocles, the great Athenian general, being
asked whether he would choose to marry his
daughter to an indigent man of merit, or to a
worthless man of an estate, replied, that he would
prefer a man without an estate, to an estate
without a man. *The Fortune Hunter*

The truth of it is, learning, like travelling, and all
other methods of improvement, as it finishes good
sense, so it makes a silly man ten thousand times
more insufferable, by supplying variety of matter
to his impertinence, and giving him an opportunity
of abounding in absurdities. *The Man of the Town*

It was said of Socrates that he brought philosophy
down from heaven to inhabit among men; and
I shall be ambitious to have it said of me that I
have brought philosophy out of closets and
libraries, schools and colleges, to dwell in clubs
and assemblies, at tea-tables and in coffee-houses.
                    Spectator, 1

Sir Roger told them, with the air of a man who
would not give his judgement rashly, that much
might be said on both sides. *Ib.* 122

I value my garden more for being full of blackbirds than of cherries, and very frankly give them
fruit for their songs. *Ib.* 477

14

When I read the several dates of the tombs, of some that died yesterday, and some six hundred years ago, I consider that great day when we shall all of us be contemporaries, and make our appearance together. *Thoughts in Westminster Abbey*

I consider woman as a beautiful, romantic animal, that may be adorned with furs and feathers, pearls and diamonds, ores and silks. *Trial of the Petticoat*

Arguments out of a pretty mouth are unanswerable. *Women and Liberty*

Ady, Thomas   c. 1655

Matthew, Mark, Luke, and John,
The Bed be blest that I lie on.
Four angels to my bed,
Four angels round my head,
One to watch, and one to pray,
And two to bear my soul away.
A Candle in the Dark (Quoted by Ady)

Aeschylus   525-456 B.C.

Things are where things are, and, as fate has willed,
So shall they be fulfilled.
Agamemnon (*Tr.* Browning)

Make not my path offensive to the gods
By spreading it with carpets. *Ib.*

The wisest of the wise may err. *Fragments*

It is always the season for the old to learn. *Ib.*

Words are the physicians of a mind diseased.
Prometheus Bound

15

His resolve is not to seem the bravest, but to be it.
Seven against Thebes

Albertano of Brescia   c. 1190-c. 1270

The angry man always thinks he can do more
than he can. *Liber Consolationis*

Qui omnes despicit, omnibus displicet. Who
despiseth all, displeaseth all. *Ib.*

Alcott, Amos Bronson   1799-1888

Civilisation degrades the many to exalt the few.
Table Talk. Pursuits

A sip is the most that mortals are permitted from
any goblet of delight. *Ib. Habits*

Alcuin   735-804

Vox populi, vox dei. The voice of the people is the
voice of God. *Letter to Charlemagne*

Alexander the Great   356-323 B.C.

Heaven cannot brook two suns, nor earth two
masters. *Apothegms*, Plutarch

I assure you I had rather excel others in the
knowledge of what is excellent, than in the extent
of my power and dominion. *Lives*, Plutarch

Alexander, Sir William, Earl of Stirling c. 1567-1640

Yet with great toil all that I can attain
By long experience, and in learned schools,
Is for to know my knowledge is but vain,
And those that think them wise, are greatest fools.
The Tragedy of Croesus, 2

D'Allainval, Léonor Jean　　　　　　　**c. 1700-1753**

L'Embarras de Richesse. The Embarrassment of
Riches. *Title of Play*, 1726

Allingham, William　　　　　　　　　**1824-1889**

Up the airy mountain,
Down the rushy glen,
We daren't go a-hunting,
For fear of little men. *The Fairies*

Four ducks on a pond,
A grass-bank beyond,
A blue sky of spring,
White clouds on the wing:
What a little thing
To remember for years—
To remember with tears. *A Memory*

Ambrose, St.　　　　　　　　　　　　**c. 340-397**

Si fueris Romae, Romano vivito more;
Si fueri alibi, vivito sicut ibi.
If you are in Rome, live in the Roman way; if
you are elsewhere, live as they do there. *Ductor
Dubitantium*, Jeremy Taylor

Amiel, Henri-Frédéric　　　　　　　**1828-1881**

Action is but coarsened thought—thought become
concrete, obscure, and unconscious. *Journal*, 1850

The age of great men is going; the epoch of the
ant-hill, of life in multiplicity, is beginning.
Ib. 1851

Every life is a profession of faith, and exercises
an inevitable and silent influence. *Ib.* 1852

A belief is not true because it is useful. *Ib.* 1876

Andersen, Hans Christian   **1805-1875**

Every man's life is a fairy-tale written by God's fingers. *Works*, preface

Andrewes, Bishop Lancelot   **1555-1626**

The nearer the Church the further from God.
                                        Sermon

Anonymous

[Of Dr. Temple, Headmaster of Rugby] A beast, but a just beast.

A rainbow in the morning
Is the Shepherd's warning;
But a rainbow at night
Is the Shepherd's delight. *Old Weather Rhyme*

A very gallant gentleman. *Inscription on grave of Capt. L. E. G. Oates,* 1912

Ad majorem Dei gloriam. To the greater glory of God. *Motto of the Society of Jesus*

All present and correct.
                        Queen's Regulations (Army)

[A lie] An abomination unto the Lord, but a very present help in time of trouble.

An army marches on its stomach.
                            Attrib. to Napoleon I

An intelligent Russian once remarked to us, "Every country has its own constitution; ours

18

Is absolutism moderated by assassination."
Political Sketches of the State of Europe, 1814-1867.
Georg Herbert, Count Münster

Are we downhearted? No! *War of 1914-18,*
(based on remark of Joseph Chamberlain)

Be happy while y'er leevin,
For y'er a lang time deid. *Scottish Motto*

*Caveant consules ne quid res publici detrimenti
caperet.* Let the consuls see to it that no harm
come to the state.
       ' *Ultimate decree*' *of the Senate of Rome*

*Cet animal est très méchant,
Quand on l'attaque il se défend.*
This animal is very wicked,
When it is attacked it defends itself.
                         La Ménagerie, 1868

[Of Bayard] *Chevalier sans peur et sans reproche.*
Knight without fear and without blame.
                     Chronicles, 1476-1524

Christmas is coming, the geese are getting fat,
Please to put a penny in the old man's hat;
If you haven't got a penny, a ha'penny will do,
If you haven't got a ha'penny, God bless you!
                          Beggar's Rhyme

Dear Sir, Your astonishment's odd:
I am always about in the Quad.
    And that's why the tree
    Will continue to be,
Since observed by Yours faithfully, God.
           Reply to limerick on Idealism (cf. p. 266)

Esau selleth his birthright for a mess of potage.
Geneva Bible (heading to Genesis, 25)

Every minute dies a man,
And one and one-sixteenth is born.
Statistician's Parody of Tennyson (cf. p. 417)

For so long as but a hundred of us remain alive,
we will in no way yield ourselves to the dominion
of the English. For it is not for glory, nor riches,
nor honour that we fight, but for Freedom only,
which no good man lays down but with his life.
Declaration of Arbroath, 1320

Gaudeamus igitur,
Juvenes dum sumus
Post jucundam juventutem,
Post molestam senectutem,
Nos habebit humus. Let us be happy while we are
young, for after carefree youth and careworn age,
the earth will hold us also. *Students' song* (traced
to 1267)

God be in my head,
And in my understanding;
God be in my eyes,
And in my looking;
God be in my mouth,
And in my speaking;
God be in my heart,
And in my thinking;
God be at my end,
And at my departing. *Sarum Missal*

[Of America] God's own country. *In this form,*
first found in 1921

20

If all the world were paper,
And all the sea were inke;
If all the trees were bread and cheese
How should we do for drinke? *17th cent.*

It is good to be merry and wise,
It is good to be honest and true,
It is best to be off with the old love,
Before you are on with the new. *Song*

It's the same the whole world over,
Ain't it all a blooming shame,
It's the rich wot gets the pleasure,
It's the poor wot gets the blame. *Song of World
War I (many variants)*

Laborare est orare. Work is prayer. *Unknown origin*

Liberté! Egalité! Fraternité. Liberty! Equality!
Brotherhood!   *(Used 1793)*

Monday's child is fair of face,
Tuesday's child is full of grace,
Wednesday's child is full of woe,
Thursday's child has far to go,
Friday's child is loving and giving,
Saturday's child works hard for its living,
And a child that's born on the Sabbath day
Is fair and wise and good and gay.
                          Traditions of Devon, Bray

Nemo me impune lacessit. Wha daur meddle wi' me.
                          Motto of the Scots Crown

O God, if there be a God, save my soul, if I have
a soul! *Quoted in* Newman's *Apologia*

Once a clergyman always a clergyman. *Attrib.
ruling in trial of Horne Tooke*

21

Oxford gave the world marmalade and a manner, Cambridge science and a sausage.

Revenons à nos moutons. Let us go back to the subject. (*lit.* Let us return to our sheep.) *Maistre Pierre Pathelin*

Se non è vero, è molto ben trovato. If it is not true, it is a happy invention. *16th cent.*

See the happy moron,
  He doesn't give a damn,
I wish I were a moron,
  My God! perhaps I am!
                    Eugenics Review, 1929

Since wars begin in the minds of men, it is in the minds of men that the defences of peace must be constructed. *Constitution of United Nations Educational, Scientific and Cultural Organisation*, 1946

Sumer is icumen in,
  Lhude sing cuccu!
Groweth sed, and bloweth med,
  And springeth the wude nu. *Cuckoo Song,* c. 1250 (cf. p. 335)

Tempora mutantur, et nos mutamur in illis. The times are changing, and we are changing in them. *Description of Britain*, Harrison, 1577

The almighty dollar is the only object of worship. *Philadelphia Public Ledger*, 1860

The eternal triangle. *The Daily Chronicle*, 1907

The nature of God is a circle of which the centre

ıs everywhere and the circumference is nowhere.
Attrib. to Empedocles (quoted in *Roman de la Rose*
and by S. Bonaventura)

We hold these truths to be self-evident, that all
men are created equal, that they are endowed by
their Creator with certain unalienable rights, that
among these are life, liberty and the pursuit of
happiness. *American Declaration of Independence*,
4th July, 1776 (originally drafted by Jefferson)

" Well, what sort of sport has Lord—had? "
" Oh, the young Sahib shot divinely, but God
was very merciful to the birds." *Collections and
Recollections*, G. W. E. Russell

Wha hes gud malt and makis ill drink,
Wa mot be hir werd!
I pray to God scho rot and stink,
Sevin yeir abone the erd. *A Book of Scotland*,
ed. G. F. Maine

When Adam delved, and Eve span,
Who was then a gentleman? *Attrib. to John Ball*,
Blackheath, 1381 (cf. de Hampole, p. 220)

You pays your money and you takes your choice.
Collectanea, V. S. Lean

Antiphanes of Macedonia   fl. 360 B.C.

Idly inquisitive tribe of grammarians, who dig
up the poetry of others by the roots. . . . Get away,
bugs that bite secretly at the eloquent. *Greek
Anthology*, 11

23

Apocrypha

So every carpenter and workmaster, that laboureth
night and day: and they that cut and grave seals
. . . the smith also, sitting by the anvil . . . the
potter sitting at his work . . . all these trust to
their hands; and every one is wise in his work.
Without these cannot a city be inhabited. . . .
They shall not be sought for in public council,
nor sit high in the congregation . . . but they will
maintain the state of the world, and their desire
is in their craft. *Ecclesiasticus*, 38, 27-34

Let us now praise famous men, and our fathers
that begat us. *Ib.* 44, 1

And some there be, which have no memorial. *Ib.* 9

It was an holy and good thought.
2 Maccabees, 12, 45

Arabian Nights

Who will change old lamps for new ones? . . .
New lamps for old ones? *The History of Aladdin*

Open Sesame! *The History of Ali Baba*

Archimedes   287-212 B.C.

Give me a firm place to stand, and I will move the
earth. *Collectio*, Pappus Alexander

Eureka! I've got it! *De Architectura*, Vitruvius
Pollio

Archpoet of Cologne   fl. c. 1205

Meum est propositum in taberna mori;
Vinum sit appositum sitienti ori:

24

Ut dicant cum venerint angelorum chori
'Deus sit propitius isti potatori.'
I have resolved to die in a tavern; let the wine be close to my parched lips, so that the band of angels may say when they come: " May God be gracious to this drinker." *The Confession of Golias* (also attrib. to Walter Map and others)

Aristophanes   c. 444-380 B.C.

A man may learn wisdom even from a foe.
The Birds

You cannot make a crab walk straight. *The Peace*

Aristotle   384-322 B.C.

The roots of education are bitter, but the fruit is sweet. *Aristotle*, Diogenes Laertius

What is a friend? A single soul dwelling in two bodies. *Ib.*

I count him braver who overcomes his desires than him who overcomes his enemies. *Florilegium*, Stobaeus

Where we are free to act, we are also free to refrain from acting, and where we are able to say No, we are also able to say Yes. *Nicomachean Ethics*, 3

Our characters are the result of our conduct. *Ib.*

What we have to learn to do, we learn by doing. *Ib.*

Revolutions are not about trifles, but spring from trifles. *Politics*

25

Man is by nature a political animal. *Ib.*

Armin, Robert fl. 1610

A flea in his ear. *Foole upon Foole*

Arnold, Matthew 1822-1888

And we forget because we must
And not because we will. *Absence*

Is it so small a thing
To have enjoy'd the sun,
To have liv'd light in the spring,
To have lov'd, to have thought, to have done?
Empedocles on Etna, 1

But as on some far northern strand,
Thinking of his own Gods, a Greek
In pity and mournful awe might stand
Before some fallen Runic stone—
For both were faiths, and both are gone.
The Grande Chartreuse

Wandering between two worlds, one dead,
The other powerless to be born. *Ib.*

Years hence, perhaps, may dawn an age,
More fortunate, alas, than we,
Which without hardness will be sage,
And gay without frivolity. *Ib.*

Yet they, believe me, who await
No gifts from Chance, have conquer'd Fate.
Resignation

Friends who set forth at our side,
Falter, are lost in the storm,
We, we only are left. *Rugby Chapel*

Tired of knocking at Preferment's door.
The Scholar Gipsy

This strange disease of modern life. *Ib.*

Rustum, my father; who I hoped should greet,
Should one day greet, upon some well-fought field,
His not unworthy, not inglorious son. *Sohrab and
Rustum*

Truth sits upon the lips of dying men. *Ib.*

But now in blood and battles was my youth,
And full of blood and battles is my age;

And I shall never end this life of blood. *Ib.*

The great aim of culture is the aim of setting ourselves to ascertain what perfection is, and to make
it prevail. *Culture and Anarchy*

The men of culture are the true apostles of
equality. *Ib.*

One has often wondered whether upon the whole
earth there is anything so unintelligent, so unapt
to perceive how the world is really going, as an
ordinary young Englishman of our upper class. *Ib.*

[Oxford] Beautiful city! so venerable, so lovely,
so unravaged by the fierce intellectual life of our
century. . . . Home of lost causes, and forsaken
beliefs, and unpopular names, and impossible
loyalties. *Essays in Criticism, 1st Series, preface*

My own definition of criticism; a disinterested
endeavour to learn and propagate the best that
is known and thought in the world. *Ib. Functions
of Criticism at the Present Time*

27

A beautiful and ineffectual angel, beating in the void his luminous wings in vain. *Ib. 2nd Series, Shelley*

Arnold, Thomas   1795-1842

My object will be, if possible, to form Christian men, for Christian boys I can scarcely hope to make. *Letter of* 1828

Auden, Wystan Hugh   1907-1973

To save your world you asked this man to die:
Would this man, could he see you now, ask why?
Epitaph for an Unknown Soldier

In an upper room at midnight
See us gathered on behalf
Of love according to the gospel
Of the radio-phonograph. *The Love Feast*

Augier, Émile   1820-1889

La nostalgie de la boue. Homesickness for the gutter. *Le Mariage d'Olympe,* 1

Augustine, St.   354-430

Da mihi castitatem et continentiam, sed noli modo. Give me chastity and continence, but not yet. *Confessions,* 8

Securus indicat orbis terrarum. The judgement of the world is sure. *Contra Epistolam Parmeniani,* 3

Salus extra ecclesiam non est, There is no salvation outside the church. *De Bapt.,* 4

Audi partem alteram. Hear the other side. *De Duabus Animabus,* 14

Ama et fac quod vis. Love and do what you like.
Popular variant of In Joann., 7, 8

Roma locuta est; causa finita est. Rome has
spoken; the matter is settled. *Sermons*, 1

Austen, Jane   1775-1817

Matrimony, as the origin of change, was always
disagreeable. *Emma*, 1

One half of the world cannot understand the
pleasures of the other. *Ib.* 9

Perfect happiness, even in memory, is not common
Ib. 27

Why not seize the pleasure at once? How often is
happiness destroyed by preparation, foolish preparation! *Ib.* 30

Emma denied none of it aloud, and agreed to
none of it in private. *Ib.* 42

The stain of illegitimacy, unbleached by nobility
or wealth, would have been a stain indeed. *Ib.* 55

It is happy for you that you possess the talent of
flattering with delicacy. *Mansfield Park*, 14

You must try not to mind growing up into a
pretty woman. *Ib.* 21

There seems something more speakingly incom-
prehensible in the powers, the failures, the in-
equalities of memory, than in any other of our
intelligences. *Ib.* 22

29

We all talk Shakespeare, use his similes, and describe with his descriptions. *Ib.* 34

A family of ten children will always be called a fine family, where there are heads, and arms, and legs enough for that number. *Northanger Abbey*, 1

" And what are you reading, Miss ——? " " Oh! it is only a novel! " replies the young lady; while she lays down her book with affected indifference, or momentary shame. It is only *Cecilia*, or *Camilla*, or *Belinda*; or, in short, only some work in which the greatest powers of the mind are displayed, in which the most thorough knowledge of human nature, the happiest delineations of its varieties, the liveliest effusions of wit and humour, are conveyed to the world in the best chosen language. *Ib.* 5

A woman, especially if she have the misfortune of knowing anything, should conceal it as well as she can. *Ib.* 14

One does not love a place the less for having suffered in it, unless it has all been suffering, nothing but suffering. *Persuasion*, 20

All the privilege I claim for my own sex ... is that of loving longest, when existence or when hope is gone. *Ib.* 23

It is a truth universally acknowledged, that a single man in possession of a good fortune, must be in want of a wife. *Pride and Prejudice*, 1

Happiness in marriage is entirely a matter of chance. *Ib.* 6

What is the difference in matrimonial affairs, between the mercenary, and the prudent motive? *Ib.* 26

Lord, how ashamed I should be of not being married before three and twenty! *Ib.* 39

You ought certainly to forgive them as a Christian, but never to admit them in your sight, or allow their names to be mentioned in your hearing, *Ib.* 57

[Mr. Darcy] I have been a selfish being all my life, in practice, though not in principle. *Ib.* 58

An annuity is a very serious business; it comes over and over every year, and there is no getting rid of it. *Sense and Sensibility*, 1

On every formal visit a child ought to be of the party, by way of provision for discourse. *Ib.* 6

" I am afraid," replied Elinor, " that the pleasure of an employment does not always evince its propriety." *Ib.* 13

Bacon, Francis   1561-1626

If a man will begin with certainties, he shall end in doubts; but if he will be content to begin with doubts, he shall end in certainties. *Advancement of Learning*, 1

[Knowledge is] a rich storehouse, for the glory of the Creator and the relief of man's estate. *Ib*

They are ill discoverers that think there is no land, when they can see nothing but sea. *Ib.* 2

A man must make his opportunity, as oft as find it. *Ib.*

Fortunes . . . come tumbling into some men's laps.
Ib.

Hope is a good breakfast, but it is a bad supper.
Apothegms, 36

One of the Seven was wont to say: " That laws
were like cobwebs; where the small flies were
caught, and the great brake through." *Ib.* 181

Silence is the virtue of fools. *De Augmentis
Scientiarum* 1, 6

What is Truth? said jesting Pilate; and would
not stay for an Answer. *Essays* 1, *Of Truth*

This same Truth is a naked and open daylight,
that doth not show the masques and mummeries
and triumphs of the world half so stately and
daintily as candlelights. *Ib.*

Doth any man doubt, that if there were taken out
of men's minds, vaine opinions, flattering hopes,
false valuations, imaginations as one would, and
the like; but it would leave the minds of a
number of men poor shrunken things. *Ib.*

The inquiry of Truth, which is the love-making,
or wooing of it, the knowledge of Truth, which is
the presence of it, and the belief of Truth which
is the enjoying of it, is the sovereign good of
human nature. *Ib.*

But it is not the lie that passeth through the Mind, but the lie that sinketh in, and settleth in it, that doth the hurt. *Ib.*

To say that a man lieth, is as much to say, as that he is brave towards God, and a coward towards Men. *Ib.*

Men fear Death as children fear to go in the dark; and as that natural fear in children is increased with tales, so is the other. *Ib. 2, Of Death*

Revenge triumphs over Death; Love slights it; Honour aspireth to it; Grief flieth to it. *Ib.*

Prosperity is not without many fears and distastes; and Adversity is not without comforts and hopes.
Ib. 5, Of Adversity

Prosperity doth best discover Vice, but Adversity doth best discover Virtue. *Ib.*

He that hath Wife and Children, hath given Hostages to Fortune; for they are impediments to great enterprises, either of Virtue or Mischief.
Ib. 8, Of Marriage and Single Life

But the most ordinary cause of a single life, is Liberty; especially in certain self-pleasing and humorous minds, which are so sensible of every restraint as they will goe neare to think their girdles and garters to be bonds and shackles. *Ib.*

Certainly, Wife and Children are a Kind of Discipline of Humanity. *Ib.*

Wives are young men's Mistresses; companions for Middle Age; and old men's Nurses. *Ib.*

33

They do best who, if they cannot but admit Love, yet make it keep quarter; and sever it wholly from their serious affairs and actions of life: for if it checke once with Business, it troubleth Men's Fortunes, and maketh Men, that they can no wayes be true to their own ends. *Ib.* 10, *Of Love*

Men in Great Place are thrice Servants: Servants of the Soveraigne or State; Servants of Fame; and Servants of Businesse. . . . It is a strange desire to seek Power and to lose Libertie. *Ib.* 11, *Of Great Place*

All rising to Great Place is by a winding stair. *Ib.*

If the Hill will not come to Mahomet, Mahomet will go to the Hill. *Ib.* 12, *Boldness*

And Money is like Muck, not good except it be spread. *Ib.* 15, *Of Seditions and Troubles*

It is true, that a little Philosophy inclineth Man's Minde to Atheism; but depth in Philosophy bringeth Men's Mindes about to Religion. *Ib.* 16, *Atheism*

Travel, in the younger sort, is a part of Education; in the Elder, a part of Experience. He that travelleth into a country before he hath some entrance into the language, goeth to School, and not to Travel. *Ib.* 18, *Of Travel*

And he that will not apply New Remedies, must expect New Evils; for Time is the greatest Innovator. *Ib.* 24, *Of Innovations*

Whosoever is delighted in solitude, is either a Wilde Beast, or a God. *Ib.* 27, *Of Friendships*

This communicating of a Man's Selfe to his Frend works two contrarie effects; for it redoubleth Joys, and cutteth Griefs in halves. *Ib.*

Some in their Discourse, desire rather Commendation of Wit, in being able to hold all Arguments, than of Judgement in discerning what is true. *Ib.* 32, *Of Discourse*

I knew One, was wont to say in scorn: He must needs be a wise man, he speaks so much of Himself. *Ib.*

Of great Riches, there is no real use, except it be in distribution; the rest is but Conceit. *Ib.* 34, *Of Riches*

Nature is often hidden; sometimes overcome; seldom extinguished. *Ib.* 38, *Of Nature in Men*

A Man that is young in yeares, may be Old in hours, if he have lost no Time. But that happeneth rarely. *Ib.* 42, *Of Youth and Age*

There is no Excellent Beauty, that hath not some strangeness in the proportion. *Ib.* 43, *Of Beauty*

God Almighty first planted a Garden. And indeed, it is the purest of human Pleasures. *Ib.* 46, *Of Gardens*

To spend too much Time in Studies, is Sloth; To use them too much for Ornament, is Affectation; To make Judgement wholly by their rules is the humour of a Scholar. *Ib.* 50, *Of Studies*

Crafty Men contemn Studies; Simple Men admire them; and Wise Men use them. *Ib.*

Some Books are to be Tasted, others to be Swallowed, and some few to be Chewed and Digested; that is, some Books are to be read only in Parts; others to be read but not Curiously; and some few to be read wholly, and with Diligence and Attention. *Ib.*

Opportunity makes a thief. *Letter to the Earl of Essex*, 1598

Nam et ipsa scientia potestas est. Knowledge itself is power. *Religious Meditations. Of Heresies*

The world's a bubble; and the life of man Less than a span. *The World*

Bagehot, Walter   1826-1877

A constitutional statesman is in general a man of common opinions and uncommon abilities.
                                    Biographical Studies

The Times has made many ministries. *The English Constitution*, 1

Women—one half the human race at least—care fifty times more for a marriage than a ministry. *Ib.* 2

So long as the human heart is strong and the human reason weak, Royalty will be strong. *Ib.*

Of all the nations in the world the English are perhaps the least a nation of pure philosophers. *Ib.*

A Parliament is nothing less than a big meeting of more or less idle people. *Ib.* 4

The habit of common and continuous speech is a symptom of mental deficiency. *Literary Studies,* 1

A man who has not read Homer is like a man who has not seen the ocean. There is a great object of which he has no idea. *Ib.*

Poverty is an anomaly to rich people. It is very difficult to make out why people who want dinner do not ring the bell. *Ib.* 2

Nothing is more unpleasant than a virtuous person with a mean mind. *Ib.*

So long as there are earnest believers in the world, they will always wish to punish opinions, even if their judgement tells them it is unwise, and their conscience that it is wrong. *Ib.*

The whole history of civilisation is strewn with creeds and institutions which were invaluable at first, and deadly afterwards. *Physics and Politics*

One of the greatest pains to human nature is the pain of a new idea. *Ib.*

The most melancholy of human reflections, perhaps, is that, on the whole, it is a question whether the benevolence of mankind does most good or harm. *Ib.*

Baillie, Joanna   1762-1851

What custom hath endeared
We part with sadly, though we prize it not. *Basil,* 1

But woman's grief is like a summer storm,
Short as it violent is. *Ib.* 5

Bairnsfather, Charles Bruce   **1888-1959**

Well, if you knows of a better 'ole, go to it.
> *Fragments of France*

Ball, John   **d. 1381**

When Adam delved and Eve span,
Who was then the gentleman?
> *Sermon on the outbreak of the Peasants' Revolt*
> *(attrib.)*

Ballads

*N.B. Most ballads are of uncertain date and exist
in many versions*

" Annan water's wading deep,
And my love Annie's wond'rous bonnie;
And I am laith she should weet her feet,
Because I love her best of ony." *Annan Water*

O cherry, cherry was her cheek,
And golden was her hair;
But clay-cauld were her rosy lips—
Nae spark of life was there. *Annie of Lochryan*

In Scarlet town, where I was born,
There was a fair maid dwellin',
Mack every youth cry *Well-a-way!*
Her name was Barbara Allen. *Barbara Allen*

It fell about the Lammas tide,
When the muir-men win their hay,
The doughty Douglas bound him to ride
Into England, to drive a prey. *Battle of Otter-bourne*

38

" But I hae dream'd a dreary dream,
Beyond the Isle of Skye;
I saw a dead man win a fight,
And I think that man was I."   *Ib.*

There were twa sisters lived in a bower—
Binnorie, O Binnorie!
There came a knight to be their wooer,
By the bonnie mill-dams o' Binnorie. Binnorie

He courted the eldest wi' glove an' ring,
But he loved the youngest above a' thing. *Ib.*

Ye Highlands and ye Lawlands,
O where hae ye been?
They hae slain the Earl of Murray,
And hae laid him on the green. *The Bonny Earl
of Murray*

O lang will his Lady
Look owre the Castle Doune,
Ere she see the Earl of Murray,
Come sounding through the toun.   *Ib.*

O are ye come to drink the wine,
As ye hae doon before, oh?
Or are ye come to wield the brand,
On the bonny banks o' Yarrow? *The Dowie
Houms o' Yarrow*

" Why does your brand sae drap with bluid?
Edward! Edward!
Why does your brand sae drap with bluid,
And why sae sad gang ye, O ? " *Edward! Edward!*

I wish I were where Helen lies
Night and day on me she cries;
O that I were where Helen lies
On fair Kirkconnell lea! *Helen of Kirkconnell*

I lighted down my sword to draw,
I hacked him in pieces sma',
I hacked him in pieces sma',
For her sake that died for me.   *Ib.*

" Oh, it's Hynde Horn fair, and it's Hynde Horn
    free;
Oh, where were you born, and in what countrie?"
" In a far distant countrie I was born;
But of home and friends I am quite forlorn."
                                    Hynde Horn

O Johnny was as brave a knight
As ever sailed the sea,
An he's done him to the English court,
To serve for meat and fee. *Johnny Scott*

There was a May, and a weel-far'd May.
Lived high up in yon glen;
Her name was Katherine Janfarie
Weel loved by mony men. *Katherine Janfarie*

O is my basnet a widow's curch?
Or my lance a wand of the willow tree?
Or my arm a lady's lily hand,
That an English lord should lightly me? *Kinmons
Willie*

The Laird o' Drum is a-wooing gane,
It was on a morning early,
And he has fawn in wi' a bonny may
A-shearing at her barley. *The Laird o' Drum*

" For an' I war dead, and ye war dead,
And baith in ae grave laid, O,
And ye and I war tane up again,
Wha could distan your moulds frae mine, O?" *Ib.*

40

" Where hae ye been hunting Lord Randal, my
   son?
Where hae ye been hunting, my handsome young
   man? "
" In yon wild wood, O mither; so make my bed
   soon,
For I'm weary wi' huntin', and fain wad lie
   doun." *Lord Randal*

There liv'd a lord on yon sea-side,
   And he thought on a wile,
How he would go o'er the salt-sea,
   A lady to beguile. *Lord Thomas and Fair Annie*

The ane was buried in Marie's kirk,
   The other in Marie's quire;
And out of the ane there sprang a birk,
   And out of the other a brier. *Prince Robert*

Marie Hamilton's to the kirk gane,
   Wi' gloves upon her hands;
The king thought mair o' Marie Hamilton
   Than the Queen and a' her lands. *The Queen's
Maries*

Yestreen the Queen had four Maries,
   The night she'll hae but three;
There was Marie Seaton, and Marie Beaton
   And Mary Carmichael and me.

O little did my mother ken,
   The day she cradled me,
The lands I was to travel in
   Or the death I was to dee! *Ib.*

She sought him east, she sought him west,
   She sought him braid and narrow;

Sine, in the lifting of a craig,
  She found him drown'd in Yarrow. *Rare Willie Drowned in Yarrow*

The king sits in Dunfermline town,
  Drinking the blude-red wine:
" Oh, where will I get a gude skipper
  To sail this ship of mine?" *Sir Patrick Spens*

" I saw the new moon late yestreen
  Wi' the auld moon in her arm;
And if we gang to sea, master,
  I fear we'll come to harm." *Ib.*

Then she has kilted her green kirtle
  A little abune her knee;
And she has braided her yellow hair
  A little abune her bree. *Tamlane*

True Thomas lay on Huntly bank;
  A ferlie he spied with his e'e;
And there he saw a ladye bright,
  Came riding down by the Eildon tree. *Thomas the Rhymer, First part*

" O, see ye na that braid, braid road,
  That lies across the lily leven?
That is the path of wickedness,
  Tho' some call it the road to heaven.

And see ye not yon narrow road,
  Sae thick beset with thorns and briars?
That is the path of righteousness,
  Tho' after it but few inquires." *Ib.*

When seven years were come and gane,
  The sun blink'd fair on pool and stream;

And Thomas lay on Huntlie bank,
  Like one awaken'd from a dream.
                              Ib. Second part

As I was walking all alane,
I heard twa corbies making a mane:
The tane unto the tither did say,
" Whaur sall we gang and dine the day?"
                              The Twa Corbies

There lived a wife at Usher's Well,
And a wealthy wife was she;
She had three stout and stalwart sons,
And sent them o'er the sea. *The Wife of Usher's Well*

Balzac, Honoré de   1799-1850

L'ironie est le fond du caractère de la Providence.
Irony is the essence of the character of Providence.
                              Eugénie Grandet

Penser, c'est voir. To think is to see. *Louis Lambert*

*Je préfère la pensée à l'action, une idée à une affaire,
la contemplation au mouvement.* I prefer thought
to action, an idea to an event, reflection to activity.
                              Ib.

*Que signifie adieu, à moins de mourir? Mais la
mort serait-elle un adieu?* What does farewell
mean, if not death? But will death itself be a
farewell? *Ib.*

*La fin est le retour de toutes choses à l'unité qui est
Dieu.* The final aim is the reversion of everything
to the unity which is God. *Ib.*

43

To kill the emotions and so live to old age, or to accept the martyrdom of our passions and die young is our doom. *La Peau de Chagrin*

Barbour, John   c. 1316-1395

A! fredome is a noble thing!
Fredome mayss man to haiff liking;
Fredome all solace to man giffio:
He levys at ess that frely levys! *The Brus, 1*

Na he that ay hass levyt free,
May nocht knaw weill the propyrté,
The angyr, na the wrechyt dome,
That is cowpyt to foule thyrldome. *Ib.*

And suld think fredome mar to pryss,
Than all the gold in warld that is. *Ib.*

[Of loyalty]
For quhar it failyeis, na vertu
May be of price, na of value,
To mak a man sa gud, that he
May symply gud man callyt be. *Ib.*

For certis, I trow, thar is no man
That he ne will rew up-on woman. *Ib.*

Barham, Rev. Richard Harris   1788-1845

There, too, full many an Aldermanic nose
Roll'd its loud diapason after dinner.
                    The Ingoldsby Legends. The Ghost

The Jackdaw sat on the Cardinal's chair! *Ib.*
The Jackdaw of Rheims

So put that in your pipe, my Lord Otto, and smoke it! *Ib. Lay of St. Odille*

44

Barnum, Phineas T.   1810-1891

There's a sucker born every minute. *Attrib.*

Barrie, James Matthew   1860-1937

As Dr. Johnson never said, is there any Scotsman without charm? *Address, Edinburgh University*

I'm a second eleven sort of chap. *The Admirable Crichton*, 3

You canna expect to be baith grand and comfortable. *The Little Minister*, 3

When the first baby laughed for the first time, the laugh broke into a thousand pieces and they all went skipping about, and that was the beginning of fairies. *Peter Pan*, 1

Every time a child says " I don't believe in fairies," there is a little fairy somewhere that falls down dead. *Ib.*

To die will be an awfully big adventure. *Ib.* 3

[Charm] It's a sort of bloom on a woman. If you have it, you don't need to have anything else; and if you don't have it, it doesn't much matter what else you have. *What Every Woman Knows*, 1

A young Scotsman of your ability let loose upon the world with £300, what could he not do? It's almost appalling to think of; especially if he went among the English. *Ib.*

You've forgotten the grandest moral attribute of a Scotsman, Maggie, that he'll do nothing which might damage his career. *Ib.* 2

There are few more impressive sights in the world than a Scotsman on the make. *Ib.*

Baudelaire, Charles   1821-1867

*L'air est plein du frisson des choses qui s'enfuient,
Et l'homme est las d'écrire et la femme d'aimer.*
There is a shiver in the air, of things which pass;
And man is tired of writing, and woman of loving.
Le Crépuscule du Matin

*Là, tout n'est qu'ordre et beauté,
Luxe, calme et volupté.* For all things there are
ordered, lovely, profuse, serene and pleasureable.
L'Invitation au Voyage

J'ai plus de souvenirs que si j'avais mille ans. I have
more memories than if I were a thousand. *Spleen*

Bayly, Thomas Haynes   1797-1839

Absence makes the heart grow fonder,
  Isle of Beauty, Fare thee well! *Isle of Beauty*

I'm saddest when I sing. *Title of poem*

Beatty, David, Earl   1871-1936

There's something wrong with our bloody ships
to-day, Chatfield. Steer two points nearer the
enemy. *Remark during the Battle of Jutland,* 1916.
(*The second sentence may be apocryphal*)

Beaumarchais, Pierre-Augustin de   1732-1799

*Je me presse de rire de tout, de peur d'être obligé
d'en pleurer.* I make myself laugh at everything,
in case I should have to weep. *Le Barbier de
Séville,* 1

Parce que vous êtes un grand seigneur, vous vous croyez un grand génie! . . . Vous vous êtes donné la peine de naître, et rien de plus. Because you are a great lord, you think you are a great genius. You have taken the trouble to be born, but no more. *Mariage de Figaro*, 5

Tout finit par des chansons. Everything ends in songs. *Ib.* (last line)

Beaumont, Francis, 1584-1616 and John Fletcher 1579-1625

Deeds, not words shall speak me. *The Lover's Progress*, 3

Faith Sir, he went away with a flea in's ear. *Ib.* 4

I'll put a spoke among your wheels. *The Mad Lover*, 3

All your better deeds
Shall be in water writ, but this in marble. *The Nice Valour*, 5

Kiss till the cow comes home. *Scornful Lady*, 2

There is no other purgatory but a woman. *Ib.* 3

Beckford, William 1759-1844

He did not think with the Caliph Omar Ben Adalaziz, that it was necessary to make a hell of this world to enjoy paradise in the next. *Vathek*

Bee, Bernard Elliot 1823-1861

Let us determine to die here, and we will conquer.

There is Jackson standing like a stone wall. Rally behind the Virginians.
First Battle of Bull Run, 1861

Beer, Thomas   1889-1940

I agree with one of your reputable critics that a taste for drawing-rooms has spoiled more poets than ever did a taste for gutters. *The Mauve Decade*

Beerbohm, Sir Max   1872-1956

Most women are not so young as they are painted.
A Defence of Cosmetics

" After all," as a pretty girl once said to me, " women are a sex by themselves, so to speak."
The Pervasion of Rouge

" I don't," she added, " know anything about music, really. But I know what I like." *Zuleika Dobson*, 16

Beers, Ethel Lynn   1827-1879

All quiet along the Potomac to-night,
  No sound save the rush of the river,
While soft falls the dew on the face of the dead—
  The picket's off duty forever. *All Quiet Along the Potomac* (cf. p. 283)

Behan, Brendan   1923-1964

Pound notes is the best religion in the world.
The Hostage

Never throw stones at your mother,
  You'll be sorry for it when she's dead,
Never throw stones at your mother,
  Throw bricks at your father instead. *Ib.*

Behn, Aphra   1640-1689

Of all that writ, he was the wisest bard, who spoke
this mighty truth—
He that knew all that ever learning writ,
Knew only this—that he knew nothing yet. *The
Emperor of the Moon*, 1

Love ceases to be a pleasure, when it ceases to be
a secret. *The Lover's Watch, Four o'clock*

Faith, Sir, we are here to-day, and gone to-
morrow. *The Lucky Chance*, 4

Money speaks sense in a language all nations
understand. *The Rover*, 2

Belloc, Hilaire   1870-1953

Child! Do not throw this book about;
Refrain from the unholy pleasure
Of cutting all the pictures out!
Preserve it as your chiefest treasure. *Bad Child's
Book of Beasts*, dedication

A manner rude and wild
Is common at your age. *Ib.* introduction

There's nothing worth the wear of winning,
    But laughter and the love of friends.
                                    Dedicatory Ode

But I will sit beside my fire,
And put my hand before my eyes,
And trace, to fill my heart's desire,
The last of all our Odysseys. *Ib.*

When I am dead, I hope it may be said
" His sins were scarlet, but his books were read."
                                    On His Books

It is the best of all trades, to make songs, and the second best to sing them. *On Everything*

I will hold my house in the high wood
Within a walk of the sea,
And the men that were boys when I was a boy
Shall sit and drink with me.
The South Country

Benes, Eduard 1884-1948

To make peace in Europe possible, the last representative of the pre-war generation must die and take his pre-war mentality into the grave with him.
Interview, 1929

Benét, Stephen 1898-1943

. . . the lounging mirth of cracker-barrel men,
Snowed in by winter, spitting at the fire,
And telling the disreputable truth
With the sad eye that marks the perfect liar. *Poem*

Bennett, Enoch Arnold 1867-1931

"Ye can call it influenza if ye like," said Mrs. Machin. "There was no influenza in my young days. We called a cold a cold." *The Card*, 8

"And yet," demanded Councillor Barlow . . . "what great cause is he identified with?"—"He is identified," said the speaker, "with the great cause of cheering us all up." *Ib.* 12

My general impression is that Englishmen act better than Frenchmen, and French women better than English women. *The Crisis in the Theatre*

50

Pessimism, when you get used to it, is just as agreeable as optimism. *Things That Have Interested Me*

The price of justice is eternal publicity. *Ib.*

The test of a first-rate work, and a test of your sincerity in calling it a first-rate work, is that you finish it. *Ib.*

Journalists say a thing that they know isn't true, in the hope that if they keep on saying it long enough it *will* be true. *The Title*

Being a husband is a whole-time job. That is why so many husbands fail. They cannot give their entire attention to it. *Ib.*

Bentham, Jeremy   **1748-1832**

Stretching his hand out to catch the stars, he forgets the flowers at his feet. *Deontology*

. . . this sacred truth—that the greatest happiness of the greatest number is the foundation of morals and legislation. *Works*, 10 (quoting Francis Hutcheson, 1694-1746)

Bentley, Edmund Clerihew   **1875-1956**

The art of Biography
Is different from Geography.
Geography is about Maps,
But Biography is about chaps.
                              Biography for Beginners

John Stuart Mill,
By a mighty effort of will,

Overcame his natural bonhomie
And wrote ' Principles of Political Economy.'
Ib. John Stuart Mill

Bernard, William Bayle　　　　　**1807-1875**

A Storm in a Teacup. *Title of a Farce,* 1854

Bethell, Richard, Baron Westbury　　　**1800-1873**

His Lordship says he will turn it over in what he is pleased to call his mind. *Life of Westbury,* Nash

Betterton, Thomas　　　　　**1635-1710**

Actors speak of things imaginary as if they were real, while you preachers too often speak of things real as if they were imaginary. *Reply to Archbishop of Canterbury*

Bickerstaff, Isaac　　　　　**c. 1735-1812**

Perhaps it was right to dissemble your love,
But—why did you kick me downstairs?
An Expostulation

We all love a pretty girl—under the rose.
Love in a Village, 1

Bigod, Roger　　　　　**1245-1306**

(Edward I: " By God, earl, you shall either go or hang! ")
" O King I will neither go nor hang! " *Hemingburgh's Chronicle*

Binyon, Laurence　　　　　**1869-1943**

They shall grow not old, as we that are left grow old:

52

Age shall not weary them, nor the years condemn.
At the going down of the sun and in the morning
We will remember them. *Poems for the Fallen*

Bismarck, Otto Von   **1815-1898**

To youth I have but three words of counsel—
work, work, work. *Sayings of Bismarck*

Lieber Spitzkugeln als Spitzreden. Better pointed
bullets than pointed speeches. *Speech, 1850*

Sie macht sich nur durch Blut und Eisen. It can
only be done by blood and iron. *Speech, 1886*

Blackstone, Sir William   **1723-1780**

That the king can do no wrong, is a necessary
and fundamental principle of the English constitution. *Commentaries, 3*

Blake, William   **1757-1827**

Tell me the acts, O historian, and leave me to
reason upon them as I please; away with your
reasoning and your rubbish! *The Ancient Britons*

To see a World in a Grain of Sand,
And a Heaven in a Wild Flower,
Hold Infinity in the palm of your hand,
And Eternity in an hour. *Auguries of Innocence*

A truth that's told with bad intent
Beats all the lies you can invent. *Ib.*

The soldier armed with sword and gun
Palsied strikes the summer sun. *Ib.*

53

Nought can deform the human race
Like to the armourer's iron brace. *Ib.*

The whore and gambler, by the state
Licensed, build that nation's fate. *Ib.*

As, long agone,
When men were first a nation grown,
Lawless they lived, till wantonness
And liberty began to increase,
And one man lay in another's way;
Then laws were made to keep fair play.
Blind-Man's Buff

Can Wisdom be put in a silver rod,
Or Love in a golden bowl? *Book of Thel*

Great things are done when men and mountains
meet;
This is not done by jostling in the street.
Gnomic Verses

But vain the sword, and vain the bow—
They never can work war's overthrow. *The Grey
Monk*

The hand of vengeance found the bed
To which the purple tyrant fled;
The iron hand crushed the tyrant's head,
And became a tyrant in his stead. *Ib.*

The god of war is drunk with blood,
    The earth doth faint and fail;
The stench of blood makes sick the heavens;
    Ghosts glut the throat of hell!
Gwin, King of Norway

I must Create a System, or be enslaved by another
Man's;

54

I will not Reason and Compare: my business
is to Create. *Jerusalem*

I care not whether a man is Good or Evil; all
that I care
Is whether he is a Wise man or a Fool. Go! put
off Holiness,
And put on Intellect. *Ib.*

Sweet Prince, the arts of peace are great,
And no less glorious than those of war.
King Edward the Third

Ambition is the growth of every clime. *Ib.*

Justice hath heaved a sword to plunge in Albion's
breast; for Albion's sins are crimson-dyed.
Prologue to King John

Bring me my bow of burning gold!
Bring me my arrows of desire!
Bring me my spear! O clouds, unfold!
Bring me my chariot of fire!

I will not cease from Mental Strife
Nor shall my Sword sleep in my hand
Till we have built Jerusalem,
In England's green and pleasant Land.
Milton, preface

Mock on, mock on, Voltaire, Rousseau;
Mock on, mock on; 'tis all in vain!

You throw the sand against the wind,
And the wind blows it back again. *Mock On*

Drive your cart and your plough over the bones
of the dead. *Proverbs of Hell*

55

No bird soars too high if he soars with his own wings. *Ib.*

Prisons are built with stones of Law, brothels with bricks of Religion. *Ib.*

Prudence is a rich, ugly, old maid courted by incapacity. *Ib.*

Truth can never be told so as to be understood, and not be believed. *Ib.*

You never know what is enough, unless you know what is more than enough. *Ib.*

Samson, the strongest of the children of men, I sing; how he was foiled by woman's arts. *Samson*

Ten thousand spears are like the summer grass. *Ib.*

Manoa left his fields to sit in the house, and take his evening's rest from labour—the sweetest time that God hath allotted mortal man. *Ib.*

Oppression stretches his rod over our land, our country is ploughed with swords, and reaped in blood. *Ib.*

How sweet I roamed from field to field,
And tasted all the summer's pride,
Till I the Prince of Love beheld
Who in the sunny beams did glide. *Song*

Love seeketh not itself to please,
Nor for itself hath any care,
But for another gives its ease,
And builds a heaven in hell's despair.
    Songs of Experience. The Clod and the Pebble

Is this a holy thing to see
In a rich and fruitful land,
Babes reduced to misery,
Fed with cold and usurous hand?
Ib. Holy Thursday

I was angry with my friend,
I told my wrath, my wrath did end.
I was angry with my foe,
I told it not, my wrath did grow. *Ib. A Poison Tree*

Tiger! Tiger! burning bright
In the forests of the night,
What immortal hand or eye,
Could frame thy fearful symmetry? *Ib. The Tiger*

In every cry of every man,
In every infant's cry of fear,
In every voice, in every ban,
The mind-forged manacles I hear. *Ib. London*

Little Lamb, who made thee?
Dost thou know who made thee?
Songs of Innocence. The Lamb

My mother bore me in the southern wild,
And I am black, but O! my soul is white;
White as an angel is the English child,
But I am black, as if bereaved of light.
Ib. The Little Black Boy

Blind Harry the Minstrel   **fl. 1470**

Now leiff thi myrth, now leiff thi haill plesance;
Now leiff thi bliss, now leiff thi childis age;
Now leiff thi youth, now folow thi hard chance;
Now leiff thi lust, now leiff thi mariage;

Now leiff thi luff, for thou sall loss a gage
Quhilk never in erd sall be redemyt agayne.
                    Wallace (attrib. to Blind Harry)

In thee was wyt, fredom, and hardines;
In thee was truth, manheid, and nobilnes;
In thee was rewll, in thee was governans;
In thee was wertu withoutys warians. *Ib.*

Boccaccio, Giovanni   c. 1313-1375

Do as we say, and not as we do. *Decameron*, 3

Boethius, Ancius Manlius Severinus   c. 480-525

*In omni adversitate fortunae, infelicissimum est
genus infortunii, fuisse felicem.* At every blow of
fate, the cruellest kind of misfortune is to have
been happy. *De Consolatione Philosophiae*, 2

*Nihil est miserum nisi cum putes; contraque beata
sors omnis est aequanimatate tolerantis.* Nothing
is miserable unless you think it so; conversely,
every lot is happy if you are content with it. *Ib.*

*Quis legem dat amantibus? Major lex amor est
sibi.* Who can give a law to lovers? Love is a
greater law unto itself. *Ib.* 3

Bolingbroke, Henry St. John, Viscount   1678-1751

Plain truth will influence half a score of men at
most in a nation, or an age, while mystery will
lead millions by the nose. *Letter*, 1721

I have read somewhere or other—in Dionysius
of Halicarnassus, I think—that History is Philosophy teaching by examples. *On the Study of
History*

The Idea of a Patriot King. *Title of Book*

Bonaparte, Napoleon   **1769-1821**

L'Angleterre est une nation de boutiquiers. England
is a nation of shopkeepers. *Attrib.*

Du sublime au ridicule il n'y a qu'un pas. It is
but a step from the sublime to the ridiculous.
Attrib.

*Soldats, songez que, du haut de ces pyramides
quarante siècles vous contemplent.* Think of it,
soldiers, from the summit of these pyramids, forty
centuries look down upon you. *Speech, Battle
of the Pyramids, 1798*

*Tout soldat français porte dans sa giberne le bâton
de maréchal de France.* Every French soldier
carries a French marshal's baton in his knapsack.
La Vie Militaire sous l'Empire, E. Blaze

*Quant au courage moral, il avait trouvé fort rare,
disait-il, celui de deux heures après minuit; c'est-
à-dire le courage de l'improviste.* As for moral
courage, he had, he said, very rarely encountered
two o'clock in the morning courage; that is, the
courage of the unprepared. *Memorial de Ste.
Hélène*, Las Cases

Borgia, Cesare   **1476-1507**

Aut Caesar aut nihil. Emperor or nothing. *Motto*

Borrow, George   **1803-1881**

"Life is sweet, brother." "Do you think so?"
"Think so! —There's night and day, brother,
both sweet things; sun, moon and stars, brother,

all sweet things; there's likewise a wind on the
heath. Life is very sweet, brother; who would
wish to die?" *Lavengro*, 25

Youth will be served, every dog has his day, and
mine has been a fine one. *Ib.* 92

Bosquet, Pierre François Joseph   1810-1861

C'est magnifique mais ce n'est pas la guerre. It is
magnificent, but it is not war. *At the Battle of
Balaclava*, Oct., 1854

Boyd, Mark Alexander   1563-1601

Twa gods guides me; the ane of tham is blin',
Yea and a bairn brocht up in vanitie;
The next a wife ingenrit of the sea,
And lichter nor a dauphin with her fin.

Sonnet

Braxfield, Lord   1722-1799

[To an eloquent culprit at the bar] Ye're a vera
clever chiel, man, but ye wad be nane the waur
o' a hanging. *Life of Scott*, 48, Lockhart

[The butler gave up his place because Lady Brax-
field was always scolding him.] Lord! Ye've little
to complain o': ye may be thankfu' ye're no
married to her. *Memorials*, 2, Cockburn

[To a juryman.] Come awa, Maister Horner,
come awa, and help us to hang ane o' thae
daamned scoondrels. *Ib.*

[Gerald, a political prisoner, remarked that Christ
had been a reformer.] Muckle he made o' that;
he was hanget. *Ib.*

60

Let them bring me prisoners, and I'll find them law. *Attrib. by* Cockburn

Bridges, Robert   1844-1930

I never shall love the snow again
Since Maurice died. *I Never Shall Love the Snow Again*

Bridie, James (Dr. O. H. Mavor)   1888-1951

"London! Pompous Ignorance sits enthroned there and welcomes Pretentious Mediocrity with flattery and gifts. Oh, dull and witless city! Very hell for the restless, inquiring, sensitive soul. Paradise for the snob, the parasite and the prig; the pimp, the placeman and the cheapjack." *The Anatomist*, 3

"The Heart of Man, we are told, is deceitful and desperately wicked. However that may be, it consists of four chambers, the right ventricle, the left ventricle, the left auricle, the right auricle. . . ." *Ib.*

Boredom is a sign of satisfied ignorance, blunted apprehension, crass sympathies, dull understanding, feeble powers of attention and irreclaimable weakness of character. *Mr. Bolfry*

Bright, John   1811-1889

The angel of death has been abroad throughout the land; you may almost hear the beating of his wings. *Speech in House of Commons*, 1855

England is the mother of Parliaments.
Ib., Birmingham 1865

Force is not a remedy. *Ib.* 1880

Brontë, Anne   **1820-1849**

The human heart is like Indian rubber: a little
swells it, but a great deal will not burst it. *Agnes
Grey*, 13

There is always a " but " in this imperfect world.
            The Tenant of Wildfell Hall, 22

All our talents increase in the using, and every
faculty, both good and bad, strengthens by
exercise. *Ib.* 23

Brontë, Charlotte   **1816-1855**

Conventionality is not morality. Self-righteousness is not religion. To attack the first is not to
assail the last. To pluck the mask from the face
of the Pharisee, is not to lift an impious hand to
the Crown of Thorns. *Jane Eyre*, preface

Life, believe, is not a dream,
    So dark as sages say;
Oft a little morning rain
    Foretells a pleasant day! *Life*

Had I been in anything inferior to him, he would
not have hated me so thoroughly, but I knew all
that he knew, and, what was worse, he suspected
that I kept the padlock of silence on mental
wealth in which he was no sharer. *The Professor*, 4

Novelists should never allow themselves to weary
of the study of real life. *Ib.* 19

If there is one notion I hate more than another,
it is that of marriage—I mean marriage in the
vulgar, weak sense, as a mere matter of sentiment.
                                Shirley, 2

Alfred and I intended to be married in this way
almost from the first; we never meant to be
spliced in the humdrum way of other people.
Villette, 42

Brontë, Emily   1818-1848

Oh, for the time when I shall sleep
Without identity. *Oh, For the Time When I Shall
Sleep*

No coward soul is mine,
No trembler in the world's storm-troubled sphere:
I see Heaven's glories shine,
And faith shines equal, arming me from fear.
Last Lines

Vain are the thousand creeds
That move men's hearts: unutterably vain;
Worthless as withered weeds. *Ib.*

Oh dreadful is the check—intense the agony—
When the ear begins to hear and the eye begins
   to see;
When the pulse begins to throb, the brain to
   think again;
The soul to feel the flesh and the flesh to feel the
   chain! *The Prisoner*

Sweet Love of youth, forgive if I forget thee
While the World's tide is bearing me along;
Sterner desires and darker hopes beset me,
Hopes which obscure but cannot do thee wrong.
Remembrance

He was, and is yet, most likely, the wearisomest,
self-righteous pharisee that ever ransacked a Bible

to rake the promises to himself and fling the curses on his neighbours. *Wuthering Heights*, 5

I lingered round them, under that benign sky: watched the moths fluttering among the heath and hare-bells; listened to the soft wind breathing through the grass; and wondered how anyone could ever imagine unquiet slumbers for the sleepers in that quiet earth. *Ib.* last lines

Brooke, Rupert   **1887-1915**

And I shall find some girl perhaps,
And a better one than you,
With eyes as wise, but kindlier,
And lips as soft, but true
And I dare say she will do.   *The Chilterns*

Blow out, you bugles, over the rich Dead!
                                                      The Dead

These laid the world away; poured out the red
Sweet wine of youth. *Ib.*

Because God put His adamantine fate
    Between my sullen heart and its desire,
I swore that I would burst the Iron Gate,
    Rise up, and curse Him on His throne of fire.
                                                      Failure

For Cambridge people rarely smile,
Being urban, squat, and packed with guile.
                                                      Grantchester

I thought when love for you died, I should die.
It's dead. Alone, mostly strangely, I live on. *The Life Beyond*

64

Nothing to shake the laughing heart's long peace
   there
But only agony and that has ending;
And the worst friend and enemy is but Death.
Peace

Leave the sick hearts that honour could not move,
And half-men, and their dirty songs and dreary,
And all the little emptiness of love. *Ib.*

If I should die, think only this of me:
That there's some corner of a foreign field
That is for ever England. *The Soldier*

A dust whom England bore, shaped, made aware,
Gave once, her flowers to love, her ways to roam,
A body of England's breathing English air,
Washed by the rivers, blest by the suns of home.
Ib.

And laughter, learnt of friends; and gentleness,
In hearts at peace, under an English heaven. *Ib.*

Brown, Thomas   **1663-1704**

A leap into the dark. *Letters from the Dead*

I do not love you, Dr. Fell,
But why I cannot tell;
But this I know full well,
I do not love you, Dr. Fell.
Trans. of an Epigram of Martial

Brown, Thomas Edward   **1830-1897**

A garden is a lovesome thing, God wot!
My Garden

Browne, Sir Thomas   **1605-1682**

He who discommendeth others obliquely commendeth himself. *Christian Morals*

What song the Sirens sang, or what name Achilles assumed when he hid himself among the women, though puzzling questions, are not beyond all conjecture. *Hydriotaphia*

I am not so much afraid of death, as ashamed thereof; 'tis the very disgrace and ignominy of our natures. *Religio Medici*

No man can justly censure or condemn another, because indeed no man truly knows another. *Ib.*

There is surely a piece of divinity in us, something that was before the elements, and owes no homage unto the sun. *Ib.*

Browne, Sir William   **1692-1774**

The King to Oxford sent a troop of horse,
For Tories own no argument but force:
With equal skill to Cambridge books he sent,
For Whigs admit no force but argument.
                    A Reply to Trapp's Epigram, q.v.

Browning, Elizabeth Barrett   **1806-1861**

Of writing many books there is no end.
                    Aurora Leigh, 1

        Let no one till his death
Be called unhappy. Measure not the work
Until the day's out and the labour done. *Ib.* 5

Since when was genius found respectable? *Ib.* 6

The devil's most devilish when respectable. *Ib.* 7

> Earth's crammed with heaven,
And every common bush afire with God. *Ib.*

"Yes," I answered you last night;
"No," this morning, sir, I say.
Colours seen by candle-light
Will not look the same by day.   *The Lady's Yes*

If thou must love me, let it be for naught
Except for love's sake only.
Sonnets from the Portuguese, 14

There, Shakespeare, on whose forehead climb
The crowns o' the world. Oh, eyes sublime,
With tears and laughters for all time!
A Vision of Poets, 100

Browning, Robert   **1812-1889**

Ah, but a man's reach should exceed his grasp,
Or what's a heaven for?   *Andrea del Sarto*

I am grown peaceful as old age tonight.
I regret a little, I would change still less. *Ib.*

There up and spoke a brisk little somebody,
Critic and whippersnapper, in a rage
To set things right.   *Balaustion's Adventure*

> Truth that peeps
Over the edge when dinner's done,
And body gets its sop and holds its noise
And leaves soul free a little. *Bishop Blougram's Apology*

67

The common problem, yours, mine, everyone's,
Is not to fancy what were fair in life
Provided it could be,—but, finding first
What may be, then find how to make it fair. *Ib.*

Just when we are safest, there's a sunset-touch,
A fancy from a flower-bell, some one's death,
A chorus-ending from Euripides,—
And that's enough for fifty hopes and fears
As old and new at once as Nature's self,
To rap and knock and enter in our soul. *Ib.*

All we have gained then by our unbelief
Is a life of doubt diversified by faith,
For one of faith diversified by doubt:
We called the chess-board white,—we call it black.
                                             Ib.
If once we choose belief, on all accounts
We can't be too decisive in our faith. *Ib.*

Brave with the needlework of Noodledom. *Ib.*

I show you doubt, to prove that faith exists. *Ib.*

        Gigadibs the literary man,
Who played with spoons. *Ib.*

Blue as a vein o'er the Madonna's breast.
The Bishop Orders his Tomb in St. Praxed's Church

                And brown Greek manuscripts,
And mistresses with great smooth marbly limbs.
                                             Ib.

Letting the rank tongue blossom into speech.
                        Caliban upon Setebos

He must be wicked to deserve such pain.
Childe Roland to the Dark Tower Came

Toads in a poisoned tank,
Or wild cats in a red-hot iron cage. *Ib.*

He took such cognisance of men and things. *Ib.*

In youth I looked to these very skies,
And probing their immensities,
I found God there. *Christmas Eve*

For the loving worm within its clod,
Were diviner than a loveless god. *Ib.*

And I have written three books on the soul,
Proving absurd all written hitherto,
And putting us to ignorance again. *Cleon*

There's a world of capability
For joy, spread round about us, meant for us,
Inviting us. *Ib.*

She should never have looked at me,
If she meant I should not love her! *Cristina*

Stung by the splendour of a sudden thought.
A Death in the Desert

Open my heart and you will see
Graved inside of it, ' Italy.' *De Gustibus*

Karshish, the picker up of learning's crumbs,
The not-incurious in God's handiwork.
An Epistle

That puff of vapour from his mouth, man's soul.
Ib.

The man's fantastic will is the man's law.   *Ib.*

Truth never hurts the teller.   *Fifine at the Fair*

    Where the haters meet
In the crowded city's horrible street.
                The Flight of the Duchess

When the liquor's out, why clink the cannikin?
                                    Ib.

Your business is to paint the souls of men.
                           Fra Lippo Lippi

If you get simple beauty and nought else,
You get about the best thing God invents.   *Ib.*

You should not take a fellow eight years old
And make him swear to never kiss the girls.   *Ib.*

Oh, if we draw a circle premature,
  Heedless of far gain,
Greedy for quick returns of profit, sure,
  Bad is our bargain.
                A Grammarian's Funeral

The low man goes on adding one to one,
  His hundred's soon hit;
This high man, aiming at a million
  Misses a unit.   *Ib.*

God help all poor souls lost in the dark!
                The Heretic's Tragedy

Oh, to be in England,
Now that April's there.
             Home-Thoughts from Abroad

That's the wise thrush; he sings each song twice
over,
Lest you should think he never could recapture
The first fine careless rapture! *Ib.*

Nobly, nobly Cape St. Vincent to the North-
west died away.
Home-Thoughts from the Sea

I sprang to the stirrup, and Joris, and he;
I galloped, Dirck galloped, we galloped all three.
'*How they brought the Good News from Ghent
to Aix.*'

Women hate a debt as men a gift.
In a Balcony

I count life just a stuff
To try the soul's strength on, educe the man. *Ib.*

Who knows but the world may end to-night?
The Last Ride Together

Just for a handful of silver he left us,
Just for a riband to stick in his coat.
The Lost Leader

One more devils'-triumph, and sorrow for angels,
One wrong more to man, one more insult to God!
Ib.

She liked whate'er
She looked on, and her looks went everywhere.
My Last Duchess

I gave commands
Then all smiles stopped together. *Ib.*

Never the time and the place
  And the loved one all together!
Never the Time and the Place

Works done least rapidly, Art most cherishes.
Old Pictures in Florence

God be thanked, the meanest of his creatures
Boasts two soul-sides, one to face the world with,
One to show a woman when he loves her.
One Word More

Truth is within ourselves. *Paracelsus*

    God is the perfect poet,
Who in his person acts his own creations. *Ib.*

I give the fight up: let there be an end,
A privacy, an obscure nook for me.
I want to be forgotten even by God. *Ib.*

It is the glory and good of Art,
That Art remains the one way possible
Of speaking truths, to mouths like mine at least.
Ib.

It was roses, roses, all the way,
With myrtle mixed in my path like mad.
The Patriot

Ah, thought which saddens while it soothes!
Pictor Ignotus

Rats!
They fought the dogs and killed the cats,
And bit the babies in the cradles.
The Pied Piper of Hamelin

And the muttering grew to a grumbling
And the grumbling grew to a mighty rumbling
And out of the houses rats came tumbling. *Ib.*

So munch on, crunch on, take your nuncheon,
Breakfast, supper, dinner, luncheon! *Ib.*

The lark's on the wing
The snail's on the thorn
    God's in his heaven—
All's right with the world. *Pippa Passes*

In the morning of the world,
    When earth was nigher heaven than now. *Ib.*

    Whoso mounts the throne
For beauty, knowledge, strength, should stand
    alone,
And mortals love the letters of his name. *Protus*

    Grow old along with me!
    The best is yet to be,
The last of life for which the first was made:
    Our times are in His hand
    Who saith, " A whole I planned,
Youth shows but half; trust God: see all, nor
    be afraid! " *Rabbi Ben Ezra*

Irks care the crop-full bird? Frets doubt the
    maw-crammed beast? *Ib.*

    Now, who shall arbitrate?
    Ten men love what I hate,
Shun what I follow, slight what I receive. *Ib.*

My times be in Thy hand!
Perfect the cup as planned!

73

Let age approve of youth, and death complete
the same! *Ib.*

Well, British Public, ye who like me not.
The Ring and the Book

Youth means love,
Vows can't change nature, priests are only men.
Ib.

The story always old and always new. *Ib.*

White shall not neutralise the black, nor good
Compensate bad in man, absolve him so:
Life's business being just the terrible choice. *Ib.*

Faultless to a fault. *Ib.*

'Tis not what man does which exalts him, but
what a man would do! *Saul*

Plague take all your pedants, say I!
Sibrandus Schafraburgensis

If hate killed men, Brother Lawrence,
God's blood, would not mine kill you!
Soliloquy of the Spanish Cloister

One who never turned his back but marched breast
forward,
Never doubted clouds would break,
Never dreamed, though right were worsted, wrong
would triumph
Held we fall to rise, are baffled to fight better,
Sleep to wake. *Summum Bonum*, epilogue

What of soul was left, I wonder, when the kissing
had to stop? *A Toccata of Galuppi's*

Bang, whang, whang, goes the drum, *tootle-te-tootle,* the fife
Oh a day in the city square, there is no such pleasure in life.
Up at a Villa—Down in the City

Ichabod, Ichabod,
The glory is departed! *Waring*

Bryan, William Jennings　　　　　　　**1860-1925**

I shall not help crucify mankind upon a cross of gold. I shall not aid in pressing down upon the bleeding brow of labor this crown of thorns.
Speech, 1894

The humblest citizen of all the land, when clad in the armor of a righteous cause is stronger than all the hosts of error. *Ib. Chicago,* 1896

An orator is a man who says what he thinks and feels what he says. *The Peerless Leader,* Hibben

Buchanan, Robert Williams　　　　　**1841-1901**

All that is beautiful shall abide,
All that is base shall die. *Balder the Beautiful*

The buying and the selling, and the strife
Of little natures. *De Berney*

But his eddication to his ruination had not been over nice,
And his stupid skull was choking full of vulgar prejudice. *Phil Blood's Leap*

A race that binds
Its body in chains and calls them Liberty,
And calls each fresh link Progress.
Titan and Avatar

Beauty and Truth, though never found, are worthy
to be sought. *To David in Heaven*

Buckingham, George Villiers, Second Duke of
1628-1687

The world is made up for the most part of fools and
knaves. *To Mr. Clifford, on his Humane Reason*

Bullet, Gerald 1893-1958
So, when a new book comes his way,
By someone still alive to-day,
Our Honest John, with right good will,
Sharpens his pencil for the kill. *A Reviewer*

Bunyan, John 1628-1688

It beareth the name of Vanity-Fair, because the
town where 'tis kept, is lighter than vanity.
Pilgrim's Progress, 1

Hanging is too good for him, said Mr. Cruelty. *Ib.*

Now Giant Despair had a wife, and her name was
Diffidence. *Ib.*

Then I saw there was a way to hell, even from
the gates of heaven. *Ib.*

. . . a man that could look no way but downwards,
with a muck-rake in his hand. . . . The man did
neither look up nor regard, but raked to himself
the straws, the small sticks, and dust of the
floor. *Ib.* 2

76

One leak will sink a ship, and one sin will destroy a sinner. *Ib.*

He that is down need fear no fall,
He that is low no pride. *Ib.*

Who would true valour see,
  Let him come hither. *Ib.*

My sword, I give to him that shall succeed me in my pilgrimage, and my courage and skill to him that can get it. *Ib.*

So he passed over, and all the trumpets sounded for him on the other side. *Ib.*

Burgess, Gelett   **1866-1951**

I never saw a Purple Cow,
I never hope to see one;
But I can tell you, anyhow,
I'd rather see than be one!
Appeared in The Lark, San Francisco, May, 1895

Ah, yes! I wrote the " Purple Cow "—
I'm sorry, now, I wrote it!
But I can tell you, anyhow,
I'll kill you if you quote it!
               Burgess Nonsense Book, The Purple Cow

Love is only chatter,
Friends are all that matter. *Willy and the Lady.*

Bromides and sulphites. *First used by Burgess in 1907 to mean respectively, the majority of mankind who think and talk alike, and the select majority who " eliminate the obvious from their conversation."*

It is the nature of all greatness not to be exact.
    Speech (on American taxation), 1774

Passion for fame; a passion which is the instinct
of all great souls. *Ib.*

To tax and to please, no more than to love and
to be wise, is not given to men. *Ib.*

Young man, there is America—which at this day
serves for little more than to amuse you with
stories of savage men, and uncouth manners; yet
shall, before you taste of death, show itself equal
to the whole of that commerce which now
attracts the envy of the world. *Ib. (on conciliation
with America),* 1775

The use of force alone is but *temporary.* It may
subdue for a moment; but it does not remove
the necessity of subduing again: and a nation
is not governed, which is perpetually to be
conquered. *Ib.*

The mysterious virtue of wax and parchment. *Ib.*

I do not know the method of drawing up an indictment against a whole people. *Ib.*

The people are the masters. *Speech,* 1780

The people never give up their liberties but under
some delusion. *Ib.* 1784

An event . . . upon which it is difficult to speak,
and impossible to be silent. *Ib. (on impeachment
of Warren Hastings),* 1789

A state without the means of some change is without the means of its conservation. *Reflections on the Revolution in France*

The only infallible criterion of wisdom to vulgar judgements—success. *Letter*, 1791

Tyrants seldom want pretexts. *Ib.*

Burne-Jones, Sir Edward   1833-1898

I mean by a picture a beautiful, romantic dream of something that never was, never will be—in a light better than any lights that ever shone—in a land no one can define or remember, only desire—and the forms divinely beautiful—and then I wake up, with the waking of Brynhild.
Letter

Burney, Fanny [Mme. D'Arblay]   1752-1840

Dancing? Oh, dreadful! How it was ever adopted in a civilised country I cannot find out; 'tis certainly a Barbarian exercise, and of savage origin. *Cecilia*, 3

"Do you come to the play without knowing what it is?" "Oh, yes, sir, yes, very frequently. I have no time to read play-bills. One merely comes to meet one's friends, and show that one's alive." *Evelina*, 20

Nothing is so delicate as the reputation of a woman; it is at once the most beautiful and most brittle of all human things. *Ib.* 39

Indeed, the freedom with which Dr. Johnson condemns whatever he disapproves is astonishing.
Diary, 23 Aug., 1778

Burns, Robert **1759-1796**

O Thou! Whatever title suit thee—
Auld Hornie, Satan, Nick, or Clootie.
Address to the Deil

Then gently scan your brother man,
Still gentler sister woman;
Tho' they may gang a kennin wrang,
To step aside is human.
Address to the Unco Guid

Freedom and whisky gang thegither,
Tak aff your dram!
Author's Earnest Cry and Prayer

To see her is to love her,
And love but her for ever,
For Nature made her what she is,
And ne'er made anither! *Bonnie Lesley*

Scots wha hae wi' Wallace bled.
Bruce before Bannockburn

By Oppression's woes and pains!
By your sons in servile chains!
We will drain our dearest veins,
   But they shall be free! *Ib.*

Contented wi' little and cantie wi' mair,
Whene'er I foregather wi' Sorrow and Care,
I gie them a skelp, as they're creepin' alang,
Wi' a cog o' guid swats and an auld Scottish sang.
Contented wi' Little

From scenes like these old Scotia's grandeur
   springs,
That makes her loved at home, revered abroad:

80

Princes and lords are but the breath of kings,
" An honest man's the noblest work of God."
The Cotter's Saturday Night

I wasna fou, but just had plenty.
Death and Dr. Hornbook

Who will not sing *God Save the King*
    Shall hang as high's the steeple;
But while we sing *God Save the King*,
    We'll ne'er forget the People!
Does Haughty Gaul Invasion Threat?

But Facts are chiels that winna ding,
An' downa be disputed. *A Dream*

A Gentleman who held the patent for his honours
immediately from Almighty God. *Elegy on Capt.
Matthew Henderson.*

The heart ay's the part ay
That makes us right or wrang. *Epistle to Davie*

What's a' your jargon o' your schools,
Your Latin names for horns and stools;
If honest Nature made you fools,
    What sairs your grammars?
First Epistle to Lapraik

Gie me ae spark o' Nature's fire,
That's a' the learning I desire. *Ib.*

Some rhyme a neebor's name to lash;
Some rhyme (vain thought!) for needfu' cash;
Some rhyme to court the contra clash,
    An' raise a din;
For me, an aim I never fash:
    I rhyme for fun. *Epistle to James Smith*

An' fareweel dear, deludıng Woman,
   The joy of joys. *Ib.*

Leeze me on drink! it gies us mair
    Than either school or college;
It ken'les wit, it waukens lear,
    It pangs us fou o' knowledge. *The Holy Fair*

There's some are fou o' love divine,
There's some are fou o' brandy;
An' monie jobs that day begin,
May end in houghmagandie
       Some ither day. *Ib.*

O Thou that in the heavens does dwell,
Wha, as it pleases best Thysel,
Sends ane to heaven, and ten to hell,
    A' for Thy glory,
And no' for ony guid or ill
    They've done afore Thee! *Holy Willie's Prayer*

Yet I am here, a chosen sample,
To show Thy grace is great and ample:
I'm here a pillar o' Thy temple,
    Strong as a rock,
A guide, a buckler, and example
    To a' Thy flock! *Ib.*

But yet, O Lord! confess I must,
At times I'm fashed wi' fleshly lust;
And sometimes, too, wi' warldly trust,
    Vile self gets in;
But Thou remembers we are dust,
    Defil'd wi' sin. *Ib.*

The rank is but the guinea's stamp,
The man's the gowd for a' that.
      Is there for Honest Poverty ?

For a' that, an' a' that,
It's comin yet for a' that,
That man to man the world o'er
Shall brithers be for a' that. *Ib.*

Wae worth thy power, thou cursed leaf!
Fell source of a' my woe and grief,
For lack o' thee I've lost my lass,
For lack o' thee I scrimp my glass.
Lines written on a Bank Note

Poor Andrew that tumbles for sport
Let naebody name wi' a jeer:
There's even, I'm tauld, i' the Court
A tumbler ca'd the Premier.
Love and Liberty (or *The Jolly Beggars*)

But och! they catch'd him at the last,
And bound him in a dungeon fast.
My curse upon them every one—
They've hang'd my braw John Highlandman! *Ib.*

Whistle owre the lave o't. *Ib.*

[Of women]
Their tricks an' craft hae put me daft,
They've taen me in, an' a' that;
But clear your decks, an' here's the Sex!
I like the jads for a' that. *Ib.*

A fig for those by law protected!
Liberty's a glorious feast!
Courts for cowards were erected,
Churches built to please the priest! *Ib.*

83

May coward shame distain his name,
The wretch that dares not die!
                    Macpherson's Farewell

Man's inhumanity to man
Makes countless thousands mourn!
                    Man was made to Mourn

If I'm design'd yon lordling's slave—
By Nature's law design'd—
Why was an independent wish
E'er planted in my mind? *Ib.*

Hear, Land o' Cakes, and brither Scots.
          On Captain Grose's Peregrinations

A child's amang you taking notes,
          And, faith, he'll prent it. *Ib.*

An idiot race, to honour lost—
Who know them best, despise them most.
  On Seeing the Royal Palace at Stirling in Ruins

Hail, Poesie! thou nymph reserv'd!
In chase o' thee, what crowds hae swerv'd
Frae Common Sense, or sunk ennerv'd
            'Mang heaps o' clavers;
And Och! o'er aft thy joes hae starv'd
    'Mid a' thy favors!   *Sketch*

But pleasures are like poppies spread—
You seize the flow'r, its bloom is shed;
Or like the snow falls in the river—
A moment white—then melts for ever;
Or like the Borealis race,
That flit ere you can point their place;
Or like the rainbow's lovely form
Evanishing amid the storm.   *Tam o' Shanter*

We labour soon, we labour late,
To feed the titled knave, man,
And a' the comfort we're to get,
Is that ayont the grave, man. *The Tree of Liberty*

I see how folk live that hae riches;
But surely poor-folk maun be wretches!
The Twa Dogs

But human bodies are sic fools,
For a' their colleges and schools,
That when nae real ills perplex them,
They mak enow themsels to vex them. *Ib.*

He'll hae misfortunes great and sma',
But aye a heart aboon them a'.
There was a Lad

That I for poor auld Scotland's sake,
Some usefu' plan or beuk could make,
Or sing a sang at least.
To the Guidwife of Wauchope House

O wad some Power the giftie gie us
To see oursels as others see us!
It wad frae monie a blunder free us,
   An' foolish notion:
What airs in dress an' gait wad lea'e us
   An' ev'n devotion! *To a Louse.*

I'm truly sorry man's dominion
Has broken Nature's social union,
An' justifies that ill opinion
   Which makes thee startle
At me, thy poor, earth-born companion
   An' fellow mortal. *To a Mouse*

The best laid schemes o' mice an' men
Gang aft a-gley. *Ib.*

85

Their sighin', cantin', grace-proud faces,
Their three mile prayers, and half mile graces.
To the Rev. John McMath

We are na fou, we're nae that fou,
    But just a drappie in our e'e!
The cock may craw, the day may daw,
    And ay we'll taste the barley-bree!
Willie Brew'd a Peck o' Maut

Her nose and chin they threaten ither.
Willie's Wife

To be overtopped in anything else I can bear: but in the tests of generous love I defy all mankind. *Letter to Clarinda*

I am quite transported at the thought that ere long, perhaps very soon, I shall bid an eternal adieu to all the pains, and uneasiness and disquietudes of this weary life; for I assure you I am heartily tired of it, and, if I do not very much deceive myself I could contentedly and gladly resign it.
Letter to his Father

As for this world I despair of ever making a figure in it—I am not formed for the bustle of the busy nor the flutter of the gay. I shall never again be capable of it. *Ib.*

. . . the story of Wallace poured a Scottish prejudice in my veins, which will boil along there till the floodgates of life shut in eternal rest.
Letters to Dr. John Moore

Whatever mitigates the woes or increases the happiness of others, this is my criterion of goodness; and whatever injures society at large, or any individual in it, this is my measure of iniquity. *Ib.*

What a rocky-hearted, perfidious Succubus was that Queen Elizabeth! Judas Iscariot was a sad dog to be sure, but still his demerits sink to insignificance, compared with the doings of the infernal Bess Tudor. *Ib.*

I am a strict economist; not, indeed, for the sake of the money; but one of the principal parts in my composition is a kind of pride of stomach; and I scorn to fear the face of any man living.
Letter to John Murdoch

After all my boasted independence, curst necessity compels me to implore you for five pounds. . . . Do, for God's Sake, send me that sum, and that by return of post. . . . Forgive, forgive me! *Letter to George Thomson*

Burton, Robert   1577-1640

All my joys to this are folly,
Naught so sweet as Melancholy. *Anatomy of Melancholy. Author's Abstract of Melancholy*

Hinc quam sit calamus saevior ense patet. Hence it is clear how much more cruel the pen is than the sword. *Ib.* 1

Tobacco, divine, rare, superexcellent tobacco, which goes far beyond all their panaceas, potable gold, and philosopher's stones, a sovereign remedy to all diseases. *Ib.* 2

Diogenes struck the father when the son swore.
Ib. 3

England is a paradise for women, and hell for
horses: Italy a paradise for horses, hell for
women. *Ib.*

One religion is as true as another. *Ib.*

Bussy-Rabutin, Comte de 1618-1693

*L'absence est à l'amour ce qu'est au feu le vent;
il éteint le petit, il allume le grand.* Absence is to
love what wind is to fire; it extinguishes the
small, it inflames the great. *Histoire amoureuse
des Gaules*

Butler, Samuel 1612-1680

For he, by geometric scale,
Could take the size of pots of ale; . . .
And wisely tell what hour o' th' day
The clock doth strike, by algebra. *Hudibras*, 1

And prove their doctrine orthodox
By apostolic blows and knocks. *Ib.*

For rhyme the rudder is of verses,
With which like ships they steer their courses. *Ib.*

Some have been beaten till they know
What wood a cudgel's of by th' blow;
Some kick'd, until they can feel whether
A shoe be Spanish or neats-leather. *Ib.* 2

She that with poetry is won
Is but a desk to write upon. *Ib.*

Oaths are but words, and words but wind. *Ib.*

> As the ancients
> Say wisely, Have a care o' th' main chance,
> And look before you ere you leap;
> For, as you sow, you are like to reap. *Ib.*

What makes all doctrines plain and clear?
About two hundred pounds a year.
And that which was prov'd true before,
Prove false again? Two hundred more. *Ib.* 3

Butler, Samuel   1835-1902

Life is one long process of getting tired. *Note Books*

Life is the art of drawing sufficient conclusions from insufficient premises. *Ib.*

All progress is based upon a universal innate desire on the part of every organism to live beyond its income. *Ib.*

When the righteous man turneth away from his righteousness that he hath committed and doeth that which is neither quite lawful nor quite right, he will generally be found to have gained in amiability what he has lost in holiness. *Ib.*

To himself every one is an immortal; he may know that he is going to die, but he can never know that he is dead. *Ib.*

We think as we do, mainly because other people think so. *Ib.*

The history of art is the history of revivals. *Ib.*

The phrase " unconscious humour " is the one contribution I have made to the current literature of the day. *Ib.*

An apology for the Devil: it must be remembered that we have only heard one side of the case. God has written all the books. *Ib.*

God is Love, I dare say. But what a mischievous devil Love is. *Ib.*

To live is like love, all reason is against it, and all healthy instinct for it. *Ib.*

The public buys its opinions as it buys its meat, or takes in its milk, on the principle that it is cheaper to do this than keep a cow. So it is, but the milk is more likely to be watered. *Ib.*

I do not mind lying, but I hate inaccuracy. *Ib.*

The world will, in the end, follow only those who have despised as well as served it. *Ib.*

An honest God's the noblest work of man. *Further Extracts from the Note-Books* (cf. p. 241)

'Tis better to have loved and lost than never to have lost at all. *The Way of All Flesh* (cf. Tennyson, *In Memoriam*, p. 414)

Byrom, John   1692-1763

Where you find
Bright passages that strike your mind,

90

And which perhaps you may have reason
To think on at another season,—
—Take them down in black and white.
Hint to a Young Person

God bless the King!—I mean the Faith's
    Defender;
God bless (no harm in blessing) the Pretender!
But who Pretender is, or who is King,
God bless us all!—that's quite another thing.
To an Officer in the Army

Byron, George Gordon, Lord   1788-1824

His heart was one of those which most enamour
    us,
Wax to receive, and marble to retain. *Beppo*

Mark! where his carnage and his conquests cease!
He makes a solitude, and calls it—peace!
The Bride of Abydos

Adieu, adieu! my native shore
    Fades o'er the waters blue. *Childe Harold*, 1

Convention is the dwarfish demon styled
That foiled the knights in Marialva's dome. *Ib.*

Ambition's honoured fools. *Ib.*

And must they fall? the young, the proud, the
    brave,
To swell one bloated Chief's unwholesome reign?
Ib.

Here all were noble, save Nobility;
None hugged a Conqueror's chain, save fallen
    Chivalry! *Ib.*

91

A schoolboy's tale, the wonder of an hour. *Ib.* 2

The last, the worst, dull spoiler, who was he? *Ib.*

The Ocean Queen, the free Britannia, bears
The last poor plunder from a bleeding land. *Ib.*

But midst the crowd, the hum, the shock of men,
To hear, to see, to feel, and to possess. *Ib.*

Hereditary Bondsmen! know ye not
Who would be free themselves must strike the
    blow? *Ib.*

Death in the front, Destruction in the rear! *Ib.*

What is the worst of woes that wait on Age?
What stamps the wrinkle deeper on the brow?
To view each loved one blotted from Life's page,
And be alone on earth, as I am now. *Ib.*

Since my young days of passion—joy or pain—
Perchance my heart and harp have lost a string—
And both may jar. *Ib.* 3

                               Years steal
Fire from the mind as vigour from the limb;
And Life's enchanted cup but sparkles near the
    brim. *Ib.*

He would not yield dominion of his mind
To Spirits against whom his own rebelled.   *Ib.*

On with the dance! let joy be unconfined;
No sleep till morn, when Youth and Pleasure meet
To chase the glowing Hours with flying feet. *Ib.*

There is a very life in our despair,
Vitality of poison. *Ib.*

      That untaught innate philosophy,
Which, be it Wisdom, Coldness, or deep Pride,
Is gall and wormwood to an enemy. *Ib.*

. . . . the madmen who have made men mad
By their contagion; Conquerors and Kings,
Founders of sects and systems. *Ib.*

He who ascends to mountain tops, shall find
The loftiest peaks most wrapt in clouds and
    snow;
He who surpasses or subdues mankind,
Must look down on the hate of those below. *Ib.*

To fly from, need not be to hate, mankind. *Ib.*

I live not in myself, but I become
Portion of that around me; and to me
High mountains are a feeling, but the hum
Of human cities torture. *Ib.*

Are not the mountains, waves, and skies, a part
Of me and of my Soul, as I of them?   *Ib.*

For 'tis his nature to advance or die.   *Ib.*

I have not loved the World, nor the World me;
I have not flattered its rank breath, nor bowed
To its idolatries a patient knee,
Nor coined my cheek to smiles. *Ib.*

I stood in Venice, on the Bridge of Sighs;
A palace and a prison on each hand.   *Ib.* 4

The Moon is up, and yet it is not night—
Sunset divides the sky with her—a sea
Of glory streams along the Alpine height
Of blue Friuli's mountain. *Ib.*

Then farewell, Horace; whom I hated so,
Not for thy faults but mine. *Ib.*

> His manly brow
Consents to death, but conquers agony. *Ib.*

He heard it, but he heeded not—his eyes
Were with his heart, and that was far away. *Ib.*

> He, their sire,
Butcher'd to make a Roman holiday. *Ib.*

While stands the Coliseum, Rome shall stand:
When falls the Coliseum, Rome shall fall;
And when Rome falls—the World. *Ib.*

Such hath it been—shall be—beneath the sun
The many still must labour for the one.
The Corsair, 1

The weak alone repent. *Ib.* 2

The fountain moves without a wind: but shall
The ripple of a spring change my resolve?
The Deformed Transformed

The flower of Adam's bastards. *Ib.*

> Your old philosophers
Beheld mankind as mere spectators of
The Olympic games. When I behold a prize
Worth wrestling for I may be found a Milo. *Ib.*

94

The Assyrian came down like the wolf on the fold.
Destruction of Sennacherib

I wish he would explain his explanation.
Don Juan, dedication

What men call gallantry, and gods adultery,
Is much more common where the climate's sultry.
Ib. 1

Even innocence itself has many a wile,
And will not dare to trust itself with truth,
And love is taught hypocrisy from youth. *Ib.*

Christians have burnt each other, quite persuaded
That all the Apostles would have done as they
did. *Ib.*

Whether it was she did not see, or would not,
Or, like all very clever people, could not. *Ib.*

A little still she strove, and much repented,
And whispering " I will ne'er consent "—consented. *Ib.*

Thou shalt believe in Milton, Dryden, Pope;
Thou shalt not set up Wordsworth, Coleridge,
Southey. *Ib.*

A solitary shriek, the bubbling cry
Of some strong swimmer in his agony. *Ib.* 2

Let us have wine and women, mirth and laughter,
Sermons and soda water the day after. *Ib.*

Man, being reasonable, must get drunk;
The best of life is but intoxication:
Glory, the grape, love, gold, in these are sunk
The hopes of all men, and of every nation. *Ib.*

Each kiss a heart-quake,—for a kiss's strength,
I think it must be reckon'd by its length.   *Ib.*

Think you, if Laura had been Petrarch's wife,
He would have written sonnets all his life? *Ib.* 3

He was the mildest manner'd man
That ever scuttled ship or cut a throat.   *Ib.*

The mountains look on Marathon—
And Marathon looks on the sea;
And musing there an hour alone,
I dream'd that Greece might still be free.   *Ib.*

We learn from Horace, "Homer sometimes
    sleeps";
We feel without him, Wordsworth sometimes
    wakes. *Ib.*

Nothing so difficult as a beginning
In poesy, unless perhaps the end. *Ib.* 4

And if I laugh at any mortal thing,
'Tis that I may not weep. *Ib.*

"Whom the gods love die young" was said of
    yore. *Ib.*

That all-softening, overpowering knell,
The tocsin of the soul—the dinner-bell.   *Ib.* 5

There is a tide in the affairs of women,
Which, taken at the flood, leads—God knows
    where.   *Ib.* 6

A lady of a "certain age," which means
Certainly aged. *Ib.*

" Let there be light! " said God, " and there was
    light! "
" Let there be blood! " says man, and there's a
    sea! *Ib.* 7

And, after all, what is a lie? 'Tis but
    The truth in masquerade. *Ib.* 11

'Tis strange the mind, that very fiery particle,
Should let itself be snuff'd out by an article. *Ib.*

And hold up to the sun my little taper. *Ib.* 12

Merely innocent flirtation.
Not quite adultery, but adulteration. *Ib.*

Now hatred is by far the longest pleasure;
Men love in haste, but they detest at leisure. *Ib.* 13

The English winter—ending in July,
To recommence in August. *Ib.*

Society is now one polish'd horde,
Form'd of two mighty tribes, the *Bores* and
    Bored. Ib.

Of all the horrid, hideous notes of woe,
    Sadder than owl-songs or the midnight blast,
Is that portentous phrase, " I told you so." *Ib.* 14

'Tis strange—but true; for truth is always strange;
Stranger than fiction. *Ib.*

'Tis pleasant, sure, to see one's name in print;
A Book's a Book, altho' there is nothing in't.
            English Bards and Scotch Reviewers

With just enough of learning to misquote. *Ib.*

97

Better to err with Pope than shine with Pye. *Ib.*

[Of Wordsworth]
Who, both by precept and example, shows
That prose is verse, and verse is merely prose.

Ib.

Be warm but pure: be amorous but chaste. *Ib.*

Who killed John Keats?
  " I," says the Quarterly,
    So savage and Tartarly;
" 'Twas one of my feats."   *John Keats*

Maid of Athens, ere we part,
Give, oh give me back my heart!
Or, since that has left my breast,
Keep it now, and take the rest!   *Maid of Athens*

I know thee for a man of many thoughts.
                     Manfred, 2

          I passed
The nights of years in sciences untaught.   *Ib.*

Her faults were mine—her virtues were her own.
                     Ib.

We are the fools of time and terror: Days
Steal on us, and steal from us; yet we live,
Loathing our life, and dreading still to die.   *Ib.*

    Knowledge is not happiness, and science
But an exchange of ignorance for that
Which is another kind of ignorance.   *Ib., 2*

        There is an order
Of mortals on the earth, who do become
Old in their youth, and die ere middle age.   *Ib., 3*

Old man! 'tis not so difficult to die.   *Ib.*

So we'll go no more a-roving
　　So late into the night
Though the heart be still as loving,
　　And the moon be still as bright.
　　　　　　　So We'll Go No More A-Roving

'Tis vain to struggle—let me perish young—
Live as I lived, and love as I have loved;
To dust if I return, from dust I sprung.
　　　　　　　Stanzas to the Po

Saint Peter sat by the celestial gate:
　　His keys were rusty, and the lock was dull,
So little trouble had been given of late.
　　　　　　The Vision of Judgement

　　That household virtue, most uncommon,
Of constancy to a bad, ugly woman.   *Ib.*

　　For by many stories,
And true, we learn the angels all are Tories. *Ib.*

When a proposal is made to emancipate or relieve,
you hesitate, you deliberate for years, you tem-
porise and tamper with the minds of men; but a
death-bill must be passed off-hand, without a
thought of the consequences. *Maiden speech in
House of Lords*, 27th Feb., 1812

But I am convinced of the advantages of looking
at mankind instead of reading about them,
and the bitter effects of staying at home with
all the narrow prejudices of an islander, that
I think there should be a law amongst us, to set
our young men abroad for a term, among the
few allies our wars have left us. *Letter to Mrs.
Byron*

99

But I never see any one much improved by matrimony. All my coupled contemporaries are bald and discontented. *Journal,* 1813

Cleopatra strikes me as the epitome of her sex— fond, lively, sad, tender, teasing, humble, haughty, beautiful, the devil!—coquettish to the last, as well with the "asp" as with Antony. *Ib.*

The more I see of men, the less I like them. If I could but say so of women too, all would be well. *Ib.* 1814

If I could always read, I should never feel the want of society. *Ib.*

There is something to me very softening in the presence of a woman,—some strange influence, even if one is not in love with them—which I cannot at all account for, having no very high opinion of the sex. *Ib.*

The only pleasure of fame is that it paves the way to pleasure, and the more intellectual our pleasure, the better for the pleasure and for us too. It was, however, agreeable to have heard our fame before dinner, and a girl's harp after. *Ib.* 1821

What is poetry? The feeling of a Former world and Future. *Ib.*

The Impression of Parliament upon me was that it's members are not formidable as *speakers,* but very much so as an audience.

Detached Thoughts, 11, 1821

Cicero himself, and probably the Messiah, could never have alter'd the vote of a single Lord of the Bedchamber or Bishop. *Ib.* 12

Caesar, Augustus   63 B.C.-A.D. 14

Urbem . . . excoluit adeo, uti iure sit gloriatus marmoream se relinquere, quam latericiam accepisset. He so improved the city that he justly boasted that he found it brick and left it marble.
Divus Augustus, Suetonius

Ad Graecas Kalendas. At the Greek Kalends (i.e. never). *Ib.*

Caesar, Gaius Julius   c. 102-44 B.C.

Iacta alea est. The die is cast. *Remark on crossing the Rubicon*

Veni, vidi, vici. I came, I saw, I conquered. *Letter to Amantius, 47 B.C.*

Et tu, Brute! You too, Brutus! *Dying words, 15th March, 44 B.C.*

Gallia est omnis divisa in partas tres. All Gaul is divided into three parts. *De Bello Gallico,* 1

Calderón de la Barca, Pedro   1600-1681

Fame, like water, bears up the lighter things, and lets the weighty sink. *Adventures of Five Hours*

Calverley, Charles Stuart   1831-1884

For I've read in many a novel that, unless they've souls that grovel,
Folks *prefer* in fact a hovel to your dreary marble halls. *In the Gloaming*

How Eugene Aram, though a thief, a liar, and a murderer,
Yet, being intellectual, was amongst the noblest of mankind. *Of Reading*

Cameron, Simon   1789-1889

An honest politician is one who, when he is bought, will stay bought.   *Remark*

Campbell, Roy   1901-1957

You praise the firm restraint with which they write—
I'm with you there, of course:
They use the snaffle and the curb all right,
But where's the bloody horse?
    Adamastor: On Some South African Novelists

Campbell, Thomas   1777-1844

O leave this barren spot to me!
Spare, woodman, spare the beechen tree.
                          The Beech-Tree's Petition

On Linden, when the sun was low,
All bloodless lay the untrodden snow,
And dark as winter was the flow
Of Iser, rolling rapidly.   *Hohenlinden*

The combat deepens. On, ye brave,
Who rush to glory, or the grave!   *Ib.*

Better be courted and jilted
Than never be courted at all.   *The Jilted Nymph*

'Tis distance lends enchantment to the view,
And robes the mountain in its azure hue.
                          Pleasures of Hopes, 1

And muse on Nature with a poet's eye.   *Ib.* 2

What millions died—that Caesar might be great!
                                          Ib.

One moment may with bliss repay
Unnumbered hours of pain.   *The Ritter Bann*

The sentinel stars set their watch in the sky.
                              The Soldier's Dream

Campion, Thomas   1567-1620

There is a garden in her face,
Where roses and white lilies grow. *Book of Airs*

There cherries grow, which none may buy
Till " Cherry ripe" themselves do cry. *Ib.*

Camus, Albert   1913-1960

*Il semblait être l'ami de tous les plaisirs normaux,
sans en être l'esclave.* He seemed to indulge in
all the usual pleasures without being enslaved by
any of them. *La Peste*

*Là était la certitude, dans le travail de tous les
jours. . . . L'essentiel était de bien faire son métier.*
There, in day-to-day work, was certainty. . . .
Doing one's job well was what mattered. *Ib.*

*. . . la peste avait enlevé à tous le pouvoir de
l'amour et même de l'amitié. Car l'amour demande
un peu d'avenir, et il n'y avait plus pour nous que
des instants.* The plague had deprived us all of
the capacity for love and even for friendship. For
love must have some future, and for us there were
only moments. *Ib.*

Ils savaient maintenant que s'il est une chose qu'on puisse désirer toujours et obtenir quelquefois, c'est la tendresse humaine. They now knew that if there is one thing which can always be desired and sometimes obtained, it is human kindness.   *Ib.*

Canning, George   **1770-1827**

I called the New World into existence, to redress the balance of the Old.   *Speech,* 1826

Carew, Thomas   **c. 1595- c. 1639**

Thou didst pay
The debts of our penurious bankrupt age.
An Elegy upon the Death of Dr. John Donne

Here lies a King that rul'd, as he thought fit
The universal Monarchy of wit;
Here lie two Flamens, and both those, the best,
Apollo's first, at last, the true God's Priest.   *Ib.*

I was foretold, your rebel sex,
Nor love, nor pity knew.   *A Deposition from Love*

Carey, Henry   **c. 1693-1743**

God save our gracious king!
Long live our noble king!
    God Save the King. (also attrib. to others)

Of all the girls that are so smart
    There's none like pretty Sally,
She is the darling of my heart,
    And she lives in our alley.   *Sally in our Alley*

Carlyle, Thomas   **1795-1881**

The barrenest of all mortals is the sentimentalist.
                                    Characteristics

The life of man, says our friend Herr Sauerteig, the life of even the meanest man, it were good to remember, is a poem.
Critical and Miscellaneous Essays, Count Cagliostro. Flight First

The three great elements of modern civilisation, Gunpowder, Printing, and the Protestant Religion.
Ib. State of German Literature

What is all knowledge too but recorded experience, and a product of history; of which, therefore, reasoning and belief, no less than action and passion, are essential materials? *Ib. On History*

For, as I take it, Universal History, the history of what man has accomplished in this world, is at bottom the History of the Great Men who have worked here. *Heroes and Hero Worship*, 1

It is well said, in every sense, that a man's religion is the chief fact with regard to him. A man's or a nation of men's. By religion I do not mean here the church creed which he professes, the articles of faith which he will sign and, in words or otherwise, assert; not this wholly, in many cases not this at all. We see men of all kinds of professed creeds attain to almost all degrees of worth or worthlessness under each or any of them. This is not what I call religion, this profession and assertion, which is often only a profession and assertion from the outworks of man, from the mere argumentative region of him, if even so deep as that. But the thing a man does practically believe (and this is often enough *without* asserting it even to himself, much less to others). *Ib.*

The illimitable, silent, never-resting thing called Time, rolling, rushing on, swift, silent, like an all embracing ocean-tide, on which we and all the Universe swim like exhalations. *Ib.*

A whiff of grapeshot. *History of the French Revolution,* 1

The sea-green Incorruptible. *Ib.* 2

Aristocracy of the Money bag. *Ib.*

Cash payment is not the sole nexus of man with man. *Past and Present,* 3

Blessed is he who has found his work; let him ask no other blessedness. *Ib.*

Captains of industry. *Ib.,* 4

If Jesus Christ were to come to-day, people would not even crucify him. They would ask him to dinner, and hear what he had to say, and make fun of it. *Remark*

Man is a tool-using animal. *Sartor Resartus,* 1

An unmetaphorical style you shall in vain seek for: is not your very *Attention* a *Stretching-to*? *Ib.*

Any road, this simple Entepfuhl road, will lead you to the end of the world! *Ib.* 2

But the world is an old woman, and mistakes any gilt farthing for a gold coin; whereby being often cheated, she will thenceforth trust nothing but the common copper. *Ib.*

O thou who art able to write a Book, which once in the two centuries or oftener there is a man gifted to do, envy not him whom they name the City-builder, and inexpressibly pity him whom they name Conqueror or City-burner! *Ib.*

Man's unhappiness, as I construe, comes of his greatness; it is because there is an Infinite in him, which with all his cunning he cannot quite bury under the Finite. *Ib.*

It is a mathematical fact that the casting of this pebble from my hand alters the centre of gravity of the universe. *Ib.* 3

That tough faculty of reading. *Ib.*

Carnegie, Andrew   1835-1919

Surplus wealth is a sacred trust which its possessor is bound to administer in his lifetime for the good of the community. *The Gospel of Wealth*

Pioneering does not pay. *Life*, Hendrick

Carroll, Lewis   1832-1898

"What is the use of a book," thought Alice, "without pictures or conversations?" *Alice in Wonderland*, 1

"Curiouser and curiouser!" cried Alice. *Ib.* 2

How cheerfully he seems to grin,
  How neatly spreads his claws,
And welcomes little fishes in
  With gently smiling jaws! *Ib.*

" You are old, Father William," the young man said,
  " And your hair has become very white;
And yet you incessantly stand on your head—
    Do you think, at your age, it is right?" *Ib.* 5

Twinkle, twinkle, little bat!
How I wonder what you're at!
Up above the world you fly!
Like a tea tray in the sky. *Ib.* 7

The Queen was in a furious passion, and went stamping about, and shouting, " Off with his head!" or " Off with her head!" about once in a minute. *Ib.* 8

" A cat may look at a king," said Alice. *Ib.*

And the moral of that is—" Oh, 'tis love, 'tis love that makes the world go round!" *Ib.* 9

Take care of the sense, and the sounds will take care of themselves. *Ib.*

" Will you walk a little faster?" said a whiting to a snail,
" There's a porpoise close behind us, and he's treading on my tail." *Ib.* 10

The Queen of Hearts, she made some tarts,
  All on a summer day:
The Knave of Hearts, he stole those tarts,
  And took them quite away! *Ib.* 11

" Begin at the beginning," the King said, gravely,
" and go on till you come to the end: then stop."
                                                   Ib. 12

'Twas brillig, and the slithy toves
  Did gyre and gimble in the wabe;
All mimsy were the borogoves,
  And the mome raths outgrabe.
            Alice Through the Looking-Glass, 1

"Now, *here*, you see, it takes all the running you
can do, to keep in the same place. If you want
to get somewhere else, you must run at least twice
as fast as that!" *Ib.* 2

"Contrariwise," continued Tweedledee, "if it
was so, it might be; and if it were so, it would be:
but as it isn't, it ain't. That's logic." *Ib.* 4

"The time has come," the Walrus said,
"To talk of many things:
Of shoes—and ships—and sealing wax—
Of cabbages—and kings—
And why the sea is boiling hot
And whether pigs have wings." *Ib.*

The rule is, jam tomorrow and jam yesterday—
but never jam to-day. *Ib.* 5

"There's no use trying," she said: "one *can't*
believe impossible things." "I dare say you haven't
had much practice," said the Queen. "When I
was your age, I always did it for half an hour a
day. Why, sometimes I've believed as many as
six impossible things before breakfast." *Ib.*

"When *I* use a word," Humpty Dumpty said in
a rather scornful tone, "it means just what I
choose it to mean,—neither more nor less." *Ib.* 6

It's as large as life and twice as natural. *Ib.* 7

What I tell you three times is true.

Hunting of the Snark, 1

Catechism [Shorter]

Man's chief end is to glorify God, and to enjoy him forever. *Answer* 1

The Scriptures principally teach what man is to believe concerning God, and what duty God requires of man. *Ib.* 3

All mankind by their fall lost communion with God, are under his wrath and curse, and so made liable to all the miseries in this life, to death itself, and to the pains of hell for ever. *Ib.* 19

Christ, the Son of God, became man, by taking to himself a true body, and a reasonable soul, being conceived by the power of the Holy Ghost, in the womb of the Virgin Mary, and born of her, yet without sin. *Ib.* 22

No mere man since the fall is able in this life perfectly to keep the commandments of God, but doth daily break them in thought, word, and deed. *Ib.* 82

Cato, Marcus Porcius (The Censor)   234-149 B.C.

Ceterum censeo, Carthaginem esse delendam. Moreover, I think that Carthage should be destroyed. *Life of Cato*, Plutarch

I would rather see a young man blush than turn pale. *Ib.*

I would much rather have men ask why I have no statue than why I have one. *Ib.*

In all my life, I have never repented but of three things: that I trusted a woman with a secret, that I went by sea when I might have gone by land and that I passed a day in idleness. *Ib.*

Do not buy what you want, but what you need; what you do not need is dear at a farthing.
Reliquae

Catullus, Caius Valerius   87- c. 54 B.C.

Vivamus, mea Lesbia, atque amemus,
Rumoresque senum severiorum
Omnes unius aestimemus assis.
Lesbia, let us live and love, and pay no heed to all the tales of grim old men. *Carmina, 5*

Da mi basia mille. Give me a thousand kisses. *Ib.*

Sed mulier cupido quod dicit amanti
In vento et rapida scribere oportet aqua
But a woman's words to an eager love
Should be written in wind and running water.
Ib. 70

Cavell, Edith   1865-1915

I realise that patriotism is not enough. I must have no hatred or bitterness towards anyone.
Last Words, 1915

Cervantes, Miguel de   1547-1616

El Caballero de la Triste Figura
The Knight of the Sorrowful Countenance.
Don Quixote, 1

La mejor salsa del mundo es el hambre.
The best sauce in the world is hunger. *Ib.* 2

Muchos pucos hacen un mucho.
Mony a mickle maks a muckle. *Ib.*

Es un entreverado loco, lleno de lúcidos intervalos.
He's a muddled fool, full of lucid intervals. *Ib.*

Dos linages sólos hay en el mundo, como decía una abuela mia, que son el tenir y el no tenir. There are but two families in the world as my grandmother used to say, the Haves and the Have-nots. *Ib.*

Los buenos pintores imitan la naturaleza, pero los malos la vomitan. Good painters imitate nature, bad ones vomit it. *El Licenciado Vidriera*

Chalmers, Patrick Reginald   1872-1942

What's lost upon the roundabouts we pulls up on the swings! *Green Days and Blue Days: Roundabouts and Swings*

Chamberlain, Joseph   1836-1914

We are not downhearted. The only trouble is, we cannot understand what is happening to our neighbours. *Speech*, 1906

Chamberlain, Neville   1869-1940

In war, whichever side may call itself the victor, there are no winners, but all are losers. *Speech*, 1938

I believe it is peace for our time . . . peace with honour. *Speech after Munich Agreement*, 1938

Hitler has missed the bus. *Speech*, 1940

Chapman, George   c. 1559- c. 1634

And let a scholar all Earth's volumes carry,
He will be but a walking dictionary.
Tears of Peace

Charles II, King of Britain   1630-1685

[Of Nell Gwynn]Let not poor Nelly starve. *Attrib.*

Brother, I am too old to go again to my travels.
Attrib.

He had been, he said, an unconscionable time
dying; but he hoped that they would excuse it.
History of England, Macaulay

Chaucer, Geoffrey   c. 1340-1400

She was so ferforth yeven hym to plese,
That al that lyked him hit dyde her ese.
Anelida and Arcite

So thirleth with the poynt of remembraunce
The swerde of sorowe, ywhet with fals plesaunce. *Ib*

Whan that Aprill with his shoures soote
The droghte of March hath perced to the roote.
And bathed every veyne in swich licour
Of which vertu engendred is the flour.
Canterbury Tales, prologue

He loved chivalrie,
Trouthe and honour, fredom and curteisie.
Ib. The Knight

He nevere yet no vileynye ne sayde
In al his lyf unto no maner wight.
He was a verray, parfit gentil knyght. *Ib.*

And Frenssh she spak ful faire and fetisly,
After the scole of Stratford atte Bowe,
For Frenssh of Parys was to hire unknowe.
Ib. The Prioresse

His heed was balled, that shoon as any glas,
And eek his face, as he hadde been enoynt.
Ib. The Monk

He knew the tavernes wel in every toun.
Ib. The Frere

Sownynge in moral vertu was his speche,
And gladly wolde he lerne and gladly teche.
Ib. The Clerk

Nowher so bisy a man as he ther nas,
And yet he seemed bisier than he was.
Ib. The Sergeant of the Lawe

She was a worthy womman al hir lyve:
Housbondes at chirche dore she hadde fyve,
Withouten oother coompaignye in youthe,—
But therof nedeth nat to speke as nowthe.
Ib. The Wife of Bath

But Cristes loore and his apostles twelve
He taughte, but first he folwed it hymselve.
Ib. The Persoun

With scalled browes blake and piled berd,
Of his visage children were aferd.
Ib. The Somnour

Well koude he rede a lessoun or a storie,
But alderbest he song an offertorie.

Ib. The Pardoner

Thanked be Fortune and hir false wheel,
That noon estaat assureth to be weel.

Knight's Tale

Wostow nat wel the olde clerkes sawe,
That "who shal yeve a lovere any lawe?"
Love is a gretter lawe, by my pan,
Than may be yeve to any erthely man. *Ib.*

A man moot nedes love, maugree his heed. *Ib.*

The bisy larke, messeger of day. *Ib.*

The smylere with the knyf under the cloke. *Ib.*

To maken vertu of necessitee. *Ib.*

The gretteste clerkes been noght the wysest man.

Reve's Tale

I hate hym that my vices telleth me,
And so doo mo, God woot, of us than I.

Wife of Bath's Tale, prologue

Wommen desiren have sovereynetee
As wel over hir housbond as hir love,
And for to been in maistrie hym above. *Ib.*

Wel ofter of the welle than of the tonne
She drank. *Clerkes Tale*

Though clerkes preise wommen but a lite,
Ther kan no man in humblesse hym acquite
As womman kan. *Ib.*

115

A wyf wol laste, and in thyn hous endure,
Wel lenger than thee list, paraventure.
Merchant's Tale

My theme is alwey oon, and evere was—
Radix mabrum est cupiditas. (Greed is the root
of evil—Old proverb) *Pardoner's Tale,* prologue

Nay, I wol drynke licour of the vyne,
And have a joly wenche in every toun.   *Ib.*

What is bettre than wisdom? Womman. And
what is bettre than a good womman? No-thing.
Tale of Melibee

No deyntee morsel passed thurgh hir throte;
Hir diete was accordant to hir cote.
Nun's Priesi's Tale

Of al the floures in the mede,
Thanne love I most thise floures white and rede,
Swiche as men callen daysyes in our toun.
The Legend of Good Women, prologue

Welcome, somer, oure governour and lord!   *Ib.*

Wel by reson, men it calle may
The "dayesye," or elles the "ye of day."   *Ib.*

The lyf so short, the craft so long to lerne,
Th'assay so hard, so sharp the conquerynge.
The Parliament of Fowls (cf. Hippocrates, p. 230)

For out of olde feldes, as men seith,
Cometh al this newe corn from yere to yere;
And out of olde bokes, in good feith,
Cometh al this newe science that men lere.   *Ib.*

Know thyself first immortal,
And loke ay besyly thow werche and wysse
To commune profit, and thow shalt not mysse
To comen swiftly to that place deere
That full of blysse is and of soules cleere.   *Ib.*

The tyme, that may not sojourne,
But goth, and may never retourne,
As watir that doun renneth ay,
But never drope retourne may.
                                    Romaunt of the Rose

        Povert al aloon,
That not a penny had in wolde,
All though she hir clothis solde,
And though she shulde anhonged be;
For nakid as a worm was she.   *Ib.*

O blynde world, O blynde entencioun!
How often falleth all the effect contraire
Of surquidrie and foul presumpcion;
For kaught is proud, and kaught is debonaire.
                                    Troilus and Criseyde, 1

For it is seyd "man maketh ofte a yerde
With which the maker is hymself ybeten."   *Ib.*

It is nought good a sleping hound to wake.   *Ib.* 3

The worst kinde of infortune is this,
A man to have ben in prosperitce,
And it remembren, when it passed is.   *Ib.*

Oon ere it herde, at the other out it wente. *Ib.* 4

Chekhov, Anton   **1860-1904**

He was a rationalist, but he had to confess that
he liked the ringing of church bells. *Note Book*

117

Chesterfield, Philip Dormer Stanhope, Earl of
1694-1773

In scandal, as in robbery, the receiver is always thought as bad as the thief. *Advice to his Son. Rules for Conversation*

In my mind, there is nothing so illiberal and so ill-bred, as audible laughter. *Ib. Graces*

In my opinion, parsons are very like other men, and neither the better nor the worse, for wearing a black gown. *Letters to his Son*, 1746

The knowledge of the world is only to be acquired in the world, and not in a closet. *Ib.*

An injury is much sooner forgotten than an insult. *Ib.*

There is a Spanish proverb, which says very justly, Tell me whom you live with, and I will tell you who you are. *Ib.* 1747

Do as you would be done by is the surest method that I know of pleasing. *Ib.*

I recommend you to take care of the minutes; for hours will take care of themselves. *Ib.*

Advice is seldom welcome; and those who want it the most always like it the least. *Ib.* 1748

Speak of the moderns without contempt, and of the ancients without idolatry. *Ib.*

Wear your learning, like your watch, in a private pocket: and do not merely pull it out and strike it; merely to show that you have one. *Ib.*

If Shakespeare's genius had been cultivated, those beauties, which we so justly admire in him, would have been undisgraced by those extravagancies, and that nonsense, with which they are so frequently accompanied. *Ib.*

Women, then, are only children of a larger growth: they have an entertaining tattle, and sometimes wit; but for solid, reasoning good-sense, I never knew in my life one that had it, or who reasoned or acted consequentially for four and twenty hours together. *Ib.*

It must be owned, that the Graces do not seem to be natives of Great Britain; and I doubt, the best of us here have more of rough than of polished diamond. *Ib.*

Idleness is only the refuge of weak minds. *Ib.* 1749

Women are much more like each other than men: they have, in truth, but two passions, vanity and love; these are their universal characteristics. *Ib.*

Swallow all your learning in the morning, but digest it in company in the evenings. *Ib.* 1751

It is an undoubted truth, that the less one has to do, the less time one finds to do it in. One yawns, one procrastinates, one can do it when one will, and therefore one seldom does it at all.
Letter, 1757

The fame of a conqueror; a cruel fame, that arises from the destruction of the human species.
Ib.

I assisted at the birth of that most significant word, flirtation, which dropped from the most beautiful mouth in the world. *The World*

Chesterton, Gilbert Keith   1874-1936

For the great Gaels of Ireland
Are the men that God made mad,
For all their wars are merry,
And all their songs are sad.

Ballad of the White Horse, 2

Fools! For I also had my hour;
One far fierce hour and sweet:
There was a shout about my ears,
And palms before my feet. *The Donkey*

The folk that live in Liverpool, their heart is in
    their boots;
They go to hell like lambs, they do, because the
    hooter hoots. *Me Heart*

John Grubby, who was short and stout
And troubled with religious doubt,
Refused about the age of three
To sit upon the curate's knee.

The New Freethinker

All the easy speeches
That comfort cruel men.

O God of Earth and Altar

Before the Roman came to Rye or out to Severn
    strode,
The rolling English drunkard made the rolling
    English road. *The Rolling English Road*

We only know the last sad squires ride slowly
    towards the sea,
And a new people takes the land: and still it is
    not we.   *The Secret People*

Smile at us, pay us, pass us; but do not quite
    forget.
For we are the people of England, that never
    have spoken yet. *Ib.*

The souls most fed with Shakespeare's flame
Still sat unconquered in a ring,
Remembering him like anything.
                        The Shakespeare Memorial

And the faith of the poor is faint and partial,
And the pride of the rich is all for sale,
And the chosen heralds of England's Marshal
Are the sandwich-men of the *Daily Mail*.
                        A Song of Defeat

Where Life was slain and Truth was slandered
On that one holier hill than Rome.
                To F. C. in Memoriam Palestine

And Noah he often said to his wife when he sat
    down to dine,
" I don't care where the water goes if it doesn't
    get into the wine."   *Wine and Water*

" My country, right or wrong," is a thing that no
patriot would think of saying except in a desperate
case. It is like saying, " My mother, drunk or
sober." *The Defendant*

To be in the weakest camp is to be in the strongest
school. *Heretics*

The human race, to which so many of my readers belong. . . .   *The Napoleon of Notting Hill*

Democracy means government by the uneducated, while aristocracy means government by the badly educated. *New York Times*, 1931

You can never have a revolution in order to establish a democracy. You must have a democracy in order to have a revolution.
        Tremendous Trifles

Chronicles, The First Book of

Let the heavens be glad, and let the earth rejoice: and let men say among the nations. The Lord reigneth. 16, 31

And he died in a good old age, full of days, riches and honour: and Solomon his son reigned in his stead. 29, 28

Chronicles, The Second Book of

And behold, the one half of the greatness of thy wisdom was not told me: for thou exceedest the fame that I heard. 9, 6

Be ye strong therefore, and let not your hands be weak: for your work shall be rewarded. 15, 7

Churchill, Charles   1731-1764

Though by whim, envy, or resentment led,
They damn those authors whom they never read.
        The Candidate

Thy danger chiefly lies in acting well;
No crime's so great as daring to excel.
        Epistle to William Hogarth

By different methods different men excel;
But where is he who can do all things well? *Ib.*

It can't be Nature, for it is not sense.
The Farewell

Just to the windward of the law. *The Ghost, 3*

Wise fear, you know,
Forbids the robbing of a foe;
But what, to serve our private ends,
Forbids the cheating of our friends? *Ib.*

So much they talk'd, so very little said.
The Rosciad

Churchill, Lord Randolph Spencer   1849-1894

Ulster will fight; Ulster will be right. *Letter,* 1886

[Of Gladstone] An old man in a hurry. *Speech
June,* 1886

The duty of an Opposition is to oppose.
Quoted by Lord Randolph Churchill

Churchill, Sir Winston Leonard Spencer   1874-1965

It cannot in the opinion of His Majesty's Government be classified as slavery in the extreme acceptance of the word without some risk of terminological inexactitude. *Speech, House of Commons,* 1906

I have nothing to offer but blood, toil, tears, and sweat. *Ib. May,* 1940

123

We shall not flag or fail. We shall fight in France, we shall fight on the seas and oceans, we shall fight with growing confidence and growing strength in the air, we shall defend our island, whatever the cost may be, we shall fight on the beaches, we shall fight on the landing grounds, we shall fight in the fields and in the streets, we shall fight in the hills; we shall never surrender.
Ib. 4th June, 1940

Let us therefore brace ourselves to our duties, and so bear ourselves that, if the British Empire and its Commonwealth last for a thousand years, men will still say, " This was their finest hour."
Ib. 18th June, 1940

The battle of Britain is about to begin.
Ib. 1st July, 1940

Never in the field of human conflict was so much owed by so many to so few. *Ib. 20th Aug., 1940*

We do not covet anything from any nation except their respect. *Broadcast to the French people, Oct., 1940*

Give us the tools, and we will finish the job.
Broadcast, Feb., 1941

The people of London with one voice would say to Hitler, " You do your worst, and we will do our best." *Speech, June, 1941*

Do not let us speak of darker days; let us rather speak of sterner days. These are not dark days; these are great days—the greatest days our country has ever lived; and we must all thank God that we have been allowed, each of us according to our stations, to play a part in making these days memorable in the history of our race. *Ib. Harrow School,* 1941

When I warned them [the French Government] that Britain would fight on alone whatever they did, their Generals told their Prime Minister and his divided Cabinet, " In three weeks England will have her neck wrung like a chicken."
Some chicken! Some neck! *Speech to the Canadian Parliament, Dec.,* 1941

The empires of the future are empires of the mind. *Speech, Harvard, Sept.,* 1943

Beware, for the time may be short. A shadow has fallen across the scenes so lately lighted by the Allied victory. Nobody knows what Soviet Russia and its Communist international organisation intend to do in the immediate future.
From Stettin in the Baltic to Trieste in the Adriatic an Iron Curtain has descended across the Continent. *Ib. Fulton, Missouri,* 1946

Cibber, Colley   **1671-1757**

Stolen sweets are best. *The Rival Fools*

Cicero, Marcus Tullius   **106-43 B.C.**

Salus populi suprema est lex. The welfare of the people is the ultimate law. *De Legibus*

Summum bonum. The greatest good. *De Officiis*

Mens culusque is est quisque. Each man's mind is the man himself. *De Republica*

O tempora! O mores! What an age! What customs! *In Catilinam*

Civis Romanus sum. I am a Roman citizen. *In Verrem*

Cui bono? Who stands to gain? *Pro Milone*

Neminem saltare sobrius, nisi forte insanit. No sober man dances, unless he happens to be mad. *Pro Murena*

Clay, Henry   1777-1852

I had rather be right than be President. *To Senator Preston of South Carolina*, 1839

Clive, Lord Robert   1725-1774

By God, Mr. Chairman, at this moment I stand astonished at my own moderation! *Reply during Parliamentary cross-examination*, 1773

Clough, Arthur Hugh   1819-1861

Whither depart the souls of the brave that die in the battle,
Die in the lost, lost fight, for the cause that perishes with them?   *Amours de Voyage*, 5

And almost everyone when age,
   Disease, or sorrows strike him,
Inclines to think there is a God,
   Or something very like Him.   *Dipsychus*

Do not adultery commit;
Advantage rarely comes of it.
               The Latest Decalogue

Thou shalt not kill; but need'st not strive
Officiously to keep alive. *Ib.*

Say not, the struggle naught availeth,
  The labour and the wounds are vain,
The enemy faints not, nor faileth,
  And as things have been they remain.
            Say Not, the Struggle Naught Availeth

If hopes were dupes, fears may be liars. *Ib.*

That out of sight is out of mind
Is true of most we leave behind.
            Songs in Absence. That Out of Sight

Cobbett, William   1762-1835

To be poor and independent is very nearly an
impossibility. *Advice to Young Men*

Nouns of number, or multitude, such as *Mob*,
Parliament, Rabble, House of Commons, Regiment, Court of King's Bench, Den of Thieves,
and the like. *English Grammar, Letter 17, Syntax
as Relating to Pronouns*

From a very early age, I had imbibed the opinion,
that it was every man's duty to do all that lay
in his power to leave his country as good as he
had found it. *Political Register*, 1832

[Of London] But what is to be the fate of the great
wen of all? The monster, called . . . "the metropolis of the empire."? *Rural Rides*, 1821

Cockburn, Lord Henry   1779-1854

[Of Robert Dundas] It was impossible not to
like the owner of the look. *Memorials*, 3

It used to be said that if Hermand had made the heavens, he would have permitted us fixed stars. His constitutional animation never failed to carry him a flight beyond ordinary mortals. *Ib.*

Cocteau, Jean   1891-1963

The worst tragedy for a poet is to be admired through being misunderstood. *Le Rappel à L'Ordre*

One does not blame an epoch; one congratulates oneself on not having belonged to it. *Ib.*

If it has to choose who will be crucified, the crowd will always save Barabbas. *Ib.*

Art is science in the flesh. *Ib.*

Coke, Sir Edward   1552-1634

Six hours in sleep, in law's grave study six,
Four spend in prayer, the rest on Nature fix.
Pandects

The house of everyone is to him as his castle and fortress, as well for his defence against injury and violence, as for his repose. *Semayne's Case.*

Coleridge, Samuel Taylor   1772-1834

It is an ancient Mariner,
And he stoppeth one of three.
" By thy long grey beard and glittering eye,
Now wherefore stopp'st thou me ? "
The Ancient Mariner, 1

He holds him with his glittering eye—
The Wedding-Guest stood still,
And listens like a three-years' child:
The Mariner hath his will. *Ib.*

128

The fair breeze blew, the white foam flew,
The furrow followed free;
We were the first that ever burst
Into that silent sea. *Ib.* 2

As idle as a painted ship
Upon a painted ocean. *Ib.*

Water, water, everywhere,
And all the boards did shrink;
Water, water, everywhere.
Nor any drop to drink. *Ib.*

The Sun's rim dips; the stars rush out:
At one stride comes the dark. *Ib.* 3

" I fear thee, ancient Mariner!
I fear thy skinny hand!
And thou art long, and lank, and brown,
As is the ribbed sea-sand." *Ib.* 4

Alone, alone, all, all alone,
Alone on a wide, wide sea!
And never a soul took pity on
My soul in agony. *Ib.*

Oh! Sleep it is a gentle thing
Beloved from pole to pole,
To Mary Queen the praise be given!
She sent the gentle sleep from Heaven,
That slid into my soul. *Ib.* 5

Then like a pawing horse let go,
She made a sudden bound. *Ib.*

Like one, that on a lonesome road
Doth walk in fear and dread,
And having once turned round walks on,
And turns no more his head;

Because he knows, a frightful fiend
Doth close behind him tread. *Ib., 6*

He prayeth best, who loveth best
All things both great and small;
For the dear God who loveth us,
He made and loveth all. *Ib., 7*

A sadder and a wiser man,
He rose the morrow morn. *Ib.*

Alas! they had been friends in youth;
But whispering tongues can poison truth.
Christabel

Often do the spirits
Of great events stride on before the events,
And in to-day already walks to-morrow.
Death of Wallenstein

For what is freedom, but the unfettered use
Of all the powers which God for use had given?
The Destiny of Nations

From his brimstone bed at break of day
A walking the Devil is gone,
To visit his snug little farm the Earth,
And see how his stock goes on.
The Devil's Thoughts

And the Devil did grin, for his darling sin
Is pride that apes humility. *Ib.*

What is an Epigram? a dwarfish whole,
Its body brevity, and wit its soul. *Epigram*

Swans sing before they die—'twere no bad thing
Should certain persons die before they sing.
Epigram on a Volunteer Singer

[Of Britain, 1798]
A vain, speech-mouthing, speech-reporting guild,
One benefit-club for mutual flattery.

Fears in Solitude

All adoration of the God in nature,
All lovely and all honourable things,
Whatever makes this mortal spirit feel
The joy and greatness of its future being?
There lives nor form nor feeling in my soul
Unborrowed from my country. *Ib.*

In Xanadu did Kubla Khan
A stately pleasure-dome decree:
Where Alph, the sacred river, ran
Through caverns measureless to man
Down to a sunless sea. *Kubla Khan*

Woman wailing for her demon lover. *Ib.*

And close your eyes with holy dread,
For he on honey-dew hath fed,
And drunk the milk of Paradise. *Ib.*

Ah! far removed from all that glads the sense,
From all that softens or ennobles Man,
The wretched Many! *Religious Musings*

The innumerable multitude of Wrongs
By man on man inflicted. *Ib.*

He who begins by loving Christianity better than
Truth will proceed by loving his own sect or
church better than Christianity, and end by loving
himself better than all. *Aids to Reflection. Moral
and Religious Aphorisms, 25*

No man was ever yet a great poet, without being at the same time a profound philosopher. *Biographia Literaria*

That willing suspension of disbelief for the moment, which constitutes poetic faith. *Ib.*

The dwarf sees farther than the giant, when he has the giant's shoulder to mount on. *The Friend*

Reviewers are usually people who would have been poets, historians, biographers, etc., if they could; they have tried their talents at one or at the other, and have failed; therefore they turn critics. *Lecture on Shakespeare and Milton*

Collingwood, Robin George   **1889-1943**

Perfect freedom is reserved for the man who lives by his own work and in that work does what he wants to do. *Speculum Mentis*

Collins, John Churton   **1848-1908**

To ask advice is in nine cases out of ten to tout for flattery. *Maxims and Reflections*, 59

Collins, Mortimer   **1827-1876**

A man is as old as he's feeling,
  A woman as old as she looks.
                         The Unknown Quantity

Collins, William   **1721-1759**

How sleep the brave, who sink to rest,
By all their country's wishes blest!
                     Ode Written in the Year 1746

Too nicely Jonson knew the critic's part,
Nature in him was almost lost in Art.
Verses to Sir Thomas Hanmer

Colossians, Epistle of Paul to the

Luke, the beloved physician. 4, 14

Colton, Charles Caleb   c. 1780-1832

When you have nothing to say, say nothing.
Lacon

Imitation is the sincerest form of flattery. *Ib.*

Examinations are formidable even to the best
prepared, for the greatest fool may ask more
than the wisest man can answer. *Ib.*

Man is an embodied paradox, a bundle of contradictions. *Ib.*

Friendship often ends in love; but love in friendship—never. *Ib.*

Subtract from many modern poets all that may
be found in Shakespeare, and trash will remain.
Ib.

Some read to think,—these are rare; some to
unite,—these are common; and some to talk,—
and these form the great majority. *Ib.*

Of the professions it may be said that soldiers are
becoming too popular, parsons too lazy, physicians too mercenary, and lawyers too powerful.
Ib.

We have erred and strayed from thy ways like
lost sheep. . . . We have left undone those things
which we ought to have done; And we have done
those things which we ought not to have done;
And there is no health in us. . . . A godly, righteous
and sober life. *Morning Prayer. General Confession*

An infinite Majesty. *Ib. Te Deum Laudamus*

The noble army of martyrs. *Ib.*

Give peace in our time, O Lord.
Because there is none other that fighteth for us,
but only thou, O God. *Ib. Versicles*

The author of peace and lover of concord, in
knowledge of whom standeth our eternal life,
whose service is perfect freedom. *Ib. Second
Collect, for Peace*

In Quires and Places where they sing. *Ib. Rubric
after Third Collect*

That peace which the world cannot give. *Evening
Prayer. Second Collect*

Lighten our darkness, we beseech thee, O Lord;
and by thy great mercy defend us from all perils
and dangers of this night. *Ib. Third Collect*

Have mercy upon us miserable sinners. *The Litany*

Deceits of the world, the flesh and the devil. *Ib.*

The fruits of the Spirit. *Ib.*

All sorts and conditions of men . . . all who profess and call themselves Christians. *Prayers and Thanksgivings upon Several Occasions*

Hear them, read, mark, learn and inwardly digest them. *Collects. 2nd Sunday in Advent*

The glory that shall be revealed. *Ib. St. Stephen's Day*

The author and giver of all good things. *Ib. 7th Sunday after Trinity*

Serve thee with a quiet mind. *Ib. 21st Sunday after Trinity*

Stir up, we beseech, O Lord, the wills of thy faithful people; that they, plenteously bringing forth the fruit of good works, may of thee be plenteously rewarded. *Ib. 25th Sunday after Trinity*

Whom truly to know is everlasting life. *Ib. St. Philip and St. James's Day*

An open and notorious evil liver. *Holy Communion. Introductory Rubric*

Truly repented and amended his former naughty life. *Ib.*

The peace of God, which passeth all understanding. *Nicene Creed. The Blessing*

Here in the sight of God, and in the face of this congregation. *Solemnization of Matrimony. Exhortation*

Let him now speak, or else hereafter forever hold his peace. *Ib.*

To have and to hold from this day forward, for better for worse, for richer for poorer, in sickness and in health, to love and to cherish, till death us do part, according to God's holy ordinance; and thereto I plight thee my troth. *Ib. Betrothal*

To love, cherish and to obey. *Ib.*

Those whom God hath joined together let no man put asunder. *Ib. The Prayer*

Consented together in holy wedlock. *Ib. Priest's Declaration*

We therefore commit his body to the ground; earth to earth, ashes to ashes, dust to dust; in sure and certain hope of the Resurrection to eternal life. *Burial of the Dead. First Anthem*

We therefore commit his body to the deep, to be turned into corruption, looking for the resurrection of the body (when the sea shall give up her dead). *Forms of Prayer to be used at sea. At the Burial of their Dead at Sea*

Of Works of Supererogation.

Articles of Religion, 14

Confucius c. 550- c.478 B.C.

True goodness springs from a man's own heart. All men are born good. *Analects*

An oppressive government is more to be feared than a tiger. *Ib.*

Gravity is only the bark of wisdom's tree, but it preserves it. *Ib.*

Men's natures are alike; it is their habits that carry them far apart. *Ib.*

The mirror reflects all objects, without being sullied. *Ib.*

Study the past, if you would divine the future. *Ib.*

The scholar who cherishes the love of comfort, is not fit to be deemed a scholar. *Ib.*

The heart of the wise, like a mirror, should reflect all objects without being sullied by any. *Ib.*

Learning without thought is labour lost; thought without learning is perilous. *Ib.*

What the superior man seeks is in himself: what the small man seeks is in others. *Ib.*

In all things, success depends upon previous preparation, and without such preparation there is sure to be failure. *Ib.*

For one word a man is often deemed to be wise, and for one word he is often deemed to be foolish. We should be careful indeed what we say. *Ib.*

Everything has its beauty but not everyone sees it. *Ib.*

They must often change who would be constant in happiness or wisdom. *Ib.*

To see what is right and not to do it is want of courage. *Ib.*

Better a diamond with a flaw than a pebble without. *Ib.*

Congreve, William   1670-1729

Retired to their tea and scandal, according to their ancient custom. *The Double Dealer*, 1

She lays it on with a trowel. *Ib.* 3

See how love and murder will out. *Ib.* 4

Music alone with sudden charms can bind
The wandering sense, and calm the troubled mind.
Hymn to Harmony

I am always of the opinion with the learned, if they speak first. *Incognita*

Music has charms to soothe a savage breast. *The Mourning Bride*, 1

Heav'n has no rage, like love to hatred turn'd,
Nor Hell a fury, like a woman scorn'd. *Ib.* 3

Courtship to marriage, as a very witty prologue to a very dull Play. *The Old Bachelor*, 5

Alack, he's gone the way of all flesh.
'*Squire Bickerstaff Detected (Attrib.)*

Beauty is the lover's gift. *The Way of the World*, 2

Let us be as strange as if we had been married a great while, and as well-bred as if we were not married at all. *Ib.* 4

Conrad, Joseph (Teodor Josef Konrad Korzeniowski)
1857-1924

Proverbs are art—cheap art. As a general rule they are not true; unless indeed they happen to be mere platitudes. *Gaspar Ruiz, 5*

Don't talk to me of your Archimedes' lever. . . . Give me the right word and the right accent and I will move the world. *A Personal Record: Preface*

All ambitions are lawful except those which climb upward on the miseries or credulities of mankind. *Ib.*

Cook, Eliza
1818-1889

I love it, I love it; and who shall dare
To chide me for loving that old armchair?
The Old Armchair

Coolidge, Calvin
1872-1933

The governments of the past could fairly be characterised as devices for maintaining in perpetuity the place and position of certain privileged classes. . . . The Government of the United States is a device for maintaining in perpetuity the rights of the people, with the ultimate extinction of all privileged classes. *Speech, 1924*

Corinthians, The First Epistle of Paul to the

Though I have all faith, so that I could remove mountains, and have not charity, I am nothing. And though I bestow all my goods to feed the poor, and though I give my body to be burned, and have not charity, it profiteth me nothing. Charity suffereth long and is kind; charity

envieth long; charity vaunteth not itself, is not puffed up,
Doth not behave itself unseemly, seeketh not her own, is not easily provoked, thinketh no evil;
Rejoiceth not in iniquity, but rejoiceth in the truth;
Beareth all things, believeth all things, hopeth all things, endureth all things.
Charity never faileth: but whether there be prophecies, they shall fail; whether there be tongues, they shall cease; whether there be knowledge, it shall vanish away. 13, 2-8

And now abideth faith, hope, charity, these three; but the greatest of these is charity. 13, 13

The last enemy that shall be destroyed is death.
15, 26

Corneille, Pierre   **1606-1684**

We triumph without glory when we conquer without danger. *Le Cid*

Et enfin la clémence est la plus belle marque
Qui fasse à l'univers connaître un vrai monarque.
Ultimately, mercy is the surest sign by which the world may distinguish a true king. *Cinna*

He who allows himself to be insulted, deserves to be. *Héraclius*

Cornford, Frances Crofts   **1886-1960**

O fat white woman whom nobody loves,
Why do you walk through the fields in gloves?
To a Fat Lady Seen from a Train

Cornuel, Madame Anne Bigot, de   **1605-1694**

Il n'y a point de grand homme pour son valet de chambre. No man is a hero to his valet. *Attrib.* (Similar sentiments are attributed to, among others, Antigonus Gonatas [319-239 B.C.] King of Thessaly, Madame de Sévigné [1626-1696], Nicolas Catinat [1637-1712], Goethe, and Montaigne.)

Coué, Sir Emile   **1857-1926**

Tous les jours, à tous points de vue, je vais de mieux en mieux. Every day, in every way, I am getting better and better. *Motto*

Coward, Sir Noel   **b. 1899**

Life without faith is an arid business.
                             Blithe Spirit, 1

Time is the reef upon which all our frail mystic ships are wrecked. *Ib.*

I don't give a hoot about posterity. Why should I worry about what people think of me when I'm dead as a doornail anyway? *Present Laughter*, 1

Everybody worships me, it's nauseating. *Ib.*

Extraordinary how potent cheap music is.
                             Private Lives, 1

Comedies of manners swiftly become obsolete when there are no longer any manners. *Relative Values*, 1

Cowley, Abraham   **1618-1667**

Love in her sunny Eyes does basking play;
Love walks the pleasant Mazes of her Haire.
The Change

God the first garden made, and the first city Cain.
The Garden

His faith perhaps, in some nice Tenets might
Be wrong; his Life, I'm sure, was in the right.
On the Death of Mr. Crashaw

Ah, yet, e'er I descend to th' grave
May I a small house, and a large garden have!
And a few friends, and many books, both true,
        Both wise, and both delightful too!
            And since Love ne'er will from me flee,
A Mistress moderately fair,
And good as guardian angels are,
        Only belov'd, and loving me!   *The Wish*

Cowley, Hannah   **1743-1809**

Five minutes! Zounds! I have been five minutes
too late all my life-time. *The Belle's Stratagem*, 1

But what is woman?—only one of Nature's
agreeable blunders. *Who's the Dupe?*, 2

Cowper William,   **1731-1800**

Rome shall perish—write that word
In the blood that she has spilt. *Boadicea*

Grief is itself a med'cine. *Charity*

He found it inconvenient to be poor. *Ib.*

Pelting each other for the public good. *Ib.*

A noisy man is always in the right. *Conversation*

War lays a burden on the reeling state,
And peace does nothing to relieve the weight.
Expostulation

Thousands . . .
Kiss the book's outside who ne'er look within. *Ib.*

O'erjoyed was he to find
That, though on pleasure she was bent,
She had a frugal mind. *John Gilpin*

But strive to be a man before your mother.
Motto to Connoisseur, 3

I am monarch of all I survey,
My right there is none to dispute.
The Solitude of Alexander Selkirk

Oh solitude! where are the charms
That sages have seen in thy face? *Ib.*

Freedom has a thousand charms to show,
That slaves, howe'er contented, never know.
Table Talk

Stamps God's own name upon a lie just made
To turn a penny in the way of trade. *Ib.*

God made the country, and man made the town.
The Task, 1, *The Sofa*

Variety's the very spice of life,
That gives it all its flavour. *Ib.* 2, *The Timepiece*

Domestic happiness, thou only bliss
Of Paradise that has surviv'd the fall!

Ib. 3, The Garden

Crabbe, George   1754-1832

Habit with him was all the test of truth,
" It must be right: I've done it from my youth."

The Borough, letter 3, The Vicar

This books can do—nor this alone: they give
New views to life, and teach us how to live;
They soothe the grieved, the stubborn they
    chastise;
Fools they admonish, and confirm the wise,
Their aid they yield to all: they never shun
The man of sorrow, nor the wretch undone;
Unlike the hard, the selfish, and the proud,
They fly not from the suppliant crowd;
Nor tell to various people various things,
But show to subjects, what they show to kings.

The Library

Secrets with girls, like loaded guns with boys,
Are never valued till they make a noise.

Tales of the Hall, 11, The Maid's Story

Crashaw, Richard   c. 1612-1649

Love, thou art absolute sole Lord
Of life and death. *Hymn to the Name and
Honour of the Admirable St. Teresa*

I would be married, but I'd have no wife,
I would be married to a single life.

On Marriage

     . . . two faithful fountaines;
Two walking baths; two weeping motions;
Portable, and compendious oceans.

Saint Mary Magdalene, or The Weeper

Two went to pray? O rather say
One went to brag, th'other to pray. *Steps to the
Temple. Two went up into the Temple to Pray*

All is Caesar's; and what odds
So long as Caesar's self is God's? *Ib. Mark 12*

A face made up,
Out of no other shop
Than what natures white hand sets ope.
Wishes to his (supposed) Mistress

A Cheeke where growes
More than a Morning Rose:
Which to no Boxe his being owes.

Lipps, where all Day
A lovers kisse may play,
Yet carry nothing thence away. *Ib.*

Creighton, Mandell   **1843-1901**

No people do so much harm as those who go
about doing good. *Life*, 1904

Croker, John Wilson   **1780-1857**

A game which a sharper once played with a dupe,
entitled, "Heads I win, tails you lose." *Croker
Papers*

We now are, as we always have been, decidedly
and conscientiously attached to what is called the
Tory, and which might with more propriety be
called the Conservative, party. *Quarterly Review,
Jan.*, 1830

Cromwell, Oliver   1599-1658

I beseech you, in the bowels of Christ, think it possible you may be mistaken. *Letter to the General Assembly of the Church of Scotland,* 1650

The dimensions of this mercy are above my thoughts. It is, for aught I know, a crowning mercy. *Letter to the Hon. W. Lenthall,* 1651

What shall we do with the bauble? Take it away! *Remark on dissolving Parliament,* 1653

Necessity hath no law. *Speech,* 1654

You have accounted yourselves happy on being environed with a great ditch from all the world beside. *Ib.* 1658

Mr. Lely, I desire you would use all your skill to paint my picture freely like me, and not flatter me at all; but remark all these roughnesses, pimples, and everything as you see me, otherwise I will never pay a farthing for it. *Remark*

Not what they want but what is good for them.
                                        Attrib. Remark

Cunningham, Allan   1784-1842

The lark shall sing me hame in my ain countree.
                    (Attrib.) It's Hame and It's Hame

Wha the deil hae we got for a King,
But a wee, wee German lairdie!
                    The Wee, Wee German Lairdie

A wet sheet and a flowing sea,
A wind that follows fast
And fills the white and rustling sail
And bends the gallant mast.
                                    A Wet Sheet and a Flowing Sea

. . . the hollow oak our palace is,
Our heritage the sea. *Ib.*

Curran, John Philpot   1750-1817

The condition upon which God hath given liberty
to man is eternal vigilance; which condition if
he break, servitude is at once the consequence of
his crime, and the punishment of his guilt.
                                    Speech, 1790

Dana, Charles Anderson   1819-1897

All the goodness of a good egg cannot make up
for the badness of a bad one. *The Making of a
Newspaper Man*

When a dog bites a man that is not news, but
when a man bites a dog that is news. *What is
News? New York Sun*, 1882

Daniel, The Book of

But if ye worship not, ye shall be cast the same
hour into the midst of a burning fiery furnace.
                                    3, 15

And this is the writing that was written, MENE,
MENE, TEKEL, UPHARSIN. 5, 25

Dante Alighieri   1265-1321

Lasciate ogni speranza voi ch'entrate. Abandon
hope, all ye who enter here. *Inferno*, 3

Questi non hanno speranza di morte. These have
not hope of death. *Ib.*

Il gran rifiuto. The great refusal. *Ib.*

L'arte vostra quella, quanto puote,
Segue, come il maestro fa il discente,
Si che vostr'arte a Dio quasi è nipote.
Art, as far as it can, follows nature, as a pupil
imitates his master; thus your art must be, as it
were, God's grandchild. *Ib.* 11

Onorate l'altissimo poeta. Honour the greatest
poet. *Ib.*

Ahi fiera compagnia! ma nella chiesa
Coi santi ed in taverna coi ghiottoni.
Ah, proud company! In church with saints and
in taverns with gluttons. *Ib.* 22

Chè, seggendo in piuma,
In fama non si vien, nè sotto coltre.
For fame is not won by lying on a feather bed
nor under a canopy. *Ib.* 24

E cortesia fu in lui esser villano. To be rude to
him was courtesy. *Ib.* 33

Tu proverai si come sa di sale
Lo pane altrui, e com' è duro calle
Lo scendere e il salir per l'altrui scale.
You will find how salt is the taste of another's
bread, and how hard is the way up and down
another's stairs. *Paradiso,* 17

Vien, retro a me, e lascia dir le genti. Come,
follow me and leave the world to chatter.
Purgatorio, 5

*Sta come torre ferma, che non crolla
Giammai la cima per soffiar de' venti.*
Be as a strong tower, that never bows its head to
the force of the wind. *Ib.*

Danton, Georges Jacques   1759–1794

*De l'audace, et encore de l'audace, et toujours de
l'audace!* Boldness, and more boldness, and
always boldness! *Speech, 1792*

Darwin, Charles Robert   1809–1882

We must, however, acknowledge, as it seems to
me, that man with all his noble qualities . . . still
bears in his bodily frame the indelible stamp of
his lowly origin. *Descent of Man*, conclusion

Believing as I do that man in the distant future
will be a far more perfect creature than he now
is, it is an intolerable thought that he and all
other sentient beings are doomed to complete
annihilation after such long-continued slow
progress. To those who fully admit the immortality of the human soul, the destruction of
our world will not appear so dreadful. *Life and
Letters*

I have called this principle, by which each slight
variation, if useful, is preserved, by the term of
Natural Selection. *The Origin of Species*, 3

The struggle for existence. *Ib.*

The expression often used by Mr. Herbert
Spencer of the Survival of the Fittest is more
accurate, and is sometimes equally convenient. *Ib.*

Daudet, Alphonse   **1840-1897**

Des coups d'épée, messieurs, des coups d'épée!
Mais pas de coups d'épingle! Strokes of the sword,
gentlemen, strokes of the sword! Not pin pricks!
                                        Tartarin de Tarascon, 1

Davenant, William   **1606-1668**

Fraile Life! in which, through Mists of humane
    breath,
We grope for Truth, and make our Progress
    slow. *The Christians Reply to the Phylosopher*

I shall sleep like a top. *The Rivals,* 3

Davidson, John   **1857-1909**

" In shuttered rooms let others grieve,
    And coffin thought in speech of lead;
I'll tie my heart upon my sleeve:
    It is the Badge of Men," he said.
                                        The Badge of Men

He wrought at one great work for years;
    The world passed by with lofty look:
Sometimes his eyes were dashed with tears;
    Sometimes his lips with laughter shook.
                                        A Ballad of Heaven

He doubted; but God said " Even so;
    Nothing is lost that's wrought with tears:
The music that you made below
    Is now the music of the spheres." *Ib.*

Seraphs and saints with one great voice
    Welcomed the soul that knew not fear;

Amazed to find it could rejoice,
Hell raised a hoarse, half-human cheer.
A Ballad of Hell

He cursed the canting moralist,
Who measures right and wrong.
A Ballad of a Poet Born

" My time is filched by toil and sleep;
My heart," he thought, " is clogged with dust;
My soul that flashed from out the deep,
A magic blade, begins to rust."
A Ballad of a Workman

For this was in the North, where Time stands still
And Change holds holiday, where Old and New
Welter upon the Borders of the world,
And savage faith works woe.
A Ballad in Blank Verse on the Making of a Poet

Davies, Sir John   1569-1626

Skill comes so slow, and life so fast doth fly,
   We learn so little and forget so much.
Nosce Teipsum, introduction

Judge not the play before the play be done.
Respice Finem

Davies, William Henry   1870-1940

What is this life if, full of care,
We have no time to stand and stare? *Leisure*

Davis, Jefferson   1808-1889

All we ask is to be let alone. *Attrib. Remark,
Inaugural Address as President of Confederate
States of America, 1861*

Debs, Eugene Victor   **1855-1926**

While there is a lower class, I am in it. While
there is a criminal class I am of it. While there
is a soul in prison, I am not free. *Labor and
Freedom*

Decatur, Stephen   **1779-1820**

Our country! In her intercourse with foreign
nations, may she always be in the right; but our
country, right or wrong. *Life of Decatur*, A. S.
Mackenzie

Defoe, Daniel   **c. 1661-1731**

Nature has left this tincture in the blood,
That all men would be tyrants if they could.
                                   The Kentish Petition

Wherever God erects a house of prayer,
The Devil always builds a chapel there;
And 'twill be found, upon examination,
The latter has the largest congregation.
                                   The True-Born Englishman, 1

From this amphibious, ill-born mob began
That vain, ill-natur'd thing, an Englishman. *Ib.*

And of all plagues with which mankind are curst,
Ecclesiastic tyranny's the worst. *Ib.* 2

When kings the sword of justice first lay down,
They art no kings, though they possess the crown.
Titles are shadows, crowns are empty things,
The good of subjects is the end of kings. *Ib.*

152

Robin, Robin, Robin Crusoe, poor Robin Crusoe!
Where are you, Robin Crusoe? Where are you?
Where have you been? *The Life and Adventures
of Robinson Crusoe*, 1

It happened one day, about noon, going towards
my boat, I was exceedingly surprised with the
print of a man's naked foot on the shore, which
was very plain to be seen in the sand. I stood like
one thunderstruck, or as if I had seen an
apparition. *Ib.*

Necessity makes an honest man a knave. *Serious
Reflections of Robinson Crusoe*, 2

Dekker, Thomas   **c. 1570- c. 1641**

                  The best of men
That e'er wore earth about him, was a sufferer
A soft, meek, patient, humble, tranquil spirit,
The first true gentleman that ever breath'd.
                              The Honest Whore, 1

Golden slumbers kiss your eyes,
Smiles awake you when you rise.
                              Patient Grissill, 1

De La Mare, Walter   **1873-1956**

I met at eve the Prince of Sleep,
His was a still and lovely face,
He wandered through a valley steep,
Lovely in a lonely place. *I Met at Eve*

" Is there anybody there? " said the traveller,
Knocking on the moonlit door. *The Listeners*

" Tell them that I came, and no one answered,
That I kept my word," he said. *Ib.*

Slowly, silently, now the moon
Walks the night in her silver shoon.   *Silver*

Demosthenes   385-322 B.C.

I decline to buy repentance at the cost of ten
thousand drachmas. *Noctes Atticae*, Aulus Gellius

The easiest thing of all is to deceive one's self;
for what a man wishes he generally believes to
be true. *Olynthiaca, 3*

There is one safeguard known generally to the
wise, which is an advantage and security to all,
but especially to democracies against despots—
suspicion. *Philippics, 2*

Dennis, John   1657-1734

A man who could make so vile a pun, would not
scruple to pick a pocket.   *The Gentleman's
Magazine*, 1781

See how the rascals use me! They will not let
my play run and yet they steal my thunder!
          Remark at a production of Macbeth

De Quincey, Thomas   1785-1859

It is most absurdly said, in popular language, of
any man, that he is *disguised* in liquor; for, on
the contrary, most men are disguised by sobriety.
          Confessions of an English Opium Eater

Better to stand ten thousand sneers than one
abiding pang, such as time could not abolish, of
bitter self-reproach. *Ib.* 1

Thou hast the keys of Paradise, oh just, subtle, and mighty opium! *Ib.* 2, *The Pleasures of Opium*

Murder Considered as One of the Fine Arts. *Title of Essay*

Descartes, René   1596-1650

Cogito, ergo sum. I think, therefore I am. *Le Discours de la Méthode*

Deuteronomy, The Book of

Man doth not live by bread only, but by every word that proceedeth out of the mouth of the Lord doth man live. 8, 3

A dreamer of dreams. 13, 1

Deutsch, Babette (Mrs. Avrahm Yarmolinsky)
b. 1895

You also, laughing one,
Tosser of balls in the sun,
Will pillow your bright head
By the incurious dead. *A Girl*

Old women sit, stiffly, mosaics of pain . . .
Their memories: a heap of tumbling stones,
Once builded stronger than a city wall.
Old Women

Dewar, Lord Thomas Robert   1864-1930

The road to success is filled with women pushing their husbands along. *Epigram*

Dewey, John   1859-1952

It is strange that the one thing that every person looks forward to, namely old age, is the one thing for which no preparation is made. *Attrib.*

There are strings . . . in the human heart that had better not be wibrated. *Barnaby Rudge*, 22

In came Mrs. Fezziwig, one vast substantial smile.
A Christmas Carol, 2

Barkis is willin'. *David Copperfield*, 5

" When a man says he's willin'," said Mr. Barkis . . . " it's as much as to say, that a man's waitin' for a answer." *Ib.* 8

Annual income twenty pounds, annual expenditure nineteen nineteen six, result happiness. Annual income twenty pounds, annual expenditure twenty pounds ought and six, result misery.
Ib. 12

We are so very 'umble. *Ib.* 17

" It was as true," said Mr. Barkis, " . . . as taxes is. And nothing's truer than them." *Ib.* 21

" People can't die, along the coast," said Mr. Peggotty, " except when the tide's pretty nigh out. They can't be born, unless it's pretty nigh in— not properly born, till flood. He's a going out with the tide." *Ib.* 30

Mrs. Crupp had indignantly assured him that there wasn't room to swing a cat there; but, as Mr. Dick justly observed to me, sitting down on the foot of the bed, nursing his leg, " You know, Trotwood, I don't want to swing a cat. I never do swing a cat. Therefore, what does that signify to *me* ! " *Ib.* 35

Circumstances beyond my individual control.
Ib. 49

I'm Gormed—and I can't say no fairer than that!
Ib. 63

Train up a fig-tree in the way it should go, and
when you are old sit under the shade of it.
Dombey and Son, 19

Your sister is given to government.
Great Expectations, 7

I had cherished a profound conviction that her
bringing me up by hand, gave her no right to
bring me up by jerks. *Ib.* 8

Get hold of portable property. *Ib.* 24

You don't object to an aged parent, I hope? *Ib.* 25

" Now, what I want is, Facts. Teach these boys
and girls nothing but Facts. Facts alone are
wanted in life. Plant nothing else, and root out
everything else. . . . Stick to Facts, sir! " *Hard
Times*, 1, 1

" I canna tell what will better aw this—but I can
tell what I know will never do't. The strong hand
will never do't. Vict'ry and triumph will never
do't. Agreeing fur to mak' one side unnat'rally
and fur ever wrong, will never do't. . . . Most of
aw, rating 'em as so much power, and reg'latin'
'em as if they was figures in a soom, or machines.
wi'out souls to weary and souls to hope—this
will never do't, sir, till God's work is unmade."
Ib. 2, 21

In company with several other old ladies of both sexes. *Little Dorrit*, 1, 17

You can't make a head and brains out of a brass knob with nothing in it. You couldn't when your Uncle George was living; much less when he's dead. *Ib.* 23

Papa, potatoes, poultry, prunes and prism, are all very good words for the lips; especially prunes and prism. *Ib.* 2, 5

Any man may be in good spirits and good temper when he's well dressed. There an't much credit in that. *Martin Chuzzlewit*, 5

With affection beaming in one eye, and calculation shining out the other. *Ib.* 8

Here's the rule, for bargains: " Do other men, for they would do you." That's the true business precept. *Ib.* 11

" She's the sort of woman now," said Mould . . . " one would almost feel disposed to bury for nothing: and do it neatly, too!" *Ib.* 25

He'd make a lovely corpse. *Ib.*

As she frequently remarked when she made any such mistake, it would all be the same a hundred years hence. *Nicholas Nickleby*, 9

There are only two styles of portrait painting; the serious and the smirk. *Ib.* 10

Language was not powerful enough to describe the infant phenomenon. *Ib.* 23

My life is one demd horrid grind! *Ib.* 64

Fan the sinking flame of hilarity with the wing of friendship; and pass the rosy wine. *The Old Curiosity Shop*, 7

It was a maxim with Foxey—our revered father, gentlemen—" Always suspect everybody." *Ib.* 66

Oliver Twist has asked for more! *Oliver Twist*, 2

" If the law supposes that," said Mr. Bumble . . . " the law is a ass—a idiot." *Ib.* 51

The question about everything was, would it bring a blush to the cheek of a young person? *Our Mutual Friend*, 1, 11

Queer Street is full of lodgers just at present. *Ib.* 3, 1

" Suppose there are two mobs?" suggested Mr. Snodgrass. " Shout with the largest," replied Mr. Pickwick. *Pickwick Papers*, 13

Tongue; well that's a wery good thing when it an't a woman's. *Ib.* 19

Wery glad to see you, indeed, and hope our acquaintance may be a long 'un, as the gen'l'm'n said to the fi' pun' note. *Ib.* 25

Our noble society for providing the infant negroes in the West Indies with flannel waistcoats and moral pocket handkerchiefs. *Ib.*

When you're a married man, Samivel, you'll understand a good many things as you don't understand now; but vether it's worth while goin' through so much to learn so little, as the charity-boy said when he got to the end of the alphabet, is a matter o' taste. *Ib.* 27

159

" Eccentricities of genius, Sam," said Mr. Pickwick. *Ib.* 30

Mr. Phunky, blushing to the very whites of his eyes, tried to look as if he didn't know that everybody was gazing at him, a thing which no man ever succeeded in doing yet, or, in all reasonable probability, ever will. *Ib.* 34

As it is, I don't think I can do with anythin' under a female markis. I might keep up with a young 'ooman o' large property as hadn't a title, if she made wery fierce love to me. Not else. *Ib.* 37

A smattering of everything and a knowledge of nothing. *Sketches by Boz. Sentiment*

Grief never mended no broken bones, and as good people's wery scarce, what I says is, make the most on 'em. *Ib. Gin Shops*

It was the best of times, it was the worst of times, it was the age of wisdom, it was the age of foolishness, it was the epoch of belief, it was the epoch of incredulity, it was the season of Light, it was the season of Darkness, it was the spring of hope, it was the winter of despair, we had everything before us, we had nothing before us, we were all going direct to Heaven, we were all going direct the other way. *A Tale of Two Cities,* 1, 1

It is a far, far better thing that I do, than I have ever done; it is a far, far better rest that I go to, than I have ever known. *Ib.* 3, 15

Dickinson, Emily   1830-1886

These are the days when skies put on
The old, old sophistries of June,—
A blue and gold mistake. *Indian Summer*

How dreary to be somebody!
How public, like a frog
To tell your name the livelong day
To an admiring bog! *Poems*

Diogenes (the Cynic)   c. 412-323 B.C.

I do not know whether there are gods, but there
ought to be. *Ad Nationes*, Tertullian

I am a citizen of the world. (*Kosmopolites:* origin
of the word "cosmopolitan.") *Diogenes*, Diogenes
Laertius

I am called a dog because I fawn on those who
give me anything, I yelp at those who refuse, and
I set my teeth in rascals. *Ib.*

If I were running in the stadium, ought I to
slacken my pace when approaching the goal?
Ought I not rather to put on speed? *Ib.*

The foundation of every state is the education of
its youth. *Florilegium*, Stobaeus

Disraeli, Benjamin, Earl of Beaconsfield 1804-1881

No Government can be long secure without a
formidable opposition. *Coningsby*, 2, 1

Conservatism discards Prescription, shrinks from
Principle, disavows Progress; having rejected all

respect for antiquity, it offers no redress for the present, and makes no preparation for the future. *Ib.* 5

A sound Conservative government. . . . Tory men and Whig measures. *Ib.* 6

Time is the great physician. *Endymion*, 6, 9

Marriage is the greatest earthly happiness when founded on complete sympathy. *Letter to Gladstone*

When a man fell into his anecdotage it was a sign for him to retire from the world. *Lothair*, 28

You know who the critics are? The men who have failed in literature and art. *Ib.* 35

I was told that the Privileged and the People formed Two Nations. *Sybil*, 4, 8

The Youth of a Nation are the Trustees of Posterity. *Ib.* 6, 13

Experience is the child of Thought, and Thought is the child of Action. We cannot learn men from books. *Vivian Grey*, 5, 1

She did not know which came first, the Greeks or the Romans, but she was a wonderful woman. *Remark to Sir William Harcourt*

Though I sit down now, the time will come when you will hear me. *Maiden Speech*, Dec., 1837

The Continent will not suffer England to be the workshop of the world. *Speech, House of Commons*, 1838

A Conservative government is an organised hypocrisy. *Ib.* 1845

Is man an ape or an angel? Now I am on the side of the angels. *Speech, Oxford,* 1864

Lord Salisbury and myself have brought you back peace—but peace, I hope, with honour. *Ib. House of Commons, July,* 1878

Donne, John   c. 1571-1631

Twice or thrice had I loved thee,
Before I knew thy face or name;
So in a voice, so in a shapelesse flame,
Angells affect us oft, and worship'd bee.
Aire and Angels

　Just such disparitie
As is twixt Aire and Angells puritie,
'Twixt womens love, and mens will ever bee. *Ib.*

All other things, to their destruction draw,
Only our love hath no decay;
This, no to morrow hath, nor yesterday,
Running it never runs from us away,
But truly keeps his first, last, everlasting day.
The Anniversarie

Come live with mee, and bee my love,
And we will some new pleasures prove
Of golden sands, and christall brookes,
With silken lines, and silver hookes. *The Baite*

For Godsake hold your tongue, and let me love.
The Canonization

Chang'd loves are but chang'd sorts of meat,
And when hee hath the kernell eate,
Who doth not fling away the shell? *Communitie*

No man is an *Island*, entire of it self. *Devotions*

Any man's *death* diminishes *me*, because I am
involved in *Mankind*; And therefore never send
to know for whom the *bell* tolls; It tolls for *thee*.
Ib.

Love built on beauty, soon as beauty, dies.
Elegy 2, The Anagram

Women are like the Arts, forc'd unto none,
Open to all searchers, unpriz'd if unknowne.
Ib. 3, Change

Oh, let mee not serve so, as those men serve
Whom honours smoakes at once fatten and
sterve. *Ib. 6*

No Spring, nor Summer Beauty hath such grace,
As I have seen in one Autumnall face.
Ib. 9, The Autumnall

So, if I dreame I have you, I have you,
For, all our joyes are but fantasticall.
Ib. 10, The Dreame

And must she needs be false because she's faire?
Ib. 15, The Expostulation

May Wolves teare out his heart, Vultures his eyes,
Swine eate his bowels, and his falser tongue,
That utter'd all, be to some Raven flung. *Ib.*

164

How happy were our Syres in ancient times,
Who held plurality of loves no crime! *Ib.* 17

So, so, breake off this last lamenting kisse,
Which sucks two soules, and vapors both away.
The Expiration

Loves mysteries in soules doe grow,
But yet the body is his booke.   *The Extasie*

Yet, because outward stormes the strongest
   breake,
And strength it selfe by confidence growes weake,
This new world may be safer, being told
The dangers and diseases of the old.
The First Anniversary

I wonder by my troth, what thou, and I
Did, till we lov'd? *The Good-Morrow*

Or snorted we in the Seven Sleepers den? *Ib.*

I am a little world made cunningly
Of Elements, and an Angelike spright.
Holy Sonnets, 5

All whom warre, dearth, age, agues, tyrannies,
Despaire, law, chance, hath slaine. *Ib.* 7

One short sleepe past, wee wake eternally,
And death shall be no more; Death, thou shalt die.
Ib. 10

What if this present were the worlds last night?
Ib. 13

Batter my heart, three person'd God; for, you
As yet but knocke. *Ib.* 14

Since I am comming to that Holy roome,
Where, with thy Quire of Saints for evermore,
I shall be made thy Musique; As I come
I tune the Instrument here at the dore,
And what I must doe then, thinke now before.
Hymne to God my God, in my Sicknesse

Wilt thou forgive that sinne where I begunne,
Which was my sin, though it were done before?
Wilt thou forgive that sinne, through which I
runne,
And doe them still: though still I do deplore?
When thou hast done, thou hast not done,
For, I have more.   *Hymne to God the Father*

When I dyed last, and, Deare, I dye
As often as from thee I goe,
Though it be but an houre agoe,
And Lovers houres be full eternity,
I can remember yet. *The Legacie*

I long to talke with some old lovers ghost,
Who dyed before the god of Love was borne.
Loves Deitie

Love's not so pure, and abstract, as they use
To say, which have no Mistresse but their Muse,
But as all else, being elemented too,
Love sometimes would contemplate, sometimes
do. *Loves Growth*

I never stoop'd so low, as they
Which on an eye, cheeke, lip can prey,
Seldome to them, which soare no higher
Then vertue or the minde to admire.
Negative Love

166

I sing the progresse of a deathlesse soule,
Whom Fate, which God made, but doth not
controule,
Plac'd in most shapes.
The Progresse of the Soule, 1

Giddie fantastique Poëts of each land. *Satyres,* 1

On a huge hill,
Cragged, and steep, Truth stands, and hee that
will
Reach her, about must, and about must goe;
And what the hills suddennes resists, winne so.
Ib. 3

But 'twere little to have chang'd our roome,
If, as we were in this our living Tombe
Oppress'd with ignorance, wee still were so.
Poore soule, in this thy flesh what dost thou know?
The Second Anniversary

And yet one watches, starves, freeses, and sweats,
To know but Catechismes and Alphabets
Of unconcerning things, matters of fact:
How others on our stage their parts did Act;
What Caesar did, yea, and what Cicero said. *Ib.*

Goe, and catche a falling starre,
Get with child a mandrake roote,
Tell me, where all past yeares are,
Or who cleft the Divel's foot. *Song*

And sweare
No where
Lives a woman true, and faire. *Ib.*

Busie old foole, unruly Sunne,
Why dost thou thus,
Through windowes, and through curtaines call on
  us? *The Sunne Rising*

Love, all alike, no season knowes, nor clyme,
Nor houres, dayes, months, which are the rags
  of time. *Ib.*

I am two fooles, I know,
For loving, and for saying so
In whining Poëtry. *The Triple Foole*

Griefe brought to numbers cannot be so fierce,
For, he tames it, that fetters it in verse. *Ib.*

But he who lovelinesse within
Hath found, all outward loathes,
For he who colour loves, and skinne,
Loves but their oldest clothes. *The Undertaking*

Man is a lumpe, where all beasts kneaded bee,
Wisdome makes him an Arke where all agree;
The foole, in whom these beasts do live at jarre,
Is sport to others, and a Theater.
                       To Sir Edward Herbert

Dull sublunary lovers love
(Whose soule is sense) cannot admit
Absence, because it doth remove
Those things which elemented it.
                  A Valediction Forbidding Mourning

But we by a love, so much refin'd,
That our selves know not what it is,
Inter-assured of the mind,
Care lesse, eyes, lips, and hands to misse. *Ib.*

Douglas, Archibald, Fifth Earl of Angus c. 1449-1514

I shall bell the cat. *Attrib.*

Douglas, Gawin   c. 1475-1522

Considir it warlie, reid oftair than anis;
Weill at ane blenk slee poetry nocht tane is.
The Prologue of the First Book of Eneados

[Of love]
Quhat is your force bot febling of the strenth?
Your curious thochtis quhat but musardry?
Your fremmyt glaidnes lestis nocht ane houris
    lenth;
Your sport for scham ye dar nocht specify;
Your frute is bot unfructuous fantasy;
Your sary joyis bene bot jangling and japis,
And your trew servandis silly goddis apes.
Ib. Fourth Book

The nycht come and all thing levand seisst;
Wery of wirk bayth byrd and brutell beist
Our all the landis war at rest ilkane—
The profund swoch of sleip had thaim ourtayne.
Eneados, bk. 8

Yit, by my self, I fynd this proverb perfyte:
The blak craw thinkis hir awin byrdis quhite.
Ib. prol. 9

The lycht begouth to quynkill out and faill,
The day to dyrkyn, decline and devaill.
Ib. prol. 13

Yondyr doun dwynis the evin sky away
And upspringys the brycht dawing of day
Intill ane other place nocht far in sundir
That to behold was plesans and half wondir. *Ib.*

169

The more featureless and commonplace a crime is, the more difficult is it to bring it home. *The Boscombe Valley Mystery*

All other men are specialists, but his specialism is omniscience. *Bruce-Partington Plans*

It has long been an axiom of mine that the little things are infinitely the most important. *A Case of Identity*

It is my belief, Watson, founded upon my experience, that the lowest and vilest alleys of London do not present a more dreadful record of sin than does the smiling and beautiful countryside. *Copper Beeches*

" Excellent ! " I [Dr. Watson] cried. " Elementary," said he [Holmes]. *The Crooked Man*

A man should keep his little brain attic stocked with all the furniture that he is likely to use, and the rest he can put away in the lumber-room of his library, where he can get it if he wants it. *Five Orange Pips*

It is quite a three-pipe problem. *The Red-Headed League*

It is a capital mistake to theorise before one has data. *Scandal in Bohemia*

An experience of women which extends over many nations and three separate continents. *The Sign of Four*

How often have I said to you that when you have eliminated the impossible, whatever remains, *however improbable*, must be the truth. *Ib.*

You know my methods. Apply them. *Ib.* (Also, with slight variations, in *The Musgrave Ritual, The Crooked Man,* etc.)

London, that great cesspool into which all the loungers of the Empire are irresistibly drained.
A Study in Scarlet

The vocabulary of Bradshaw is nervous and terse, but limited. *The Valley of Fear*

Mediocrity knows nothing higher than itself, but talent instantly recognises genius. *Ib.*

Drake, Francis   c. 1540-1596

I remember Drake, in the vaunting style of a soldier, would call the Enterprise [of Cadiz, 1587] the singeing of the King of Spain's Beard.
Considerations touching a War with Spain, Bacon

There is plenty of time to win this game, and to thrash the Spaniards too. *Attrib. in Dict. of Nat. Biog.*

Drayton, Michael   1563-1631

Ill news hath wings, and with the wind doth go,
Comfort's a cripple and comes ever slow.
The Barrons' Wars, 2

Thus when we fondly flatter our desires,
Our best conceits do prove the greatest liars. *Ib.* 6

Fair stood the wind for France
When we our sails advance,
Nor now to prove our chance
    Longer will tarry.
        To the Cambro-Britons, Agincourt

Neat Marlowe, bathed in the Thespian springs,
Had in him those brave translunary things
That the first poets had; his raptures were
All air and fire, which made his verses clear,
For that fine madness still he did retain
Which rightly should possess a poet's brain.
        Of Poets and Poesie

Since there's no help, come let us kiss and part.
        Sonnet. Idea

Dryden, John   **1631-1700**

In pious times, ere priestcraft did begin,
Before polygamy was made a sin.
        Absalom and Achitophel, 1

Whate'er he did was done with so much ease,
In him alone 'twas natural to please.   *Ib.*

Gods they had tried of every shape and size
That godsmiths could produce or priests devise.
        Ib.

Great wits are sure to madness near allied.   *Ib.*

In friendship false, implacable in hate,
Resolved to ruin or to rule the state. *Ib.*

So easy still it proves in factious times
With public zeal to cancel private crimes.   *Ib.*

All empire is no more than power in trust,
Which, when resumed, can be no longer just. *Ib.*

Better one suffer than a nation grieve.   *Ib.*
   (*N.B.—Million* in first edition instead of *nation*)

And pity never ceases to be shown
To him who makes the people's wrongs his own.
                              Ib.
Nor is the people's judgement always true:
The most may err as grossly as the few.   *Ib.*

None but the brave deserves the fair.
                       Alexander's Feast

Drinking is the soldier's pleasure. *Ib.*

At length, with love and wine at once oppressed,
The vanquished victor sunk upon her breast. *Ib.*

See the Furies arise!
See the snakes that they rear,
How they hiss in their hair,
And the sparkles that flash from their eyes. *Ib.*

And, like another Helen, fired another Troy. *Ib.*

Men are but children of a larger growth.
                    All for Love, 4

Our author by experience finds it true,
'Tis much more hard to please himself than you.
                   Aureng-Zebe, prologue

When I consider life, 'tis all a cheat;
Yet, fooled with hope, men favour the deceit. *Ib.* 4

Yet dull religion teaches us content;
But when we ask it where that blessing dwells,
It points to pedant colleges and cells.
The Conquest of Granada, 2

Fair though you are
As summer mornings, and your eyes more bright
Than stars that twinkle in a winter's night. *Ib.* 3

Treaties are but the combat of the brain,
Where still the stronger lose, the weaker gain. *Ib.*

His grandeur he derived from Heaven alone,
For he was great, ere fortune made him so.
Heroic Stanzas after Cromwell's Funeral

By education most have been misled;
So they believe, because they so were bred.
The priest continues what the nurse began,
And thus the child imposes on the man.
The Hind and the Panther, 3

All human things are subject to decay,
And, when fate summons, monarchs must obey.
Mac Flecknoe

But now the world's o'er stocked with prudent
men. *The Medal*

Dim, as the borrowed beams of moon and stars
To lonely, weary, wandering travellers
Is reason to the soul. *Religio Laic*

How can the less the greater comprehend?
Or finite reason reach Infinity? *Ib.*

174

But since men will believe more than they need;
And every man will make himself a creed,
In doubtful questions 'tis the safest way
To learn what unsuspected ancients say.   *Ib.*

A very merry, dancing, drinking,
Laughing, quaffing, and unthinking time.
                              Secular Masque

Happy the man, and happy he alone,
He, who can call to-day his own:
He who, secure within, can say,
To-morrow do thy worst, for I have lived to-day.
                    Translation of Horace, Odes, 3, 29

Dudley, Sir Henry Bate   1745-1824

Wonders will never cease. *Letter to Garrick*, 1776

Dukes, Ashley   b. 1885

Adventure must be held in delicate fingers. It
should be handled, not embraced. It should be
sipped, not swallowed at a gulp. *The Man with
a Load of Mischief*, 1

The woman who runs will never lack followers.
                                            Ib.

Men reason to strengthen their own prejudices,
and not to disturb their adversary's convictions.
                                          Ib. 2

The tender passion is much overrated by the poets.
They have their living to earn, poor fellows. *Ib.* 3

Dumas, Alexandre   1803-1870

Tous pour un, un pour tous. All for one, one for
all. *Les Trois Mousquetiers*

Du Maurier, George Louis Palmella Busson
1834-1896

She had all the virtues but one. *Trilby*

[Of a husband] Feed the brute. *Punch*, 1886

Dunbar, William   **c. 1465- c. 1530**

The Devil sa deavit was with their yell,
That in the deepest pot of hell
He smoorit them with smoke.
The Dance of the Seven Deidly Sinnis

The bank was green, the brook was full of breamis,
The stanneris clear as stern in frosty nicht.
The Golden Targe

Be merry, man! and tak nocht far in mind
The wavering of this wrechit world of sorrow;
To God be hummill, and to the friend be kind,
And with thy neebouris gladly len' and borrow.
Hermes the Philosopher

Na gude in thine save only that thou spendis. *Ib.*

Without glaidness availis no tresour. *Ib.*

Flattery wearis ane furrit gown,
And fabet with the lord does roun,
And truth stands barrit at the dune.
Into this World May None Assure

I wauk, I turn, sleep may I nocht,
I vexit am with heavy thocht;
This warld all owre I cast about,
And aye the mair I am in doubt,
The mair that I remead have socht.
Meditation in Winter

176

God give to thee ane blissed chance,
And of all virtue abundance,
And grace ay for to persevere,
In hansel of this guid new year. *New Year's Gift*

Gif thou has micht, be gentle and free;
And gif thou standis in povertie,
Of thine awn will to it consent;
And riches sall return to thee:
He has eneuch that is content. *Of Content*

Great men for taking and oppressioun,
Are set full famous at the Sessioun,
And poor tokaris are hangit hie,
Shamit for ever and their succession:
In taking suld discretioun be.
Of Discretion in Taking

Our plesance here is all vain glory,
This fals world is but transitory,
The flesh is bruckle, the Feynd is slee:
  Timor Mortis conturbat me.
      Lament for the Makaris

Unto the deid gois all Estatis,
Princis, Prelatis, and Potestatis,
Baith rich and poor of all degree:
  Timor Mortis conturbat me. Ib.

Dyer, Sir Edward   c. 1540-1607

And he that will this health deny,
Down among the dead men let him lie.
      Toast: Here's a Health to the King

Ecclesiastes

Vanity of vanities, saith the Preacher, vanity of
vanities; all is vanity. 1, 2

To everything there is a season, and a time to
every purpose under the heaven:
A time to be born and a time to die; a time to
plant and a time to pluck that which is planted;
A time to kill, and a time to heal; a time to break
down, and a time to build up;
A time to weep, and a time to laugh; a time to
mourn, and a time to dance;
A time to cast away stones, and a time to gather
stones together; a time to embrace and a time to
refrain from embracing;
A time to get, and a time to lose; a time to keep,
and a time to cast away;
A time to rend, and a time to sew; a time to keep
silence, and a time to speak;
A time to love, and a time to hate; a time of war
and a time of peace. 3, 1-8

God is in heaven, and thou upon earth: therefore
let thy words be few. 5, 2

Whatsoever thy hand findeth to do, do it with
thy might. 9, 10

Cast thy bread upon the waters: for thou shalt
find it after many days. 11, 1

Of making many books there is no end; and
much study is the weariness of the flesh. 12, 12

Edgeworth, Maria   **1767-1849**

Well! some people talk of morality, and some of
religion, but give me a little snug property.
The Absentee, 2

Business was his aversion; pleasure was his
business. *The Contrast*, 2

There is one distinguishing peculiarity of the Irish bull—its horns are tipped with brass. *Irish Bulls*, 9

Edison, Thomas Alva   1847-1931

Genius is one per cent inspiration and ninety-nine per cent perspiration. *Newspaper Interview. Life*, 24

Edward VIII (later Duke of Windsor)   b. 1894

I have found it impossible to carry the heavy burden of responsibility and to discharge my duties as King as I would wish to do without the help and support of the woman I love.
Broadcast, 11th Dec., 1936

Edwards, Oliver   1711-1791

I have tried too in my time to be a philosopher; but, I don't know how, cheerfulness was always breaking in. Boswell's *Johnson*, 1778

Einstein, Albert   1879-1955

I never think of the future. It comes soon enough.
Interview, 1930

Why does this magnificent applied science which saves work and makes life easier bring us so little happiness? The simple answer runs: Because we have not yet learned to make sensible use of it. *Address, California Institute of Technology*, 1931

Only a life lived for others is a life worthwhile.
Defining Success. Youth, 1932

If my theory of relativity is proven successful, Germany will claim me as a German and France will declare that I am a citizen of the world. Should my theory prove untrue, France will say that I am a German and Germany will declare that I am a Jew. *Address, Sorbonne, Paris*

Before God we are all equally wise—equally foolish. *Ib.*

An empty stomach is not a good political adviser. *Cosmic Religion*

Peace cannot be kept by force. It can only be achieved by understanding. *Notes on Pacifism*

Imagination is more important than knowledge. *On Science*

Eliot, George (Mary Anne Evans)   1819-1880

A prophetess? Yea, I say unto you, and more than a prophetess—a uncommon pretty young woman. *Adam Bede, 1, 1*

He was like a cock who thought the sun had risen to hear him crow. *Ib. 4, 33*

I'm not denyin' the women are foolish: God Almighty made 'em to match the men. *Ib. 6, 53*

A blush is no language: only a dubious flag-signal which may mean either of two contradictories. *Daniel Deronda, 5, 35*

Man's life was spacious in the early world:
It paused, like some slow ship with sail unfurled
Waiting in seas by scarce a wavelet curled;
Beheld the slow star-paces of the skies,
And grew from strength to strength through centuries;

Saw infant trees fill out their giant limbs,
And heard a thousand times the sweet bird's
marriage hymns. *The Legend of Jubal*

This is a puzzling world, and Old Harry's got a
finger in it. *The Mill on the Floss*, 3, 9

I should like to know what is the proper function
of women, if it is not to make reasons for husbands
to stay at home, and still stronger reasons for
bachelors to go out. *Ib.* 6, 6

There's nothing like a dairy if folks want a bit o'
worrit to make the days pass. *Silas Marner*, 2, 17

'Tis God gives skill,
But not without men's hands: He could not make
Antonio Stradivari's violins
Without Antonio. Get thee to thy easel.

Stradivarius

Eliot, Thomas Stearns   1888-1965

You shouldn't interrupt my interruptions:
That's really worse than interrupting.
The Cocktail Party

Miss Nancy Ellicot smoked
And danced all the modern dances;
And her aunts were not quite sure how they felt
about it,
But they knew that it was modern. *Cousin Nancy*

No artist produces great art by a deliberate
attempt to express his own personality. *Essay.
Four Elizabethan Dramatists*

Those to whom nothing has ever happened
Cannot understand the unimportance of events.
The Family Reunion

181

History has many cunning passages, contrived
    corridors
And issues: deceives with whispering ambitions,
Guides us by vanities. *Gerontion*

Thoughts of a dry brain in a dry season. *Ib.*

We are the hollow men
We are the stuffed men
Leaning together
Headpiece filled with straw.
                    The Hollow Men, 1

This is the way the world ends
Not with a bang but a whimper. *Ib.* 5

Let us go then, you and I,
When the evening is spread out against the sky
Like a patient etherised upon a table.
                    Love Song of J. Alfred Prufrock

In the room the women come and go
Talking of Michelangelo. *Ib.*

The yellow fog that rubs its back upon the
    window-panes. *Ib.*

Have known the evenings, mornings, afternoons,
I have measured out my life with coffee spoons.
                                        Ib.

They are rattling breakfast plates in the basement
    kitchens,
And along the trampled edges of the street
I am aware of the damp souls of housemaids
Sprouting despondently at area gates.
                    Morning at the Window

Men will not hate you
Enough to defame or to execrate you,
But pondering the qualities that you lacked
Will only try to find the historical fact.
Murder in the Cathedral

However certain our expectation
The moment foreseen may be unexpected
When it arrives. *Ib. 2*

Human kind cannot bear very much reality. *Ib.*
(also in *Burnt Norton*)

The last temptation is the greatest treason:
To do the right deed for the wrong reason. *Ib.*

The winter evening settles down
With smell of steaks in passageways.
Six o'clock.
The burnt-out ends of smoky days. *Preludes, 1*

Let us take air, in a tobacco trance,
Admire the monuments,
Discuss the late events,
Correct our watches by the public clocks.
Then sit for half an hour and drink our bocks.
Portrait of a Lady

Every son would have his motor-cycle,
And daughters ride away on casual pillions.
The Rock

In the land of lobelias and tennis flannels,
The rabbit shall burrow and the thorn revisit,
The nettle shall flourish on the gravel court,
And the wind shall say " Here were decent, god-
less people;
Their only monument the asphalt road
And a thousand lost golf balls." *Ib.*

Many are engaged in writing books and printing
  them
Many desire to see their names in print,
Many read nothing but the race reports.   *Ib*.

And I will show you something different from
  either
Your shadow at morning striding behind you,
Or your shadow at evening rising to meet you
I will show you fear in a handful of dust.
            The Waste Land. The Burial of the Dead

When lovely woman stoops to folly and
Paces about her room again, alone,
She smoothes her hair with automatic hand,
And puts a record on the gramophone.
                        Ib. The Fire Sermon

Elizabeth I, Queen   1533-1603

I am your anointed Queen. I will never be by
violence constrained to do anything. I thank
God I am endued with such qualities that if I
were turned out of the Realm in my petticoat I
were able to live in any place in Christome. *Attrib.*

I know I have the body of a weak and feeble
woman, but I have the heart and stomach of a
king, and of a king of England too; and think
foul scorn that Parma or Spain, or any prince of
Europe, should dare to invade the borders of my
realm. *Speech to the Troops on the Approach of
the Armada*, 1588

Though God hath raised me high, yet this I
count the glory of my crown: that I have reigned
with your loves. *The Golden Speech*, 1601

Elliot, Jane   **1727-1805**

I've heard them lilting, at the ewe milking.
  Lasses a' lilting, before dawn of day;
But now they are moaning, on ilka green loaning;
  The flowers of the forest are a' wede awae.
                                    The Flowers of the Forest

Ellis, Henry Havelock   **1859-1939**

What we call " Progress " is the exchange of one
nuisance for another nuisance.   *Impressions and
Comments*

God is an unutterable Sigh in the Human Heart,
said the old German mystic. And therewith said
the last word. *Ib.*

The absence of flaw in beauty is itself a flaw.
                                                    Ib.

The whole religious complexion of the modern
world is due to the absence from Jerusalem of a
lunatic asylum. *Ib.*

Every artist writes his own autobiography. *The
New Spirit*

Beauty is the child of love. *Ib.*

In many a war it has been the vanquished, not
the victor, who has carried off the finest spoils.
                                    The Soul of Spain

Ellwood, Thomas   **1639-1713**

Thou hast said much here of " Paradise Lost ";
but what hast thou to say of " Paradise found " ?
    Remark to Milton at Chalfont St. Giles, 1665

Novels are as useful as Bibles if they teach you the secret that the best of life is conversation, and the greatest success is confidence. *Conduct of Life. Behaviour*

As there is use in medicine for poison, so the world cannot move without rogues. *Ib. Power*

Art is a jealous mistress, and if a man have a genius for painting, poetry, music, architecture, or philosophy, he makes a bad husband and an ill provider. *Ib. Wealth*

The manly part is to do with might and main what you can do. *Ib.*

The Frenchman invented the ruffle, the Englishman added the shirt. *English Traits*

They [the English] think him the best dressed man, whose dress is so fit for his use that you cannot notice or remember to describe it. *Ib.*

Adhere to your own act, and congratulate yourself if you have done something strange and extravagant, and broken the monotony of a decorous age. *Essays*

Fear is an instructor of great sagacity and the herald of all revolutions. *Ib. Compensation*

A friend may well be reckoned the masterpiece of Nature. *Ib. Friendship*

Let the soul be assured that somewhere in the universe it should rejoin its friend, and it would be content and cheerful alone for a thousand years. *Ib.*

It was a high counsel that I once heard given to a young person, " Always do what you are afraid to do." *Ib. Heroism*

Living blood and a passion of kindness does at last distinguish God's gentlemen from Fashion's.
Ib. Manners

To believe your own thought, to believe that what is true for you in your private heart is true for all men—that is genius. *Ib. Self Reliance*

Society everywhere is in conspiracy against the manhood of every one of its members. *Ib.*

Whoso would be a man, must be a nonconformist.
Ib.

A foolish consistency is the hobgoblin of little minds, adored by little statesmen and philosophers and divines. With consistency a great soul has simply nothing to do. *Ib.*

Shove Jesus and Judas equally aside. *Ib.*

I like the silent church before the service begins, better than any preaching. *Ib.*

No law can be sacred to me but that of my nature. Good and bad are but names very readily transferable to that or this; the only right is what is after my own constitution; the only wrong is what is against it. *Ib.*

It is easy in the world to live after the world's opinion; it is easy in solitude after our own; but the great man is he who in the midst of the crowd keeps with perfect sweetness the independence of solitude. *Ib.*

Earth laughs in flowers. *Hamatreya*

In your sane hour, you shall see that not a line has yet been written; for that for all the poetry that is in the world your first sensation on entering a wood or standing on the shore of a lake has not been chanted yet. . . . And yet for all this it must be owned that literature has truly told us that the cock crows in the mornings. *Journals*

A day is a miniature eternity. *Ib.*

When divine souls appear men are compelled by their own self-respect to distinguish them. *Ib.*

I trust a good deal to common fame, as we all must. If a man has good corn, or wood, or boards, or pigs, to sell, or can make better chairs or knives, crucibles, or church organs, than anybody else, you will find a broad, hard-beaten road to his house, though it be in the woods. *Ib. Common Fame*

Artists must be sacrificed to their art. Like bees, they must put their lives into the sting they give. *Letters and Social Aims. Inspiration*

When Shakespeare is charged with debts to his authors, Landor replies: " Yet he was more original than his originals. He breathed upon dead bodies and brought them into life." *Ib. Quotation and Originality*

Good manners are made up of petty sacrifices.
Ib. Social Aims

It is only when the mind and character slumber that the dress can be seen. *Ib.*

It is a lesson which all history teaches wise men, to put trust in ideas, and not in circumstances. *Miscellanies. War*

Light is the first of painters. There is no object so foul that intense light will not make it beautiful. *Nature*

The Americans have little faith. They rely on the power of the dollar. *Nature, Addresses and Lectures. Man the Reformer*

We are taught by great actions that the universe is the property of every individual in it. *Ib. Beauty*

There is a little formula, couched in pure Saxon, which you may hear in the corners of the streets and in the yard of the dame's school, from very little republicans: " I'm as good as you be," which contains the essence of the Massachusetts Bill of Rights and of the American Declaration of Independence. *Natural History of Intellect. Boston*

The bitterest tragic element in life is the belief in a brute Fate or Destiny. *Ib. The Tragic*

" Well," said Red Jacket (to one who complained he had not enough time), " I suppose you have all there is." *Society and Solitude. Works and Days*

The machine unmakes the man. Now that the machine is so perfect, the engineer is nobody. *Ib.*

Life is good only when it is magical and musical, a perfect timing and consent, and when we do not anatomise it. . . . You must hear the bird's song without attempting to render it into nouns and verbs. *Ib.*

A man builds a fine house; and now he has a master, and a task for life; he is to furnish, watch, show it, and keep it in repair, the rest of his days.
Ib.

Write it on your heart that every day is the best day in the year. No man has learned anything rightly until he knows that every day is Dooms-day. *Ib.*

Now that is the wisdom of a man, in every instance of his labour, to hitch his wagon to a star, and see his chore done by the gods themselves. *Ib. Civilisation*

Nature is full of freaks, and now puts an old head on young shoulders, and then a young heart beating under fourscore winters. *Ib. Old Age*

There is no knowledge that is not power. *Ib.*

As soon as there is life there is danger. *Ib. Public and Private*

Other world! There is no other world! Here or nowhere is the whole fact. *Uncollected Lectures. Natural Religion*

Spring still makes spring in the mind
When sixty years are told. *The World Soul*

Ennius

Simia, quam similis turpissima bestia, nobis. How
like us is the ape, most horrible of beasts. *De
Natura Deorum,* Cicero

[Of Q. Fabius Maximus] *Unus homo nobis
cunctando restituit rem.* One man by delaying
saved the situation for us. *De Senectute,* Cicero

Quem metuunt, oderunt. They hate whom they
fear. *Thyestes*

Ephesians, The Epistle of Paul to the

. . . children, tossed to and fro, and carried about
with every wind of doctrine, by the sleight of men,
and cunning craftiness. 4, 14

We are members one of another. 4, 25

Be ye angry, and sin not; let not the sun go down
upon your wrath. 4, 26

Put on the whole armour of God. 6, 11

For we wrestle not against flesh and blood, but
against principalities, against powers, against the
rulers of the darkness of this world, against
spiritual wickedness in high places. 6, 12

Erasmus, Gerard Didier
c. 1465-1536

Scitum est inter caecos luscum regnare posse. It
is well known, that among the blind the one-eyed
man is king. *Adagia*

A fronte praecipitium, a tergo lupi. A precipice in
front, wolves behind. *Ib.*

Dulce bellum inexpertis. War is sweet to those who do not fight. *Ib.*

Estienne, Henri   **1531-1598**

Si jeunesse savoit; si vieillesse pouvoit. If only youth had the knowledge; if only age had the strength. *Les Prémices*

Euclid   **fl. c. 300 B.C.**

[To Ptolemy 1] There is no royal road to geometry.
Commentaria in Euclidem, Proclus

Ewer, William Norman   **b. 1885**

I gave my life for freedom—This I know:
For those who bade me fight had told me so.
Five Souls

Exodus, The Book of

Who made thee a prince and a judge over us? 2, 14

I have been a stranger in a strange land. 2, 22

Behold, the bush burned with fire, and the bush was not consumed. 3, 2

A land flowing with milk and honey. 3, 8

The Lord God of your fathers, the God of Abraham, the God of Isaac, and the God of Jacob. 3, 15

Thou shalt have no other gods before me. 20, 3

Thou shalt not make unto thee any graven image, or any likeness of anything that is in heaven above, or that is in the earth beneath, or that is in the water under the earth:

Thou shalt not bow down thyself to them, nor serve them: for I the Lord thy God am a jealous God, visiting the iniquity of the fathers upon the children unto the third and fourth generation of them that hate me. 20, 4-5

Thou shalt not take the name of the Lord thy God in vain. 20, 7

Remember the sabbath day, to keep it holy. 20, 8

Six days shalt thou labour, and do all thy work. But the seventh day is the sabbath of the Lord thy God: in it thou shalt not do any work. 20, 9-10

For in six days the Lord made heaven and earth, the sea and all that in them is, and rested the seventh day: wherefore the Lord blessed the sabbath day, and hallowed it. 20, 11

Honour thy father and thy mother: that thy days may be long upon the land which the Lord thy God giveth thee. 20, 12

Thou shalt not kill. 20, 13

Thou shalt not commit adultery. 20, 14

Thou shalt not steal. 20, 15

Thou shalt not bear false witness against thy neighbour. 20, 16

Thou shalt not covet thy neighbour's house, thou shalt not covet thy neighbour's wife, nor his manservant, nor his maidservant, nor his ox, nor his ass, nor anything that is thy neighbours. 20, 17

Life for life,
Eye for eye, tooth for tooth, hand for hand, foot for foot,
Burning for burning, wound for wound, stripe for stripe. 21, 23-25

Ezekiel, The Book of the Prophet

The fathers have eaten sour grapes, and the children's teeth are set on edge. 18, 2

O ye dry bones, hear the word of the Lord. 37, 4

Faraday, Michael   1791-1867

It may be a weed instead of a fish that, after all my labour, I may at last pull up. *Letter to R. Phillips*, 1831

Farquhar, George   1678-1707

My Lady Bountiful. *The Beaux Stratagem*, 1

'Tis still my maxim, that there is no scandal like rags, nor any crime so shameful as poverty. *Ib.*

There are secrets in all families. *Ib.* 3

How a little love and good company improves a woman. *Ib.* 4

Charming women can true converts make,
We love the precepts for the teacher's sake. *The Constant Couple*, 5

Money is the sinews of love, as of war. *Love and a Bottle*, 2

194

Ferdinand I, Emperor   **1503-1564**

Fiat justitia, et pereat mundus. Let justice be
done though the world perish. *Attrib.*
or *Fiat justitia ruat caelum.* Let justice be done
though the heavens fall.

Fergusson, Sir James   **1832-1907**

I have heard many arguments which influenced
my opinion, but never one which influenced my
vote. *Attrib.*

Fergusson, Robert   **1750-1774**

[Sunday]
Ane wad maist trow some people chose
To change their faces wi' their clo'es,
And fain wad gar ilk neibour think
They thirst for goodness as for drink.
                                            Auld Reekie

And thou, great god of *Aquavitae!*
Wha sway'st the empire o' this city;—
Whan fou, we're sometimes capernoity;—
          Be thou prepar'd
To hedge us frae that black banditti,
          The City Guard.   *The Daft Days*

So, Delia, when her beauty's flown,
Trades on a bottom not her own,
And labours to escape detection
By putting on a false complexion.
                    On Seeing a Lady Paint Herself

Fielding, Henry   **1707-1754**

The devil take me, if I think anything but love
to be the object of love. *Amelia,* 5

I am as sober as a judge. *Don Quixote in England*, 3

Oh! The roast beef of England,
And old England's roast beef.
The Grub Street Opera, 3

There were particularly two parties . . . the former were called *cavaliers* and *tory rory ranter boys*.
Jonathan Wild

Greatness consists in bringing all manner of mischief on mankind, and goodness in removing it from them. *Ib.*

It hath been thought a vast commendation of a painter to say his figures seem to breathe; but surely it is much greater and nobler applause, that they appear to think. *Joseph Andrews*

To whom nothing is given, of him can nothing be required. *Ib.* 2

What a silly fellow must he be who would do the devil's work for nothing. *Ib.*

Public schools are the nurseries of all vice and immorality. *Ib.* 3

Some folks rail against other folks because other folks have what some folks would be glad of. *Ib.* 4

Love and scandal are the best sweeteners of tea.
Love in Several Masques, 4

A newspaper, which consists of just the same number of words, whether there be news in it or not. . . . may, likewise, be compared to a stage-coach, which performs constantly the same course, empty as well as full. *Tom Jones*, 2

Thwackum was for doing justice, and leaving mercy to Heaven. *Ib.* 3

O! more than Gothic ignorance. *Ib.* 7

FitzGerald, Edward   1809-1883

Awake! for Morning in the Bowl of Night
Has flung the Stone that puts the Stars to Flight:
And Lo! the Hunter of the East has caught
The Sultan's Turret in a Noose of Light.
Rubáiyát of Omar Khayyám, 1st Ed.

Come, fill the Cup, and in the Fire of Spring
The Winter Garment of Repentance fling:
The Bird of Time has but a little way
To fly—and Lo! the Bird is on the Wing. *Ib.*

Here with a Loaf of Bread beneath the Bough,
A Flask of Wine, a Book of Verse—and Thou
Beside me singing in the Wilderness—
And Wilderness is Paradise enow! *Ib.*

I sometimes think that never blows so red
The Rose as where some buried Caesar bled. *Ib.*

Lo! some we loved, the loveliest and best
That Time and Fate of all their Vintage prest,
Have drunk their Cup a Round or two before,
And one by one crept silently to Rest.   *Ib.*

Ah, fill the Cup:—what boots it to repeat
How Time is slipping underneath our Feet:
Unborn TO-MORROW and dead YESTERDAY,
Why fret about them if TO-DAY be sweet! *Ib.*

The Grape that can with Logic absolute
The Two-and-Seventy jarring Sects confute. *Ib.*

'Tis all a Chequer-board of Nights and Days
Where Destiny with Men for Pieces plays:
Hither and thither moves, and mates, and slays,
And one by one back in the Closet lays. *Ib.*

The Ball no question makes of Ayes and Noes,
But Right or Left, as strikes the Player goes. *Ib.*

The Moving Finger writes; and, having writ,
Moves on: nor all thy Piety nor Wit
Shall lure it back to cancel half a Line,
Nor all thy Tears wash out a Word of it. *Ib.*

. . . that inverted Bowl they call the Sky. *Ib.*

I often wonder what the Vintners buy
One half so precious as the Goods they sell. *Ib.*

Ah Love! Could you and I with Fate conspire
To grasp this sorry Scheme of Things entire,
Would we not shatter it to bits—and then
Re-mould it nearer to the Heart's Desire. *Ib.*

Flecker, James Elroy   **1884-1915**

Half to forget the wandering and the pain,
Half to remember days that have gone by,
And dream and dream that I am home again!
Brumana

And with great lies about his wooden horse
Set the crew laughing, and forgot his course.
The Old Ships

Fletcher, Andrew, of Saltoun   **1655-1716**

Like his that lights a candle to the sun.
Letter to Sir Walter Aston

I knew a very wise man who believed that . . . if a man were permitted to make all the ballads, he need not care who should make the laws of a nation. And we find that most of the ancient legislators thought they could not well reform the manners of any city without the help of a lyric, and sometimes of a dramatic poet. *Letter to Marquis of Montrose*, 1704

Foch, Ferdinand   1851-1929

Hostilities will cease along the whole front at the 11th hour, French o'clock, on Nov. 11. Allied troops will not cross, until further orders, the line reached on that date and that hour. *Command announcing the armistice*, 1914

Fontaine, Jean de la   1621-1695

Je plie et ne romps pas. I bend and do not break.
Fables: Le Chêne et le Roseau

La mort ne surprend point le sage,
Il est toujours prêt à partir.
Death does not surprise a wise man, he is always ready to leave. *Ib. La Mort et le Mourant*

Aucun chemin de fleurs ne conduit à la gloire.
No road of flowers leads to glory. *Ib. Les Deux Aventuriers et le Talisman*

De la peau de lion l'âne s'étant vêtu
Etoit craint partout à la ronde.
Dressed in the lion's skin, the ass spread terror far and wide. *Ib. L'Ane vêtu de la peau du Lion*

Hélas! on voit que de tout temps,
Les Petits ont pâti des sottises des Grands.
Alas, it seems that for all time the Small have suffered from the folly of the Great. *Ib. Les Deux Taureaux et la Grenouille*

Foote, Samuel   **1720-1777**

Born in a cellar . . . and living in a garret.
The Author

He is not only dull in himself, but the cause of dullness in others. *Remark.* Boswell's *Life of Johnson*

For as the old saying is,
When house and land are gone and spent
Then learning is most excellent. *Taste*

Ford, Henry   **1863-1947**

History is bunk. *Remark in court, July,* 1919

Ford, John   **c. 1586-1639**

Green indiscretion, flattery of greatness,
Rawness of judgement, wilfulness in folly,
Thoughts vagrant as the wind, and as uncertain.
The Broken Heart

Parthenophil is lost, and I would see him;
For he is like to something I remember,
A great while since, a long, long time ago.
The Lover's Melancholy

Forgy, Howell   **b. 1908**

Praise the Lord and pass the ammunition. *Attrib.*
Pearl Harbour, Dec., 1941

Fourier, François Charles Marie   **1772-1837**

Instead of by battles and Ecumenical Councils, the rival portions of humanity will one day dispute each other's excellence in the manufacture of little cakes. *Lectures and Biographical Sketches*, Emerson

France, Anatole (Jacques Anatole Thibault)
                                                    1844-1924

Le hasard c'est peut-être le pseudonyme de Dieu, quand il ne veut pas signer. Chance is perhaps God's pseudonym when he does not want to sign. *Le Jardin d'Epicure*

The law, in its majestic equality, forbids the rich as well as the poor to sleep under bridges, to beg in the streets, and to steal bread. *Modern Plutarch*, Cournos

It is better to understand little than to misunderstand a lot. *Revolt of the Angels*

Le bon critique est celui qui raconte les aventures de son âme au milieu des chefs-d'oeuvre. The good critic is one who recounts the adventures of his soul among masterpieces. *La Vie Litteraire*

Franklin, Benjamin
                                                    1706-1790

Remember that time is money. *Advice to Young Tradesman*

Here Skugg lies snug
As a bug in a rug. *Letter to Miss Shipley*, 1772

There never was a good war, or a bad peace. *Ib. to Quincey*, 1783

In this world nothing can be said to be certain, except death and taxes. *Ib. to J. B. Le Roy*, 1789

Be in general virtuous, and you will be happy.
On Early Marriages

He's the best physician that knows the worthlessness of the most medicines. *Poor Richard's Almanac*, 1733

To lengthen thy life, lessen thy meals. *Ib.*

Where there's marriage without love, there will be love without marriage. *Ib.* 1734

Necessity never made a good bargain. *Ib.* 1735

Three may keep a secret, if two of them are dead. *Ib.*

At twenty years of age, the will reigns; at thirty, the wit; and at forty, the judgement. *Ib.* 1741

Experience keeps a dear school, but fools will learn in no other. *Ib.* 1743

Dost thou love life? Then do not squander time, for that's the stuff life is made of. *Ib.* 1746

Many have been ruined by buying good pennyworths. *Ib.* 1747

All would live long; but none would be old. *Ib.* 1749

Many foxes grow grey, but few grow good. *Ib.*

The golden age never was the present age. *Ib.* 1750

Little strokes fell great oaks. *Ib.*

Old boys have their playthings as well as young ones; the difference is only in price. *Ib.* 1752

If you would know the value of money, go and try to borrow some; for he that goes a borrowing goes a sorrowing. *Ib.* 1754

He that lives upon hope will die fasting.

Ib. 1758, preface

A little neglect may breed mischief . . . for want of a nail, the shoe was lost; for want of a shoe, the horse was lost; and for want of a horse the rider was lost. *Ib.*

Early to bed and early to rise,
Makes a man healthy, wealthy and wise. *Ib.* 1758

Creditors have better memories than debtors. *Ib.*

We must all hang together, or, most assuredly, we shall all hang separately. *Remark to John Hancock, Independence Day,* 1776

No nation was ever ruined by trade. *Thoughts on Commercial Subjects*

Frederick the Great   1712-1786

My people and I have come to an agreement which satisfies us both. They are to say what they please, and I am to do what I please. *Attrib.*

Frost, Robert   1875-1963

Home is the place where, when you have to go there,
They have to take you in.

The Death of the Hired Man

Some say the world will end in fire,
Some say in ice.
From what I've tasted of desire
I hold with those who favour fire.   *Fire and Ice*

I would have written of me on my stone:
I had a lover's quarrel with the world.
                    The Lesson for Today

I never dared be radical when young
For fear it would make me conservative when old.
                    Precaution

We dance round in a ring and suppose,
But the Secret sits in the middle and knows.
                    The Secret Sits

Scholars get theirs (knowledge) with concientious
thoroughness along projected lines of logic; poets
theirs cavalierly and as it happens in and out of
books. They stick to nothing deliberately, but let
what will stick to them like burrs where they
walk in the fields. *The Figure a Poem Makes*

A poem may be worked over once it is in being,
but may not be worried into being. *Ib.*

Froude, James Anthony   1818-1894

Wild animals never kill for sport. Man is the
only one to whom the torture and death of his
fellow creatures is amusing in itself. *Oceana, 5*

Fear is the parent of cruelty. *Party Politics*

Fry, Christopher   b. 1907

Who should question then
Why we lean our bicycle against a hedge

And go into the house of God?
Who shall question
That coming out from our doorsteps
We have discerned a little, we have known
More than the gossip that comes to us over our
gates?   *The Boy with a Cart*

I've begun to believe that the reasonable
Is an invention of man, altogether in opposition
To the facts of creation. *The Firstborn, 3*

What is official
Is incontestable. It undercuts
The problematical world and sells us life
At a discount. *The Lady's Not for Burning, 1*

I know I am not
A practical person; legal matters and so forth
Are Greek to me, except, of course,
That I understand Greek. *Ib. 2*

Where in this small-talking world can I find
A longitude with no platitude?   *Ib. 3*

Oh, the unholy mantrap of love! *Ib.*

Life and death
Is cat and dog in this double-bed of a world.
                              A Phoenix Too Frequent

It doesn't do a man any good, daylight.
It means up and doing, and that means up to no
good.
The best life is led horizontal.
                              Thor, With Angels

Fuller, Thomas   **1608-1661**

It is always darkest just before the day dawneth.
Pisgah Sight, 2

Fyleman, Rose   **1877-1957**

There are fairies at the bottom of our garden.
Fairies

Galileo Galilei   **1564-1642**

Eppur si muove. But it does move.
Attrib., probably apocryphal

Gallacher, William   **b. 1881**

We are for our own people. We want to see them
happy, healthy and wise, drawing strength from
co-operation with the peoples of other lands, but
also contributing their full share to the general
well-being. Not a broken-down pauper and
mendicant, but a strong, living partner in the
progressive advancement of civilisation. *The Case
for Communism*

Gauguin, Paul   **1848-1903**

Many excellent cooks are spoiled by going into
the arts. *Modern Plutarch*, Cournos

Civilisation is paralysis. *Ib.*

Art is either a plagiarist or a revolutionist. *Pathos
of Distance*, Huneker

Gavarni   **1801-1866**

Les enfants terribles. The embarassing young
Title of a series of prints

206

I rage, I melt, I burn,
The feeble God has stabb'd me to the heart.
Acis and Galatea, 2

Do you think your mother and I should have
liv'd comfortably so long together, if ever we **had**
been married? *The Beggar's Opera*, 1

How happy could I be with either,
Were t'other dear charmer away! *Ib.* 2

She who has never lov'd, has never liv'd.
The Captives, 2

Then nature rul'd, and love, devoid of art,
Spoke the consenting language of the heart.
Dione, prologue

Whence is thy learning? Hath thy toil
O'er books consum'd the midnight oil. *Fables,
Series I*, introduction

Lighter than a feather. *A New Song of New
Similes*

Brown as a berry. *Ib.*

Sharp as a needle. *Ib.*

Happy as a king. *Ib.*

No, sir, tho' I was born and bred in England,
I can dare to be poor, which is the only thing
now-a-days men are ashamed of. *Polly*, 1

In the beginning God created the heaven and the earth.
And the earth was without form, and void; and darkness was upon the face of the deep. And the Spirit of God moved upon the face of the waters. And God said, Let there be light: and there was light. 1, 1-3

And the evening and the morning were the first day. 1, 5

And God saw that it was good. 1, 10

And God said, Let us make man in our image, after our likeness, 1, 26

And the rib, which the Lord God had taken from man, made he a woman. 2, 22

The woman whom thou gavest to be with me, she gave me of the tree, and I did eat. 3, 12

What is this that thou hast done? 3, 13

Am I my brother's keeper? 4, 9

And God remembered Noah. 8, 1

Let there be no strife, I pray thee, between thee and me . . . for we be brethren. 13, 8

But his wife looked back from behind him, and she became a pillar of salt. 19, 26

And he sold his birthright unto Jacob. 25, 33

And he dreamed, and behold a ladder set upon the earth and the top of it reached to heaven: and behold the angels of God ascending and descending on it. 28, 12

Surely the Lord is in this place; and I knew it not. 28, 16

Now Israel loved Joseph more than all his children, because he was the son of his old age; and he made him a coat of many colours. 37, 3

Behold, this dreamer cometh. 37, 19

Ye shall eat the fat of the land. 45, 18

George, Henry   1839-1897

So long as all the increased wealth which modern progress brings goes but to build up great fortunes, to increase luxury and make sharper the contrast between the House of Have and the House of Want, progress is not real and cannot be permanent. *Progress and Poverty, Introductory*

The man who gives me employment, which I must have or suffer, that man is my master, let me call him what I will. *Social Problems, 5*

Gibbon, Edward   1737-1794

I spent fourteen months at Magdalen College; they proved the fourteen months the most idle and unprofitable of my whole life. *Autobiography*

It was at Rome, on the 15th of October, 1764, as I sat musing amidst the ruins of the Capitol, while the barefooted friars were singing vespers in the Temple of Jupiter, that the idea of writing the decline and fall of the city first started to my mind. *Ib.*

The first of earthly blessings, independence. *Ib.*

The various modes of worship, which prevailed in the Roman world, were all considered by the people as equally true; by the philosopher as equally false; and by the magistrate as equally useful. *Decline and Fall of the Roman Empire*, 2

The principles of a free constitution are irrecoverably lost, when the legislative power is nominated by the executive. *Ib.* 3

History . . . is, indeed, little more than the register of the crimes, follies, and misfortunes of mankind. *Ib.*

All that is human must retrograde if it does not advance. *Ib.* 71

My early and invincible love of reading . . . I would not exchange for the treasures of India.
Memoirs

I was never less alone than when by myself. *Ib.*

Gilbert, William Schwenck   1836-1911

In all the woes that curse our race
There is a lady in the case. *Fallen Fairies*, 2

The padre said, " Whatever have you been and gone and done? " *Gentle Alice Brown*

[Of the Duke of Plaza Toro]
He led his regiment from behind—
He found it less exciting. *The Gondoliers*, 1

Of that there is no manner of doubt—
No probable, possible shadow of doubt—
No possible doubt whatever. *Ib.*

Now, that's the kind of king for me—
He wished all men as rich as he,
So to the top of every tree
Promoted everybody. *Ib.* 2

When everyone is somebodee
Then no one's anybody! *Ib.*

The House of Peers, throughout the war,
Did nothing in particular,
And did it very well. *Iolanthe*, 2

A wandering minstrel I—
A thing of shreds and patches,
Of ballads, songs and snatches,
And dreamy lullaby! *The Mikado*, 1

I can trace my ancestry back to a protoplasmal
primordial atomic globule. Consequently, my
family pride is something inconceivable. *Ib.*

It revolts me, but I do it! *Ib.*

I accept refreshment at any hands, however lowly.
Ib.

I've got a little list
Of society offenders who might well be under-
ground
And who never would be missed. *Ib.*

My object all sublime
I shall achieve in time—
To let the punishment fit the crime—
The punishment fit the crime. *Ib.* 2

Something lingering, with boiling oil in it, I
fancy.   *Ib.*

Merely corroborative detail, intended to give
artistic verisimilitude to an otherwise bald and
unconvincing narrative. *Ib.*

The flowers that bloom in the spring,
Tra la, have nothing to do with the case. *Ib.*

But the peripatetics
Of long-haired aesthetics
Are very much more to their taste. *Patience, 1*

Though the Philistines may jostle, you will
    rank as an apostle in the high aesthetic band,
If you walk down Piccadilly with a poppy or a
    lily in your mediaeval hand. *Ib.*

I always voted at my party's call,
And I never thought of thinking for myself at all.
                               H.M.S. Pinafore, 1

I never use a big, big D. *Ib.*

But in spite of all temptations
To belong to other nations,
He remains an Englishman. *Ib. 2*

When a felon's not engaged in his employment—
Or maturing his felonious little plans—
His capacity for innocent enjoyment—
Is just as great as any honest man's.
                        The Pirates of Penzance, 2

A policeman's lot is not a happy one. *Ib.*

He combines the manners of a Marquis with the
morals of a Methodist. *Ruddigore, 1*

All baronets are bad. *Ib.*

If you wish in this world to advance
Your merits you're bound to enhance,
    You must stir it and stump it,
    And blow your own trumpet,
Or, trust me, you haven't a chance! *Ib.*

For duty, duty must be done;
The rule applies to everyone. *Ib.*

I can't say fairer than that, can I? *Ib.*

Oh! a Baronet's rank is exceedingly nice,
But the title's uncommonly dear at the price! *Ib.* 2

Wherever valour true is found,
True modesty will there abound.
                    Yeomen of the Guard, 1

It's a song of a merryman, moping mum,
Whose soul was sad, and whose glance was glum,
Who sipped no sup, and who craved no crumb,
As he sighed for the love of a ladye. *Ib.*

Gladstone, William Ewart   1809-1898

[On Naples] This is the negation of God erected
into a system of government. *Letter to Lord
Aberdeen,* 1851

The resources of civilisation are not yet exhausted.
                    Speech, Leeds, 1881

All the world over, I will back the masses against
the classes. *Ib. Liverpool,* 1886

Godwin, William   **1756-1836**

The log was burning brightly,
'Twas a night that should banish all sin,
For the bells were ringing the Old Year out,
And the New Year in.
The Miner's Dream of Home

Goering, Hermann   **1893-1946**

Guns will make us powerful; butter will only
make us fat. *Broadcast*, 1936

Goethe, Johann Wolfgang von   **1749-1832**

Wer reitet so spät durch Nacht und Wind?
Es ist der Vater mit seinem Kind.
Who rides so late through the night and storm?
It is the father with his child. *Erlkönig*

Es irrt der Mensch, so lang er strebt.
While man aspires, he errs. *Faust*, 1

Grau, teuer Freund, ist alle Theorie
Und grün des Lebens goldner Baum.
All theory, dear friend, is grey; but the precious
tree of life is green. *Ib.*

Die Tat ist alles, nicht der Ruhm.
The act is all, the reputation nothing. *Ib.* 2

Sah ein Knab' ein Röslein stehn,
Röslein auf der Heiden.
In the woods a boy one day, saw a wild rose
growing. *Heidenröslein*

Entzwei' und gebiete! Tüchtig Wort;
Verein' und leite! Bess 'rer Hort.
Divide and rule, a sound motto. Unite and lead
a better one. *Sprüche in Reimen*

214

Es bildet ein Talent sich in der Stille,
Sich ein Charakter in dem Strom der Welt.
Ability grows in peace, character in the current
of affairs. *Tasso,* 1

Mein Vermächtniss, wie herrlich weit und breit!
Die Zeit ist mein Vermächtniss mein Acker ist die
Zeit.
How great is my inheritance, how wide and
spacious.
Time is my inheritance, my estate is time.
Wilhelm Meisters Wanderjahre

Goldoni, Carlo   1707-1793

Bello è il rossore, ma è incommodo qualche volta.
The blush is beautiful, but it is sometimes inconvenient. *Pamela*

Goldsmith, Oliver   1728-1774

Ill fares the land, to hast'ning ills a prey,
Where wealth accumulates, and men decay.
The Deserted Village

But a bold peasantry, their country's pride,
When once destroyed, can never be supplied. *Ib.*

Trade's unfeeling train
Usurp the land and dispossess the swain.   *Ib.*

And the loud laugh that spoke the vacant mind.
Ib.

And still they gazed, and still the wonder grew,
That one small head could carry all he knew. *Ib.*

And, e'en while fashion's brightest arts decoy,
The heart distrusting asks, if this be joy. *Ib.*

Ye friends to truth, ye statesmen, who survey
The rich man's joys increase, the poor's decay,
'Tis yours to judge, how wide the limits stand
Between a splendid and a happy land. *Ib.*

    The man of wealth and pride
Takes up a space that many poor supplied. *Ib.*

    Ten thousand baneful arts combined
To pamper luxury, and thin mankind. *Ib.*

As writers become more numerous, it is natural
for readers to become more indolent. *The Bee*

On whatever side we regard the history of
Europe, we shall perceive it to be a tissue of
crimes, follies and misfortunes. *The Citizen of
the World*

All his faults are such that one loves him still the
better for them. *The Good-Natured Man*, 1

Don't let us make imaginary evils, when you
know we have so many real ones to encounter. *Ib.*

I love everything that's old; old friends, old
times, old manners, old books, old wine. *She
Stoops to Conquer*, 1

And honour sinks where commerce long prevails.
                      The Traveller

I . . . showed her that books were sweet, unre-
proaching companions to the miserable, and that
if they could not bring us to enjoy life, they
could at least teach us to endure it. *The Vicar
of Wakefield*, 22

As ten millions of circles can never make a square, so the united voice of myriads cannot lend the smallest foundation to falsehood. *Ib.* 26

Grafton, Richard   d. c. 1572

Thirty days hath November,
April, June, and September,
February hath twenty-eight alone,
And all the rest have thirty-one.
    Abridgement of the Chronicles of England, intro.
                                   (1570)

Grahame, Kenneth   1859-1932

Believe me, my young friend, there is *nothing*—absolutely nothing—half so much worth doing as simply messing about in boats. *The Wind in the Willows*, 1

Graves, Robert von Ranke   b. 1895

He grips the tankard of brown ale
That spills a generous foam:
Oft-times he drinks, they say, and winks
    At drunk men lurching home.
                        The General Elliott

The moral of the Scilly Islanders who earned a precarious livelihood by taking in one another's washing is that they never upset their carefully balanced island economy by trying to horn into the laundry trade of the mainland; and that nowhere in the Western Hemisphere was washing so well done. *Collected Poems, 1938-1945*, preface

Gray, Thomas   1716-1771

Ruin seize thee, ruthless King!
Confusion on thy banners wait.   *The Bard*

In gallant trim the gilded vessel goes,
Youth on the prow, and Pleasure at the helm. *Ib.*

The curfew tolls the knell of parting day,
The lowing herd wind slowly o'er the lea,
The ploughman homeward plods his weary way,
And leaves the world to darkness and to me.
                    Elegy Written in a Country Churchyard

Each in his narrow cell for ever laid,
The rude forefathers of the hamlet sleep.   *Ib.*

The short and simple annals of the poor.   *Ib.*

The paths of glory lead but to the grave.   *Ib.*

Full many a gem of purest ray serene. *Ib.*

Full many a flower is born to blush unseen,
And waste its sweetness on the desert air.   *Ib.*

Far from the madding crowd's ignoble strife. *Ib.*

Gregory I   540-604

Responsum est, quod Angli vocarentur. At ille:
"*Bene,*" *inquit,* "*nam et angelicam habent
faciem, et tales angelorum in caelis decet esse
coheredes.*" They replied that they were called
Angles. But he said, "It is good; for they have
the countenance of angels, and such should be
the co-heirs of the angels in heaven."
                    Historia Ecclesiastica, Bede

Gregory VII   c. 1020-1085

*Dilexi justitiam et odivi iniquitatem: propterea
morior in exilio.* I have loved justice and hated
iniquity: therefore I die in exile. *Last Words*

Grellet, Stephen   **1773-1855**

I expect to pass through this world but once;
any good thing therefore that I can do, or any
kindness that I can show to any fellow-creature,
let me do it now; let me not defer or neglect it,
for I shall not pass this way again. *Attrib.*

Greville, Fulke, First Baron Brooke   **1554-1628**

Fire and people do in this agree,
They both good servants, both ill masters be.
Inquisition upon Fame

Grey, Edward, Viscount of Falloden   **1862-1933**

The lamps are going out all over Europe; we
shall not see them lit again in our lifetime.
August, 1914

Guinan, Texas   **1884-1933**

Fifty million Frenchmen can't be wrong. *Attrib.*

Haig, Douglas, First Earl   **1861-1928**

Every position must be held to the last man:
there must be no retirement. With our backs to
the wall, and believing in the justice of our cause,
each one of us must fight on to the end. *Order,
12th April, 1918*

Halifax, George Savile, Marquis of   **1633-1695**

Love is a passion that hath friends in the garrison.
Advice to a Daughter

This innocent word "Trimmer" signifies no
more than this, that if men are together in a boat,
and one part of the company would weigh it

down on one side, another would make it lean as much to the contrary. *Character of a Trimmer*, preface

Hammond, Percy   1873-1936

The human knee is a joint and not an entertainment. *Our Times*, Mark Sullivan

Hampole, Richard Rolle de   c. 1290-1349

When Adam dalfe and Eve spane
So spire if thou may spede,
Whare was then the pride of man,
That nowe merres his mede?
           Religious Pieces in Proses and Verse, 7
(cf. John Ball, p. 23)

Hardy, Thomas   1840-1928

Yet saw he something in the lives
Of those who ceased to live
That rounded them with majesty,
Which living failed to give.
           The Casterbridge Captains

So little cause for carolings
Of such ecstatic sound
Was written on terrestial things
Afar or nigh around,
That I could think there trembled through
His happy good-night air
Some blessed Hope, whereof he knew
And I was unaware.   *The Darkling Thrush*

When shall the softer, saner politics,
Whereof we dream, have play in each proud land?
           Departure

A local cult called Christianity. *The Dynasts*, 1

My argument is that War makes rattling good history; but Peace is poor reading. *Ib.* 2

But what's one woman's fortune more or less Beside the schemes of kings. *Ib.*

Of course poets have morals and manners of their own, and custom is no argument with them. *Hand of Ethelberta*, 2

Good, but not religious good. *Under the Greenwood Tree*, 2

Harris, Joel Chandler   1848-1908

De wimmin, dey does de talkin' en de flyin', en de mens, dey does de walkin' en de pryin', en betwixt en betweenst um, dey ain't much dat don't come out. *Brother Rabbit and His Famous Foot*

Tar-baby ain't sayin' nuthin', en Brer Fox, he lay low. *Legends of the Old Plantation*

Hit look lak sparrer-grass, hit feel lak sparrer-grass, hit tas'e lak sparrer-grass, en I bless ef 'taint sparrer-grass. *Nights with Uncle Remus*

Licker talks mighty loud w'en it git loose from de jug. *Uncle Remus. Plantation Proverbs*

Lazy fokes' stummucks don't git tired. *Ib.*

Youk'n hide de fier, but w'at you gwine do wid de smoke? *Ib.*

Haskins, Minnie Louise   **b. 1875**

I said to a man who stood at the gate of the
year: "Give me a light that I may tread safely
into the unknown." And he replied: "Go out
into the darkness and put your hand into the
hand of God. That shall be to you better than a
light, and safer than a known way." *God Knows*

Hawker, Robert Stephen   **1803-1875**

And have they fixed the where and when?
And shall Trelawney die?
Here's twenty thousand Cornishmen
Will know the reason why!
                              Song of the Western Men

Hazlitt, William   **1778-1830**

[Of Scott] His worst is better than any other
person's best. *English Literature*, 14

You will hear more good things on the outside
of a stagecoach from London to Oxford than if
you were to pass a twelvemonth with the undergraduates, or heads of colleges, of that famous
city. *The Ignorance of the Learned*

[Of Coleridge] He talked on for ever; and you
wished him to talk on for ever. *Lectures on the
English Poets*

The art of pleasing consists in being pleased.
                              Round Table. On Manner

Rules and models destroy genius and art. *Sketches
and Essays. On Taste*

The English (it must be owned) are rather a foul-mouthed nation. *Table-Talk. On Criticism*

So have I loitered my life away, reading books, looking at pictures, going to plays, hearing, thinking, writing on what pleased me best. I have wanted only one thing to keep me happy, but wanting that have wanted everything. *Winterslow. My First Acquaintance with Poets*

Hegel, Georg Wilhelm   1770-1831

Was die Erfahrung aber und die Geschichte lehren, ist dieses das Völker und Regierungen niemals etwas aus der Geschichte gelernt. But what experience and history teach is this, that peoples and governments have never learned anything from history.
Philosophy of History

Was vernünftig ist, das ist wirklich: und was wirklich ist, das ist vernünftig. What is reasonable is true, and what is true is reasonable.
Rechtsphilosophie

Heine, Heinrich   1797-1856

*Ich weiss nicht, was soll es bedeuten
Das ich so traurig bin,
Ein Märchen aus alten Zeiten,
Dass kommt mir nicht aus dem Sinn.*
I do not know why I am so sad; there is an old-time fairy tale that I cannot get out of my mind.
Die Lorelei

*Es ist eine alte Geschichte,
Doch bleibt sie immer neu.*
It is an ancient story, yet it is ever new. *Lyrisches Intermezzo*

When people talk about a wealthy man of my
creed, they call him an Israelite; but if he is poor
they call him a Jew. *MS. Papers*

Helps, Sir Arthur   1813-1875

Reading is sometimes an ingenious device for
avoiding thought. *Friends in Council*

What a blessing this smoking is! perhaps the
greatest that we owe to the discovery of America.
Ib.

There is one statesman of the present day, of
whom I always say that he would have escaped
making the blunders that he has made if he had
only ridden more in omnibuses. *Ib.*

Hemans, Felicia Dorothea   1793-1835

The boy stood on the burning deck
Whence all but he had fled;
The flame that lit the battle's wreck
Shone round him o'er the dead.   *Casabianca*

The stately homes of England,
How beautiful they stand!
                        The Homes of England

Hemingway, Ernest   1898-1961

The world is a fine place and worth fighting for.
                        For Whom the Bell Tolls

Henley, William Ernest   1849-1903

I thank whatever gods may be
For my unconquerable soul.   *Echoes. Invictus*

In the fell clutch of circumstance,
I have not winced nor cried aloud:
Under the bludgeonings of chance
My head is bloody, but unbowed. *Ib.*

I am the master of my fate:
I am the captain of my soul. *Ib.*

Henri IV, King of France   1553-1610

One catches more flies with a spoonful of honey
than with twenty casks of vinegar. *Attrib.*

*Les grands mangeurs et les grands dormeurs sont
incapables de rien faire de grand.* Great eaters
and great sleepers are incapable of doing anything
great. *Attrib.*

[Of James VI and I] The wisest fool in Christendom. *Attrib. to Henri and to Sully*

Paris vaut bien une messe. Paris is well worth a
mass. *Ib.*

Henry II, King of England   1133-1189

[Of Becket] Will no one free me of this turbulent
priest? *Attrib.*

Henry, Patrick   1736-1799

Caesar had his Brutus—Charles the First, his
Cromwell and George the Third—("Treason,"
cried the Speaker) . . . *may profit by their example.*
If *this* be treason, make the most of it. *Speech
in the Virginia Convention, 1765*

Henryson, Robert   c. 1425- c. 1506

Her hat suld be of fair-having,
And her tepat of truth;
Her patelet of gude pansing;
Her hals-ribbon of ruth.
                              The Garmont of Gude Ladies

There was no solace mycht his sobbing cease,
Bot cryit aye, with cairis cauld and keen:
"Where art thou gane, my luve Eurydices?"

Orpheus and Eurydice

O youth, be glad into thy flouris green!
O youth, thy flouris fadis ferly sone!

The Reasoning Betwixt Youth and Age

The man that will nocht when he may
Sall have nocht when he wald.

Robene and Makyne

Yit efter joy ofttimes cumis care,
And trouble efter great prosperitie.

*The Taill of the Uponlandis Mous and the Burges
Mous*

I sall excuse, als far furth as I may,
Thy womanheid, thy wisdom and fairness:
The whilk Fortune has put to sic distress
As her pleasit, and nathing through the guilt
Of thee, through wicked language to be spilt.

The Testament of Cresseid

Nocht is your fairness bot ane fading flour,
Nocht is your famous laud ánd high honour
Bot wind inflate in other mennis earis;
Your rosing reid to rotting sall retour. *Ib.*

I lat you wit, thair is richt few thairout
Quhome ye may traist to have trew lufe againe.
Preif quhen ye will, your labour is in vaine.
Thairfoir, I reid, ye tak theme as ye find;
For they ar sad as widdercock in wind. *Ib.*

226

Don't let's go to the dogs to-night
For mother will be there.
> *Don't Let's Go to the Dogs*

A highbrow is the kind of person who looks at
a sausage and thinks of Picasso.   *The Highbrow*

I'm not a jealous woman, but I can't see what
he sees in her. *I Can't Think What He Sees in Her*

I wouldn't be too ladylike in love if I were you.
> *I Wouldn't be Too Ladylike*

Let's find out what everyone is doing,
And then stop everyone from doing it.
> *Let's Stop Somebody*

Once people start on all this Art
Goodbye, moralitee! *Lines for a Worthy Person*

This high official, all allow,
Is grossly overpaid.
There wasn't any Board; and now
There isn't any trade.
> *On the President of the Board of Trade*

People must not do things for fun. We are not
here for fun. There is no reference to fun in any
Act of Parliament. *Uncommon Law*

The Englishman never enjoys himself except for
a noble purpose. *Ib.*

An Act of God was defined as *something which
no reasonable man could have expected. Ib.*

Herbert, Edward, Baron Herbert of Cherbury
1583-1648

O that our love might take no end
Or never had beginning took!
*An Ode upon a Question moved, Whether Love
should continue for ever?*

For where God doth admit the fair.
Think you that he excludeth Love? *Ib.*

Herbert, George   **1593-1633**

A verse may finde him who a sermon flies,
And turn delight into a sacrifice.
                         The Temple. The Church Porch

Drink not the third glasse,—which thou can'st
    not tame
When once it is within thee. *Ib.*

The stormie working soul spits lies and froth. *Ib.*

Kneeling ne're spoil'd silk stocking. *Ib.*

I struck the board, and cry'd, " No more
I will abroad."
What, shall I ever sigh and pine?
My lines and life are free; free as the road,
Loose as the winde. *Ib. The Collar*

Thy rope of sands
Which pettie thoughts have made. *Ib.*

Man is all symmetrie,
Full of proportions, one limbe to another,
And all to all the world besides. *Ib. Man*

My God, my verse is not a crown,
No point of honour, or gay suit,

228

No hawk, or banquet, or renown,
Nor a good sword, nor yet a lute.
Ib. The Quiddity

The God of Love my Shepherd is,
And He that doth me feed,
While He is mine, and I am His,
What can I want or need?   *Ib. 23rd Psalm*

Take heed of a young wench, a prophetess, and a
Latin-bred woman. *Jacula Prudentum*

Herford, Oliver   1863-1935

The bubble winked at me, and said,
"You'll miss me brother, when you're dead."
Toast. The Bubble Winked

Herrick, Robert   1591-1674

I write of youth, of love, and have accesse
By these, to sing of cleanly-wantonnesse.
Hesperides. The Argument of his Book

Cherrie-ripe, ripe, ripe I cry,
Full and faire ones; come and buy.
Ib. Cherrie-Ripe

Fair daffodils, we weep to see
You haste away so soon.   *Ib. Daffodils*

A sweet disorder in the dresse
Kindles in cloathes a wantonnesse.
Ib. Delight in Disorder

Gather ye rose-buds while ye may,
Old Time is still a-flying:
And this same flower that smiles to-day,
To-morrow will be dying.
Ib. To the Virgins, to Make Much of Time

Hickson, William Edward   **1803-1870**

If at first you don't succeed,
Try, try, again. *Try and Try Again*

Hill, Rowland   **1744-1833**

He did not see any reason why the devil should
have all the good tunes.
           Rev. Rowland Hill, E. W. Broome

Hippocrates   **c. 460-357 B.C.**

[Of medicine] The life so short, the art so long to
learn, opportunity fleeting, experience treacherous,
judgement difficult. *Aphorisms*, 1

Hitler, Adolf   **1889-1945**

My patience is now at an end.
           Speech, 26th Sept., 1938

Hobbes, Thomas   **1588-1679**

No arts; no letters; no society; and which is
worst of all, continual fear and danger of violent
death; and the life of man, solitary, poor, nasty,
brutish, and short. *Leviathan*

The praise of ancient authors proceeds not from
the reverence of the dead, but from the competition and mutual envy of the living. *Ib.*

I am about to take my last voyage, a great leap
in the dark. *Last Words*

Hoch, Edward Wallis   **1849-1925**

There is so much good in the worst of us,
And so much bad in the best of us,
That it hardly becomes any of us
To talk about the rest of us.
           Good and Bad. Attrib. to others

Hogg, James   **1770-1835**

And Charlie is my darling,
The young Chevalier. *Jacobite Relics of Scotland*

Better lo'ed ye canna be,
Will ye no come back again? *Ib.*

O, love, love, love; Love is like a dizziness;
It winna let a poor body gang about his business!
Love Is Like a Dizziness

For Kilmeny had been she knew not where,
And Kilmeny had seen what she could not declare.
The Queen's Wake

Holmes, Oliver Wendell   **1809-1894**

A country clergyman with a one-story intellect
and a one-horse vocabulary. *The Autocrat of the
Breakfast Table*

Man has his will,—but woman has her way. *Ib.*

A general flavour of mild decay. *Poems. The
Deacon's Masterpiece*

Lean, hungry, savage anti-everythings. *Ib. A
Modest Request*

Home, John   **1722-1808**

In the first days
Of my distracting grief, I found myself—
As women wish to be, who love their lords.
Douglas, 1

He seldom errs
Who thinks the worst he can of womankind. *Ib.* 3

231

Bold and erect the Caledonian stood,
Old was his mutton, and his claret good;
Let him drink port, the English statesmen cried—
He drank the poison and his spirit died.
Life of Scott, Lockhart

Homer   c. 1000 B.C.

As the generation of leaves, so is that of men.
Iliad, 6

Always to be best and distinguished above others.
Ib.

He saw the cities of many men, and knew their mind. *Odyssey*, 3

Hood, Thomas   1799-1845

Take her up tenderly
Lift her with care;
Fashioned so slenderly,
Young, and so fair! *The Bridge of Sighs*

Ben Battle was a soldier bold,
And used to war's alarms:
But a cannon-ball took off his legs,
So he laid down his arms! *Faithless Nellie Gray*

They went and told the sexton, and
The sexton toll'd the bell. *Faithless Sally Brown*

For that old enemy the gout
Had taken him in toe! *Lieutenant Luff*

Oh! God! that bread should be so dear,
And flesh and blood so cheap!
The Song of the Shirt

There is a silence where hath been no sound,
There is a silence where no sound may be,
In the cold grave—under the deep, deep sea,
Or in the wide desert where no life is found.
Sonnet. Silence

Holland . . . lies so low they're only saved by being damned. *Up the Rhine. To Rebecca Page*

Hooker, Richard   c. 1554-1600

He that goeth about to persuade a multitude, that they are not so well governed as they ought to be, shall never want attentive and favourable hearers.
Ecclesiastical Policy

Hoover, Herbert Clark   1874-1964

Rugged individualism. *Speech*, 1928

Hope, Anthony (Sir Anthony Hope Hawkins)
       1863-1933

Economy is going without something you do want in case you should, some day, want something you probably won't want. *The Dolly Dialogues*, 12

" Boys will be boys——"
" And even that . . . wouldn't matter if we could only prevent girls from being girls." *Ib.* 16

I wish you would read a little poetry sometimes. Your ignorance cramps my conversation. *Ib.* 22

Hopkins, Gerald Manley   1844-1889

The world is charged with the grandeur of God.
God's Grandeur

Look at the stars! look, look up at the skies!
O look at all the fire-folk sitting in the air!
The bright boroughs, the circle-citadels there!
The Starlight Night

Hopkins, Jane Ellice   1836-1904

Gift, like genius, I often think, only means an
infinite capacity for taking pains. *Work amongst
Working Men*

Horace, Quintus Horatius Flaccus   65-8 B.C.

Grammatici certant et adhuc sub iudice lis est.
Scholars dispute, and the case is still before the
courts. *Ars Poetica,* 78

In medias res. To the heart of the matter.
Ib. 148

Indignor quandoque bonus dormitat Homerus.
When worthy Homer nods, I am offended. *Ib.* 359

Concordia discors. Harmony in discord.
Epistles, 1, 12

*Graecia capta ferum victorem cepit et artes,
Intulit agresti Latio.*
Occupied Greece subdued her fierce conqueror,
and introduced the arts to rustic Latium. *Ib.* 2, 1

*Quodsi me lyricis vatibus inseres,
Sublimi feriam sidera vertice.*
But if you include me among the lyric poets, I
shall touch the stars with my exalted head. *Odes,*
1, 1

*Pallida Mors, aequo pulsat pede pauperum tabernas
Regumque turris.*
Pale Death, with impartial foot, strikes at poor
men's hovels and the towers of kings. *Ib.* 1, 4

Nil desperandum Teucro duce et auspice Teucro.
Nothing need be despaired under Teucer's leadership and patronage. *Ib.* 1, 7

Carpe diem, quam minimum credula postero.
Snatch at to-day and trust as little as you can
in to-morrow. *Ib.* 1, 11

Integer vitae scelerisque purus.
A man of upright life and free from guilt. *Ib.* 1, 22

*Eheu fugaces, Posthume, Posthume,
Labuntur anni.*
Alas, Posthumus, Posthumus the fleeting years are
slipping by. *Ib.* 2, 14

*Cur valle permutem Sabina
Divitias operosiores?*
Why should I exchange my Sabine valley for
wealth that brings more troubles? *Ib.* 3, 1

Dulce et decorum est pro patria mori.
It is a fine and seemly thing to die for one's country.
Ib. 3, 2

Magnas inter opes inops. A poor man surrounded
by riches. *Ib.* 3, 16

Exegi monumentum aere perennius. I have raised
a monument more lasting than bronze. *Ib.* 3, 30

Diffugere nives, redeunt iam gramina campis
Arboribusque comae.
The snows have scattered and fled; already the
grass comes again in the fields and the leaves on
the trees. *Ib.* 4, 7

Housman, Alfred Edward   1859-1936

We'll to the woods no more,
The laurels all are cut. *Last Poems*

The chestnut casts his flambeaux. *Ib.*

O often have I washed and dressed
And what's to show for all my pain?
Let me lie abed and rest:
Ten thousand times I've done my best
And all's to do again. *Ib.*

O, God will save her, fear you not:
Be you the men you've been,
Get you the sons your fathers got,
And God will save the Queen.
         A Shropshire Lad. 1887

       The man that runs away
Lives to die another day. *Ib. The Day of Battle*

O many a peer of England brews
Livelier liquor than the Muse,
And malt does more than Milton can
To justify God's ways to man. *Ib.* 62

Howell, James   c. 1594-1666

One hair of a woman can draw more than a
hundred pair of oxen. *Familiar Letters,* 2

Howitt, Mary   **1799-1888**

" Will you walk into my parlour? " said a spider
to a fly. *The Spider and the Fly*

Hubbard, Elbert   **1859-1915**

Life is just one damned thing after another.
                    A Thousand and One Epigrams

Hughes, Thomas   **1822-1896**

Life isn't all beer and skittles. *Tom Brown's
Schooldays, 1*

He never wants anything but what's right and
fair; only when you come to settle what's right
and fair, it's everything that he wants and nothing
that you want. And that's his idea of a compromise. Give me the Brown compromise when
I'm on his side. *Ib., 2*

Hugo, Victor Marie   **1802-1885**

In the twentieth century, war will be dead, the
scaffold will be dead, hatred will be dead, frontier
boundaries will be dead, dogmas will be dead; man
will live. He will possess something higher than all
these—a great country, the whole earth, and a great
hope, the whole heaven. *The Future of Man*

*On résiste à l'invasion des armées; on ne résiste pas
à l'invasion des idées.* The invasion of armies is
resisted; the invasion of ideas is not. *Histoire
d'un Crime*

Le beau est aussi utile que l'utile. Plus peut-être.
The beautiful is as useful as the useful. Perhaps
more so. *Les Misérables: Fantine*

Art has its fanatics and even its monomaniacs.
Ninety-three

Jesus wept; Voltaire smiled.
Oration on Voltaire, 1878

Hume, David   1711-1776

Nothing appears more surprising to those who consider human affairs with a philosophical eye, than the ease with which the many are governed by the few. *First Principles of Government*

Never literary attempt was more unfortunate than my Treatise of Human Nature. It fell *dead-born from the press. My Own Life*

Avarice, the spur of industry. *Of Civil Liberty*

Hunt, James Henry Leigh   1784-1859

Abou Ben Adhem (may his tribe increase!)
Awoke one night from a deep dream of peace.
Abou Ben Adhem and the Angel

Huxley, Aldous   1894-1963

The proper study of mankind is books. *Chrome Yellow*

A poor degenerate from the ape,
Whose hands are four, whose tail's a limb,
I contemplate my flaccid shape
And know I may not rival him
Save with my mind. *First Philosopher's Song*

It is far easier to write ten passably effective sonnets, good enough to take in the not too inquiring critic, than one effective advertisement

238

that will take in a few thousand of the uncritical buying public. *On the Margin*

The solemn foolery of scholarship for scholarship's sake. *The Perennial Philosophy*

There is no substitute for talent. Industry and all the virtues are of no avail. *Point Counter Point*

Silence is as full of potential wisdom and wit as the unhewn marble of great sculpture. *Ib.*

That all men are equal is a proposition to which, at ordinary times, no sane individual has ever given his assent. *Proper Studies*

Those who believe that they are exclusively in the right are generally those who achieve something. *Ib.*

Facts do not cease to exist because they are ignored. *Ib.*

Defined in psychological terms, a fanatic is a man who consciously over-compensates a secret doubt. *Ib.*

Success—"the bitch-goddess, Success," in William James's phrase—demands strange sacrifices from those who worship her. *Ib.*

Living is an art; and, to practise it well, men need, not only acquired skill, but also a native tact and taste. *Texts and Pretexts*

In the upper and lower churches of St. Francis, Giotto and Cimabue showed that art had once worshipped something other than itself. *Those Barren Leaves*

There's only one corner of the universe you can be certain of improving, and that's your own self.
Time Must Have a Stop

Huxley, Sir Julian Sorell   b. 1887

The ant herself cannot philosophise—
While man does that, and sees, and keeps a wife,
And flies, and talks, and is extremely wise.
For a Book of Essays

Huxley, Thomas Henry   1825-1895

I took thought and invented what I conceived to be the appropriate title of "agnostic." . . . To my great satisfaction, the term took: and when the *Spectator* had stood godfather to it, any suspicion in the minds of respectable people . . . was, of course, completely lulled. *Agnosticism*

That man, I think, has a liberal education who has been so trained in youth that his body is the ready servant of his will . . . whose intellect is ready like a steam engine to be turned to any kind of work, and spin the gossamers as well as the anchors of the mind; . . . one who, no stunted ascetic, is full of life and fire, but whose passions are . . . the servant of a tender conscience; who has learned to love all beauty, whether of nature or of art, to hate all violence, and to respect others as himself. *Evolution and Ethics*

If a little knowledge is dangerous, where is the man who has so much as to be out of danger?
Science and Culture

History warns us that it is the customary fate of new truths to begin as heresies and to end as superstitions. *Ib.*

Ibsen, Henrik   1828-1906

The minority is always right. *An Enemy of the People*, 4

The most dangerous foe to truth and freedom in our midst is the compact majority. Yes, the damned, compact, liberal majority. *Ib.*

One should never put on one's best trousers to go out to battle for freedom and truth. *Ib.* 5

Ignoto   fl. 1630

I would be high, but see the proudest oak
Most subject to the rending Thunder-Stroke;
I would be rich, but see men too unkind
Dig in the bowels of the richest mine;
I would be wise, but that I often see
The Fox suspected whilst the Ass goes free.
    Farewell Ye Guilded Follies, Pleasing Troubles

Then here I'll sit and sigh my hot loves folly
And learn t'affect an holy melancholy. *Ib.*

Inge, William Ralph   1860-1954

Literature flourishes best when it is half a trade and half an art. *The Victorian Age*

A man may build himself a throne of bayonets, but he cannot sit upon it. *Wit and Wisdom of Dean Inge*, Marchant

Ingersoll, Robert Greene   1833-1899

An honest God is the noblest work of man.
       Gods, 1 (cf. p. 90)

In nature there are neither rewards nor punishments—there are consequences. *Lectures and Essays, 3rd Series*

Irving, Washington   **1783-1859**

They who drink beer will think beer. *The Sketch Book. Stratford*

The almighty dollar, that great object of universal devotion throughout our land. . . . *Wolfert's Roost. The Creole Village*

Isaiah, The Book of the Prophet

They shall beat their swords into plowshares, and their spears into pruninghooks : nation shall not lift up sword against nation, neither shall they learn war any more. 2, 4

What mean ye that ye beat my people to pieces and grind the faces of the poor? saith the Lord God of hosts. 3. 15

Woe unto them that join house to house, that lay field to field, till there be no place, that they may be placed alone in the midst of the earth. 5, 8

Whom shall I send, and who will go for us? Then said I, Here am I; send me. 6, 8

For unto us a child is born, unto us a son is given: and the government shall be upon his shoulder; and his name shall be called Wonderful, Counsellor, The mighty God, The everlasting Father, The Prince of Peace. 9, 6

The wolf also shall dwell with the lamb, and the leopard shall lie down with the kid. 11, 6

Let us eat and drink; for to-morrow we shall die. 22, 13

Sorrow and sighing shall flee away. 35, 10

Set thine house in order. 38, 1

The voice of him that crieth in the wilderness,
Prepare ye the way of the Lord, make straight in
the desert a highway for our God.
Every valley shall be exalted, and every mountain
and hill shall be made low: and the crooked
shall be made straight, and the rough places plain:
And the glory of the Lord shall be revealed and
all flesh shall see it together : for the mouth of
the Lord hath spoken it. 40, 3-5

He shall feed his flock like a shepherd: he shall
gather the lambs with his arm, and carry them
in his bosom, and shall gently lead those that are
with young. 40, 11

Have ye not known? Have ye not heard? Have
it not been told you from the beginning. 40, 21

Who hath believed our report? and to whom is
the arm of the Lord revealed? 53, 1

He hath no form nor comeliness; and when we
shall see him, there is no beauty that we should
desire him.
He is despised and rejected of men; a man of
sorrows and acquainted with grief; and we hid
as it were our faces from him; he was despised,
and we esteemed him not.
Surely he hath borne our griefs and carried our
sorrows. 53, 2-4

All we like sheep have gone astray; we have turned every one to his own way; and the Lord hath laid on him the iniquity of us all. 53, 6

Seek ye the Lord while he may be found, call ye upon him while he is near. 55, 6

James I, King of Scots   1394-1437

The bird, the beast, the fish eke in the sea,
They live in freedom everich in his kind;
And I a man, and lackith liberty.
The Kingis Quair

Worshippe, ye that loveris been, this May,
For of your blisse the Kalendis are begun,
And sing with us, away, Winter, away!
Come, Summer, come, the sweet seasoun and sun.
Ib.

So far I fallen was in loves dance,
That suddenly my wit, my countenance,
My heart, my will, my nature, and my mind
Was changit right clean in another kind. *Ib.*

James V of Scotland   1512-1542

It cam' wi' a lass, and it'll gang wi' a lass.
Referring to the Scottish Crown, 1542

James VI of Scotland and I of England   1566-1625

A custom loathesome to the eye, hateful to the nose, harmful to the brain, dangerous to the lungs, and in the black, stinking fume thereof, nearest resembling the horrible Stygian smoke of the pit that is bottomless. *A Counterblast to Tobacco*

No bishop, no king. *Attrib. remark, Hampton Court Conference*

James, Henry Jr.   **1843-1916**

The deep well of unconscious cerebration.
The American

Huge American rattle of gold. *The American Scene*

The only obligation to which in advance we may hold a novel, without incurring the accusation of being arbitrary, is that it be interesting.
The Art of Fiction. Partial Portraits

What is character but the determination of incident? what is incident but the illustration of character? *Ib.*

The historian, essentially, wants more documents than he can really use; the dramatist only wants more liberties than he can really take. *The Aspern Papers*

Her grace of ease was perfect, but it was all grace of ease, not a single shred of it grace of uncertainty or difficulty. *Crapy Cornelia*

It takes a great deal of history to produce a little literature. *Life of Nathanial Hawthorne*

Jefferson, Thomas   **1743-1826**

A little rebellion now and then is a good thing.
Letter, Jan. 1787

The tree of liberty must be refreshed from time to time with the blood of patriots and tyrants. It is its natural manure. *Ib. Nov. 1787*

If a due participation of office is a matter of right, how are vacancies to be obtained? Those by death are few; by resignation, none. *Ib. July* 1801

Indeed I tremble for my country when I reflect that God is just. *Notes on Virginia*

Jeremiah, The Book of the Prophet

And they shall fight against thee; but they shall not prevail against thee; for I am with thee, saith the Lord, to deliver thee. 1, 19

The harvest is past, the summer is ended, and we are not saved. 8, 20

Can the Ethiopian change his skin, or the leopard his spots? 13, 23

As the partridge sitteth on eggs, and hatcheth them not; so he that getteth riches, and not by right. 17, 11

And seekest thou great things for thyself? seek them not. 45, 5

Jerome, Jerome Klapka   1859-1927

It is impossible to enjoy idling thoroughly unless one has plenty of work to do. *Idle Thoughts of an Idle Fellow. On Being Idle*

Love is like the measles; we all have to go through it. *Ib. On Being in Love*

The world must be getting old, I think; it dresses so very soberly now. *Ib. On Dress and Deportment*

I like work; it fascinates me. I can sit and look at it for hours. I love to keep it by me: the idea of getting rid of it nearly breaks my heart. *Three Men in a Boat*, 3

Jerrold, Douglas William   1803-1857

Religion's in the heart, not in the knees.
The Devil's Ducat, 1

The ugliest of trades have their moments of pleasure. Now, if I were a grave-digger, or even a hangman, there are some people I could work for with a great deal of enjoyment. *Wit and Opinions of Douglas Jerrold*

Joan of Arc   1412-1431

You think when you have slain me you will conquer France, but that you will never do. Though there were a hundred thousand God-dammees more in France than there are, they will never conquer that kingdom. *Attrib.* 1430

Job, The Book of

The Lord gave, and the Lord hath taken away; blessed be the name of the Lord. 1, 21

All that a man hath will he give for his life. 2, 4

Curse God, and die. 2, 9

Man is born unto trouble, as the sparks fly upward. 5, 7

I know that my redeemer liveth. 19, 25

I was eyes to the blind, and feet was I to the lame. 29, 15

Canst thou draw out leviathan with an hook?
41, 1

Joel

I will pour out my spirit upon all flesh; and your sons and your daughters shall prophesy, your old men shall dream dreams, and your young men shall see visions. 2, 28

John, The Gospel According to Saint

In the beginning was the Word, and the Word was with God, and the Word was God. 1, 1

God so loved the world, that he gave his only begotten Son, that whosoever believeth in him should not perish, but have everlasting life. 3, 16

Rise, take up thy bed, and walk. 5, 8

He that is without sin among you, let him first cast a stone at her. 8, 7

The good shepherd giveth his life for the sheep.
10, 11

In my Father's house are many mansions. 14, 2

I am the way, the truth, and the life; no man cometh unto the Father, but by me. 14, 6

Greater love hath no man than this, that a man lay down his life for his friends. 15, 13

John, First Epistle General of

He that loveth not knoweth not God; for God is love. 4, 8

If a man say, I love God, and hateth his brother, he is a liar: for he that loveth not his brother whom he hath seen, how can he love God whom he hath not seen? 4, 20

Johnson, Samuel   1709-1784

I am sometimes disposed to think with the severer casuists of most nations that marriage is rather permitted than approved, and that none, but by the instigation of a passion too much indulged, entangle themselves with indissoluble compacts. *The History of Rasselas, Prince of Abyssinia*

He [Charles James Fox] talked to me at club one day concerning Catiline's conspiracy—so I withdrew my attention and thought about Tom Thumb. *Johnsonian Miscellanies*, 1

It is very strange, and very melancholy, that the paucity of human pleasures should persuade us ever to call hunting one of them. *Ib.*

A man is in general better pleased when he has a good dinner upon his table, than when his wife talks Greek. *Ib.* 2

I dogmatise and am contradicted, and in this conflict of opinions and sentiments I find delight. *Ib.*

Abstinence is as easy to me as temperance would be difficult. *Ib.*

What is written without effort is in general read without pleasure. *Ib.*

Love is the wisdom of the fool and the folly of the wise. *Ib.*

I know not whether it be not peculiar to the Scots to have attained the liberal without the manual arts, to have excelled in ornamental knowledge, and to have wanted not only the elegancies, but the conveniences of common life.
Journey to the Western Isles

A Scotchman must be a very sturdy moralist who does not love Scotland better than truth. *Ib.*

Sir, we are a nest of singing birds. *Life of Johnson*, 1 Boswell

A man, Sir, should keep his friendship in constant repair. *Ib.*

[Of literary criticism] You may scold a carpenter who has made you a bad table, though you cannot make a table. It is not your trade to make tables. *Ib.*

But, Sir, let me tell you, the noblest prospect which a Scotchman ever sees, is the high road that leads him to England! *Ib.*

Sir, a woman's preaching is like a dog's walking on his hinder legs. It is not done well; but you are surprised to find it done at all. *Ib.*

This was a good dinner enough, to be sure; but it was not a dinner to *ask* a man to. *Ib.*

Why, Sir, most schemes of political improvement are very laughable things. *Ib.* 2

Want of tenderness is want of parts, and is no less a proof of stupidity than of depravity. *Ib.*

Much may be made of a Scotchman, if he be *caught* young. *Ib.*

Read over your compositions, and where ever you meet with a passage which you think is particularly fine, strike it out. *Ib.*

[Of Thomas Gray] He was dull in a new way, and that made many people think him *great. Ib.*

[Of the Scots] Their learning is like bread in a beseiged town: every man gets a little, but no man gets a full meal. *Ib.*

Knowledge is of two kinds. We know a subject ourselves, or we know where we can find information upon it. *Ib.*

No man but a blockhead ever wrote, except for money. *Ib.* 3

Depend upon it, Sir, when a man knows he is to be hanged in a fortnight, it concentrates his mind wonderfully. *Ib.*

Though we cannot out-vote them we will out-argue them. *Ib.*

Seeing Scotland, Madam, is only seeing a worse England. It is seeing the flower fade away to the naked stalk. *Ib.*

Sir, I look upon every day to be lost, in which I do not make a new acquaintance. *Ib.* 4

Language is the dress of thought. *Lives of the English Poets: Cowley*

An acrimonious and surly republican. *Ib. Milton*

I am always sorry when any language is lost,
because languages are the pedigree of nations.
                                    Tour to the Hebrides, Boswell

The soul completes the triumph of thy face:
I thought, forgive my fair, the greatest force,
The strongest triumph of the female soul
Was but to choose the graces of a day;
To tune the tongue, to teach the eyes to roll,
Dispose the colours of the flowing robe,
And add new roses to the faded cheek. *Irene*

The stage but echoes back the public voice.
The drama's laws the drama's patrons give,
For we that live to please, must please to live.
                        Prologue at the Opening of Drury Lane

Jonah

So they cast lots, and the lot fell upon Jonah. 1, 7

Jonah was in the belly of the fish three days and
three nights. 1, 17

Jonson, Benjamin   1573-1637

        Where it concerns himself,
Who's angry at a slander makes it true.
                                    Catiline his Conspiracy, 3

        So they be ill men,
If they spake worse, 'twere better: for of such
To be dispraised, is the most perfect praise.
                                    Cynthia's Revels, 3

True happiness
Consists not in the multitude of friends,
But in the worth and choice. *Ib.*

If he were
To be made honest by an act of parliament,
I should not alter in my faith of him.
The Devil is an Ass, 4

Alas, all the castles I have, are built with air,
thou know'st. *Eastward Ho, 2*

Drink to me only with thine eyes,
And I will pledge with mine;
Or leave a kiss but in the cup,
And I'll not look for wine.
The Forest, 9. To Celia

She is Venus when she smiles
But she's Juno when she walks,
And Minerva when she talks. *Underwoods.
Celebration of Charis, 4 Her Triumph*

For a good poet's made as well as born. *To the
Memory of My Beloved, the Author, Mr. William
Shakespeare*

Sweet Swan of Avon. *Ib.*

I remember the players have often mentioned it
as an honour to Shakespeare that in his writing
(whatsoever he penned) he never blotted out a
line. My answer hath been " Would that he had
blotted a thousand. " Which they thought a
malevolent speech. I had not told posterity this,
but for their ignorance, who chose that circumstance to commend their friend by wherein he
most faulted; and to justify mine own candour;
for I loved the man, and do honour his memory,

on this side idolatry, as much as any. *Discoveries.*
De Shakespeare Nostrati, Augustus in Haterium

Jordan, Thomas   c. 1612-1685

Our God and soldier we alike adore,
Just at the brink of ruin, not before:
The danger past, both are alike requited;
God is forgotten, and our soldier slighted.
Epigram

Joshua, Book of

Be strong and of a good courage; be not afraid,
neither be thou dismayed: for the Lord thy
God is with thee, whithersoever thou goest. 1, 9

Hewers of wood and drawers of water. 9, 21

Judges, Book of

Faint, yet pursuing. 8, 4

Junius,   fl. 1769

To be acquainted with the merit of a ministry,
we need only observe the condition of the people.
Letters, 1

The right of election is the very essence of the
constitution. *Ib.* 2, 1769

Is this the wisdom of a great minister? or is it
the ominous vibration of a pendulum? *Ib.* 12

There is a holy mistaken zeal in politics as well
as in religion. By persuading others, we convince
ourselves. *Ib.* 35

Juvenal, Decimus Junius   c. 60-130

Rara avis in terris nigroque simillima cycno. A
rare bird upon the earth, and very like a black
swan. *Satires,* 6

Duas tantum res anxius optat,
Panem et circenses. The troubled (Roman people)
long for two things only: bread and games.
Ib. 10

Orandum est ut sit mens sana in corpore sano.
You should pray for a healthy mind in a healthy
body. *Ib.*

Karr, Alphonse   1808-1890

Plus ça change, plus c'est la même chose. The
more things change the more they are the same.
Les Guêpes, 1849

Every man has three characters: that which he
exhibits, that which he has, and that which he
thinks he has. *Attrib.*

Keats, John   1795-1821

Season of mists and mellow fruitfulness.
To Autumn

Who hath not seen thee oft amid thy store? *Ib.*

Where are the songs of Spring? Ay, where are
they? *Ib.*

O what can ail thee, Knight-at-arms
Alone and palely loitering;
The sedge has wither'd from the lake,
And no birds sing.
La Belle Dame Sans Merci

La belle Dame sans Merci
Hath thee in thrall! *Ib.*

. . . the fam'd memoirs of a thousand years,
Written by Crafticant, and published
By Parpaglion and Co.   *The Cap and Bells*

A thing of beauty is a joy for ever:
Its loveliness increases; it will never
Pass into nothingness. *Endymion*, 1

. . . the inhuman dearth
Of noble natures. *Ib.*

Wherein lies happiness? In that which becks
Our ready minds to fellowship divine,
A fellowship with essence. *Ib.*

A hope beyond the shadow of a dream. *Ib.*

But this is human life: the war, the deeds,
The disappointment, the anxiety,
Imagination's struggles, far and nigh,
All human. *Ib.* 2

He ne'er is crown'd
With immortality, who fears to follow
Where airy voices lead. *Ib.*

Since Ariadne was a vintage. *Ib.*

St. Agnes' Eve—Ah, bitter chill it was!
The owl, for all his feathers, was a-cold.
The Eve of St. Agnes

The joys of all his life were said and sung. *Ib.*

The silver, snarling trumpets 'gan to chide. *Ib.*

Sudden a thought came like a full-blown rose,
Flushing his brow. *Ib.*

Full on this casement shone the wintry moon,
And threw warm gules on Madeline's fair breast.
Ib.

Fanatics have their dreams, wherewith they weave
A paradise for a sect; the savage too
From forth the loftiest fashion of his sleep
Guesses at Heaven.   *The Fall of Hyperion, 1*

Every man whose soul is not a clod
Hath visions. *Ib.*

The poet and the dreamer are distinct,
Diverse, sheer opposite, antipodes.
The one pours out a balm upon the world,
The other vexes it. *Ib.*

Ever let the fancy roam,
Pleasure never is at home. *Fancy*

Where's the cheek that doth not fade,
Too much gaz'd at? Where's the maid
Whose lip mature is ever new? *Ib.*

No stir of air was there,
Not so much life as on a summer's day
Robs not one light seed from the feather'd grass.
                    Hyperion, 1

O aching time! O moments big as years.   *Ib.*

Those green-rob'd senators of mighty woods,
Tall oaks. *Ib.*

Unseen before by Gods or wondering men. *Ib.*

And only blind from sheer supremacy. *Ib. 2*

To bear all naked truths,
And to envisage circumstance, all calm,
That is the top of sovereignty. *Ib.*

For 'tis the eternal law
That first in beauty should be first in might. *Ib.*

But vain is now the burning and the strife,
Pangs are in vain, until I grow high-rife
        With old Philosophy.
                Lines on Seeing a Lock of Milton's Hair

Thou still unravish'd bride of quietness,
Thou foster-child of silence and slow time.
                Ode on a Grecian Urn

Heard melodies are sweet, but those unheard
Are sweeter. *Ib.*

' Beauty is truth, truth beauty,'—that is all
Ye know on earth, and all ye need know.   *Ib.*

Evenings steep'd in honied indolence.
                Ode on Indolence

For I would not be dieted with praise,
A pet-lamb in a sentimental farce. *Ib.*

No, no, go not to Lethe, neither twist
Wolf's-bane, tight-rooted, for its poisonous wine.
                Ode on Melancholy

Or if thy mistress some rich anger shows,
Emprison her soft hand, and let her rave,
And feed deep, deep upon her peerless eyes. *Ib.*

Ay, in the very temple of Delight
Veil'd Melancholy has her sovran shrine.   *Ib.*

My heart aches, and a drowsy numbness pains
My sense. *Ode to a Nightingale*

O for a draught of vintage! that hath been
Cool'd a long age in the deep-delved earth. *Ib.*

Full of the true, the blushful Hippocrene,
With beaded bubbles winking at the brim. *Ib.*

Fade far away, dissolve, and quite forget
What thou among the leaves hast never known,
The weariness, the fever and the fret
Here, where men sit and hear each other groan.
Ib.

Darkling I listen. *Ib.*

The voice I hear this passing night was heard
In ancient days by emperor and clown:
Perhaps the self-same song that found a path
Through the sad heart of Ruth, when, sick for
home,
She stood in tears amid the alien corn. *Ib.*

O latest born and loveliest vision far
Of all Olympus' faded hierarchy.
Ode to Psyche

A bright torch, and a casement ope at night,
To let the warm Love in! *Ib.*

Stop and consider! life is but a day;
A fragile dewdrop on its perilous way
From a tree's summit. *Sleep and Poetry*

O for ten years, that I may overwhelm
Myself in poesy; so I may do the deed
That my own soul has to itself decreed. *Ib.*

A thousand handicraftsmen wore the mask
Of Poesy. Ill-fated, impious race! *Ib.*

259

A drainless shower
Of light is poesy; 'tis the supreme of power;
'Tis might half slumb'ring on its own right arm. *Ib.*

And they shall be accounted poet kings
Who simply tell the most heart-easing things. *Ib.*

To sit upon an Alp as on a throne,
And half forget what world or worldling meant.
                    Sonnet. Happy is England

There is a budding morrow in midnight. *Ib. To
Homer*

Fame, like a wayward girl, will still be coy
To those who woo her with too slavish knees.
                              Ib. On Fame

Much have I travell'd in the realms of gold,
And many goodly states and kingdoms seen.
            Ib. On First Looking into Chapman's Homer

Then felt I like some watcher of the skies
When a new planet swings into his ken;
Or like stout Cortez when with eagle eyes
He star'd at the Pacific—and all his men
Look'd at each other with a wild surmise—
Silent, upon a peak in Darien.   *Ib.*

The poetry of earth is never dead. *Ib. On the
Grasshopper and Cricket*

To one who has been long in city pent,
'Tis very sweet to look into the fair
And open face of heaven.
                    Ib. To One Who Has Been Long

When I have fears that I may cease to be
Before my pen has glean'd my teeming brain.
Ib. When I have Fears

What can I do to drive away
Remembrance from my eyes? *What can I Do?*

Woman! when I behold thee flippant, vain,
Inconstant, childish, proud, and full of fancies.
Woman! When I Behold Thee

I am certain of nothing but the holiness of the
heart's affections and the truth of imagination—
what the imagination seizes as beauty must be
truth—whether it existed before or not. *Letter to
Benjamin Bailey*, 1817

I have never yet been able to perceive how any
thing can be known for truth by consecutive
reasoning—and yet it must be. *Ib.*

I do think better of womankind than to suppose
they care whether Mister John Keats five feet
high likes them or not. *Ib.* 1818

I have met with women whom I really think would
like to be married to a poem, and to be given
away by a novel. *Letter to Fanny Brawne*, 1819

The excellence of every art is its intensity, capable
of making all disagreeables evaporate, from their
being in close relationship with beauty and truth.
Letter to G. and T. Keats, 1817

Negative Capability, that is, when a man is
capable of being in uncertainties, mysteries,
doubts, without any irritable reaching after fact
and reason. *Ib.*

So I do believe . . . that works of genius are the first things in this world. *Ib.* 1818

The roaring of the wind is my wife and the stars through the window pane are my children. The mighty abstract idea I have of beauty in all things stifles the more divided and minute domestic happiness. . . . The opinion I have of the generality of women—who appear to me as children to whom I would rather give a sugar plum than my time, forms a barrier against matrimony which I rejoice in. *To George and Georgiana Keats*, 1818

Load every rift of your subject with ore. *Letter to Shelley*, 1820

Poetry should surprise by a fine excess, and not by singularity; it should strike the reader as a wording of his own highest thoughts, and appear almost a remembrance. *Letter to John Taylor*, 1818

I am ambitious of doing the world some good. If I should be spared, that may be the work of maturer years—in the interval I will assay to reach to as high a summit in Poetry as the nerve bestowed upon me will suffer. *Letter to Richard Woodhouse*

Kempis, Thomas a   c. 1380-1471

Verily, when the day of judgement comes, we shall not be asked what we have read, but what we have done. *De Imitatione Christi*, 1

Sic transit gloria mundi. Thus the glory of the world passes away. *Ib.* 3

Kepler, Johann   **1571-1630**

O God, I am thinking Thy thoughts after Thee.
Remark (while studying astronomy)

Kierkegaard, Sören   **1813-1855**

Life can only be understood backwards; but it
must be lived forwards. *Life*

King, Bishop Henry   **1592-1669**

We that did nothing study but the way
To love each other, with which thoughts the day
Rose with delight to us, and with them set,
Must learn the hateful art, how to forget.
The Surrender

Kings, The First Book of the

Behold, the half was not told me. 10, 7

An handful of meal in a barrel, and a little oil
in a cruise. 17, 12

How long halt ye between two opinions? 18, 21

But the Lord was not in the wind: and after the
wind an earthquake: but the Lord was not in
the earthquake;
And after the earthquake a fire: but the Lord was
not in the fire: and after the fire a still small
voice. 19, 11-12

Hast thou found me, O mine enemy? 21, 20

Kingsley, Charles   **1819-1875**

Be good, sweet maid, and let who will be clever;
Do noble things, not dream them, all day long.
A Farewell, To C. E. G.

When all the world is young, lad,
And all the trees are green;
And every goose a swan, lad
And every lass a queen.
  Song from the Water Babies. Young and Old

For men must work, and women must weep,
And there's little to earn, and many to keep.
  The Three Fishers

The loveliest fairy in the world; and her name is
Mrs. Doasyouwouldbedoneby.
  The Water Babies, 5

More ways of killing a cat than choking her with
cream. *Westward Ho!,* 20

Kipling, Rudyard   1865-1936

England's on the anvil—hear the hammers ring—
Clanging from the Severn to the Tyne! *The Anvil*

Oh, East is East, and West is West, and never the
  twain shall meet. *The Ballad of East and West*

Four things greater than all things are,—
Women and Horses and Power and War.
  Ballad of the King's Jest

And a woman is only a woman, but a good cigar
  is a Smoke. *The Bethrothed*

O where are you going to, all you Big Steamers,
With England's own coal, up and down the salt
  seas. ? *Big Steamers*

Boots—boots—boots—boots—movin' up an'
  down again! *Boots*

264

Land of our birth, our faith, our pride,
For whose dear sake our father's died;
O Motherland, we pledge to thee
Head, heart and hand through the years to be!
The Children's Song

But the Devil whoops, as he whooped of old:
" It's clever, but is it Art? " *The Conundrum of
the Workshops*

And what should they know of England who
only England know? *The English Flag*

For the female of the species is more deadly than
the male. *The Female of the Species*

And the measure of our torment is the measure
of our youth. *Gentleman Rankers*

And the Glory of the Garden it shall never pass
away! *The Glory of the Garden*

There are nine and sixty ways of constructing
tribal lays,
And—every—single—one—of—them—is—right!
In the Neolithic Age

If you can keep your head when all about you
Are losing theirs and blaming it on you. *If*

If you can dream—and not make dreams your
master. *Ib.*

With the flannelled fools at the wicket or the
muddied oafs at the goal. *The Islanders*

We have had a jolly good lesson, and it serves
us jolly well right. *The Lesson*

Pull out, pull out, on the Long Trail—the trail
that is always new! *The Long Trail*

The tumult and the shouting dies;
The Captains and the Kings depart. *Recessional*

Lest we forget—lest we forget! *Ib.*

Them that asks no questions isn't told a lie.
A Smuggler's Song

The White Man's Burden. *Title*

He travels the fastest who travels alone.
The Winners

A man of infinite-resource-and-sagacity. *Just-So
Stories. How the Whale Got his Throat*

There lived a Parsee from whose hat the rays of
the sun were reflected in more-than-oriental-
splendour. *Ib. How the Rhinoceros Got His Skin*

Take my word for it, the silliest woman can
manage a clever man; but it needs a very clever
woman to manage a fool. *Three and—an Extra*

Knox, Ronald Arbuthnot   **1888-1957**

There was once a man who said " God
Must think it exceedingly odd
      If he finds that this tree
     Continues to be
When there's no one about in the Quad."
Attrib. (cf. p.19)

" Presents," I often say, " endear Absents."
Essays of Elia. A Dissertation upon Roast Pig

We are nothing; less than nothing, and dreams.
We are only what might have been, and must
wait upon the tedious shores of Lethe millions
of ages before we have existence, and a name.
Ib. Dream Children

I have been trying all my life to like Scotchmen,
and am obliged to desist from the experiment in
despair. *Ib. Imperfect Sympathies*

There is an order of imperfect intellects (under
which mine must be content to rank) which . . . is
essentially anti-Caledonian. *Ib.*

In everything that relates to science, I am a whole
Encyclopaedia behind the rest of the world.
Ib.   The Old and New Schoolmaster

The human species, according to the best theory
I can form of it, is composed of two distinct races,
the men who borrow, and *the men who lend.*
Ib. The Two Races of Men

[Of tobacco]
Stinking'st of the stinking kind,
Filth of the mouth and fog of the mind,
Africa, that brags her foison
Breeds no such prodigious poison.
A Farewell to Tobacco

I love to lose myself in other men's minds. When
I am not walking, I am reading; I cannot sit
and think. Books think for me. *Last Essays of
Elia. Detached Thoughts on Books and Reading*

I can read anything which I call *a book*. There are things in that shape which I cannot allow for such. In this catalogue of *books which are no books*—*biblia a-biblia*—I reckon Court Calendars, Directories, . . . Almanacs, Statutes at Large, the works of Hume, Gibbon . . . and, generally, all those volumes which "no gentleman's library should be without." *Ib.*

I came home . . . hungry as a hunter. *Letter to Coleridge,* 1800

How I like to be liked, and what I do to be liked!
  Letter to D. Wordsworth, 1821

All, all are gone, the old familiar faces. *The Old Familiar Faces*

Landor, Walter Savage   **1775-1864**

George the First was always reckoned
Vile, but viler George the Second;
And what mortal ever heard
Any good of George the Third?
When from earth the Fourth descended
God be praised, the Georges ended!
  Epigram. The Atlas, 1855

Prose on certain occasions can bear a great deal of poetry: on the other hand, poetry sinks and swoons under a moderate weight of prose. *Imaginary Conversations. Archdeacon Hare and Walter Landor*

I shall dine late; but the dining-room will be well lighted, the guests few and select. *Ib.*

Lang, Andrew   **1844-1912**

St. Andrews by the Northern Sea,
That is a haunted town to me!   *Almae Matres*

Our hearts are young 'neath wrinkled rind:
Life's more amusing than we thought.
                          Ballade of Middle Age

A house full of books, and a garden full of
flowers. *Ballade of True Wisdom*

Langbridge, Frederick   **1849-1923**

Two men look out through the same bars:
One sees the mud, and one the stars.
                    A Cluster of Quiet Thoughts

Langland, William   **c. 1330-c. 1400**

A glotoun of wordes. *Piers Plowman, B Text,*
prologue

Grammere, that grounde is of alle. *Ib. C Text*, 18

Lao-tsze   **fl. c. 550 B.C.**

Acting without design, occupying oneself without
making a business of it, finding the great in what
is small and the many in the few, repaying injury
with kindness, effecting difficult things while they
are easy, and managing great things in their
beginnings: this is the method of Tao.
                                    The Simple Way

To joy in conquest is to joy in the loss of human
life. *Ib.*

La Rochefoucauld, François, Duc de   **1613-1680**

On n'est jamais si heureux ni si malheureux qu'on

s'imagine. One is never so happy or so unhappy as one thinks. *Ib.* 49

On peut trouver des femmes qui n'ont jamais eu de galanterie, mais il est rare d'en trouver qui n'en aient jamais eu qu'une. One can find women who have never had a love affair, but it is rare to find a woman who has had only one. *Maximes,* 73

La gloire des grands hommes se doit toujours mesurer aux moyens dont ils se sont servis pour l'acquérir. The glory of great men must always be measured by the means they have used to obtain it. *Ib.* 157

On peut être plus fin qu'un autre, mais non pas plus fin que tous les autres. One can be astuter than another, but not astuter than all the others. *Maximes,* 394

Latimer, Bishop Hugh   c. 1485-1555

Be of good comfort, Master Ridley, and play the man. We shall this day light such a candle by God's grace in England, as (I trust) shall never be put out. *Actes and Monuments,* Foxe

Lawrence, David Herbert   1885-1930

Love is the great Asker. *End of Another Home Holiday*

Once God was all negroid, as now he is fair·
Grapes

Money is our madness, our vast collective madness. *Money Madness*

Loud peace propaganda makes war seem imminent. *Peace and War*

Leacock, Stephen Butler   **1869-1944**

Lord Ronald said nothing; he flung himself
from the room, flung himself upon his horse and
rode madly off in all directions. *Gertrude the
Governess*

The parent who could see his boy as he really is,
would shake his head and say: " Willie is no
good: I'll sell him." *The Lot of the Schoolmaster*

Lear, Edward   **1812-1888**

Far and few, far and few
Are the lands where the Jumblies live.
                    Nonsense Songs. The Jumblies

The Owl and the Pussy-Cat went to sea
In a beautiful pea-green boat.
                    Ib. The Owl and the Pussy Cat

Lee, Robert Edward   **1807-1870**

Duty then is the sublimest word in our language.
Do your duty in all things. You cannot do more.
You should never wish to do less. *Inscription in
the Hall of Fame*

Lessing, Doris   **b. 1919**

. . . never in the whole history of the world have
people made a battle-cry out of being ordinary.
Never. Suppose we all said to the politicians—
we refuse to be heroic. We refuse to be brave.
We are bored with all the noble gestures—what
then? . . . *Each His Own Wilderness*, 3

L'Estrange, Sir Roger
1616-1704

It is with our passions as it is with fire and water, they are good servants, but bad masters. *Æsop's Fables*, 38. *Reflection*

Lewis, Sinclair
1885-1951

Our American professors like their literature clear, cold, pure, and very dead. *Address to Swedish Academy*, 1930

His name was George F. Babbitt, and . . . he was nimble in the calling of selling houses for more than people could afford to pay. *Babbitt*

It Can't Happen Here. *Title of Novel*

Lewis, Wyndham
1884-1957

. . . I lived in Great Britain. It follows that I found it necessary to become a pamphleteer to defend my paintings against attack and a critic that I might expound the doctrines responsible for the difficulties that so bewildered the public. *Note on " One Way Song"*

In its essence the purpose of satire—whether verse or prose—is aggression. (When whimsical, sentimental, or "poetic," it is a sort of bastard humour.) Satire has a great big blaring target. If successful, it blasts a great big hole in the centre. Directness there must be and singleness of aim: it is all aim, all trajectory. *Note on Verse-Satire*

Lichtenberg, Georg Cristoph
1742-1799

There can hardly be a stranger commodity in the world than books. Printed by people who don't understand them; sold by people who don't

understand them; bound, criticised and read by
people who don't understand them, and now even
written by people who don't understand them.
A Doctrine of Scattered Occasions

Lincoln, Abraham   1809-1865

You can fool some of the people all of the time,
and all of the people some of the time, but you
cannot fool all of the people all the time.
Attrib. Speech, 1856

I believe this government cannot endure per-
manently half-slave and half-free. I do not expect
the Union to be dissolved ... but I do expect it
will cease to be divided. *Ib. June, 1858*

I leave you, hoping that the lamp of liberty will
burn in your bosoms, until there shall no longer
be a doubt that all men are created free and
equal. *Ib. July, 1858*

The probability that we may fail in the struggle
ought not to deter us from the support of a cause
we believe to be just. *Ib. 1859*

Fourscore and seven years ago, our fathers
brought forth upon this continent a new nation
conceived in liberty, and dedicated to the proposition that all men are created equal. *Address,
Gettysburg National Cemetery, Nov., 1863*

The world will little note nor long remember
what we say here, but it can never forget what
they did here. . . . It is rather for us to be here
dedicated to the great task remaining before us—
that from these honoured dead we take increased

273

devotion to that cause for which they gave the last full measure of devotion; that we here highly resolve that these dead shall not have died in vain; that this nation, under God, shall have a new birth of freedom; and that government of the people, by the people, for the people, shall not perish from the earth. *Ib.*

With malice toward none, with charity for all, with firmness in the right, as God gives us to see the right. *Second Inaugural Address, 1865*

When you have got an elephant by the hind leg, and he is trying to run away, it's best to let him run. *Remark, 1865*

I don't know who my grandfather was; I am much more concerned to know what his grandson will be. *Lincoln's Own Stories, Gross*

Character is like a tree and reputation like its shadow. The shadow is what we think of it; the tree is the real thing. *Ib.*

He reminds me of the man who murdered both his parents, and then, when sentence was about to be pronounced, pleaded for mercy on the grounds that he was an orphan. *Ib.*

Better to remain silent and be thought a fool than to speak out and remove all doubt. *Attrib.*

Lindsay, Sir David   **c. 1490-1555**

Let everie man keip weil ane toung,
And everie woman tway.
                                    Ane Satyre of the Thrie Estaitis

274

What vails your kingdome, and your rent,
And all your great treasure;
Without ye haif ane mirrie lyfe,
And cast aside all sturt, and stryfe. *Ib.*

We think them verray naturall fules,
That lernis ouir mekle at the sculis.
The Complaynt to the King

[John the Common Weill]
Thare sall na Scot have comforting
Of me, till that I see the country guidit
By wisdom of ane gude, auld prudent king,
Whilk sall delight him maist abune all thing,
To put justice till execution,
And on strang traitouris mak punitioun.
The Dreme

Linklater, Eric   b. 1899

. . . weaklings, fools, and knaves; dullards, fat
profiteers, and starving dole men; the chatterers,
the rushers to and fro, the self-doubters and the
self-satisfied; with snivelling piety and super-
cilious unbelief; with empty heads and full bellies;
with ossified Tories and rattle-brained Socialists;
with pimping prettiness and ugliness too mean to
hide itself. . . . *Magnus Merriman*

While swordless Scotland, sadder than its psalms,
Fosters its sober youth on national alms
To breed a dull provincial discipline,
Commerce its god and golf its anodyne.
Preamble to a Satire

For the scientific acquisition of knowledge is
almost as tedious as a routine acquisition of
wealth. *White Man's Saga*

Livy   **59 B.C.-A.D. 17**

Vae Victis. Woe to the vanquished. *History, 5*

*In rebus asperis et tenui spe fortissima quaeque
consilia tutissima sunt.* In grave difficulties and
with little hope, the boldest measures are the
safest. *Ib. 25*

Lloyd, Robert   **1733-1764**

Who teach the mind its proper face to scan,
And hold the faithful mirror up to man.
                                              The Actor

Slow and steady wins the race. *The Hare and the
Tortoise*

Lloyd George, David   **1863-1945**

What is our task? To make Britain a fit country
for heroes to live in. *Speech, 1918*

The finest eloquence is that which gets things
done; the worst is that which delays them.
Speech at the Peace Conference, Paris, Jan., 1919

Logau, Friedrich von   **1605-1655**

*Gottesmühlen mahlen langsam, mahlen aber trefflich
klein.* The mills of God grind slow, but they
grind exceeding small. *Sinngedichte, 3*

Longfellow, Henry Wadsworth   **1807-1882**

I shot an arrow into the air,
It fell to earth, I knew not where.
                                      The Arrow and the Song

Ye are better than all the ballads
That ever were sung or said;
For ye are living poems,
And all the rest are dead.   *Children*

The cares that infest the day
Shall fold their tents, like the Arabs,
And as silently steal away.   *The Day is Done*

The shades of night were falling fast,
As through an Alpine village passed
A youth, who bore, 'mid snow and ice,
A banner with the strange device,
Excelsior! *Excelsior*

When she was good
She was very, very good,
But when she was bad she was horrid.
                    Home Life of Longfellow

You would attain to the divine perfection,
And yet not turn your back upon the world.
                    Michael Angelo, 1

The men that women marry,
And why they marry them, will always be
A marvel and a mystery to the world.   *Ib.*

A boy's will is the wind's will,
And the thoughts of youth are long, long thoughts.
                    My Lost Youth

Not in the clamour of the crowded street,
Not in the shouts and plaudits of the throng,
But in ourselves, are triumph and defeat.
                    The Poets

Life is real! Life is earnest!
And the grave is not its goal.   *A Psalm of Life*

Footprints on the sands of time. *Ib.*

By the shores of Gitche Gumee,
By the shining Big-Sea-Water,
Stood the wigwam of Nokomis,
Daughter of the Moon, Nokomis.
   The Song of Hiawatha. Hiawatha's Childhood

As unto the bow the cord is,
So unto the man is woman;
Though she bends him, she obeys him,
Though she draws him, yet she follows;
Useless each without the other!
   Ib. Hiawatha's Wooing

Ships that pass in the night, and speak each other
   in passing. *Tales of a Wayside Inn, 3, The*
   Theologian's Tale

Under the spreading chestnut tree
The village smithy stands. *The Village Blacksmith*

Something attempted, something done.   *Ib.*

Louis XIV of France   **1638-1715**

L'Etat c'est moi. I am the State. *Attrib.*

Lovelace, Richard   **1618-1658**

Stone Walls do not a Prison make
Nor Iron bars a Cage;
Minds innocent and quiet take
That for an hermitage. *To Althea, From Prison*

I could not love thee (Dear) so much,
Lov'd I not Honour more.
   To Lucasta, Going to the Wars

Lady, it is already Morn,
And 'twas last night I swore to thee
That fond impossibility. *The Scrutinie*

With spoyles of meaner Beauties crown'd,
I laden will returne to thee. *Ib.*

Lover, Samuel   **1797-1868**

When once the itch of literature comes over a
man, nothing can cure it but the scratching of a
pen. *Handy Andy*

Lowell, James Russell   **1819-1891**

It's wal enough agin a king
   To dror resolves an' triggers,—
But libbaty's a kind o' thing
   Thet don't agree with niggers.
              The Pious Editor's Creed

I mean in preyin' till one bursts
   On wut the party chooses,
An' in convartin' public trusts
   To very privit uses. *Ib.*

I don't care how hard money is
   Ez long ez mine's paid punctooal. *Ib.*

I *don't* believe in princerple,
   But O, I *du* in interest. *Ib.*

And what is so rare as a day in June?
Then, if ever, come perfect days.
              Vision of Sir Launfal, 1

Luke, The Gospel according to Saint

Because there was no room for them in the inn.
                              2, 7

And, lo, the angel of the Lord came upon them, and the glory of the Lord shone round about them: and they were sore afraid. 2, 9

Glory to God in the highest, and on earth peace, good will toward men. 2, 14

Lord, now lettest thou thy servant depart in peace, according to thy word. 2, 29

Wist ye not that I must be about my Father's business? 2, 49

Physician, heal thyself. 4, 23

He passed by on the other side, 10, 31

Go, and do thou likewise. 10, 37

He that is not with me is against me. 11, 23

The poor, and the maimed, and the halt, and the blind. 14, 21

Joy shall be in heaven over one sinner that repenteth, more than over ninety and nine just persons, which need no repentance. 15, 7

Bring hither the fatted calf, and kill it. 15, 23

Nevertheless not my will, but thine, be done.
22, 42

Father, forgive them; for they know not what they do. 23, 34

Father, into thy hands I commend my spirit.
23, 46

Luther, Martin   **1483-1546**

Ein feste Burg ist unser Gott,
Ein gute Wehr und Waffen.
A safe stronghold our God is still,
A trusty shield and weapon.
Klug'sche Gesangbuch (Tr. Carlyle)

Ich kann nicht anders. I can do no other.
Speech, Diet of Worms, 1521

Macaulay, Thomas Babington, Lord
                                                     1800-1859
Obadiah Bind-their-kings-in-chains-and-their-
    nobles-with-links-of-iron. *The Battle of Naseby*

To every man upon this earth
Death cometh soon or late.
And how can man die better
Than facing fearful odds,
For the ashes of his fathers,
And the temples of his Gods?
Lays of Ancient Rome. Horatius, 27

Now who will stand on either hand,
And keep the bridge with me? *Ib.* 29

But those behind cried " Forward! "
And those before cried " Back! " *Ib.* 50

O Tiber! father Tiber!
To whom the Romans pray,
A Roman's life, a Roman's arms,
Take thou in charge this day! *Ib.* 59

And even the ranks of Tuscany
Could scarce forbear to cheer. *Ib.* 60

281

The English Bible, a book which, if everything else in our language should perish, would alone suffice to show the whole extent of its beauty and power. *Edinburgh Review*, 1828

The gallery in which the reporters sit has become a fourth estate of the realm. *Historical Essays, Edinburgh Review*, 1828

Every schoolboy knows who imprisoned Montezuma, and who strangled Atahualpa. *Ib.* 1840

Thus our democracy was, from an early period, the most aristocratic, and our aristocracy the most democratic in the world.
History of England, 1

The Puritan hated bear-baiting, not because it gave pain to the bear, but because it gave pleaure to the spectators. *Ib.*

There were gentleman and there were seamen in the navy of Charles the Second. But the seamen were not gentlemen; and the gentlemen were not seamen. *Ib.*

We know of no spectacle so ridiculous as the British public in one of its periodical fits of morality. *Literary Essay, Edinburgh Review*, 1830

We prefer a gipsy by Reynolds to his Majesty's head on a sign-post. *Ib.*

[Of Richard Steele] He was a rake among scholars, and a scholar among rakes. *Ib.* 1843

McClellan, George   **1826-1885**

All quiet along the Potomac. *Attrib. in American Civil War* (cf. p. 48)

McCrae, John   **1872-1918**

Take up our quarrel with the foe:
To you from failing hands we throw
The torch; be yours to hold it high.
If ye break faith with us who die
We shall not sleep, though poppies grow
   In Flanders fields.   *In Flanders Fields*

MacDiarmid, Hugh (C. M. Grieve)   **b. 1892**

Oot o' the way, my senses five,
I ken a' you can tell,
Oot o' the way, my thochts, for noo'
I maun face God mysel'.
                    Ballad of the Five Senses

It's easier to lo'e Prince Charlie
Than Scotland—mair's the shame!
                    Bonnie Prince Charlie

He's no' a man ava',
And lacks a proper pride,
Gin less than a' the warld
Can ser' him for a bride!
          A Drunk Man Looks at the Thistle

And as at sicna times am I,
I wad ha'e Scotland to my eye
Until I saw a timeless flame
Tak' Auchtermuchty for a name,
And kent that Ecclefechan stood
As pairt o' an eternal mood. *Ib.*

Other masters may conceivably write
Even yet in C major,
But we—we take the perhaps "primrose path"
To the dodecaphonic bonfire.
In Memoriam James Joyce

And I lo'e love
Wi' a scunner in't. *Scunner*

Macdonald   fl. 1855

[Of Florence Nightingale] When all the medical
officers have retired for the night, and silence and
darkness have settled down upon those miles of
prostrate sick, she may be observed alone, with
a little lamp in her hand, making her solitary
rounds. *Letter to The Times*

MacDonald, George   1824-1905

Where did you come from, baby dear?
Out of the everywhere into here.
At the Back of the North Wind, 33

Here lie I, Martin Elginbrodde:
Hae mercy o' my soul, Lord God;
As I wad do, were I Lord God,
And you were Martin Elginbrodde.
David Elginbrod, 1

Machiavelli, Niccolo di Bernardo dei   1469-1527

For titles do not reflect honour on men, but
rather men on their titles. *Dei Discorsi*, 3

So it happened that all the armed prophets were
victorious, and all the unarmed perished.
Il Principe, 6

Fortune is a woman, and therefore friendly to the young, who command her with audacity. *Ib.* 25

Mackenzie, Sir Compton   b. 1883

The slavery of being waited upon that is more deadening than the slavery of waiting upon other people. *The Adventures of Sylvia Scarlett*

I don't believe in principles. Principles are only excuses for what we want to think or what we want to do. *Ib.*

Prostitution. Selling one's body to keep one's soul: this is the meaning of the sins that were forgiven to the woman because she loved much: one might say of most marriages that they were selling one's soul to keep one's body. *Ib.*

MacNeice, Louis   1907-1963

It's no go the merrygoround, it's no go the rickshaw,
All we want is a limousine and a ticket for the peep show. *Bagpipe Music*

The drunkenness of things being various. *Snow*

Madariaga, Salvador de   b. 1886

First, the sweetheart of the nation, then her aunt, woman governs America because America is a land where boys refuse to grow up. *Americans are Boys*

Mansfield, Katherine   1888-1923

England is merely an island of beef flesh swimming in a warm gulf stream of gravy. *The Modern Soul*

Marie-Antoinette   **1755-1793**

Qu'ils mangent de la brioche. Let them eat cake.
                                     Attrib. (but much older)

Mark, The Gospel according to Saint

The sabbath was made for man, and not man for
the sabbath. 2, 27

And they that did eat of the loaves were about
five thousand men. 6, 44

Suffer the little children to come unto me, and
forbid them not: for such is the kingdom of
God. 10, 14

It is easier for a camel to go through the eye of
a needle than for a rich man to enter into the
kingdom of God. 10, 25 (cf. St. Matthew, 19, 24)

Marlowe, Christopher   **1564-1593**

My heart is as an anvil unto sorrow,
Which beats upon it like the Cyclops' hammers,
And with the noise turns up my giddy brain,
And makes me frantic for my Gaveston.
                                    Edward II, 1

Fair blows the wind for France. *Ib.*

What doctrine call you this, *Che sera, sera,*
What will be, shall be? *Faustus*

Christ cannot save thy soul, for he is just. *Ib.*

Why this is hell, nor am I out of it:
Thinkst thou that I who saw the face of God,
And tasted the eternal joys of heaven,
Am not tormented with ten thousand hells
In being deprived of everlasting bliss? *Ib.*

286

Was this the face that launch'd a thousand ships
And burnt the topless towers of Ilium?
Sweet Helen, make me immortal with a kiss! *Ib.*

O, thou art fairer than the evening air
Clad in the beauty of a thousand stars. *Ib.*

O lente, lente currite, noctis equi:
The stars move still, time runs, the clock will
    strike,
The devil will come, and Faustus must be damn'd.
                                                    Ib.

Cut is the branch that might have grown full
    straight,
And burnèd is Apollo's laurel bough,
That some time grew within this learnèd man. *Ib.*

It lies not in our power to love, or hate,
For will in us is over-rul'd by fate.
                                Hero and Leander, 1

Where both deliberate, the love is slight;
Whoever loved that loved not at first sight? *Ib.*

Like untun'd golden strings all women are
Which long time lie untouch'd, will harshly jar.
                                                    Ib.

Albeit the world think Machiavel is dead,
Yet was his soul but flown beyond the Alps.
                                The Jew of Malta, prologue

I count religion but a childish toy,
And hold there is no sin but ignorance.
                                The Jew of Malta

287

Thus tralls our fortune in by land and sea,
And thus are we on every side enrich'd. *Ib.*

And better one want for a common good,
Than many perish for a private man. *Ib.*

Thou hast committed—
Fornication: but that was in another country;
And besides, the wench is dead. *Ib.*

Come live with me, and be my love,
And we will all the pleasures prove,
That hills and valleys, dales and fields,
Woods or steepy mountain yields.
The Passionate Shepherd to his Love.

The last couplet is also given as:

That hills and valleys, dale and field,
And all the craggy mountains yield.

From jigging veins of rhyming mother-wits,
And such conceits as clownage keeps in pay,
We'll lead you to the stately tent of war.
Tamburlaine the Great, 1, prologue

Zenocrate, lovelier than the love of Jove,
Brighter than is the silver Rhodope,
Fairer than whitest snow on Scythian Hills. *Ib.* I

Accurs'd be he that first invented war! *Ib.*

Is it not passing brave to be a King,
And ride in triumph through Persepolis? *Ib.*

Nature that framed us of four elements,
Warring within our breasts for regiment,
Doth teach us all to have aspiring minds. *Ib.*

Not all the curses which the Furies breathe
Shall make me leave so rich a prize as this.   *Ib.*

Whose eyes are brighter than the lamps of heaven
And speech more pleasant than sweet harmony;
That with thy looks canst clear the darken'd sky,
And calm the rage of thundering Jupiter.   *Ib.*

Holla, ye pampered jades of Asia!
What, can ye draw but twenty miles a-day? *Ib.* 2

Marryat, Frederick   1792-1848

We always took care of number one. *Frank
Mildmay*, 19

As you are not prepared, as the Americans say,
to go the whole hog, we will part good friends.
                                    Japhet, 54

She call me a damned nigger, and say like massa
like man. *King's Own*, 19

[Of an illegitimate baby] If you please, ma'am,
it was a very little one. *Midshipman Easy*, 3

As melancholy as a sick monkey. *Ib.* 21

It's just six of one and half-a-dozen of the other.
                                    The Pirate, 4

Every man paddle his own canoe.
                          Settlers in Canada, 8

Martial, Marcus Valerius M.   c. 43-104

*Quod tam grande sophos clamat tibi turba togata,
Non tu, Pomponi, cena diserta tua est.*
When your crowd of followers applaud you so

loudly, Pomponius, it is not you but your banquet
that is eloquent. *Epigrams, 6*

Marvell, Andrew   **1621-1678**

My Love is of a birth as rare
As 'tis for object strange and high:
It was begotten by despair
Upon Impossibility.   *The Definition of Love*

As Lines so Loves *oblique* may well
Themselves in every Angle greet:
But ours so truly *Paralel*,
Though infinite can never meet.   *Ib.*

Earth cannot shew so brave a Sight
As when a single Soul does fence
The Batteries of alluring Sense,
And Heaven views it with delight.
*A Dialogue between the Resolved Soul and Created
Pleasure*

But all resistance against her is vain,
Who has the advantage both of Eyes and Voice.
And all my Forces needs must be undone,
She having gained both the Wind and Sun.
The Fair Singer

Engines more keen than ever yet
Adorned Tyrants Cabinet;
Of which the most tormenting are
Black Eyes, red Lips, and curled Hair.
The Gallery

How vainly men themselves amaze
To win the Palm, the Oke, or Bayes.   *The Garden*

No white nor red was ever seen
So am'rous as this lovely green.   *Ib.*

Meanwhile the Mind, from pleasure less,
Withdraws into its happiness:
The Mind, that Ocean where each kind
Does streight its own resemblance find.   *Ib.*

Annihilating all that's made
To a green Thought in a green Shade. *Ib.*

But at my back I alwaies hear
Times wingèd Charriot hurrying near.
                    To His Coy Mistress

The Grave's a fine and private place
But none I think do there embrace. *Ib.*

Who can foretell for what high cause
This Darling of the Gods was born!
The Picture of Little T.C. in a Prospect of Flowers

Marx, Karl Heinrich   1818-1883

Without doubt machinery has greatly increased
the number of well-to-do idlers. *Capital*

*Die Proletarier haben nichts in ihr zu verlieren als
ihre Ketten. Sie haben eine Welt zu gewinnen.
Proletarier aller Länder, vereinigt euch!* The
workers have nothing to lose but their chains in
this. They have a world to win. Workers of the
world, unite! *Communist Manifesto*

*Jeder nach seinen Fähigkeiten, jedem nach seinen
Bedürfnissen.* From each according to his
abilities, to each according to his needs. *Critique
of the Gotha Programme*

Die Religion . . . ist das Opium des Volkes. Religion
. . . is the opium of the people. *Kritik der Hegelschen
Rechtsphilosophie*

Mary Tudor   **1516-1558**

When I am dead and opened, you shall find
" Calais " lying in my heart. *Attrib.*

Masefield, John   **1878-1966**

Quinquireme of Nineveh from distant Ophir
Rowing home to haven in sunny Palestine,
With a cargo of ivory,
And apes and peacocks,
Sandalwood, cedarwood and sweet white wine.
Cargoes

I must go down to the seas again, to the vagrant
    gypsy life,
To the gull's way and the whale's way where the
    wind's like a whetted knife;
And all I ask is a merry yarn from a laughing
    fellow rover,
And a quiet sleep and a sweet dream when the
    long trick's over. *Sea Fever*

It's good to be out on the road, and going one
    knows not where. *Tewkesbury Road*

I never hear the west wind but tears are in my
    eyes.
For it comes from the west lands, the old brown
    hills,
And April's in the west wind, and daffodils.
                                      The West Wind

Matthew, The Gospel according to Saint

And she shall bring forth a son, and thou shalt
call his name JESUS: for he shall save his
people from their sins. 1, 21

There came wise men from the east to Jerusalem,
Saying, Where is he that is born King of the Jews?
for we have seen his star in the east, and are come
to worship him. 2, 1-2

They presented unto him gifts; gold, and
frankincense, and myrrh. 2, 11

The voice of one crying in the wilderness, Prepare
ye the way of the Lord, make his paths straight.
3, 3

This is my beloved Son, in whom I am well
pleased. 3, 17

Man shall not live by bread alone, but by every
word that proceedeth out of the mouth of God.
4, 4

Thou shalt not tempt the Lord thy God. 4, 7

Angels came and ministered unto him. 4, 11

Fishers of men. 4, 19

Blessed are the poor in spirit: for theirs is the
kingdom of heaven.
Blessed are they that mourn: for they shall be
comforted.
Blessed are the meek: for they shall inherit the
earth.
Blessed are they which do hunger and thirst after
righteousness: for they shall be filled.
Blessed are the merciful: for they shall obtain
mercy.
Blessed are the pure in heart: for they shall see
God.
Blessed are the peacemakers: for they shall be
called the children of God. 5, 3-9

Whosoever shall compel thee to go a mile, go with him twain. 5, 41

Love your enemies, bless them that curse you, do good to them that hate you, and pray for them which spitefully use you, and persecute you. 5, 44

Be ye therefore perfect, even as your Father which is in heaven is perfect. 5, 48

After this manner therefore pray ye: Our Father which art in heaven, Hallowed be thy name. Thy kingdom come. Thy will be done in earth, as it is in heaven. Give us this day our daily bread. And forgive us our debts, as we forgive our debtors. And lead us not into temptation, but deliver us from evil: For thine is the kingdom, and the power, and the glory, for ever. Amen. 6, 9-13

Lay not up for yourself treasures upon earth. 6, 19

Lay up for yourselves treasures in heaven. 6, 20

Where your treasure is, there will your heart be also. 6, 21

Ye cannot serve God and mammon. 6, 24

Seek ye first the kingdom of God, and his righteousness; and all these things shall be added unto you. 6, 33

Take therefore no thought for the morrow; for the morrow shall take thought for the things of itself. Sufficient unto the day is the evil thereof. 6, 34

Judge not, that ye be not judged. 7, 1

Neither cast ye your pearls before swine. 7, 6

Ask, and it shall be given you; seek, and ye shall
find; knock, and it shall be opened unto you.
7, 7

I have not found so great faith, no, not in Israel.
8, 10

I am not come to call the righteous, but sinners
to repentance. 9, 13

Are not two sparrows sold for a farthing? and
one of them shall not fall on the ground without
your Father. 10, 29

He that findeth his life shall lose it: and he that
loseth his life for my sake shall find it. 10, 39

He that is not with me is against me. 12, 30

The kingdom of heaven is like to a grain of
mustard seed. 13, 31

Be of good cheer; it is I; be not afraid. 14, 27

O thou of little faith, wherefore didst thou doubt?
14, 31

Thou art Peter, and upon this rock I will build
my church; and the gates of hell shall not
prevail against it. 16, 18

Get thee behind me, Satan. 16, 23

What is a man profited, if he shall gain the whole
world, and lose his own soul. 16, 26

For where two or three are gathered together in my name, there am I in the midst of them. 18, 20

Thou shalt love thy neighbour as thyself. 19, 19

With men this is impossible; but with God all things are possible. 19, 26

For many are called, but few are chosen, 22, 14

Well done, thou good and faithful servant, 25, 21

I was a stranger and ye took me in:
Naked and ye clothed me: I was sick, and ye visited me: I was in prison, and ye came unto me.
25, 35-36

If it be possible, let this cup pass from me. 26, 39

The spirit indeed is willing, but the flesh is weak.
26, 41

He took water, and washed his hands before the multitude, saying, I am innocent of the blood of this just person: see ye to it. 27, 24

Maturin, Charles Robert   1782-1824

'Tis well to be merry and wise,
'Tis well to be honest and true;
'Tis well to be off with the old love,
Before you are on with the new. *Bertram: Motto*

Maugham, William Somerset   1874-1965

People ask you for criticism, but they only want praise. *Of Human Bondage*

It's no use crying over spilt milk, because all the forces of the universe were bent on spilling it. *Ib.*

Beauty is something wonderful and strange that the artist fashions out of the chaos of the world in the torment of his soul. *The Moon and Sixpence*

Melbourne, William Lamb, Viscount   1779-1848

Things have come to a pretty pass when religion is allowed to invade the sphere of private life.
Remark

It is not much matter which we say, but mind, we must all say *the same*. *Attrib.*

Mencken, Henry Louis   1880-1956

Every normal man must be tempted, at times, to spit on his hands, hoist the black flag, and begin slitting throats. *Prejudices, 1*

Women hate revolutions and revolutionists. They like men who are docile, and well-regarded at the bank, and never late at meals. *Ib. 4*

Meredith, George   1828-1909

They need their pious exercises less
Than schooling in the Pleasures.
A Certain People

    We'll sit contentedly
And eat our pot of honey on the grave.
Modern Love

More brain, O Lord, more brain! *Ib.*

The sun is coming down to earth, and the fields
and the waters shout to him golden shouts.
The Ordeal of Richard Fevere

Kissing don't last: cookery do! *Ib.*

Cynicism is intellectual dandyism. *The Egoist*, 7

To plod on and still keep the passion fresh. *Ib.* 12

Merritt, Dixon Lanier   1879-1954

A wonderful bird is the pelican,
His bill will hold more than his belican.
He can take in his beak
Food enough for a week,
But I'm damned if I see how the helican.
The Pelican

Mill, John Stuart   1806-1873

Ask yourself whether you are happy, and you
cease to be so. *Autobiography*, 5

No great improvements in the lot of mankind are
possible, until a great change takes place in the
fundamental constitution of their modes of
thought. *Ib.* 7

Protection, therefore, against the tyranny of the
magistrate is not enough: there needs protection
also against the tyranny of the prevailing opinion
and feeling. *On Liberty*, introduction

Another grand determining principle of the rules
of conduct . . . has been the servility of mankind
towards the supposed preferences or aversions
of their temporal masters, or of their gods. *Ib.*

The sole end for which mankind are warranted,
individually or collectively, in interfering with

the liberty of action of any of their number, is self-protection. *Ib.*

If all mankind minus one, were of one opinion, and only one person were of the contrary opinion, mankind would be no more justified in silencing that one person, then he, if he had the power, would be justified in silencing mankind. *Ib.* 2

History teems with instances of truth put down by persecution . . . It is a piece of idle sentimentality that truth, merely as truth, has any inherent power denied to error, of prevailing against the dungeon and the stake. *Ib.*

A people, it appears, may be progressive for a certain length of time, and then stop. When does it stop? When it ceases to possess individuality. *Ib.* 3

Whatever crushes individuality is despotism, by whatever name it may be called. *Ib.*

. . . mere conformers to commonplace, or time-servers for truth, whose arguments on all great subjects are meant for their hearers, and are not those which have convinced themselves. *Ib.*

Persons require to possess a title, or some other badge of rank, or of the consideration of people of rank, to be able to indulge somewhat in the luxury of doing as they like without detriment to their estimation. *Ib.*

I am not aware that any community has a right to force another to be civilised. *Ib.* 4

When the land is cultivated entirely by the spade and no horses are kept, a cow is kept for every three acres of land. *Political Economy*, 2, 6

Unearned increment. *Ib.* 5, 2

Milne, Alan Alexander   1882-1956

They're changing guard at Buckingham Palace—
Christopher Robin went down with Alice.
When We Were Very Young. Buckingham Palace

You must never go down to the end of the town
   if you don't go down with me. *Ib. Disobedience*

I do like a little bit of butter to my bread! *Ib. The King's Breakfast*

Little Boy kneels at the foot of the bed,
Drops on the little hands, little gold head;
Hush! Hush! Whisper who dares!
Christopher Robin is saying his prayers.
                 Ib. Vespers

I am a Bear of Very Little Brain, and long words
Bother me. *Winnie-the-Pooh*, 4

Time for a little something. *Ib.* 6

" Pathetic," he said. " That's what it is. Pathetic."
                       Ib.

Milner, Lord Alfred   1854-1925

If we believe a thing to be bad, and if we have a right to prevent it, it is our duty to try to prevent it and to damn the consequences. *Speech*, 1909

Come, knit hands, and beat the ground,
In a light fantastic round. *Comus*

         . . . it was the sound
Of Riot, and ill-manag'd Merriment. *Ib.*

               . . . courtesy,
Which oft is sooner found in lowly sheds
With smoky rafters, then in tap'stry Halls
And Courts of Princes, where it first was nam'd,
And yet is most pretended. *Ib.*

Himself is his own dungeon. *Ib.*

Beauty is nature's coin, must not be hoarded,
But must be current, and the good thereof
Consists in mutual and partak'n bliss. *Ib.*

Hence vain, deluding joys,
The brood of folly without father bred.
                     Il Penseroso

With even step, and musing gait,
And looks commercing with the skies. *Ib.*

And add to these retired Leisure,
That in trim Gardens takes his pleasure. *Ib.*

Or let my Lamp at midnight hour,
Be seen in some high lonely Tower,
Where I may oft outwatch the Bear,
With thrice great Hermes. *Ib.*

. . . th' unseen Genius of the Wood. *Ib.*

And storied Windows richly dight,
Casting a dim religious light. *Ib.*

Hence, loathed Melancholy,
Of Cerberus, and blackest midnight born.

L'Allegro

Sport that wrinkled Care derides,
And Laughter holding both his sides.
Come, and trip it as ye go
On the light fantastic toe. *Ib.*

And if I give thee honour due,
Mirth, admit me of thy crew
To live with her, and live with thee,
In unreproved pleasures free. *Ib.*

While the Cock with lively din,
Scatters the rear of darkness thin. *Ib.*

. . . many a youth, and many a maid,
Dancing in the Chequer'd shade;
And young and old come forth to play
On a Sunshine Holyday,
Till the live-long daylight fail,
Then to the Spicy Nut-brown Ale. *Ib.*

Or sweetest Shakespeare, fancy's child,
Warble his native Wood-notes wild. *Ib.*

The melting voice through mazes running. *Ib.*

Yet once more, O ye Laurels, and once more
Ye Myrtles brown, with Ivy never-sear,
I come to pluck your Berries, harsh and crude.

Lycidas

For we were nursed upon the self-same hill,
Fed the same flock, by fountain, shade, and rill.

Ib.

Were it not better done as others use,
To sport with Amaryllis in the shade,
Or with the tangles of Neaera's hair? *Ib.*

Fame is the spur that the clear spirit doth raise
(That last infirmity of Noble mind)
To scorn delights, and live laborious days. *Ib.*

Comes the blind Fury with th' abhorred shears,
And slits the thin-spun life. *Ib.*

Fame is no plant that grows on mortal soil,
Nor in the glistering foil
Set off to th' world, nor in broad rumour lies. *Ib.*

The Pilot of the Galilean lake,
Two massy Keys he bore of metals twain;
(The Golden opes, the Iron shuts amain.) *Ib.*

Blind mouths! that scarce themselves know how
    to hold
A Sheep-hook. *Ib.*

    . . . their lean and flashy songs
Grate on their scrannel Pipes of wretched straw,
The hungry Sheep look up, and are not fed. *Ib.*

But that two-handed engine at the door,
Stands ready to smite once, and smite no more.
                                              Ib.

Return, Alpheus, the dread voice is past,
That shrunk thy streams. *Ib.*

At last he rose, and twitch'd his Mantle blue:
Tomorrow to fresh Woods, and Pastures new. *Ib.*

303

It was the Winter wild,
While the Heav'n-borne child,
All meanly wrapt in the rude manger lies.
On the Morning of Christ's Nativity. The Hymn

Ring out ye Crystal spheres,
Once bless our human ears. *Ib.*

Time will run back, and fetch the age of gold,
And speckl'd vanity
Will sicken soon and die. *Ib.*

Rime being no necessary Adjunct or true Ornament of Poem or good Verse, in longer Works
especially, but the Invention of a barbarous Age,
to set off wretched matter and lame Metre.
Paradise Lost, introduction

Of Man's First Disobedience, and the Fruit
Of that Forbidden Tree, whose mortal taste
Brought Death into the World, and all our woe.
Ib. 1

Things unattempted yet in Prose or Rhyme.

I may assert Eternal Providence,
And justify the ways of God to men. *Ib.*   *Ib.*

                            . . . aspiring
To set himself in Glory above his Peers,
He trusted to have equal'd the most High. *Ib.*

        Him the Almighty Power
Hurl'd headlong flaming from th' Ethereal Sky
With hideous ruin and combustion down
To bottomless perdition. *Ib.*

        What though the field be lost?
All is not lost; the unconquerable Will,

And study of revenge, immortal hate,
And courage never to submit or yield. *Ib.*

The mind is its own place, and in itself
Can make a Heav'n of Hell, a Hell of Heav'n. *Ib.*

To reign is worth ambition though in Hell:
Better to reign in Hell, than serve in Heav'n. *Ib.*

Thick as Autumnal Leaves that strow the Brooks
In Vallambrosa, where th' Etrurian shades
High overarch'd imbowcr. *Ib.*

    . . . the Sons
Of Belial, flown with insolence and wine. *Ib.*

    . . . and instead of rage
Deliberate valour breath'd, firm and unmov'd. *Ib.*

Tears such as Angels weep, burst forth. *Ib.*

For who can yet believe, though after loss,
That all these puissant Legions, whose exile
Hath emptied Heav'n, shall fail to re-ascend
Self-rais'd, and repossess their native seat? *Ib.*

    . . . who overcomes
By force, hath overcome but half his foe. *Ib.*

Space may produce new Worlds. *Ib.*

To Noon he fell, from Noon to dewy Eve,
A Summer's day; and with the setting Sun
Dropt from the Zenith like a falling Star. *Ib.*

   Where there is then no good
For which to strive, no strife can grow up there
From Faction. *Ib.* 2

His trust was with th' Eternal to be deem'd
Equal in strength, and rather then be less
Car'd not to be at all. *Ib.*

[Belial] . . . his Tongue
Dropt Manna, and could make the worse appear
The better reason. *Ib.*

I should be much for open War, O Peers,
As not behind in hate. *Ib.*

To be no more; sad cure; for who would loose,
Though full of pain, this intellectual being,
Those thoughts that wander through Eternity. *Ib.*

Thus Belial with words cloth'd in reason's garb
Counsel'd ignoble ease, and peaceful sloth. *Ib.*

. . . preferring
Hard liberty before the easy yoke
Of servile Pomp. *Ib.*

Advise if this be worth
Attempting, or to sit in darkness here
Hatching vain Empires. *Ib.*

But first whom shall we send
In search of this new World, whom shall we find
Sufficient? who shall tempt with wandering feet
The dark unbottom'd infinite Abyss? *Ib.*

O shame to men! Devil with Devil damn'd
Firm concord holds: men only disagree
Of Creatures rational, though under hope
Of heavenly Grace; and God proclaiming peace,
Yet live in hatred, emnity, and strife
Among themselves, and levy cruel wars,
Wasting the Earth, each other to destroy. *Ib.*

I fled, and cry'd out Death;
Hell trembl'd at the hideous Name, and sigh'd
From all her Caves, and back resounded Death.
Ib.

Confusion worse confounded. *Ib.*

Which way I fly is Hell; myself am Hell. *Ib.* 4

Imparadis'd in one another's arms. · *Ib.*

With thee conversing I forget all time. *Ib.*

But what if better counsels might erect
Our minds and teach us to cast off this Yoke?
Will ye submit your necks, and choose to bend
The supple knee? *Ib.* 5

Headlong themselves they threw
Down from the verge of Heav'n, eternal wrath
Burnt after them to the bottomless pit. *Ib.* 6

That Man may know he dwells not in his own;
An Edifice too large for him to fill,
Lodg'd in a small partition, and the rest
Ordain'd for uses to his Lord best known. *Ib.* 8

... the sum of earthly bliss. *Ib.*

        ... nothing lovelier can be found
In woman, then to study houshold good,
And good works in her Husband to promote.
Ib. 9

On all sides, from innumerable tongues
A dismal universal hiss, the sound
Of public scorn. *Ib.* 10

The World was all before them, where to choose
Their place of rest, and Providence their guide:
They hand in hand with wand'ring steps and slow,
Through Eden took their solitary way.   *Ib.* 12

I who ere while the happy Garden sung,
By one man's disobedience lost, now sing
Recover'd Paradise to all mankind.
                    Paradise Regained, 1

Women, when nothing else, beguil'd the heart
Of wisest Solomon, and made him build,
And made him bow to the Gods of his Wives.
                                    Ib. 2

Riches are needless then, both for themselves,
And for thy reason why they should be sought,
To gain a Sceptre, oftest better miss'd. *Ib.*

They err who count it glorious to subdue
By Conquest far and wide, to over-run
Large Countries, and in field great Battles win.
                                    Ib. 3

            The childhood shews the man,
As morning shews the day. *Ib.* 4

The first and wisest of them all profess'd
To know this only, that he nothing knew. *Ib.*

Ask for this great Deliverer now, and find him
Eyeless in Gaza, at the Mill with slaves.
                            Samson Agonistes

O impotence of mind, in body strong!
But what is strength without a double share
Of wisdom. *Ib.*

O dark, dark, dark, amid the blaze of noon,
Irrecoverably dark, total Eclipse
Without all hope of day! *Ib.*

For him I reckon not in high estate
Whom long descent of birth
Or the sphere of fortune raises. *Ib.*

       . . . that grounded maxim
So rife and celebrated in the mouths
Of wisest men; that to the public good
Private respects must yield. *Ib.*

Oh how comely it is and how reviving
To the Spirits of just men long oppres'd!
When God into the hands of their deliverer
Puts invincible might
To quell the mighty of the Earth. *Ib.*

And calm of mind all passion spent. *Ib.*

But headlong joy is ever on the wing,
In Wintry solstice like the shortn'd light
Soon swallow'd up in dark and long out-living
    night. *The Passion*

Now the bright morning Star, Day's harbinger,
Comes dancing from the East, and leads with her
The Flow'ry May   *Song on May Morning*

Time, the subtle thief of youth. *Sonnets,* 7

Licence they mean when they cry liberty. *Ib.* 12

Avenge, O Lord, thy slaughtered Saints, whose
    bones

Lie scattered on the Alpine mountains cold;
Ev'n them who kept thy truth so pure of old,
When all our Father's worshipped Stocks and
  Stones.
Ib. 15. *On the late Massacre at Piedmont*

When I consider how my light is spent,
E're half my days, in this dark world and wide,
And that one Talent which is death to hide,
Lodg'd with me useless. *Ib.* 16. *On His Blindness*

Thousands at his bidding speed
And post or'e Land and Ocean without rest:
They also serve who only stand and wait.   *Ib.*

New Presbyter is but Old Priest writ Large. *Ib. On
the New Forcers of Conscience under the Long
Parliament*

For what can War, but endless war still breed?
                          Ib. On Fairfax

In vain doth Valour bleed
While Avarice, and Rapine share the land.   *Ib.*

. . . peace hath her victories
No less renowned than war. *Ib. To Cromwell*

Help us to save free Conscience from the paw
Of hireling wolves whose Gospel is their maw.
                                              Ib.

I cannot praise a fugitive and cloistered virtue,
unexercised and unbreathed, that never sallies
out and sees her adversary, but slinks out of the
race where that immortal garland is to be run for,
not without dust and heat. *Areopagitica*
310

Though all the winds of doctrine were let loose to play upon the earth, so Truth be in the field, we do injuriously, by licensing and prohibiting to misdoubt her strength. *Ib.*

... the right path of a virtuous and noble Education, laborious indeed at the first ascent, but else so smooth, so green, so full of goodly prospect, and melodious sounds on every side, that the harp of Orpheus was not more charming. *On Education*

Mitford, Mary Russell   1787-1855

I have discovered that our great favourite, Miss Austen, is my country-woman ... with whom mamma before her marriage was acquainted. Mamma says that she was then the prettiest, silliest, most affected, husband-hunting butterfly she ever remembers. *Letter to Sir William Elford,* 1815

Molière (Jean Baptiste Poquelin)   1622-1673

Il faut manger pour vivre et non pas vivre pour manger. One should eat to live, not live to eat.
L'Avare, 3

Par ma foi! il y a plus de quarante ans que je dis de la prose sans que j'en susse rien. Good Heavens! For more than forty years I have been speaking prose without knowing it. *Le Bourgeois Gentilhomme,* 2

Mais qui rit d'autrui
Doit craindre qu'en revanche on rie aussi de lui. But the man who laughs at anyone must be afraid that in return the other also laughs at him. *L'Ecole des Femmes,* 1

Le mariage, Agnès, n'est pas un badinage.
Marriage, Agnes, is not a joke. *Ib.* 3

La beauté du visage est un frêle ornement,
Une fleur passagère, un éclat d'un moment,
Et qui n'est attaché qu' à la simple epiderme.
Beauty of face is a frail ornament, a passing flower,
a momentary brightness belonging only to the
skin. *Les Femmes Savantes,* 3

Oui, cela était autrefois ainsi, mais nous avons
changé tout cela. Yes, it used to be so, but we
have changed all that. *Le Médecin Malgré Lui,* 2

On est aisément dupé par ce qu 'on aime. One is
easily deceived by what one loves. *Le Tartuffe,* 4

L'homme est, je vous l'avoue, un méchant animal.
Man, I can assure you, is a wicked creature. *Ib.* 5

L'utilité de vivre n'est pas en l'espace, elle est en
l'usage. The value of life is not the end of it, but
the use we make of it. *Essais,* 1, 20

Il se faut réserver une arrière boutique ... en laquelle
nous établissons notre vraie liberté. We must
keep a little back shop ... where we may establish
our own true liberty. *Ib.* 39

Pour juger des choses grandes et hautes, il faut une
âme de même. To judge great and lofty matters,
a man must have such a soul. *Ib.* 42

Mon métier et mon art, c'est vivre. To know how
to live is all my calling and all my art. *Ib.* 2, 6

Montesquieu, Charles de Secondat, Baron de
1689-1755

*Les Anglais sont occupés; ils n'ont pas le temps
d'être polis.* The English are busy; they do not
have time to be polite. *Pensées Diverses*

Montgomery, Bernard Law, Viscount of El Alamein
b. 1887

Anyone who votes Labour ought to be locked up.
Speech at Woodford, Oct., 1959

Montrose, James Graham, Marquis of 1612-1650

He either fears his fate too much,
    Or his deserts are small,
That dare not put it to the touch,
    To win or lose it all. *My Dear and Only Love*

Moore, Edward 1712-1757

This is adding insult to injuries. *The Foundling,* 5

Moore, George 1852-1933

All reformers are bachelors. *The Bending of the
Bough,* 1

Art must be parochial in the beginning to be
cosmopolitan in the end. *Hail and Farewell*

The lot of critics is to be remembered by what
they failed to understand. *Impressions and
Opinions*

Moore, Thomas 1779-1852

Yet, who can help loving the land that has taught
us
Six hundred and eighty-five ways to dress eggs?
The Fudge Family in Paris

You may break, you may shatter the vase, if you will,
But the scent of the roses will hang round it still.
Irish Melodies. Farewell! But Whenever

That prophet ill sustains his holy call
Who finds not heav'ns to suit the tastes of all.
Lalla Rookh. The Veiled Prophet

Mordaunt, Thomas Osbert   1730-1809

Sound, sound the clarion, fill the fife,
Throughout the sensual world proclaim,
One crowded hour of glorious life
Is worth an age without a name.   *The Bee*

More, Hannah   1745-1833

He lik'd those literary cooks
Who skim the cream of others' books;
And ruin half an author's graces
By plucking bon-mots from their places.
Daniel

More, Sir Thomas   1478-1535

Your sheep, that were wont to be so meek and tame, and so small eaters, now, as I hear say, be become so great devourers, and so wild, that they eat up and swallow down the very men themselves. *Utopia*, 1

Morell, Thomas   1703-1784

See, the conquering hero comes!
Sound the trumpets, beat the drums! *Joshua*

Morgan, Charles   1894-1958

One cannot shut one's eyes to things not seen with eyes. *The River Line*, 3

Morgan, Augustus de   **1806-1871**

Great fleas have little fleas upon their backs to
bite 'em.
And little fleas have lesser fleas, and so *ad infinitum*.
A Budget of Paradoxes

Morris, William   **1834-1896**

Dreamer of dreams, born out of my due time,
Why should I strive to set the crooked straight?
The Earthly Paradise. An Apology

The majesty
That from man's soul looks through his eager
eyes. *Life and Death of Jason*

All their devices for cheapening labour simply
resulted in increasing the burden of labour.
News from Nowhere

Motteux, Peter Anthony   **1660-1718**

The devil was sick, the devil a monk would be;
The devil was well, and the devil a monk he'd be.
Gargantua and Pantagruel. Translation of Rabelais

Munro, Hector Hugh   **1870-1916**

See SAKI, page 353.

Nash, Ogden   **1902-1971**

If I could but spot a conclusion, I should race to
it. *All, All Are Gone*

I am a conscientious man, when I throw rocks
at seabirds I leave no tern unstoned. *Everybody's
Mind to Me a Kingdom Is*

You two can be what you like, but since I am
the big fromage in this family, I prefer to think
of myself as the Gorgon Zola. *Medusa and the
Mot Juste*

Any kiddie in school can love like a fool,
But hating, my boy, is an art.
Plea for Less Malice Toward None

Candy Is dandy
But liquor Is quicker. *Reflection on Ice-Breaking*

Nelson, Viscount Horatio   1758-1805

Westminster Abbey or victory. *Remark at the
Battle of Cape St. Vincent*

I have only one eye—I have a right to be blind
sometimes: . . . I really do not see the signal. *Ib.
Battle of Copenhagen*

England expects every man will do his duty. *Ib.
Battle of Trafalgar*

Thank God, I have done my duty. *Ib.*

Kiss me, Hardy. *Ib.*

Nero   A.D. 37-68

Qualis artifex pereo! What an artist dies with
me! *Attrib.*

Newton, Isaac   1642-1727

I do not know what I may appear to the world,
but to myself I seem to have been only a boy
playing on the seashore, and diverting myself in
now and then finding a smoother pebble or a

prettier shell than ordinary, whilst the great ocean of truth lay all undiscovered before me.
Memoirs of Newton, Brewster

If I have done the public any service, it is due to patient thought. *Letter to Dr. Bentley*

Nicholas I, Emperor of Russia   1796-1855

Russia has two generals in whom she can confide —Generals Janvier and Février. *Punch*, 1853

Nietzsche, Friedrich Wilhelm   1844-1900

Ich lehre euch den Übermenschen. Der Mensch ist etwas, das überwunden werden soll. I teach you the superman. Man is something to be surpassed.
Thus Spake Zarathustra

North, Christopher (John Wilson)   1785-1854

Minds like ours, my dear James, must always be above national prejudices, and in all companies it gives me true pleasure to declare, that, as a people, the English are very little indeed inferior to the Scotch. *Noctes Ambrosianae*, 9

Laws were made to be broken. *Ib.*, 24

Noyes, Alfred   1880-1958

And you shall wander hand in hand with love in summer's wonderland;
Go down to Kew in lilac-time (it isn't far from London!) *Barrel Organ*

The wind was a torrent of darkness among the gusty trees,
The moon was a ghostly galleon tossed upon cloudy seas. *The Highwayman*

Numbers, Book of

The Lord bless thee, and keep thee:
The Lord make his face shine upon thee, and be
  gracious unto thee:
The Lord lift up his countenance upon thee, and
give thee peace.   6, 24-26

Be sure your sin will find you out.   32, 23

Nursery Rhymes

As I was going to St. Ives. *Harley MS.*, c. 1730

Baa, Baa, Black Sheep. *Tommy Thumb's Pretty
Song Book*, c. 1744

Bye, Baby Bunting. *Gammer Gurton's Garland*,
1784

Cock a Doodle Doo! *Quoted in " The Most
Cruel and Bloody Murder Committed by an Inn-
keeper's Wife,"* 1606

Curly Locks. *Infant Institutes*, 1797

Ding, Dong, Bell. *Mother Goose's Melody*,
c. 1765

Georgie Porgie. *Nursery Rhymes, ed. J. O.
Halliwell*, 1842

Goosey Goosey Gander. *Gammer Gurton's
Garland*, 1784

Hey Diddle Diddle. *Mother Goose's Melody*,
c. 1765

Hickory, Dickory, Dock. *Tommy Thumb's Pretty Song Book*, c. 1744

Humpty Dumpty. *From the addition to a copy of Mother Goose's Melody*, c. 1803

I Had a Little Nut-tree. *Newest Christmas Box*, c. 1797

Jack and Jill. *Mother Goose's Melody*, c. 1765

Jack Sprat. *Paroemiologia Anglo-Latina*, John Clarke, 1639

Little Bo-Peep. *Douce MS.*, c. 1805

Little Boy Blue. *The Famous Tommy Thumb's Little Story Book*, c. 1760

Little Jack Horner. *Quoted by* Henry Carey, *Namby Pamby*, c. 1720

Little Polly Flinders. *Original Ditties for the Nursery*, c. 1805

Mary, Mary, Quite Contrary. *Tommy Thumb's Pretty Song Book*, c. 1744

Old King Cole. *Quoted by* William King, *Useful Translations in Philosophy*, 1708-1709

Old Mother Hubbard. *The Comic Adventures of Old Mother Hubbard*, 1805, Sarah Catherine Martin.

One, Two, Buckle My Shoe. *Songs for the Nursery*, 1805

Oranges and Lemons. *Tommy Thumb's Pretty Song Book*, c. 1744

Peter Piper. *Peter Piper's Practical Principles of Plain and Perfect Pronunciation*, 1819

Pussy Cat, Pussy Cat, Where Have you Been?
Songs for the Nursery, 1805

Simple Simon. *Simple Simon* (a chapbook advertisement, 1764)

Sing a Song of Sixpence. *Tommy Thumb's Pretty Song Book*, c. 1744

Solomon Grundy. *Nursery Rhymes, ed.* J. O. Halliwell, 1842

There Was an Old Woman Who Lived in a Shoe. *Gammer Gurton's Garland*, 1784

Thirty days hath September,
April, June, and November;
All the rest have thirty-one,
Excepting February alone,
And that has twenty-eight days clear
And twenty-nine in each leap year.
Stevins MS., c. 1555

Three Blind Mice. *Deuteromelia*, Thomas Ravenscroft, 1609

Tom, the Piper's Son. c. 1795

Twinkle, Twinkle, Little Star. *The Way to be Happy*, Jane Taylor (1783-1827)

21

Wee Willie Winkie
Runs through the town. *Willie Winkie*, William
Miller (1810-1872)

What Are Little Boys Made of? *Nursery Rhymes,
ed.* J. O. Halliwell, 1844

Who Killed Cock Robin? *Tommy Thumb's Pretty
Song Book*, c. 1744

Wynken, Blynken, and Nod. Eugene Field (1850-
1895)

O'Casey, Sean   1884-1964

" I am going where life is more like life than it
is here." *Cock-a-Doodle Dandy*, 3

Th' whole worl's . . . in a terr . . . ible state o' . . .
chassis! *Juno and the Paycock*, 1

Orczy, Baroness   1864-1947

We seek him here, we seek him there,
Those Frenchies seek him everywhere.
Is he in heaven?—Is he in hell?
That demmed, elusive Pimpernel?
                                    The Scarlet Pimpernel, 12

Orwell, George (Eric Blair)   1903-1950

All animals are equal, but some animals are
more equal than others. *Animal Farm*, 10

England is not the jewelled isle of Shakespeare's
much-quoted passage, nor is it the inferno depicted
by Dr. Goebbels. More than either it resembles
a family, a rather stuffy Victorian family, with not
many black sheep in it but with all its cupboards

bursting with skeletons. It has rich relations who have to be kow-towed to and poor relations who are horribly sat upon, and there is a deep conspiracy about the source of the family income. It is a family in which the young are generally thwarted and most of the power is in the hands of irresponsible uncles and bedridden aunts. Still, it is a family. *England, Your England*

. . . a cult of cheeriness and manliness, beer and cricket, briar pipes and monogamy, and it was at all times possible to earn a few guineas by writing an article denouncing "highbrows."
Inside the Whale

Osborne, John   b. 1929

Do the Sunday papers make *you* feel ignorant?
Look Back in Anger, 1

How I long for a little ordinary human enthusiasm. Vast enthusiasm—that's all. I want to hear a warm, thrilling voice cry out Hallelujah! Hallelujah! I'm alive! *Ib.*

I keep looking back, as far as I can remember, and I can't think what it was like to feel young, really young. *Ib.*

There aren't any good, brave causes left. If the big bang does come, and we all get killed off, it won't be in aid of the old-fashioned, gr and design. It'll just be for the Brave New-nothing-very-much-thank-you. *Ib.* 3

The injustice of it is almost perfect! The wrong people going hungry, the wrong people being loved, the wrong people dying. *Ib.*

The heaviest, strongest creatures in this world seem to be the loneliest. *Ib.*

Ovid, Publius O. Naso   43 B.C.-A.D. 18

Delectant etiam castas praeconia formae;
Virginibus curae grataque forma sua est.
Even honest girls like to hear their beauty praised; even the innocent are worried and pleased by their looks. *Ars Amatoria*, 1

Quae dant, quaeque negant, gaudent tamen esse rogatae. Whether they give or refuse, women are glad to have been asked. *Ib.*

Virginibus cordi grataque forma suaest. Dear to girls' hearts is their own beauty. *De Medicamine Faciei*

Iam seges est ubi Troia fuit. There is now a cornfield where Troy once was. *Heroides*, 1

Tempus edax rerum. Time the devourer of all things. *Metamorphoses*, 15

Owen, John   c. 1560-1622

Tempora mutantur nos et mutamur in illis. The times are changing, and we are changing in them.
Epigrams (cf. p. 22)

Owen, Roderic   b. 1921

The important thing is to know when to laugh, or since laughing is somewhat undignified, to smile. But the smile must be of the right kind; and the right kind must have understanding in it, and friendliness, and a good deal of patience.
The Golden Bubble

Page, William Tyler   1868-1942

I believe in the United States of America as a government of the people, by the people, for the people; whose just powers are derived from the consent of the governed; a democracy in a republic; a sovereign nation of many sovereign states; a perfect union, one and inseparable; established upon those principles of freedom, equality, justice and humanity for which American patriots sacrificed their lives and fortunes. I therefore believe it is my duty to my country to love it, to support its constitution, to obey its laws, to respect its flag, and to defend it against all enemies. *The American's Creed*

Paine, Thomas   1737-1809

The sublime and the ridiculous are often so nearly related, that it is difficult to class them separately.
Age of Reason, 2

Government, even in its best state, is but a necessary evil; in its worst state, an intolerable one. *Common Sense*, 1

[Of Burke] As he rose like a rocket, he fell like the stick. *Letter to His Addressers*, 1792

He pities the plumage, but forgets the dying bird.
Rights of Man

Palmerston, Henry John Temple, Viscount   1784-1865

Die, my dear Doctor, that's the last thing I shall do! *Attrib. last words*

Parkman, Francis　　　　　　　　　　**1823-1893**

The public demands elocution rather than reason of those who address it; something to excite the feelings and captivate the fancy rather than something to instruct the understanding. It rejoices in sweeping statements, confident assertions, bright lights and black shadows alternating with something funny. . . . On matters of the greatest interest it craves to be excited or amused. *The Tale of the " Ripe Scholar."*

To direct popular education, not to stuffing the mind with crude aggregations of imperfect knowledge, but rather to the development of its powers of observation, comparison, analysis, and reasoning, to strengthening and instructing its moral sense, and leading it to self-knowledge and consequent modesty. *Ib.*

Pascal, Blaise　　　　　　　　　　**1623-1662**

Je n'ai fait celle-ci plus longue que parceque je n'ai pas eu le loisir de la faire plus courte. I have only made this letter longer because I have not had time to make it shorter. *Lettres Provinciales*

Le nez de Cléopâtre: s'il eût été plus court, toute la face de la terre aurait changé. If Cleopatra's nose had been shorter the whole history of the world would have been different. *Pensées 2, 162*

Le cœur a ses raisons que la raison ne connaît point. The heart has its reasons which the mind knows nothing of. *Ib. 4, 277*

Peacock, Thomas Love   1785-1866

Respectable means rich, and decent means poor.
I should die if I heard my family called decent.
Crotchet Castle, 3

I almost think it is the ultimate destiny of science
to exterminate the human race. *Gryll Grange*

If ifs and ands were pots and pans
There'd be no work for the tinkers. *Manley*

Pemberton, Max   1863-1950

A negro preacher having vainly attempted to
collect money from a peripatetic flock, thanked
God that he had got his hat back. *Attrib.*

Pepys, Samuel   1633-1703

And so to bed. *Diary*, 1660

A good, honest and painful sermon. *Ib.* 1661

But it is pretty to see what money will do. *Ib.* 1667

Persius Flaccus, Aulus   A.D. 34-62

Nec te quaesiveris extra. Ask no opinion but your
own. *Satires* 1, 7

Pétain, Marshal Henri Phillipe   1856-1951

Ils ne passeront pas. They shall not pass.
Verdun, 1916

Petronius   d. c. A.D. 66

Cave canem. Beware of the dog. *Satyricon*

Scimus te prae litteras fatuum esse. We know that you are mad with much learning. *Ib.*

Curiosa felicitas. A painstaking facility (of style). *Ib.*

Litteratum esse, quos odisse divites solent. A man of letters, of the kind that rich men hate. *Ib.*

Philippians, The Epistle of Paul to the

The peace of God which passeth all understanding. 4, 7

Whatsoever things are true, whatsoever things are honest, whatsoever things are just, whatsoever things are pure, whatsoever things are lovely, whatsoever things are of good report; if there be any virtue, and if there be any praise, think on these things. 4, 8

I can do all things through Christ which strengtheneth me. 4, 13

Phillips, Stephen   1864-1915

A man not old, but mellow, like good wine.
Ulysses, 3

Phillips, Wendell   1811-1884

Every man meets his Waterloo at last.
Lecture, 1859

Pinero, Sir Arthur Wing   1855-1934

While there's tea there's hope. *The Second Mrs. Tanqueray,* 1

From forty to fifty a man is at heart either a stoic or a satyr. *Ib.*

Pitt, William, Earl of Chatham   1708-1778

The atrocious crime of being a young man . . . I shall neither attempt to palliate nor deny. *Speech, House of Commons*, 1741

Pitt, William   1759-1806

Necessity is the plea for every infringement of human freedom. It is the argument of tyrants; it is the creed of slaves. *Speech*, 1783

England has saved herself by her exertions, and will, as I trust, save Europe by her example. *Ib.* 1805

Plato   c. 429-347 B.C.

That man is wisest who, like Socrates, realises that his wisdom is worthless. *Apologia of Socrates*

Man was not born for himself but for his country. *Epistles*, 9

Time brings everything. *Greek Anthology*, 9

Through obedience learn to command. *Leges*

The good is the beautiful. *Lysis*

Poets utter great and wise things which they do not themselves understand. *Republic*, 2

The rulers of the State are the only ones who should have the privilege of lying, either at home or abroad; they may be allowed to lie for the good of the State. *Ib.* 3

Our object in the construction of the state is the greatest happiness of the whole, and not that of any one class. *Ib.* 4

Nothing in the affairs of men is worthy of great anxiety. *Ib.* 10

Every king springs from a race of slaves, and every slave has had kings among his ancestors.
Thæstetus

Pliny, Caius P. Secundus 23-79

Ex Africa semper aliquid novi. There is always something new out of Africa. *Derived from Historia Naturalis, 2, 8*

In vino veritas. Truth in wine. *Ib.* 14

Ne supra crepidam sutor iudicaret. The cobbler should not judge beyond his last. *Ib.* 35

Plautus, Titus Maccius c. 254-184 B.C.

Miles gloriosus. The boastful soldier. *Title*

Tetigisti acu. You have hit the nail on the head. (Lit. You have touched it with a needle.) *Rudens*

Plutarch c. 46-120

A traveller at Sparta, standing long upon one leg, said to a Lacedaemonian. "I do not believe you can do as much." "True," said he, "but every goose can." *Laconic Apothegms*

Alexander wept when he heard from Anaxarchus that there was an infinite number of worlds . . . he said: "Do you not think it lamentable that

with such a vast multitude of worlds, we have
not yet conquered one?" *On the Tranquillity of
the Mind*

It is indeed desirable to be well descended, but
the glory belongs to our ancestors. *On the
Training of Children*

Poe, Edgar Allan   1809-1849

But we loved with a love which was more than
love—
I and my Annabel Lee. *Annabel Lee*

The play is the tragedy, " Man,"
And its hero the Conqueror Worm.
                          The Conqueror Worm

The fever call'd " Living "
Is conquered at last.   *For Annie*

The glory that was Greece
And the grandeur that was Rome.   *To Helen*

Pompadour, Madame de   1721-1764

Après nous le déluge. After us the flood. *Remark
after Battle of Rossbach,* 1757

Pope, Alexander   1688-1744

Maggots half-form'd in rhyme exactly meet,
And learn to crawl upon poetic feet. *Dunciad,* 1

While pensive Poets painful vigils keep,
Sleepless themselves, to give their readers sleep.
                                            Ib.

Some Daemon stole my pen (forgive th' offence)
And once betray'd me into common sense. *Ib.*

And cackling save the monarchy of Tories. *Ib.*

Stretch'd on the rack of a too easy chair. *Ib.* 4

Is it, in heav'n, a crime to love too well?
Elegy to the Memory of an Unfortunate Lady

The world forgetting, by the world forgot. *Eloisa
to Abelard*

'Tis with our judgements as our watches, none
Go just alike, yet each believes his own.
Essay on Criticism

Let such teach others who themselves excel,
And censure freely who have written well. *Ib.*

Some have at first for Wits then Poets past,
Turn'd Critics next, and prov'd plain fools at last.
Ib.

A *little learning* is a dang'rous thing;
Drink deep, or taste not the Pierian spring:
There shallow draughts intoxicate the brain,
And drinking largely sobers us again. *Ib.*

True Wit is Nature to advantage dress'd,
What oft was thought, but ne'er so well express'd.
Ib.

True ease in writing comes from art, not chance.
Ib.

Fondly we think we honour merit then,
When we but praise ourselves in other men. *Ib.*

Good-nature and good-sense must ever join;
To err is human, to forgive, divine. *Ib.*

For Fools rush in where Angels fear to tread. *Ib.*

And the same age saw Learning fall, and Rome.
Ib.

Then say not Man's imperfect, Heav'n in fault;
Say rather, Man's as perfect as he ought.
Essay on Man, 1

Who sees with equal eye as God of all,
A hero perish or a sparrow fall,
Atoms or systems into ruin hurl'd,
And now a bubble burst, and now a world. *Ib.*

Hope springs eternal in the human breast:
Man never is, but always to be blest. *Ib.*

Men would be Angels, Angels would be Gods,
Aspiring to be Gods, if Angels fell,
Aspiring to be Angels, Men rebel. *Ib.*

Say what the use, were finer optics giv'n,
T' inspect a mite, nor comprehend the heav'n? *Ib.*

Know then thyself, presume not God to scan;
The proper study of Mankind is Man. *Ib.* 2

Nor God alone in the still calm we find,
He mounts the storm, and walks upon the wind.
Ib.

Pleasures are ever in our hands or eyes. *Ib.*

For Forms of Government let fools contest;
Whate'er is best administer'd is best:
For Modes of Faith let graceless zealots fight;
His can't be wrong whose life is in the right. *Ib.* 3

Thus God and Nature link'd the gen'ral frame,
And bade Self-love and Social be the same. *Ib*

Go, like the Indian, in another life
Expect thy dog, thy bottle, and thy wife. *Ib. 4*

A Wit's a feather, and a Chief a rod;
An honest Man's the noblest work of God. *Ib.*

See Cromwell, damn'd to everlasting fame! *Ib.*

Thou wert my guide, philosopher, and friend. *Ib.*

And all our Knowledge is, ourselves to know. *Ib.*

Damn with faint praise, assent with civil leer,
And without sneering, teach the rest to sneer;
Willing to wound, and yet afraid to strike,
Just hint a fault, and hesitate dislike.
                    Imitations of Horace, prologue

Learn to live well, or fairly make your will;
You've play'd and lov'd, and ate and drank, your
    fill.
Walk sober off, before a sprightlier age
Comes tittering on, and shoves you from the
    stage. *Ib. Epistles*, 2

All Manners take a tincture from our own;
Or come discolour'd thro' our Passions shown.
                    Moral Essays, 1

Chaste to her Husband, frank to all beside,
A teeming Mistress, but a barren Bride. *Ib. 2*

Virtue she finds too painful an endeavour,
Content to dwell in Decencies for ever. *Ib.*

Men, some to Bus'ness, some to Pleasure take;
But every Woman is at heart a Rake:
Men, some to Quiet, some to public Strife;
But ev'ry Lady would be Queen for life. *Ib.*

But thousands die, without or this or that,
Die, and endow a College, or a Cat. *Ib.* 3

The ruling Passion, be it what it will,
The ruling Passion conquers Reason still.   *Ib.*

Where'er you walk, cool gales shall fan the glade.
                              Pastorals. Summer

Fame is at best an unperforming cheat;
But 'tis substantial happiness, *to eat.*
                    Prologue for Mr. D'Urfey's Last Play

What dire offence from am'rous causes springs,
What mighty contests rise from trivial things,
I sing. *The Rape of the Lock,* 1

Favours to none, to all she smiles extends;
Oft she rejects, but never once offends. *Ib.* 2

If to her share some female errors fall,
Look on her face, and you'll forget 'em all. *Ib.*

Or stain her honour or her new brocade;
Forget her pray'rs, or miss a masquerade;
Or lose her heart, or necklace, at a ball. *Ib.*

Here thou, great Anna! whom three realms obey,
Dost sometimes counsel take—and sometimes
   Tea. *Ib.* 3

Not louder shrieks to pitying heav'n are cast,
When husbands, or when lap-dogs breathe their
   last. *Ib.*

Beauties in vain their pretty eyes may roll;
Charms strike the sight, but merit wins the soul.
Ib. 5

Then teach me Heav'n! to scorn the guilty bays;
Drive from my breast that wretched lust of praise;
Unblemish'd let me live, or die unknown:
Oh, grant an honest Fame, or grant me none!
The Temple of Fame

And seas but join the regions they divide.
Windsor Forest

" Blessed is the man who expects nothing, for he
shall never be disappointed," was the ninth
beatitude which a man of wit (who like a man of
wit was a long time in gaol) added to the eighth.
Letter, 1725

Pound, Ezra Loomis   b. 1885

Winter is icumen in,
Lhude sing Goddamn,
Raineth drop and staineth slop
And how the wind doth ramm!
Sing: Goddamn. *Ancient Music* (cf. p. 22)

As a bathtub lined with white porcelain,
When the hot water gives out or goes tepid,
So is the slow cooling of our chivalrous passion,
O my much praised but-not-altogether-satisfactory
    lady. *The Bath Tub*

Bah! I have sung women in three cities,
But it is all the same;
And I will sing of the sun. *Cino*

335

O how hideous it is
To see three generations of one house gathered
    together!
It is like an old tree with shoots,
And with some branches rotted and falling.
                                            Commission

            Nay, whatever comes
One hour was sunlit and the most high gods
May not make boast of any better thing
Than to have watched that hour as it passed.
                                            Erat Hora

    Free us for we perish
In this ever-flowing monotony
Of ugly print marks, black
Upon white parchment. *The Eyes*

Come, let us pity those who are better off than
    we are.
Come, my friend, and remember
        that the rich have butlers and no friends,
And we have friends and no butlers.
Come, let us pity the married and unmarried.
                                            The Garret

When I carefully consider the curious habits of
    dogs
I am compelled to conclude
That man is the superior animal.
When I consider the curious habits of man
I confess, my friend, I am puzzled.   *Meditatio*

So many thousand fair are gone down to Avernus,
Ye might let one remain above with us.
                                Prayer for his Lady's Life

336

O generation of the thoroughly smug and
  thoroughly uncomfortable. *Salutation*

Come, my songs, let us speak of perfection—
We shall get ourselves rather disliked.
                                         Salvationists

Will people accept them?
  (i.e. these songs).
As a timorous wench from a centaur
  (or a centurion),
Already they flee, howling in terror. *Tenzone*

Wining the ghosts of yester-year. *Villonaud for
  this Yule*

Preston, Keith   **1884-1927**

[Of democracy] An institution in which the whole
is equal to the scum of all the parts. *Pot Shots
from Pegasus*

Propertius, Sextus Aurelius   **fl. 50 B.C.**

Magnum iter ascendo, sed dat mihi gloria vires.
The road is hard to climb, but glory gives me
strength. *Elegies, 4*

Proudhon, Pierre-Joseph   **1809-1865**

If I were asked to answer the following question:
" What is slavery?" and I should answer in one
word, " Murder! " my meaning would be understood at once. No further argument would be
required to show that the power to take from a
man his thought, his will, his personality, is a
power of life and death, and that to enslave a man
is to kill him. Why, then, to this other question:
" What is property? " may I not likewise answer
" Theft "? *Qu'est-ce que la Propriété?*

337

Proverbs, The

Her ways are ways of pleasantness, and all her paths are peace. 3, 17

The path of the just is as the shining light that shineth more and more unto the perfect day.
4, 18

As an ox goeth to the slaughter, 7, 22

Stolen waters are sweet, 9, 17

Hope deferred maketh the heart sick. 13, 12

He that spareth his rod hateth his son. 13, 24

Pride goeth before destruction, and an haughty spirit before a fall. 16, 18

Train up a child in the way he should go: and when he is old he will not depart from it. 22, 6

Heap coals of fire upon his head. 25, 22

Answer a fool according to his folly. 26, 5

Her children arise up and call her blessed. 31, 28

Psalms, Book of

The Lord is my rock, and my fortress, and my deliverer; my God, my strength, in whom I will trust. 18, 2

The Lord is my shepherd; I shall not want.
He maketh me to lie down in green pastures:
he leadeth me beside the still waters.
He restoreth my soul: he leadeth me in the paths
of righteousness for his name's sake.
Yea, though I walk through the valley of the
shadow of death, I will fear no evil: for thou art
with me; thy rod and thy staff they comfort me.
Thou preparest a table before me in the presence
of mine enemies: thou anointest my head with
oil: my cup runneth over.
Surely goodness and mercy shall follow me all
the days of my life: and I will dwell in the house
of the Lord for ever. 23, 1-6

The earth is the Lord's, and the fulness thereof;
the world, and they that dwell therein. 24, 1

I waited patiently for the Lord; and he inclined
unto me, and heard my cry. 40, 1

God is our refuge and strength, a very present
help in trouble.
Therefore will not we fear, though the earth be
removed, and though the mountains be carried
into the midst of the sea. 46, 1-2

O God, thou art my God; early will I seek thee:
my soul thirsteth for thee, my flesh longeth for
thee in a dry and thirsty land, where no water is.
63, 1

How amiable are thy tabernacles, O Lord of
hosts!
My soul longeth, yea, even fainteth for the courts
of the Lord: my heart and my flesh crieth out
for the living God.
Yea, the sparrow hath found an house, and the

swallow a nest for herself, where she may lay her
young, even thine altars, O Lord of hosts, my
King, and my God.
Blessed are they that dwell in thy house: they
will be still praising thee. 84, 1-4

It is a good thing to give thanks unto the Lord,
and to sing praises unto thy name, O most High;
To shew forth thy loving kindness in the morning,
and thy faithfulness every night,
Upon an instrument of ten strings, and upon the
psaltery; upon the harp with a solemn sound.
92, 1-3

O come, let us sing unto the Lord; let us make a
joyful noise to the rock of our salvation.
Let us come before his presence with thanksgiving,
and make a joyful noise unto him with psalms.
For the Lord is a great God, and a great King
above all gods.
In his hand are the deep places of the earth: the
strength of the hills is his also.
The sea is his, and he made it: and his hands
formed the dry land.
O come, let us worship and bow down: let us
kneel before the Lord our maker. 95, 1-6

O sing unto the Lord a new song: sing unto the
Lord, all the earth.
Sing unto the Lord, bless his name; shew forth
his salvation from day to day.
Declare his glory among the heathen, his wonders
among all people.
For the Lord is great, and greatly to be praised:
he is to be feared above all gods. 96, 1-4

Bless the Lord, O my soul: and all that is within
me, bless his holy name. 103, 1

Thy word is a lamp unto my feet, and a light unto my path. 119, 105

I will lift up mine eyes unto the hills, from whence cometh my help.
My help cometh from the Lord, which made heaven and earth.
He will not suffer thy foot to be moved: he that keepeth thee will not slumber. 121, 1-3

The Lord shall preserve thee from all evil: he shall preserve thy soul.
The Lord shall preserve thy going out and thy coming in from this time forth, and even for evermore. *Ib.* 7-8

I was glad when they said unto me, Let us go into the house of the Lord. 122, 1

Except the Lord build the house, they labour in vain that build it: except the Lord keep the city, the watchman waketh but in vain. 127, 1

Lord, I cry unto thee: make haste unto me; give ear unto my voice, when I cry unto thee.
141, 1

Praise ye the Lord. Praise the Lord, O my soul. While I live will I praise the Lord: I will sing praises unto my God while I have any being.
Put not your trust in princes, nor in the son of man, in whom there is no help. 146, 1-3

Punch

Advice to persons about to marry—" Don't! "
1845

What is better than presence of mind in a railway accident? Absence of body. 1849

Never do to-day what you can put off till to-morrow. 1849

Mun, a had na' been the-erre abune two hours when—*bang*—went saxpence!!! 1868

Go directly—see what she's doing, and tell her she mustn't. 1872

It's worse than wicked, my dear, it's vulgar. 1876

I'm afraid you've got a bad egg, Mr. Jones. Oh no, my Lord, I assure you! Parts of it are excellent! 1895

Putnam, Israel   1718-1790

Men, you are all marksmen—don't one of you fire until you see the whites of their eyes. *Bunker Hill*, 1775, *also attrib. to* William Prescott (1726-1795)

Quesnay, François   1694-1774

[Of government interference] *Laissez faire, laissez passer.* Leave it alone, and let it happen. *Attrib.*

Quiller-Couch, Sir Arthur   1863-1944

He that loves but half of Earth
Loves but half enough for me.   *The Comrade*

The lion is the beast to fight:
He leaps along the plain,
And if you run with all your might,
He runs with all his mane.   *Sage Counsel*

Rabelais, François   **c. 1494-1553**

L'appétit vient en mangeant. The appetite comes with eating. *Gargantua*

Tirez le rideau, la farce est jouée. Draw the curtain, the farce is played. *Attrib.*

Je m'en vais chercher un grand peut-être. I go to seek a great perhaps. *Attrib.*

Racine, Jean   **1639-1699**

Elle s'endormit du sommeil des justes. She slept the sleep of the just. *Abrégé de l'Histoire de Port Royal*

Elle flotte, elle hésite; en un mot, elle est femme. She wavers, she hesitates, in a word, she is a woman. *Athalie, 3*

Tel qui rit vendredi, dimanche pleurera. He who laughs on Friday will weep on Sunday. *Les Plaideurs, 1*

Raleigh, Sir Walter   **c. 1552-1618**

If all the world and love were young,
And truth in every shepherd's tongue,
These pretty pleasures might me move
To live with thee, and be my love.
The Nymph's Reply to the Shepherd

Give me my scallop-shell of quiet,
My staff of faith to walk upon,
My scrip of joy, immortal diet,
My bottle of salvation,
My gown of glory, hope's true gage,
And thus I'll make my pilgrimage.
The Passionate Man's Pilgrimage

Raleigh, Sir Walter A.   **1861-1922**

I wish I loved the Human Race;
I wish I loved its silly face;
I wish I liked the way it walks;
I wish I liked the way it talks;
And when I'm introduced to one,
I wish I thought *What Jolly Fun!*
Laughter From a Cloud. Wishes of an Elderly Man

Ramsay, Allan   **1686-1758**

Ane canna wive an' thrive baith in ae year. *Scots Proverbs*

A Scots mist will weet an Englishman to the skin.
                                                    Ib.

A woman's mind is like wind in a winter's night.
                                                    Ib.

Be aye the same thing as you wad be ca'd.   *Ib.*

Better a finger aff than aye wagging. *Ib.*

The Revelation of St. John the Divine

I am Alpha and Omega, the beginning and the ending, saith the Lord. 1, 8

I am he that liveth, and was dead; and behold, I am alive for evermore, Amen. 1, 18

I will not blot out his name out of the book of life. 3, 5

Behold, I stand at the door, and knock. 3, 20

And I saw a new heaven and a new earth: for the first heaven and the first earth were passed away; and there was no more sea. 21, 1

I will give unto him that is athirst of the fountain of the water of life freely. 21, 6

The grace of our Lord Jesus Christ be with you all. Amen. 22, 21

Reynolds, Frederic   1765-1841

How goes the enemy? [Said by Mr. Ennui, " the time-killer."] *The Dramatist,* 1

Rhodes, Cecil John   1853-1902

The unctuous rectitude of my countrymen.
Speech, 1896

So little done, so much to do! *Attrib. last words*

Richard I of England   1157-1199

Dieu et mon droit. God and my right.
Attrib. 1198

Richardson, Samuel   1689-1761

She [my mother] says, I am too witty; An glicè too pert; I, that she is too wise; that is to say, being likewise put into English, not so young as she has been. *Clarissa,* 2

Desert and reward, I can assure her, seldom keep company. *Ib.* 4

Pity is but one remove from love. *Sir Charles Grandison,* 1

That's the beauty of it; to offend and make up
at pleasure. *Ib.* 3

Rochester, Earl of   1647-1680

Here lies our sovereign lord the King
Whose word no man relies on,
Who never said a foolish thing,
Nor ever did a wise one.
Humorous Epitaph written for Charles II

Rogers, Samuel   1763-1855

Think nothing done while aught remains to do.
Human Life

Many a temple half as old as time.
Italy. A Farewell

Roland, Madame (Marie Jeanne Philipon)
1754-1793

O liberté! que de crimes on commet en ton nom!
O liberty! what crimes are committed in thy name!
Remark on mounting the scaffold

Romans, The Epistle of Paul to the

The wages of sin is death. 6, 23

If God be for us, who can be against us? 8, 31

For I am persuaded, that neither death, nor life,
nor angels, nor principalities, nor powers, nor
things present, nor things to come,
Nor height, nor depth, nor any other creature,
shall be able to separate us from the love of God,
which is in Jesus Christ our Lord. 8, 38-39

per cent Americanism, only for those who are Americans and nothing else. *Ib. Saratoga*

I wish to preach not the doctrine of ignoble ease, but the doctrine of the strenuous life. *Ib. 1899*

The first requisite of a good citizen in this republic of ours is that he shall be able and willing to pull his weight. *Ib. 1902*

No man needs sympathy because he has to work. . . . Far and away the best prize that life offers is the chance to work hard at work worth doing. *Address, 1903*

If I have erred, I err in company with Abraham Lincoln. *Speech, 1912*

Hyphenated Americans. *Metropolitan Magazine, 1915*

Nine-tenths of wisdom is being wise in time. *Speech, June, 1917*

I want to see you shoot the way you shout. *Ib. Oct., 1917*

Rossetti, Christina Georgina   1830-1894

This downhill path is easy, but there's no turning back. *Amor Mundi*

Remember me when I am gone away,
Gone far away into the silent land. *Remember*

Better by far you should forget and smile
Than you should remember and be sad. *Ib.*

Silence more musical than any song. *Rest*

When I am dead, my dearest,
Sing no sad songs for me. *When I am Dead*

And if thou wilt, remember,
And if thou wilt, forget. *Ib.*

Rossetti, Dante Gabriel 1828-1882

A sonnet is a moment's monument,—
Memorial from the Soul's eternity
To one dead deathless hour.
The House of Life, 1, introduction

Sleepless with cold commemorative eyes. *Ib.* 2,
A Superscription

When vain desire at last and vain regret
Go hand in hand to death. *Ib. The One Hope*

Teach the unforgetful to forget. *Ib.*

I have been here before,
But when or how I cannot tell:
I know the grass beyond the door,
The sweet keen smell,
The sighing sound, the lights around the shore.
Sudden Light

The sea hath no king but God alone.
The White Ship

Rousseau, Jean-Jacques 1712-1778

L'homme est né libre, et partout il est dans les fers.
Man is born free, and everywhere he is in chains.
Du Contrat Social, 1

Roux, Joseph 1834-1886

Science is for those who learn; poetry, for those
who know. *Meditations of Parish Priest* 1

We love justice greatly, and just men but little. *Ib.* 4

Evil often triumphs, but never conquers. *Ib.* 5

The egoist does not tolerate egoism. *Ib.* 9

Friends are rare for the good reason that men are not common. *Ib.*

Rowe, Nicholas   1674-1718

Like Helen, in the night when Troy was sack'd,
Spectatress of the mischief which she made.
                                    The Fair Penitent, 5

Death is the privilege of human nature,
And life without it were not worth our taking. *Ib.*

Ruskin, John   1819-1900

If a book is worth reading, it is worth buying
                                    Sesame and Lilies

It ought to be quite as natural and straightforward a matter for a labourer to take his pension from his parish, because he has deserved well of his parish, as for a man in higher rank to take his pension from his country, because he has deserved well of his country.
                                    Unto this Last, preface

Government and co-operation are in all things the laws of life; anarchy and competition, the laws of death. *Ib.* 3

Whereas it has long been known and declared that the poor have no right to the property of the

rich, I wish it also to be known and declared that the rich have no right to the property of the poor.
Ib.

Russell, Bertrand Arthur William   1872-1970

America . . where law and custom alike are based upon the dreams of spinsters. *Marriage and Morals*

Every man, wherever he goes, is encompassed by a cloud of comforting convictions, which move with him like flies on a summer day. *Sceptical Essays*

Machines are worshipped because they are beautiful, and valued because they confer power; they are hated because they are hideous, and loathed because they impose slavery. *Ib.*

Russell, Lord John   1792-1878

If peace cannot be maintained with honour, it is no longer peace. *Speech,* 1853

Ruth, The Book of

Intreat me not to leave thee, or to return from following after thee: for whither thou goest, I will go; and where thou lodgest I will lodge: thy people shall be my people, and thy God my God: Where thou diest, will I die, and there will I be buried: the Lord do so to me, and more also, if ought but death part thee and me. 1, 16-17

Saikaku, Ihara   1642-1693

Marrying off your daughter is a piece of business you may expect to do only once in a lifetime, and, bearing in mind that none of the losses are recoverable later, you should approach the matter with extreme caution. *Nippon Eitai-gura*

And why do people wilfully exhaust their strength in promiscuous living, when their wives are on hand from bridal night till old age—to be taken when required, like fish from a private pond. *Ib.*

"Saki" (Hector Hugh Munro) 1870-1916

Waldo is one of those people who would be enormously improved by death. *Beasts and Super-Beasts. The Feast of Nemesis*

He's simply got the instinct for being unhappy highly developed. *Chronicles of Clovis. The Match-Maker*

The cook was a good cook, as cooks go; and as cooks go she went. *Reginald, on Besetting Sins*

Women and elephants never forget an injury. *Ib.*

But, good gracious, yot've got to educate him first. You can't expect a boy to be vicious till he's been to a good school. *Reginald in Russia. The Baker's Dozen*

The Western custom of one wife and hardly any mistresses. *Ib. A Young Turkish Catastrophe*

In baiting a mouse-trap with cheese, always leave room for the mouse. *The Square Egg. The Infernal Parliament*

Salisbury, Robert Cecil, Lord 1830-1903

By office boys for office boys. *Remark about the Daily Mail*

Sallust 86-34 B.C.

Saltare elegantius, quam necesse est probae. She
could dance more skilfully than an honest woman
need. *Catiline, 25*

Pro patria, pro liberis, pro aris atque focis suis.
On behalf of their country, their children, their
altars, and their hearths. *Ib. 59*

Punica fide. With Carthaginian faith [i.e.
treachery]. *Jugurtha, 35*

It is always easy to begin a war, but very difficult
to stop one, since its beginning and end are not
under the control of the same man. *Ib. 83*

Salvandy, Narcisse Achille 1795-1856

Nous dansons sur un volcan. We are dancing on
a volcano. *Remark, 1830*

Samuel, The First Book of

Speak, Lord; for thy servant heareth. 3, 9

God save the king. 10, 24

A man after his own heart. 13, 14

For the Lord seeth not as man seeth: for man
looketh on the outward appearance, but the
Lord looketh on the heart. 16, 7

Go, and the Lord be with thee. 17, 37

Samuel, The Second Book of

Saul and Jonathan were lovely and pleasant in
their lives, and in their death they were not
divided. 1, 23

How are the mighty fallen, and the weapons of war perished. 1, 27

Would God I had died for thee, O Absalom, my son, my son! 18, 33

The sweet psalmist of Israel. 23, 1

Santayana, George   1863-1952

Fanaticism consists in redoubling your effort when you have forgotten your aim.
Life of Reason, 1

Nothing is so poor and melancholy as art that is interested in itself and not in its subject. *Ib.* 4

To be interested in the changing seasons is, in this middling zone, a happier state of mind than to be hopelessly in love with spring. *Little Essays*

Schiller, Friedrich von   1759-1805

Freude, schöner Götterfunken,
Tochter aus Elysium,
Wir betreten feuertrunken,
Himmlische, dein Heiligtum.
O Joy, lovely gift of the gods, daughter of Paradise, divinity, we are inspired as we approach your sanctuary. *An die Freude* (the words of Beethoven's Ninth Symphony)

Alle Menschen werden Brüder,
Wo dein sanfter Flügel weilt.
In the shade of your soft wings, all men will be brothers. *Ib.*

Time consecrates;
And what is grey with age becomes religion.
Die Piccolomini, 4

Die Weltgeschichte ist das Weltgericht.
The world's history is the world's judgement.
Lecture, Jena, 1789

Und siegt Natur, so muss die Kunst entweichen.
When Nature conquers, Art must then give way.
Remark to Goethe

Scott, Alexander   c. 1525-c. 1584

Luve is ane fervent fire,
Kendillit without desire:
Short plesour, lang displesour,
Repentance is the hire. *Lo! What it is to Luve*

Scott, Charles Prestwich   1846-1932

The newspaper is of necessity something of a
monopoly, and its first duty is to shun the temptations of monopoly. Its primary office is the
gathering of news. At the peril of its soul it must
see that the supply is not tainted. Neither in
what it gives, nor in what it does not give, nor
in the mode of presentation, must the unclouded
face of truth suffer wrong. Comment is free but
facts are sacred. *In the Manchester Guardian,
6th May,* 1926

Scott, Robert Falcon   1868-1912

Great God! this is an awful place [the South
Pole]. *Journal,* 17th Jan., 1912

Had we lived, I should have had a tale to tell of
the hardihood, endurance, and courage of my
companions which would have stirred the heart
of every Englishman. These rough notes and
our dead bodies must tell the tale. *Message to
the Public*

So let each cavalier who loves honour and me,
Come follow the bonnets of Bonny Dundee.
Bonny Dundee (in *The Doom of Devorgoil*)

The stag at eve had drunk his fill,
Where danced the moon on Monan's rill,
And deep his midnight lair had made
In lone Glenartney's hazel shade.
The Lady of the Lake, 1

Soldier, rest! thy warfare o'er,
Sleep the sleep that knows not breaking,
Dream of battled fields no more,
Days of danger, nights of waking. *Ib.*

Like the dew on the mountain,
Like the foam on the river,
Like the bubble on the fountain,
Thou art gone, and for ever! *Ib.* 3

These are Clan Alpine's warriors true;
And, Saxon,—I am Roderick Dhu! *Ib.* 5

The stern joy which warriors feel
In foemen worthy of their steel. *Ib.*

The way was long, the wind was cold,
The Minstrel was infirm and old;
His wither'd cheek and tresses grey,
Seemed to have known a better day.
The Lay of the Last Minstrel, introduction

Love rules the court, the camp, the grove,
And men below, and saints above;
For love is heaven, and heaven is love. *Ib.* 3

Breathes there the man, with soul so dead,
Who never to himself hath said,
This is my own, my native land!
Whose heart hath ne'er within him burned
As home his footsteps he hath turned
From wandering on a foreign strand!   *Ib.* 6

O Caledonia! stern and wild,
Meet nurse for a poetic child!
Land of brown heath and shaggy wood,
Land of the mountain and the flood.   *Ib.*

Thus, then, my noble foe I greet:
Health and high fortune till we meet
And then—what pleases Heaven.
                              Lord of the Isles, 3

To that dark inn, the grave!   *Ib.* 6

And come he slow, or come he fast,
It is but Death who comes at last.   *Marmion,* 2

O young Lochinvar is come out of the West
Through all the wide border his steed was the
    best;
And save his good broadsword, he weapons had
    none,
He rode all unarm'd, and he rode all alone.
So faithful in love, and so dauntless in war,
There never was knight like the young Lochinvar.
                                           Ib. 5

O what a tangled web we weave,
When first we practise to deceive.   *Ib.* 6

And such a yell was there,
Of sudden and portentous birth,

358

As if men fought upon the earth,
And fiends in upper air. *Ib.*

O Woman! in our hours of ease,
Uncertain, coy, and hard to please,
And variable as the shade. *Ib.*

The stubborn spearmen still made good
Their dark impenetrable wood,
Each stepping where his comrade stood,
The instant that he fell. *Ib.*

But no one shall find me rowing against the
stream. I care not who knows it—I write for
the general amusement. *The Fortunes of Nigel*,
introductory epistle

The hour is come, but not the man.
The Heart of Midlothian, 4

Jock, when ye hae naething else to do, ye may
be ay sticking in a tree; it will be growing, Jock,
when ye're sleeping. *Ib.* 8

When we had a king, and a chancellor, and
parliament men o' our ain, we could aye pebble
them wi stanes when they werena guid bairns;
but naebody's nails can reach the length o'
Lunnon. *Malachi Malagrowther*

The ae half of the warld thinks the tither daft.
Redgauntlet, 7

But with morning cool repentance came.
Rob Roy, 12

There's a gude time coming. *Ib.* 32

Speak out, sir, and do not Maister or Campbell
me—my foot is on my native heath, and my name
is Macgregor! *Ib.* 34

A man may drink and not be drunk;
A man may fight and not be slain;
A man may kiss a bonny lass,
And yet be welcome home again.

Woodstock, 27

Seaman, Sir Owen   1861-1936

She must know all the needs of a rational being
Be skilled to keep counsel, to comfort, to coax
And, above all things else, be accomplished a
   seeing
My jokes. *A Plea for Trigamy*

Seeger, Alan   1888-1916

I have a rendezvous with Death,
At some disputed barricade,
At midnight in some flaming town.
I Have a Rendezvous with Death

Seeley, Sir John Robert   1834-1895

We [the English] seem as it were to have conquered
and peopled half the world in a fit of absence of
mind. *The Expansion of England*

History is past politics, and politics present
history. *Growth of British Policy*

Selden, John   1584-1654

There is not anything in the world so much
abused as this sentence, *Salus populi suprema
lex esto* (Let public safety be the supreme law).
Table Talk. People

Philosophy is nothing but discretion. *Ib. Philosophy*

Sellar, Walter Carruthers   **1898-1951**
    and Yeatman, Robert Julian   **b. 1897**

1066, And All That. *Title of Book*

The National Debt is a very Good Thing and it
would be dangerous to pay it off for fear of
Political Economy. 1066, *And All That*

Napoleon's armies always used to march on their
stomachs, shouting: " *Vive l'Interiéur!* " *Ib.*

Seneca, Lucius Annaeus   **c. 4 B.C.-A.D. 65**

Illi mors gravis incubat
Qui notus nimis omnibus
Ignotus moritur sibi.
On him does death lie heavily who, but too well
known to all, dies to himself unknown. *Thyestes,*
2, *chorus* (*Tr.* Miller)

   There can be slaine
No sacrifice to God more acceptable
Than an unjust and wicked king.
               Hercules Furens (*Tr.* Milton)

Shacklock, Richard   **fl. 1575**

Proud as peacocks. *Hatchet of Heresies*

Shadwell, Thomas   **c. 1642-1692**

'Tis the way of all flesh. *The Sullen Lovers,* 5

And wit's the noblest frailty of the mind.
               A True Widow, 2

I am, out of the ladies' company, like a fish out
of the water. *Ib. 3*

Every man loves what he is good at. *Ib. 5*

Shakespeare, William   **1564-1616**

My salad days,
When I was green in judgement, cold in blood.
Anthony and Cleopatra, 1

Age cannot wither her, nor custom stale
Her infinite variety; other women cloy
The appetites they feed, but she makes hungry
Where most she satisfies.   *Ib. 2*

Sweet are the uses of adversity,
Which like a toad, ugly and venomous,
Wears yet a precious jewel in his head.
As You Like It, 2

All the world's a stage,
And all the men and women merely players. *Ib.*

Blow, blow, thou winter wind,
Thou art not so unkind
As man's ingratitude. *Ib.*

It was a lover and his lass. *Ib. 5*

Hark! hark! the lark at heaven's gate sings,
And Phoebus 'gins arise. *Cymbeline, 2*

Fear no more the heat o' the sun. *Ib. 4*

Golden lads and girls all must,
As chimney-sweeps, come to dust. *Ib.*

But look, the morn, in russet mantle clad,
Walks o'er the dew of yon high eastward hill.
Hamlet, 1

O! that this too too solid flesh would melt,
Thaw, and resolve itself into a dew. *Ib.*

Frailty, thy name is woman!   *Ib.*

He was a man, take him for all in all,
I shall not look upon his like again. *Ib.*

Neither a borrower, nor a lender be. *Ib.*

Angels and ministers of grace defend us!   *Ib.*

Something is rotten in the state of Denmark. *Ib.*

There are more things in heaven and earth,
  Horatio,
Than are dreamt of in your philosophy.   *Ib.*

Brevity is the soul of wit. *Ib.* 2

Though this be madness, yet there is method in it.
                                              Ib.
There is nothing either good or bad, but thinking
  makes it so. *Ib.*

What a piece of work is a man! *Ib.*

I know a hawk from a handsaw. *Ib.*

The play, I remember, pleased not the million;
  'twas caviare to the general. *Ib.*

  The play's the thing
Wherein I'll catch the conscience of the king. *Ib.*

To be, or not to be: that is the question:
Whether 'tis nobler in the mind to suffer
The slings and arrows of outrageous fortune,
Or to take arms against a sea of troubles,
And by opposing end them? *Ib.* 3

The undiscover'd country from whose bourn
No traveller returns. *Ib.*

And thus the native hue of resolution
Is sicklied o'er with the pale cast of thought. *Ib.*

It out-herods Herod. *Ib.*

          Give me that man
That is not passion's slave. *Ib.*

The lady doth protest too much, methinks. *Ib.*

A king of shreds and patches. *Ib.*

I must be cruel, only to be kind. *Ib.*

To what base uses we may return, Horatio. *Ib.* 5

A ministering angel shall my sister be. *Ib.*

The rest is silence. *Ib.*

You blocks, you stones, you worse than senseless
    things!
O you hard hearts, you cruel men of Rome,
Knew you not Pompey? *Julius Caesar,* 1

Beware the Ides of March. *Ib.*

Why, man, he doth bestride the narrow world
Like a Colossus; and we petty men
Walk under his huge legs. *Ib.*

Let me have men about me that are fat;
Sleek-headed men and such as sleep o' nights;
Yond' Cassius has a lean and hungry look;
He thinks too much: such men are dangerous.
Ib.

For mine own part, it was Greek to me. *Ib.*

But men may construe things after their own
fashion,
Clean from the purpose of the things themselves.
Ib.

It is the bright day that brings forth the adder;
And that craves wary walking. *Ib.* 2

Lowliness is young ambition's ladder,
Whereto the climber-upward turns his face;
But when he once attains the upmost round,
He then unto the ladder turns his back,
Looks in the clouds, scorning the base degrees
By which he did ascend. *Ib.*

Cowards die many times before their deaths,
The valiant never taste of death but once. **Ib.**

But I am constant as the northern star,
Of whose true-fix'd and resting quality
There is no fellow in the firmament. *Ib.* 3

Et tu, Brute! *Ib.*

Cry, " Havoc! " and let slip the dogs of war. *Ib.*

Not that I loved Caesar less, but that I loved
Rome more. *Ib.*

Friends, Romans, countrymen, lend me your ears;
I come to bury Caesar, not to praise him.

The evil that men do lives after them
The good is oft interred with their bones.   *Ib.*

See what a rent the envious Casca made.   *Ib.*

A friendly eye could never see such faults.   *Ib.* 4

There is a tide in the affairs of men,
Which taken at the flood, leads on to fortune;
Omitted, all the voyage of their life
Is bound in shallows and in miseries.   *Ib.*

This was the noblest Roman of them all.   *Ib.* 5

His life was gentle, and the elements
So mix'd in him that Nature might stand up,
And say to all the world, " This was a man!"
                                                     Ib.

If all the year were playing holidays,
To sport would be as tedious as to work.
                                       King Henry IV, Pt. 1, 1

[Falstaff] lards the lean earth as he walks along.
                                                     Ib. 2

O monstrous! but one half-pennyworth of bread
   to this intolerable deal of sack!   *Ib.*

Honour pricks me on. Yea, but how if honour
prick me off when I come on?   *Ib.* 5

When that this body did contain a spirit,
A kingdom for it was too small a bound;
But now two paces of the vilest earth
Is room enough.   *Ib.*

The better part of valour is discretion.   *Ib.*

I can get no remedy against this consumption of
the purse: borrowing only lingers and lingers it
out, but the disease is incurable. *Ib. Pt. 2, 1*

Uneasy lies the head that wears a crown. *Ib. 3*

There is a history in all men's lives,
Figuring the nature of the times deceas'd.   *Ib.*

Once more unto the breach, dear friends, once
    more;
Or close the wall up with our English dead!
                                        King Henry V, 3

I see you stand like greyhounds in the slips,
Straining upon the start. *Ib.*

But if it be a sin to covet honour
I am the most offending soul alive. *Ib. 4*

This day is called the feast of Crispian. *Ib.*

We few, we happy few, we band of brothers. *Ib.*

        The naked, poor, and mangled Peace,
Dear nurse of arts, plenties, and joyful births.
                                                Ib. 5

Saint Martin's summer, halcyon days. *King
Henry VI, Pt. 1, 1*

She's beautiful and therefore to be woo'd;
She is a woman, therefore to be won.
            Ib. 5 (cf. *Titus Andronicus*, 2, p. 375)

Thrice is he arm'd that hath his quarrel just.
                                King Henry VI, Pt. 2, 3

Bell, book, and candle shall not drive me back,
When gold and silver becks me to come on.
King John, 3

To gild refined gold, to paint the lily,
To throw a perfume on the violet. *Ib*. 4

The spirit of the time shall teach me speed. *Ib*.

Nought shall make us rue,
If England to itself do rest but true. *Ib*. 5

We make guilty of our disasters the sun, the
moon, and the stars; as if we were villains by
necessity, fools by heavenly compulsion. *King
Lear*, 1

How sharper than a serpent's tooth it is
To have a thankless child. *Ib*.

Blow, winds, and crack your cheeks! *Ib*. 3

There was never yet fair woman but she made
    mouths in a glass. *Ib*.

The prince of darkness is a gentleman. *Ib*.

Child Roland to the dark tower came,
His word was still, Fie, foh, and fum,
I smell the blood of a British man. *Ib*.

As flies to wanton boys, are we to the gods;
They kill us for their sport. *Ib*. 4

    Get thee glass eyes;
And, like a scurvy politician, seem
To see the things thou dost not. *Ib*.

        Men must endure
Their going hence, even as their coming hither:
Ripeness is all. *Ib.* 5

Teach thy necessity to reason thus;
There is no virtue like necessity.
                              King Richard II, 1

This royal throne of kings, this scepter'd isle
This earth of majesty, this seat of Mars,
This other Eden, demi-Paradise. *Ib.* 2

This happy breed of men. *Ib.*

This land of such dear souls, this dear, dear
    land. *Ib.*

A little, little grave, an obscure grave. *Ib.* 3

Now is the winter of our discontent
Made glorious summer by this sun of York.
                              King Richard III, 1

And therefore, since I cannot prove a lover, . . .
I am determined to prove a villain. *Ib.*

A horse! a horse! my kingdom for a horse! *Ib.* 5

For where is any author in the world
Teaches such beauty as a woman's eye?
Learning is but an adjunct to ourself.
                              Love's Labour's Lost, 4

He draweth out the thread of his verbosity finer
than the staple of his argument. *Ib.* 5

        Nothing in his life
Became him like the leaving it. *Macbeth*, 1

Yet do I fear thy nature;
It is too full o' the milk of human kindness
To catch the nearest way. *Ib.*

If it were done when 'tis done, then 'twere well
It were done quickly. *Ib.*

       I have no spur
To prick the sides of my intent, but only
Vaulting ambition, which o'erleaps itself
And falls on the other. *Ib.*

I dare do all that may become a man;
Who dares do more is none. *Ib.*

But screw your courage to the sticking-place,
And we'll not fail. *Ib.*

Is this a dagger which I see before me
The handle toward my hand? *Ib.* 2

A dagger of the mind, a false creation,
Proceeding from the heat-oppressèd brain. *Ib.*

That which hath made them drunk hath made
   me bold. *Ib.*

Will all great Neptune's ocean wash this blood
Clean from my hand? No, this my hand will
   rather
The multitudinous seas incarnadine,
Making the green one red. *Ib.*

A little water clears us of this deed. *Ib.*

The primrose way to the everlasting bonfire. *Ib.*

We have scotch'd the snake, not killed it. *Ib.* 3

But now I am cabin'd, cribb'd, confin'd, bound in
To saucy doubts and fears. *Ib.*

Stand not upon the order of your going,
But go at once. *Ib.*

What! will the line stretch out to the crack of
   doom? *Ib.* 4

Stands Scotland where it did? *Ib.*

Yet who would have thought the old man had
so much blood in him? *Ib.* 5

All the perfumes of Arabia will not sweeten this
little hand. *Ib.*

To-morrow, and to-morrow, and to-morrow,
Creeps in this petty pace from day to day,
To the last syllable of recorded time.   *Ib.*

       Fear not, till Birnam wood
Do come to Dunsinane. *Ib.*

I bear a charmed life. *Ib.*

       Lay on, Macduff;
And damn'd be him that first cries, " Hold,
   enough! " *Ib.*

'Tis one thing to be tempted, Escalus,
Another thing to fall.   *Measure for Measure*, 2

Gratiano speaks an infinite deal of nothing, more
than any man in all Venice. His reasons are as
two grains of wheat, hid in two bushels of chaff:
you shall seek all day ere you find them; and,

when you have found them, they are not worth the search. *The Merchant of Venice,* 1

Sometimes from her eyes
I did receive fair speechless messages. *Ib.*

They are as sick that surfeit with too much, as they that starve with nothing. *Ib.*

God made him, and therefore let him pass for a man. *Ib.*

The devil can cite Scripture for his purpose. *Ib.*

It is a wise father that knows his own child. *Ib.* 2

Hath not a Jew eyes? hath not a Jew hands, organs, dimensions, senses, affections, passions?
Ib. 3

If you prick us, do we not bleed? if you tickle us, do we not laugh? if you poison us do we not die? and if you wrong us, shall we not revenge?
Ib.

So may the outward shows be least themselves: The world is still deceived with ornament. *Ib.*

I am a tainted wether of the flock. *Ib.*

The quality of mercy is not strain'd,
It droppeth as the gentle rain from heaven
Upon the place beneath. *Ib.* 4

And earthly power doth then show likest God's When mercy seasons justice. *Ib.*

To do a great right, do a little wrong. *Ib.*

A Daniel come to judgement. *Ib.*

How sweet the moonlight sleeps upon this bank!
Here we will sit, and let the sounds of music
Creep in our ears. *Ib. 5*

I am never merry when I hear sweet music. *Ib.*

How far that little candle throws his beams!
So shines a good deed in a naughty world. *Ib.*

Why, then the world's mine oyster. *The Merry Wives of Windsor, 2*

Marry, this is the short and long of it. *Ib.*

I cannot tell what the dickens his name is. *Ib. 3*

Love looks not with the eyes, but with the mind,
And therefore is wing'd Cupid painted blind.
A Midsummer Night's Dream, 1

I'll put a girdle round about the earth
In forty minutes. *Ib. 2*

I know a bank whereon the wild thyme blows.
Ib.

Lord, what fools these mortals be! *Ib. 3*

The lunatic, the lover, and the poet,
Are of imagination all compact. *Ib. 4*

Comparisons are odorous. *Much Ado About Nothing, 3*

Patch grief with proverbs. *Ib. 5*

Your daughter and the Moor are now making
the beast with two backs. *Othello*, 1

The wealthy curled darlings of our nation. *Ib.*

Who steals my purse steals trash; 'tis something,
    nothing;
'Twas mine, 'tis his, and has been slave to
    thousands;
But he that filches from me my good name
Robs me of that which not enriches him,
And makes me poor indeed. *Ib.* 3

O! beware, my lord, of jealousy;
It is the green-ey'd monster which doth mock
The meat it feeds on. *Ib.*

But yet the pity of it, Iago! O! Iago, the pity
of it, Iago! *Ib.* 4

       Then, must you speak
Of one that lov'd not wisely but too well. *Ib.* 5

Crabbed age and youth cannot live together:
Youth is full of pleasance, age is full of care.
       The Passionate Pilgrim, 12

  And 'tis not hard, I think,
For men so old as we to keep the peace.
       —*Romeo and Juliet*, 1

What's in a name? that which we call a rose
By any other name would smell as sweet. *Ib.* 2

Good-night, good-night! parting is such sweet
    sorrow
That I shall say good-night till it be morrow. *Ib.*

Night's candles are burnt out, and jocund day
Stands tiptoe on the misty mountain tops. *Ib.* 3

And thereby hangs a tale. *The Taming of the
Shrew*, 4 (and other plays)

This is the way to kill a wife with kindness. *Ib.*

Full fathom five thy father lies;
Of his bones are coral made.   *The Tempest*, 1

Misery acquaints a man with strange bedfellows.
Ib. 2

We are such stuff
As dreams are made on, and our little life
Is rounded with a sleep! *Ib.* 4

O brave new world,
That has such people in't. *Ib.* 5

The strain of man's bred out
Into baboon and monkey. *Timon of Athens*, 1

She is a woman, therefore may be woo'd;
She is a woman, therefore may be won.
Titus Andronicus, 2 (cf. *King Henry VI*, Pt. 1,
p. 367)

If music be the food of love, play on;
Give me excess of it, that, surfeiting,
The appetite may sicken, and so die.
Twelfth Night, 1

Youth's a stuff will not endure. *Ib.* 2

Be not afraid of greatness: some are born
great, some achieve greatness, and some have
greatness thrust upon them. *Ib.*

Love sought is good, but giv'n unsought is better.
Ib. 3

Exit, pursued by a bear. *The Winter's Tale, 3*
(stage direction)

A snapper-up of unconsidered trifles. *Ib. 4*

Shall I compare thee to a summer's day?
Thou art more lovely and more temperate.
Rough winds do shake the darling buds of May
And summer's lease hath all too short a date.
Sonnets, 18

When in disgrace with Fortune and men's eyes,
I all alone beweep my outcast state. *Ib. 29*

Roses have thorns, and silver fountains mud.
Ib. 35

No longer mourn for me when I am dead
Than you shall hear the surly sullen bell. *Ib. 71*

Let me not to the marriage of true minds
Admit impediments. *Ib. 116*

Shaw, George Bernard   1856-1950
You can always tell an old soldier by the inside
of his holsters and cartridge boxes. The young
ones carry pistols and cartridges: the old ones,
grub. *Arms and the Man, 1*

He who has never hoped can never despair.
Caesar and Cleopatra, 4

We have no more right to consume happiness without producing it than to consume wealth without producing it. *Candida*, 1

Man can climb to the highest summits, but he cannot dwell there long. *Ib*. 3

The British soldier can stand up to anything—except the British War Office. *The Devil's Disciple*, 3

It's all that the young can do for the old, to shock them and keep them up to date. *Fanny's First Play*

Reminiscences make one feel so deliciously aged and sad. *The Irrational Knot*, 14

An Irishman's heart is nothing but his imagination. *John Bull's Other Island*, 1

What really flatters a man is that you think him worth flattering. *Ib*. 4

Nothing is ever done in this world until men are prepared to kill one another if it is not done.
Major Barbara, 3

The true artist will let his wife starve, his children go barefoot, his mother drudge for his living at seventy, sooner than work at anything but his art. *Man and Superman*, 1

There is no love sincerer than the love of food.
Ib.

A lifetime of happiness! No man alive could bear it: it would be hell on earth. *Ib*.

377

An Englishman thinks he is moral when he is only uncomfortable. *Ib.* 3

This creature man, who in his own selfish affairs is a coward to the backbone, will fight for an idea like a hero. *Ib.*

At every one of those concerts in England you will find rows of weary people who are there, not because they really like classical music, but because they think they ought to like it. *Ib.*

There are two tragedies in life. One is not to get your heart's desire. The other is to get it. *Ib.* 4

There is no satisfaction in hanging a man who does not object to it. *The Man of Destiny*

There is only one universal passion: fear. *Ib.*

There is nothing so bad or so good that you will not find Englishmen doing it; but you will never find an Englishman in the wrong. He does everything on principle. He fights you on patriotic principles; he robs you on business principles; he enslaves you on imperial principles; he supports his king on royal principles and cuts off his king's head on republican principles. *Ib.*

Beware of the man whose god is in the skies. *Maxims for Revolutionists*

Do not do unto others as you would they should do unto you. Their tastes may not be the same. *Ib*

Marriage is popular because it combines the maximum of temptation with the maximum of opportunity. *Ib.*

He who can, does. He who cannot teaches. *Ib.*

Activity is the only road to knowledge. *Ib.*

The golden rule is that there are no golden rules. *Ib.*

The populace cannot understand the bureaucracy: it can only worship national idols. *Ib.*

Equality is fundamental in every department of social organisation. *Ib.*

Every man over forty is a scoundrel. *Ib.*

Titles distinguish the mediocre, embarrass the superior, and are disgraced by the inferior. *Ib.*

In heaven an angel is nobody in particular. *Ib.*

Life levels all men: death reveals the eminent. *Ib.*

Decency is Indecency's Conspiracy of Silence. *Ib.*

Liberty means responsibility. That is why most men dread it. *Ib.*

Man is a creature of habit. You cannot write three plays and then stop. *Plays Pleasant*, preface

There is only one religion, though there are a hundred versions of it. *Plays Unpleasant*, preface

Not bloody likely. *Pygmalion*, 2

I have never sneered in my life. Sneering doesn't become either the human face or the human soul. *Ib. 5*

An all-night sitting in a theatre would be at least as enjoyable as an all-night sitting in the House of Commons, and much more useful. *St. Joan*, preface

Must then a Christ perish in torment in every age to save those that have no imagination?
Ib. epilogue

O God that madest this beautiful earth, when will it be ready to receive Thy saints? How long, O Lord, how long? *Ib.*

A day's work is a day's work, neither more nor less, and the man who does it needs a day's sustenance, a night's repose, and due leisure, whether he be painter or ploughman. *An Unsocial Socialist*, 5

We don't bother much about dress and manners in England, because as a nation we don't dress well and we've no manners. *You Never Can Tell*, 1

Shelley, Percy Bysshe   **1792-1822**

It might make one in love with death, to think that one should be buried in so sweet a place.
Adonais, preface

To that high Capital, where kingly Death
Keeps his pale court in beauty and decay.
Adonais, 7

Whence are we, and why are we? of what scene
The actors or spectators? *Ib.* 21

Why didst thou leave the trodden paths of men
Too soon? *Ib.* 27

From the contagion of the world's slow stain
He is secure. *Ib.* 40

What Adonais is, why fear we to become? *Ib.* 51

The One remains, the many change and pass;
Heaven's light forever shines, Earth's shadows fly;
Life, like a dome of many-coloured glass,
Stains the white radiance of Eternity,
Until Death tramples it to fragments. *Ib.* 52

The fountains of divine philosophy
Fled not his thirsting lips. *Alastor*

Day after day a weary waste of hours. *Ib.*

England, farewell! thou, who hast been my cradle,
Shalt never be my dungeon or my grave.
                    Charles I (Hampden's speech)

That orbèd maiden with white fire laden,
  Whom mortals call the Moon. *The Cloud*

I silently laugh at my own cenotaph,
  And out of the caverns of rain,
Like a child from the womb, like a ghost from
    the tomb,
  I arise and unbuild it again. *Ib.*

How wonderful is Death,
Death and his brother Sleep!
The Daemon of the World, 1 (also the opening
of *Queen Mab*)

My Song, I fear that thou will find but few
Who fitly shall conceive thy reasoning,
Of such hard matter dost thou entertain.
                    Epipsychidion, Advertisement

My last delight! tell them that they are dull,
And bid them own that thou art beautiful. *Ib.*

The spirit of the worm beneath the sod
In love and worship, blends itself with God.
                    Epipsychidion (cf. *To Byron* p. 388)

We—are we not formed, as notes of music are,
For one another, though dissimilar? *Ib.*

I never was attached to that great sect,
Whose doctrine is, that each one should select
Out of the crowd a mistress or a friend,
And all the rest, though fair and wise, commend
To cold oblivion. *Ib.*

True Love in this differs from gold and clay,
That to divide is not to take away. *Ib.*

The breath of her false mouth was like faint
    flowers,
Her touch was as electric poison. *Ib.*

A ship is floating in the harbour now,
A wind is hovering o'er the mountain's brow;
There is a path on the sea's azure floor,
No keel has ever ploughed that path before. *Ib.*

One Heaven, one Hell, one immortality. *Ib.*

Fame is love disguised. *An Exhortation*

I hated thee, fallen tyrant! I did groan
To think that a most unambitious slave,
Like thou shouldst dance and revel on the grave
Of Liberty.
Feelings of a Republican on the Fall of Bonaparte

Virtue owns a more eternal foe
Than Force or Fraud: old Custom, legal Crime,
And bloody Faith the foulest birth of Time. *Ib.*

Youth will stand foremost ever. *Goethe's Faust*

Good-night? ah! no; the hour is ill
  Which severs those it should unite;
Let us remain together still,
  Then it will be *good* night.   *Good Night*

Let there be light! said Liberty,
And like sunrise from the sea,
Athens arose! *Hellas*

Oh, cease! must hate and death return?
Cease! must men kill and die?
Cease! drain not to its dregs the urn
  Of bitter prophecy.
The world is weary of the past
Oh, might it die or rest at last! *Ib.*

The awful shadow of some unseen Power
  Floats though unseen among us.
          Hymn to the Intellectual Beauty

Spirit of Beauty, that dost consecrate
With thine own hues all thou dost shine upon
Of human thought or form. *Ib.*

      Most wretched men
Are cradled into poetry by wrong:
They learn in suffering what they teach in song.
          Julian and Maddalo

The self-impelling steam-wheels of the mind.
          Letter to Maria Gisborne

London, that great sea, whose ebb and flow
At once is deaf and loud, and on the shore
Vomits its wrecks, and still howls on for more.
Ib.

We'll have tea and toast;
Custards for supper, and an endless host
Of syllabubs and jellies and mince-pies,
And other such lady-like luxuries. *Ib.*

Alas, good friend, what profit can you see
In hating such a hateless thing as me?
Lines to a Critic

I met Murder on the way—
He had a mask like Castlereagh.
The Mask of Anarchy

Some say that gleams of a remoter world
Visit the soul in sleep,—that death is slumber.
Mont Blanc

Power dwells apart in its tranquillity,
Remote, serene, and inaccessible. *Ib.*

The flower that smiles to-day
      To-morrow dies. *Mutability*

O wild West Wind, thou breath of Autumn's
    being,
Thou, from whose unseen presence the leaves
    dead
Are driven, like ghosts from an enchanter fleeing.
Ode to the West Wind

O, Wind,
If Winter comes, can Spring be far behind? *Ib.*

My name is Ozymandias, king of kings:
Look on my works, ye Mighty, and despair!

Ozymandias

Hell is a city much like London—
A populous and a smoky city.

Peter Bell the Third

Things whose trade is, over ladies
  To lean, and flirt, and stare, and simper,
Till all that is divine in woman
Grows cruel, courteous, smooth, inhuman,
  Crucified 'twixt a smile and whimper.   *Ib.*

Cruel he looks, but calm and strong,
Like one who does, not suffers wrong.

Prometheus Unbound, 1

      The heaven around, the earth below
Was peopled with thick shapes of human death,
All horrible, and wrought by human hands,
And some appeared the work of human hearts,
For men were slowly killed by frowns and smiles.

Ib.

The good want power, but to weep barren tears.
The powerful goodness want: worse need for
  them.
The wise want love; and those who love want
  wisdom;
And all best things are thus confused to ill.   *Ib.*

      Peace is in the grave.
The grave hides all things beautiful and good:
I am a God and cannot find it there.   *Ib.*

From the dust of creeds outworn.   *Ib.*

To know nor faith, nor love, nor law; to be
Omnipotent but friendless is to reign. *Ib.* 2

He gave man speech, and speech created thought,
Which is the measure of the universe;
And Science struck the thrones of earth and
  heaven. *Ib.*

The soul of man, like unextinguished fire,
Yet burns towards heaven with fierce reproach.
                                        Ib. 3

Death is the veil which those who live call life:
They sleep, and it is lifted. *Ib.*

But what was he who taught them that the God
Of nature and benevolence hath given
A special sanction to the trade of blood?
                            Queen Mab, 2

    —I know
The past, and thence I will essay to glean
A warning for the future, so that man
May profit by his errors, and derive
  Experience from his folly. *Ib.* 3

        Those gilded flies
That, basking in the sunshine of a court,
Fatten on its corruption! *Ib.*

    Many faint with toil,
That few may know the cares and woe of sloth.
                                        Ib.

Nature rejects the monarch, not the man;
The subject, not the citizen: for kings
And subjects, mutual foes, forever play
A losing game into each other's hands,
Whose stakes are vice and misery. *Ib.*

Kings, priests, and statesmen, blast the human
    flower
Even in its tender bud; their influence darts
Like subtle poison through the bloodless veins
Of desolate society. *Ib.* 4

The harmony and happiness of man
Yields to the wealth of nations. *Ib.* 5

Nature impartial in munificence
Has gifted man with all-subduing will.
Matter, with all its transitory shapes
Lies subjected and plastic at his feet. *Ib.*

Yet every heart contains perfection's germ. *Ib.*

    But human pride
Is skilful to invent most serious names
To hide its ignorance. *Ib.* 7

Earth groans beneath religion's iron age
And priests dare babble of a God of peace
Even whilst their hands are red with guiltless
    blood. *Ib.*

For love, and beauty, and delight,
There is no death, no change. *The Sensitive Plant*

I love tranquil solitude,
    And such society
As is quiet, wise, and good. *Song*

An old, mad, blind, despised, and dying king.
                    Sonnet. England in 1819

If I esteemed you less, Envy would kill Pleasure.
                                    To Byron

The worm beneath the sod
May lift itself in worship to the God. *Ib.*

Less oft is peace in Shelley's mind
Than calm in water seen.
To Jane: The Recollection

Music, when soft voices die,
Vibrates in the memory.
To——: Music When Soft Voices

Beware, O Man—for knowledge must to thee
Like the great flood to Egypt, ever be.
To the Nile

The desire of the moth for the star,
   Of the night for the morrow,
The devotion to something afar
   From the sphere of our sorrow.
To——: One Word is too often Profaned

Hail to thee, blithe Spirit! *To a Skylark*

We look before and after
   And pine for what is not:
Our sincerest laughter
   With some pain is fraught;
Our sweetest songs are those that tell of saddest
   thought. *Ib.*

In honoured poverty thy voice did weave
Songs consecrate to truth and liberty,—
Deserting these, thou leavest me to grieve,
Thus having been, that thou should'st cease to be.
To Wordsworth

Poets are the unacknowledged legislators of the
world. *A Defence of Poetry*

Poetry is the record of the best and happiest moments of the happiest and best minds. *Ib.*

Shenstone, William   1714-1763

A fool and his words are soon parted; a man of genius and his money. *Essays on Men and Manners. On Reserve*

Sheridan, Philip Henry   1831-1888

The only good Indian is a dead Indian. *Attrib.*

Sheridan, Richard Brinsley   1751-1816

I open with a clock striking, to beget an awful attention in the audience: it also marks the time, which is four o'clock in the morning, and saves a description of the rising sun, and a great deal about gilding the eastern hemisphere.
The Critics, 2

O Lord, sir, when a heroine goes mad she always goes into white satin. *Ib.* 3

'Tis safest in matrimony to begin with a little aversion. *The Rivals,* 1

Our ancestors are very good kind of folks; but they are the last people I should choose to have a visiting acquaintance with. *Ib.* 4

No caparisons, miss, if you please. Caparisons don't become a young woman. *Ib.*

My valour is certainly going!—it is sneaking off! I feel it oozing out as it were at the palms of my hands! *Ib.* 5

You shall see them on a beautiful quarto page, where a neat rivulet of text shall meander through a meadow of margin. *The School for Scandal*, 1

Here is the whole set! a character dead at every word. *Ib.* 2

Here's to the maiden of bashful fifteen;
Here's to the widow of fifty;
Here's to the flaunting, extravagant quean;
And here's to the housewife that's thrifty. *Ib.* 3

Sherman, William Tecumseh   1820-1891

There is many a boy here to-day who looks on war as all glory, but, boys, it is all hell.
Speech, 1880

Shirley, James   1596-1666

Only the actions of the just
Smell sweet, and blossom in their dust.
The Contention of Ajax and Ulysses, 1

I presume you're mortal, and may err. *The Lady of Pleasure*, 2

Sidgwick, Henry   1838-1900

We think so because other people think so,
Or because—or because—after all we do think so,
Or because we were told so, and think we must think so,
Or because we once thought so, and think we still think so,
Or because having thought so, we think we will think so. *Lines Composed in his Sleep*

Sidney, Sir Philip   **1554-1586**

Who shoots at the mid-day sun, though he be sure he shall never hit the mark; yet as sure he is he shall shoot higher than who aims but at a bush. *The Arcadia, 2*

My true love hath my heart and I have his,
By just exchange one for the other giv'n;
I hold his dear, and mine he cannot miss,
There never was a better bargain driv'n. *Ib. 3*

I never heard the old song of Percy and Douglas, that I found not my heart moved more than with a trumpet. *The Defence of Poesy*

Thy necessity is greater than mine. *On giving his water-bottle to a dying soldier on the battle-field of Zutphen, 1586*

Simpson, N. F.   **b. 1919**

Each of us as he receives his private trouncings at the hands of fate is kept in good heart by the moth in his brother's parachute, and the scorpion in his neighbour's underwear. *A Resounding Tinkle*

Sitwell, Sir Osbert   **1892-1969**

The British Bourgeoisie
Is not born,
And does not die,
But, if it is ill,
It has a frightened look in its eyes.
          At the House of Mrs. Kinfoot

Smedley, Francis Edward   **1818-1864**

You are looking as fresh as paint. *Frank Fairlegh*

Smiles, Samuel   **1812-1904**

A place for everything, and everything in its place. *Thrift,* 5

Smith, Adam   **1723-1790**

No society can surely be flourishing and happy, of which the far greater part of the members are poor and miserable. *Wealth of Nations,* 1, 8

To found a great empire for the sole purpose of raising up a people of customers, may at first sight appear a project fit only for a nation of shopkeepers. It is, however, a project altogether unfit for a nation of shopkeepers; but extremely fit for a nation that is governed by shopkeepers. *Ib.* 2, 4

Smith, Logan Pearsall   **1865-1946**

Most people sell their souls and live with a good conscience on the proceeds. *Afterthoughts*

There are two things to aim at in life: First, to get what you want; and after that to enjoy it. Only the wisest of mankind achieve the second. *Ib.*

People say that life is the thing, but I prefer reading. *Ib.*

Thank heavens, the sun has gone in, and I don't have to go out and enjoy it. *All Trivia,* last words

Smith, Sydney   **1771-1845**

One of the greatest pleasures in life is conversation.
Essays (1877). *Female Education*

This great spectacle of human happiness. *Ib. Waterton's Wanderings*

Poverty is no disgrace to a man, but it is confoundedly inconvenient. *His Wit and Wisdom*

I look upon Switzerland as an inferior sort of Scotland. *Letters. To Lord Holland*

What would life be without arithmetic, but a scene of horrors. *Ib. To Miss ——*

I am convinced digestion is the great secret of life. *Ib. To Arthur Kinglake*

I have no relish for the country; it is a kind of healthy grave. *Ib. To Miss G. Harcourt*

It requires a surgical operation to get a joke well into a Scotch understanding. Their only idea of wit . . . is laughing immoderately at stated intervals. *Memoirs*, Lady Holland, 1

That knuckle-end of England—that land of Calvin, oat-cakes, and sulphur. *Ib.*

Looked as if she had walked straight out of the Ark. *Ib.*

No furniture so charming as books. *Ib.*

Madam, I have been looking for a person who disliked gravy all my life; let us swear eternal friendship. *Ib.*

How can a bishop marry? How can he flirt? The most he can say is, " I will see you in the vestry after service." *Ib.*

I have, alas, only one illusion left, and that is the Archbishop of Canterbury. *Ib.*

You find people ready enough to do the Samaritan, without the oil and twopence. *Ib.*

As the French say, there are three sexes—men, women, and clergymen. *Ib.*

Praise is the best diet for us, after all. *Ib.*

He [Macaulay] has occasional flashes of silence, that make his conversation perfectly delightful. *Ib.*

I never read a book before reviewing it; it prejudices a man so. *The Smith of Smiths*, H. Pearson

Smith, Sir Sydney b. 1883

No child is born a criminal: no child is born an angel: he's just born. *Remark*

Smollett, Tobias 1721-1771

Too coy to flatter, and too proud to serve,
Thine be the joyless dignity to starve. *Advice*

To a man of honour (said I) the unfortunate need no introduction.
Ferdinand Count Fathom, 62

Hark ye, Clinker, you are a most notorious offender. You stand convicted of sickness, hunger, wretchedness, and want. *Humphrey Clinker, Letter to Sir Watkin Phillips*

[Of Johnson] That great Cham of literature. *Letter to Wilkes*, 1759

The painful ceremony of receiving and returning visits. *Peregrine Pickle*, 5

A mere index hunter, who held the eel of science by the tail. *Ib.* 43

Some folks are wise, and some are otherwise.
Roderick Random, 6

An ounce of prudence is worth a pound of gold.
Ib. 15

He was formed for the ruin of our sex. *Ib.* 22

Death's like the best bower anchor, as the saying is, it will bring us all up. *Ib.* 24

I consider the world as made for me, not me for the world. It is my maxim therefore to enjoy it while I can, and let futurity shift for itself. *Ib.* 45

True Patriotism is of no party. *Sir Lancelot Greaves*, 9

A seafaring man may have a sweetheart in every port; but he should steer clear of a wife as he would avoid a quicksand. *Ib.* 21

I envied not the happiest swain
That ever trod th' Arcadian plain.
Ode to Leven Water

What foreign arms could never quell
By civil rage and rancour fell.
The Tears of Scotland

Somerville, William   **1675-1742**

             My hoarse-sounding horn
Invites thee to the chase, the sport of kings;
Image of war, without its guilt.   *The Chase*, 1

Hail, happy Britain! highly favoured isle,
And Heaven's peculiar care! *Ib.*

Sophocles   **495-406 B.C.**

Life is short but sweet. *Alcestis*

Marvels are many, but man is the greatest.
                             Antigone

Soule, John Babsone Lane   **1815-1891**

Go west, young man.   *Terre Haute (Indiana)
Express*, 1851

Southerne, Thomas   **1660-1746**

             And when we're worn,
Hack'd, hewn with constant service, thrown aside
To rust in peace, or rot in hospitals.
                      Loyal Brother, 1

Southey, Robert   **1774-1843**

" Now tell us all about the war,
And what they fought each other for."
                The Battle of Blenheim

But what they fought each other for,
I could not well make out. *Ib.*

" But what good came of it at last? "
Quoth little Peterkin.
" Why that I cannot tell," said he,
" But 'twas a famous victory." *Ib.*

Your true lover of literature is never fastidious
The Doctor, 17

Live as long as you may, the first twenty years
are the longest half of your life. *Ib.* 130

In the days of my youth I remembered my God!
And He hath not forgotten my age.
The Old Man's Comforts, and how he Gained them

Their wintry garment of unsullied snow
The mountains have put on.
The Poet's Pilgrimage, 1, *The Journey*

The death of Nelson was felt in England as something more than a public calamity; men started
at the intelligence, and turned pale, as if they
had heard of the loss of a dear friend. *The Life
of Nelson*, 9

Spencer, Herbert   1820-1903

Science is organised knowledge. *Education*, 2

The Republican form of Government is the
highest form of government; but because of this
it requires the highest type of human nature—a
type nowhere at present existing.
Essays. The Americans

This survival of the fittest. *Principles of Biology*

Spender, Stephen   b. 1909

I think continually of those who were truly great—
The names of those who in their lives fought for
life,
Who wore at their hearts the fire's centre.
I Think Continually of Those

The merry cuckoo, messenger of Spring,
His trumpet shrill hath thrice already sounded.
Amoretti. Sonnet 19

Most glorious Lord of life, that on this day
Didst make thy triumph over death and sin:
And, having harrow'd hell, didst bring away
Captivity thence captive, us to win.   *Ib. 68*

So let us love, dear love, like as we ought,
—Love is the lesson which the Lord us taught. *Ib.*

One day I wrote her name upon the sand
But came the waves and washed it away:
Again I wrote it with a second hand
But came the tide, and made my pains his prey.
Ib. 75

Of such deep learning little had he need,
Ne yet, of Latin, ne of Greek, that breed
Doubts 'mongst Divines, and difference of texts,
From whence arise diversity of sects,
And hateful heresies.
Complaints. Mother Hubbard's Tale

The woods shall to me answer and my echo ring.
Epithalamion

Open the temple gates unto my love,
Open them wide that she may enter in.   *Ib.*

Ah! when will this long weary day have end,
And lend me leave to come unto my love?   *Ib.*

Fierce wars and faithful loves shall moralize my
song. *The Faerie Queen, 1*

Her angel's face
As the great eye of heaven shined bright,
And made a sunshine in the shady place. *Ib.*

The noble heart, that harbours virtuous thought,
And is with child of glorious great intent,
Can never rest, until it forth have brought
Th' eternal brood of glory excellent. *Ib.*

A cruel crafty Crocodile,
Which in false grief hiding his harmful guile,
Doth weep full sore, and sheddeth tender tears.
Ib.

Sleep after toil, port after stormy seas,
Ease after war, death after life, does greatly please.
Ib.

And all for love, and nothing for reward. *Ib. 2*

Dan Chaucer, well of English undefiled,
On Fame's eternal beadroll worthy to be filed.
Ib. 4

What man that sees the ever-whirling wheel
Of Change, the which all mortal things doth sway
But that thereby doth find, and plainly fool,
How Mutability in them doth play
Her cruel sports, to many men's decay? *Ib. 7*

Sweet Thames, run softly, till I end my song.
Prothalamion

So now they have made our English tongue a
gallimaufry or hodgepodge of all other speeches.
The Shepherd's Calendar. Letter to Gabriel Harvey

Spring-Rice, Arthur Cecil   **1859-1918**

I vow to thee, my country—all earthly things
    above—
Entire and whole and perfect, the service of my
    love.   *Last Poem*

Her ways are ways of gentleness and all her
paths are peace. *Ib.*

Stanley, Sir Henry Morton   **1841-1904**

Dr. Livingstone, I presume? *How I found
Livingstone*, 2

Steele, Sir Richard   **1672-1729**

Women dissemble their Passions better than Men,
but Men subdue their Passions better than
Women. *The Lover*, 9

No Woman of spirit thinks a Man hath any
Respect for her 'till he hath plaid the Fool in her
Service. *Ib.* 17

There are so few who can grow old with a good
grace. *The Spectator*, 263

Reading is to the mind what exercise is to the
body. *The Tatler*, 147

Stephen, James Kenneth   **1859-1892**

Two voices are there: one is of the deep;

And one is of an old half-witted sheep
Which bleats articulate monotony,

And Wordsworth, both are thine.
                    Lapsus Calami. Sonnet

As an Englishman does not travel to see Englishmen, I retired to my room. *A Sentimental Journey*, preface

There are worse occupations in the world than feeling a woman's pulse. *Ib., The Pulse*

I live in a constant endeavour to fence against the infirmities of ill health, and other evils of life, by mirth; being firmly persuaded that every time a man smiles,—but much more so, when he laughs, it adds something to this Fragment of Life. *Tristram Shandy,* dedication

I wish either my father or my mother, or indeed both of them, as they were in duty both equally bound to it, had minded what they were about when they begot me. *Tristram Shandy*, 1, 1

'Tis no extravagant arithmetic to say, that for every ten jokes,—thou hast got an hundred enemies. *Ib.* 12

'Tis known by the name of perseverance in a good cause,—and of obstinacy in a bad one.
Ib. 17

My uncle Toby would never offer to answer this by any other kind of argument, than that of whistling half a dozen bars of Lillabullero. *Ib.* 21

Digressions, incontestably, are the sunshine;— they are the life, the soul of reading!—take them out of this book for instance,—you might as well take the book along with them. *Ib.* 22

Desire of knowledge, like the thirst of riches, increases ever with the acquisition of it. *Ib.* 2, 3

Whenever a man talks loudly against religion,— always suspect that it is not his reason, but his passions which have got the better of his creed. *Ib.* 17

A man's body and his mind . . . are exactly like a jerkin and a jerkin's lining;—rumple the one, —you rumple the other. *Ib.* 3, 4

All is not gain that is got into the purse. *Ib.* 30

Heat is in proportion to the want of true knowledge. *Ib.* 4 (*Slawkenbergius's Tale*)

The nonsense of the old women (of both sexes). *Ib.* 16

There is a North-west passage to the intellectual world. *Ib.* 42

Sciences may be learned by rote, but Wisdom not. *Ib.* 5, 32

Ask my pen,—it governs me,—I govern not it. *Ib.* 6, 6

The excellency of this text is that it will suit any sermon,—and of this sermon,—that it will suit any text. *Ib.* 11

Love, an' please your Honour, is exactly like war, in this; that a soldier, though he has escaped three weeks complete o' Saturday night,—may, nevertheless, be shot through his heart on Sunday morning. *Ib.* 8, 21

Honours, like impressions upon coin, may give
an ideal and local value to a bit of base metal;
but Gold and Silver will pass all the world over
without any other recommendation than their
own weight. *Ib.* 9, dedication

Said my mother, "what is all this story about?"—
"A Cock and a Bull", said Yorick. *Ib.* 33

Stevenson, Robert Louis   **1850-1894**

The pleasant land of counterpane. *A Child's
Garden of Verses. The Land of Counterpane*

O Leerie, I'll go round at night and light the lamps
with you. *Ib. The Lamplighter*

Trusty, dusky, vivid, true,
With eyes of gold and bramble-dew,
Steel-true and blade straight,
The great artificer
Made my mate. *Songs of Travel. My Wife*

Of all my verse, like not a single line;
But like my title, for it is not mine.
That title from a better man I stole;
Ah, how much better, had I stol'n the whole!
          Underwoods. Foreword

Under the wide and starry sky
Dig the grave and let me lie
Glad did I live and gladly die,
   And I laid me down with a will.
This be the verse you grave for me:
"Here he lies where he longed to be;
Home is the sailor, home from sea,
   And the hunter home from the hill."
          Ib. Requiem

" It's gey an' easy spierin'," says the beggar-wife to me. *Ib. The Spaewife*

The harmless art of knucklebones has seen the fall of the Roman Empire and the rise of the United States. *Across the Plains. The Lantern-Bearers*

The bright face of danger. *Ib.*

Everyone lives by selling something. *Ib. Beggars*

Surely we should find it both touching and inspiriting, that in a field from which success is banished, our race should not cease to labour.
Ib. Pulvis et Umbra

To be honest, to be kind—to earn a little and to spend a little less, to make upon the whole a family happier for his presence, to renounce when that shall be necessary and not be embittered, to keep a few friends, but these without capitulation—above all, on the same grim condition, to keep friends with himself—here is a task for all that a man has of fortitude and delicacy.
Ib. A Christmas Sermon

These are my politics: to change what we can; to better what we can; but still to bear in mind that man is but a devil weakly fettered by some generous beliefs and impositions; and for no word however sounding, and no cause however just and pious, to relax the stricture of these bonds. *The Dynamiter. Epilogue of the Cigar Divan*

Politics is perhaps the only profession for which no preparation is thought necessary. *Familiar Studies of Men and Books. Yoshida-Torajiro.*

"Am I no a bonny fighter?" *Kidnapped,* 10

"I've a grand memory for forgetting, David." *Ib.* 18

Is there anything in life so disenchanting as attainment? *New Arabian Nights. The Adventure of the Hansom Cab*

For my part, I travel not to go anywhere, but to go. I travel for travel's sake. The great affair is to move. *Travels with a Donkey. Cheylard and Luc*

Fifteen men on the dead man's chest
Yo-ho-ho, and a bottle of rum!
Drink and the devil had done for the rest—
Yo-ho-ho, and a bottle of rum. *Treasure Island,* 1

Tip me the black spot. *Ib.* 3

"Pieces of eight!" *Ib.* 10

"Many's the long night I've dreamed of cheese—toasted, mostly." *Ib.* 15

Even if we take matrimony at its lowest, even if we regard it as no more than a sort of friendship recognised by the police. *Virginibus Puerisque,* 1

Lastly (and this is, perhaps, the golden rule), no woman should marry a teetotaller, or a man who does not smoke. *Ib.*

Marriage is like life in this—that it is a field of battle and not a bed of roses. *Ib.*

Times are changed with him who marries; there are no more by-path meadows, where you may innocently linger, but the road lies long and straight and dusty to the grave. *Ib.*

To marry is to domesticate the Recording Angel. Once you are married, there is nothing left for you, not even suicide, but to be good. *Ib.*

Youth is the time to go flashing from one end of the world to the other both in mind and body; to try the manners of different nations; to hear the chimes at midnight; to see sunrise in town and country; to be converted at a revival; to circumnavigate the metaphysics, write halting verses, run a mile to see a fire, and wait all day long in the theatre to applaud "Hernani." *Ib.*

To love playthings well as a child, to lead an adventurous and honourable youth, and to settle when the time arrives, into a green and smiling age, is to be a good artist in life and deserve well of yourself and your neighbour. *Ib.*

There is no duty we so much underrate as the duty of being happy. *Ib.* 3

By the time a man gets well into the seventies his continued existence is a mere miracle. *Ib.* 5

To travel hopefully is a better thing than to arrive, and the true success is to labour. *Ib.* 6

Stowe, Harriet Beecher   **1812-1896**

"Who was your mother?" "Never had none!" said the child, with another grin. "Never had any mother? What do you mean? Where were

406

you born?" "Never was born!" persisted
Topsy. *Uncle Tom's Cabin*, 20

"Do you know who made you?" "Nobody, as
I knows on," said the child, with a short laugh.
. . . "I 'spect I grow'd." *Ib.*

" 'Cause I's wicked—I is. I's mighty wicked, any
how. I can't help it." *Ib.*

Suckling, Sir John   1609-1642

Her feet beneath her petticoat,
Like little mice, stole in and out,
    As if they fear'd the light.
                               Ballad. Upon a Wedding

I prithee send me back my heart,
    Since I cannot have thine:
For if from yours you will not part,
    Why then shouldst thou have mine?   *Song*

Out upon it, I have lov'd
Three whole days together;
And am like to love three more,
If it prove fair weather. *Song*

Why so pale and wan, fond lover?
Prithee, why so pale?
Will, when looking well can't move her,
Looking ill prevail? *Song*

'Tis love in love that makes the sport. *Sonnet*

Suetonius   fl. c. 120

Festina lente. Hasten slowly. *Divus Augustus*

Ave, Imperator, morituri te salutant. Hail, Emperor, those about to die salute thee. *Life of Claudius*

Surtees, Robert Smith   1803-1864

The only infallible rule we know is, that the man who is always talking about being a gentleman never is one. *Ask Mamma*

There is no secret so close as that between a rider and his horse. *Mr. Sponge's Sporting Tour*

Swift, Jonathan   1667-1745

It is the folly of too many to mistake the echo of a London coffee-house for the voice of the kingdom. *The Conduct of the Allies*

And he gave it for his opinion, that whoever could make two ears of corn or two blades of grass to grow upon a spot of ground where only one grew before, would deserve better of mankind, and do more essential service to his country than the whole race of politicians put together.
Gulliver's Travels. Voyage to Brobdingnag

Will she pass in a crowd? Will she make a figure in a country church? *Journal to Stella*, 1711

Monday is parson's holiday. *Ib.* 1712

Promises and pie-crust are made to be broken.
Polite Conversation, 1

Bachelor's fare; bread and cheese, and kisses. *Ib.*

Why, every one as they like; as the good woman said when she kissed her cow. *Ib.*

I won't quarrel with my bread and butter. *Ib.*

Faith, that's as well said, as if I had said it myself.
Ib. 2

We have just enough religion to make us hate, but
not enough to make us love one another.
Thoughts on Various Subjects

Every man desires to live long; but no man would
be old. *Ib.*

When men grow virtuous in their old age, they
only make a sacrifice to God of the devil's
leavings. *Ib.*

Swinburne, Algernon Charles   1837-1909

For a day and a night and a morrow,
That his strength might endure for a span
With travail and heavy sorrow,
The holy spirit of man. *Atlanta in Calydon.*

Sleep; and if life was bitter to thee, pardon,
If sweet give thanks; thou hast no more to live;
And to give thanks is good, and to forgive.
Ave atque Vale

For the crown of our life as it closes
Is darkness, the fruit thereof dust;
No thorns go as deep as a rose's,
And love is more cruel than lust.   *Dolores*

In a coign of the cliff between lowland and
highland,
At the sea-down's edge between windward and
lee,

Walled round with rocks as an inland island,
The ghost of a garden fronts the sea.
The Forsaken Garden

A little soul for a little bears up this corpse which
is man. *Hymn to Proserpine*

I have lost, you have won this hazard; yet per-
chance
My loss may shine yet goodlier than your gain,
When time and God give judgement.
Marino Faliero, 5

Synge, John Millington   1871-1909

A man who is not afraid of the sea will soon be
drowned, he said, for he will be going out on a
day he shouldn't. But we do be afraid of the sea,
and we do only be drowned now and again.
The Aran Islands

I have put away sorrow like a shoe that is worn
out and muddy, for it is I have had a life that
will be envied by great companies. *Deirdre of the
Sorrows, 3*

Drink a health to the wonders of the western
world, the pirates, preachers, poteen-makers, with
the jobbing jockies; parching peelers, and the
juries fill their stomachs selling judgements of the
English law. *The Playboy of the Western World, 2*

A daring fellow is the jewel of the world, and a
man did split his father's middle with a single
clout should have the bravery of ten, so may God
and Mary and St. Patrick bless you, and increase
you from this mortal day. *Ib. 3*

Lord, confound this surly sister,
Blight her brow with blotch and blister,
Cramp her larynx, lung and liver,
In her guts a galling give her.
The Curse (to the sister of an enemy who disapproved of his play)

Syrus, Publilius   fl. 1st cent. B.C.

Bis dat qui cito dat. He gives twice who gives soon.
Proverbial, attrib.

Necessitas non habet legem. Necessity has no law. *Ib.*

Tacitus, Cornelius   c. 55–c. 120

Ubi solitudinem faciunt pacem appellant. They create desolation, and call it peace. *Agricola*

[Of Galba] *Capax imperii nisi imperasset.* Suited for office if only he had not had to hold it. *Hist.*

Talleyrand, Charles-Maurice de   1754-1838

Voilà le commencement de la fin. This is the beginning of the end. *At the announcement of Napoleon's defeat at Borodino, 1812*

Tattnall, Josiah   1795-1871

Blood is thicker than water. *Remark, while helping a British squadron on the Chinese river Pei-ho, 1859*

Tawney, Richard Henry   1880-1962

It is a commonplace that the characteristic virtue of Englishmen is their power of sustained practical activity, and their characteristic vice a reluctance to test the quality of that activity by reference to principles. *The Acquisitive Society*, introduction

Taylor, Bishop Jeremy   **1613-1667**

Every school-boy knows it. *On the Real Presence*

Tennyson, Alfred, Lord   **1809-1892**

Break, break, break,
On thy cold grey stones, O Sea!
And I would that my tongue could utter
The thoughts that arise in me.
Break, Break, Break

For men may come and men may go,
But I go on for ever.   *The Brook*

You praise when you should blame
The barbarism of wars.
A juster epoch has begun.
Charge of the Heavy Brigade, epilogue

The song that nerves a nation's heart,
Is in itself a deed. *Ib.*

Their's not to make reply,
Their's not to reason why,
Their's but to do and die:
Into the valley of Death
Rode the six hundred.
Charge of the Light Brigade

But thro' all this tract of years
Wearing the white flower of a blameless life,
Before a thousand peering littlenesses,
In that fierce light which beats upon a throne.
The Idylls of the King, dedication

Where blind and naked Ignorance
Delivers brawling judgements, unashamed,
On all things all day long. *Ib. Merlin and Vivien*

He is all fault who hath no fault at all:
For who loves me must have a touch of earth.
Ib. Lancelot and Elaine

" God make thee good as thou art beautiful,"
Said Arthur, when he dubb'd him knight.
Ib. The Holy Grail

An arm
Clothed in white samite, mystic, wonderful.
Ib. The Passing of Arthur

And slowly answer'd Arthur from the barge:
" The old order changeth, yielding place to new,
And God fulfils himself in many ways,
Lest one good custom should corrupt the world."
Ib.

I have lived my life, and that which I have done
May He within Himself make pure! *Ib.*

The island-valley of Avilion;
Where falls not hail, or rain, or any snow,
Nor ever wind blows loudly; but it lies
Deep-meadow'd, happy, fair, with orchard lawns
And bowery hollows crown'd with summer sea.
Ib.

Men may rise on stepping-stones
Of their dead selves to higher things.
In Memoriam

For words, like Nature, half reveal
And half conceal the Soul within. *Ib.*

413

I hold it true, whate'er befall;
I feel it, when I sorrow most,
'Tis better to have loved and lost
Than never to have loved at all. *Ib.*

An infant crying for the light:
And with no language but a cry. *Ib.*

So many worlds, so much to do,
So little done, such things to be. *Ib.*

There lives more faith in honest doubt,
Believe me, than in half the creeds. *Ib.*

Ring out, wild bells, to the wild sky,
    The flying cloud, the frosty light:
    The year is dying in the night;
Ring out, wild bells, and let him die. *Ib.*

Ring out the feud of rich and poor,
Ring in redress to all mankind. *Ib.*

Kind hearts are more than coronets,
And simple faith than Norman blood.
            Lady Clara Vere de Vere

But who hath seen her wave her hand?
Or at the casement seen her stand?
Or is she known in all the land,
    The Lady of Shalott? *The Lady of Shalott*

"I am half sick of shadows" said
    The Lady of Shalott. *Ib.*

In the Spring a young man's fancy lightly turns
    to thoughts of love. *Locksley Hall*

Cursed be the social wants that sin against the
strength of youth!
Cursed be the social lies that warp us from the
living truth. *Ib.*

Men, my brothers, men the workers, ever reaping
something new:
That which they have done but earnest of the
things that they shall do:
For I dipt into the future, far as human eye could
see,
Saw the Vision of the world, and all the wonder
that would be. *Ib.*

Forward, forward let us range,
Let the great world spin for ever down the ringing
grooves of change. *Ib.*

She only said, " My life is dreary,
He cometh not," she said;
She said, " I am aweary, aweary,
I would that I were dead! " *Mariana*

Faultily faultless, icily regular, splendidly null.
Maud, 1, 2

Gorgonised me from head to foot
With a stony British stare. *Ib.* 13

Come into the garden, Maud,
For the black bat, night, has flown. *Ib.* 22

My life has crept so long on a broken wing
Thro' cells of madness, haunts of horror and fear,
That I come to be grateful at last for a little thing.
Ib. 3, 6

415

Not once or twice in our rough island story,
The path of duty was the way to glory.
>
> *Ode on the Death of the Duke of Wellington*

The splendour falls on castle walls
And snowy summits old in story:
The long light shakes across the lakes,
And the wild cataract leaps in glory.
>
> *The Princess*, 4, introduction

O hark, O hear! how thin and clear,
And thinner, clearer, farther going!
O sweet and far from cliff and scar
The horns of Elfland faintly blowing! *Ib.*

Man is the hunter; woman is his game. *Ib. 5*

Battering the gates of heaven with storms of
prayer. *St. Simeon Stylites*

My strength is as the strength of ten,
Because my heart is pure. *Sir Galahad*

Far on the ringing plains of windy Troy. *Ulysses*

How dull it is to pause, to make an end,
To rust unburnished, not to shine in use!
As tho' to breathe were life. *Ib.*

Some work of noble note may yet be done,
Not unbecoming men that strove with Gods. *Ib.*

> Come, my friends,
'Tis not too late to seek a newer world.
Push off, and sitting well in order smite
The sounding furrows. *Ib.*

That which we are, we are;
One equal temper of heroic hearts,
Made weak by time and fate, but strong in will
To strive, to seek, to find, and not to yield. *Ib.*

Every moment dies a man,
   Every moment one is born. *The Vision of Sin*
                              (cf. p. 20)

Terence, Publius T. Afer   **c. 190-159 B.C.**

Id arbitror
Adprime in vita esse utile, ut nequid nimis. My
view is that the most important thing in life is
never to have too much of anything. *Andria*

Amantium irae amoris integratio est. The quarrels
of lovers are the renewal of love. *Ib.*

Homo sum; humani nil a me alienum puto. I am
a man, I count nothing human indifferent to me.
                         Heauton Timorumenos

Quot homines tot sententiae. So many men, so
many opinions. *Phormio*

Thackeray, William Makepeace   **1811-1863**

He who meanly admires mean things is a Snob.
                          The Book of Snobs

'Tis not the dying for a faith that's so hard,
Master Harry—every man of every nation has
done that—'tis the living up to it that is difficult.
                        Henry Esmond, 1, 6

'Tis strange what a man may do, and a woman
yet think him an angel. *Ib.* 7

There are a thousand thoughts lying within a man that he does not know till he takes up the pen to write. *Ib.* 2, 15

The leopard follows his nature as the lamb does, and acts after leopard law; she can neither help her beauty, nor her courage, nor her cruelty; nor a single spot on her shining coat; nor the conquering spirit which impels her; nor the shot which brings her down. *Ib.* 36

And this I set down as a positive truth. A woman with fair opportunities, and without an absolute hump may marry *whom she likes. Vanity Fair,* 4

Some cynical Frenchman has said that there are two parties to a love transaction; the one who loves and the other who condescends to be so treated. *Ib.* 13

Whenever he met a great man he grovelled before him, and my-lorded him as only a free-born Briton can do. *Ib.*

When you think that the eyes of your childhood dried at the sight of a piece of gingerbread, and that a plum-cake was a compensation for the agony of parting with your mamma and sisters; O my friend and brother, you need not be too confident of your own fine feelings. *Ib.* 56

Thessalonians, First Epistle of Paul to the

Pray without ceasing. 5, 17

Thomas, Dylan   1914-1953

. . . the hockey-legged girls who laughed behind their hands. *Adventures in the Skin Trade*

These poems, with all their crudities, doubts, and confusions, are written for the love of Man and in praise of God, and I'd be a damn' fool if they weren't. *Collected Poems*, note

Do not go gentle into that good night,
Old age should burn and rave at close of day;
Rage, rage against the dying of the light.
Do Not Go Gentle

To begin at the beginning: It is spring, moonless night in the small town, starless and bible-black, the cobblestreets silent and the hunched, courters'-and-rabbits' wood limping invisible down to the sloe-black, slow, black, crowblack, fishing-boat-bobbing sea. *Under Milk Wood*, 1

And before you let the sun in, mind it wipes its shoes. *Ib.*

Thomson, James   **1834-1882**

. . . to cure the pain
Of the headache called thought in the brain.
L'Ancien Régime

Because a cold rage seizes one at whiles
To show the bitter old and wrinkled truth,
Stripped naked of all vesture that beguiles,
False dreams, false hopes, false masks and modes of youth.
The City of Dreadful Night, proem

The City is of Night; perchance of Death,
But certainly of Night; for never there
Can come the lucid morning's fragrant breath
After the dewy dawning's cold grey air. *Ib.* 1

For life is but a dream whose shapes return. *Ib.*

419

The City is of Night, but not of Sleep;
  There sweet sleep is not for the weary brain;
The pitiless hours like years and ages creep,
  A night seems termless hell. *Ib.*

I never knew another man on earth
    But had some joy and solace in his life,
    Some chance of triumph in the dreadful strife:
My doom has been unmitigated dearth.   *Ib.* 8

The vilest thing must be less vile than Thou
From whom it had its being, God and Lord! *Ib.*

Speak not of comfort where no comfort is. *Ib.* 16

And then she sang ballads olden, ballads of love
  and of woe.
Love all burningly golden, grief with heart's blood
  in its flow. *He Heard Her Sing*

From the music of mighty Beethoven to the song
of the little brown bird. *Ib.*

      The gracious power
Of sleep's fine alchemy. *Insomnia*

  Some dark Presence watching by my bed,
The awful image of a nameless dread. *Ib.*

Our poor, vast, petty life is one dark maze of
  dreams. *Ib.*

    Those pale and languid rich ones
Who are always and never free. *Sunday at
Hampstead,* 1

For thirty generations of my corn
Outlast a generation of my men,
And thirty generations of my men
Outlast a generation of their gods.
                                A Voice from the Nile.

Perfect beauty is its own sole end. *Weddah and
Om-el-Bonain*, 1

Thus beauty is that pearl a poor man found;
Which could not be surrendered, changed, or sold,
Which he might never bury in the ground,
Or hide away within his girdle-fold. *Ib.*

For verily the Tribe is all, and we
Are nothing singly save as parts of it. *Ib.* 2

She haggled for a trinket with her tongue
To veil the eager commerce of her eyes. *Ib.* 3

            Foolish ears
That should be tickled not with straws but spears.
                                                Ib.

This desert of brick and stone. *William Blake*

Thoreau, Henry David   1817-1862

The mass of men lead lives of quiet desperation.
                                Walden. Economy

It is true, I never assisted the sun materially in
rising, but, doubt not, it was of the last importance
only to be present at it. *Ib.*

Things do not change; we change. *Ib.* conclusion

Timothy, The First Epistle of Paul to

Old wives' fables. 4, 7

The love of money is the root of all evil. 6, 10

Timothy, The Second Epistle of Paul to

The husbandman that laboureth must be first partaker of the fruits. 2, 6

I have fought a good fight, I have finished my course, I have kept the faith. 4, 7

Tobin, John   **1770-1804**

The man that lays his hand upon a woman,
Save in the way of kindness, is a wretch
Whom 't were gross flattery to name a coward.
The Honeymoon, 2

Tolstoy, Leo   **1828-1910**

Pure and complete sorrow is as impossible as pure and complete joy. *War and Peace,* (*Tr. by* Maude)

Art is not a handicraft, it is a transmission of feeling the artist has experienced. *What is Art?* (*Ib.*)

I sit on a man's back, choking him and making him carry me, and yet assure myself and others that I am very sorry for him and wish to ease his lot by all possible means—except by getting off his back. *What Then Must We Do?* (*Ib.*)

Trapp, Joseph   **1679-1747**

The king, observing with judicious eyes,
The state of both his universities,

To Oxford sent a troop of horse, and why?
That learned body wanted loyalty;
To Cambridge books, as very well discerning,
How much that loyal body wanted learning.
Epigram on George I's donation of Bishop Ely's
Library to Cambridge University. (For reply, see
Sir Wm. Browne, p. 66)

Trevelyan, George Macaulay   1876-1962

Education . . . has produced a vast population
able to read but unable to distinguish what is
worth reading. *English Social History*

Trollope, Anthony   1815-1882

He must have known me had he seen me as he was
wont to see me, for he was in the habit of flogging
me constantly. Perhaps he did not recognise me
by my face. *Autobiography*, 1

Tusser, Thomas   c. 1524-1580

A fool and his money be soon at debate. *Five*
Hundred Points of Good Husbandry, 10

Make hunger thy sauce, as a medicine for health.
Ib.

At Christmas play and make good cheer,
For Christmas comes but once a year. *Ib.* 12

To dog in the manger some liken I could. *Ib.* 28

Feb, fill the dyke
With what thou dost like. *Ib.* 34

Twain, Mark [S. L. Clemens]   1835-1910

I can live for two months on a good compliment.
Attrib.

The report of my death was an exaggeration.
Cablegram, June, 1897

I don't see no p'ints about that frog that's any better'n any other frog. *The Celebrated Jumping Frog*

Persons attempting to find a motive in this narrative will be prosecuted; persons attempting to find a moral in it will be banished; persons attempting to find a plot in it will be shot.
Huckleberry Finn, introduction

There was things which he stretched, but mainly he told the truth. *Ib.* 1

Lump the whole thing! say that the Creator made Italy from designs by Michael Angelo! *Innocents Abroad*, 27

When angry count four; when very angry swear.
Pudd'nhead Wilson's Calendar

The English are mentioned in the Bible: Blessed are the meek for they shall inherit the earth. *Ib.*

Don't part with your illusions. When they are gone, you may still exist, but you have ceased to live. *Ib.*

Ustinov, Peter   **b. 1921**

I can never forgive God for having invented the French. *The Love of Four Colonels*, 3

I enjoy taking myself by surprise. *Ib.*

As for being a General, well, at the age of four
with paper hats and wooden swords we're all
Generals. Only some of us never grow out of it.
Romanoff and Juliet, 1

A diplomat these days is nothing but a headwaiter who's allowed to sit down occasionally.
Ib.

. . . the great thing about history is that it is
adaptable. *Ib.* 2

Vanbrugh, Sir John   **1664-1726**

Much of a muchness. *The Provok'd Husband*, 1

Thinking is to me the greatest fatigue in the
world. *The Relapse*

Vaughan, Henry   **1622-1695**

They are all gone into the world of light!
And I alone sit lingering here.
                    Silex Scintillans. Ascension-Hymn

Dear, beauteous death! the Jewel of the Just. *Ib.*

Man is the shuttle, to whose winding quest
And passage through these looms
God order'd motion, but ordain'd no rest.
                    Ib. Man

My soul, there is a country
   Far beyond the stars,
Where stands a wingèd sentry
   All skilful in the wars. *Ib. Peace*

Happy those early days! when I
Shin'd in my Angel-infancy. *Ib. The Retreate*

I saw Eternity the other night,
Like a great ring of pure and endless light,
All calm, as it was bright. *Ib. The World*

Vegetius, Flavius V. Renatus   **fl. c. 375**

Qui desiderat pacem, praeparet bellum. Let him
who desires peace, prepare fo rwar.
Epitome Institutionum Rei Militaris

Victoria, Queen   **1819-1901**

We are not amused. *Attrib.*

We are not interested in the possibilities of defeat.
Attrib. remark to A. J. Balfour, 1899

Villon, François   **1431-c. 1484**

Mais où sont les neiges d'antan? But where are
the snows of yesteryear? *Ballade des Dames du
Temps Jadis (Tr. by D. G. Rossetti)*

Virgil, Publius V. Maro   **70-19 B.C.**

Forsan et haec olim meminisse iuvabit. Perhaps
some day even these things will be pleasant to
remember. *Aeneid, 1*

Sunt lacrimae rerum. Events have tears. *Ib.*

Mens sibi conscia recti. A mind conscious of the
right. *Ib.*

Quidquid id est, timeo Danaos et dona ferentis.
Whatever it is, I fear the Greeks even when they
bring gifts. *Ib. 2*

Dis aliter visum. Heaven thought otherwise. *Ib*

Facilis descensus Averni:
Noctes atque dies patet atri ianua Ditis;
Sed revocare gradum superasque evadere ad auras,
Hoc opus, hic labor est.
The way to Hell is easy: night and day the gates
of black Dis stand open; but to retrace the step
and reach the breezes above, this is the task,
and in it the labour. *Ib.* 6

Procul, o procul este, profani.
Far, far from me,
Let all profane ones be. *Ib.*

Macte nova virtute, puer, sic itur ad astra. Good
luck to your young ambition, lad, that is the
way to the stars. *Ib.* 9

Latet anguis in herba. A snake lurks in the grass.
Eclogues, 3

Omnia vincit Amor: et nos cedamus Amori. Love
conquers all: and we succumb to love. *Ib.* 10

Labor omnia vincit. Work conquers all. *Georgics, 1*

Sed fugit interea, fugit inreparabile tempus. Time
meanwhile flies, flies never to return. *Ib.* 2

Hi motus animorum atque haec certamina tanta
Pulveris exigui iactu compressa quiescent.
These soul-stirrings and great conflicts are con-
tained and quelled by throwing a little dust. *Ib.* 4

Voltaire (François Marie Arouet)   1694-1778

I disapprove of what you say, but I will defend
to the death your right to say it. *Attrib.*

427

Tout est pour le mieux dans le meilleur des mondes possibles. All is for the best in the best of possible worlds. *Candide,* 1 (and elsewhere)

Dans ce pays-ci il est bon de tuer de temps en temps un amiral pour encourager les autres. In this country (England) it is considered good to kill an admiral from time to time, to encourage the others. *Ib. 23*

Il faut cultiver notre jardin—Quand l'homme fut mis dans le jardin d'Éden, il y fut mis pour qu'il travaillât; ce qui prouve que l'homme n'est pas né pour le repos.—Travaillons sans raisonner, c'est le seul moyen de rendre la vie supportable. We must look after our garden. When man was put in the garden of Eden, he was put there to work; that proves that man was not born for rest. Let us work without question, that is the only way to make life tolerable. *Ib. 30*

Si Dieu n'existait pas, il faudrait l'inventer. If God did not exist, it would be necessary to invent him. *Epîtres, 96*

All the ancient histories, as one of our wits said, are just fables that have been agreed upon.
Jeannot et Colin

Écrasez l'infâme. Wipe out the infamous. *Letter to d'Alembert,* 1760 (Voltaire's motto)

I have never made but one prayer to God, a very short one: "O Lord, make my enemies ridiculous." And God granted it. *Letter to Damilaville,* 1767

La Liberté est née en Angleterre des querelles des tyrans. Liberty was born in England from the quarrels of tyrants. *Lettres Philosophiques*

The most amazing and effective inventions are not those which do most honour to the human genius. *Ib.*

No-one will ever make me believe that I think all the time. *Ib.*

Divisés d'intérêts, et pour le crime unis. Divided by interests, and united by crime. *Mérope, 1*

Le sombre Anglais, même dans ses amours,
Veut raisonner toujours.
On est plus raisonnable en France.
The gloomy Englishman, even in his loves, always wants to reason. We are more reasonable in France. *Les Originaux, Entrée des Diverses Nations*

La crainte suit la crime, et c'est son châtiment. Fear follows crime, and is its punishment. *Semiramis, 5*

Le lâche fuit en vain; la mort vole à sa suite
C'est en la défiant que le brave l'évite.
The coward flies in vain, death follows close behind. It is by defying it that the brave escapes.
Le Triumvirat, 4

Wallace, Lew   **1827-1905**

Beauty is altogether in the eye of the beholder.
The Prince of India 3, 6

Wallace, William Ross c. 1819-1881

The hand that rocks the cradle
Is the hand that rules the world.
John o' London's Treasure Trove

Waller, Edmund 1606-1687

Go, lovely Rose!
Tell her, that wastes her time and me,
That now she knows,
When I resemble her to thee,
How sweet and fair she seems to be. *Song*

Walpole, Horace 1717-1797

They who cannot perform great things themselves
may yet have a satisfaction in doing justice to
those who can. *Attrib.*

Our supreme governors, the mob. *Letter*, 1743

Old age is no such uncomfortable thing if one
gives oneself up to it with a good grace, and
don't drag it about " To midnight dances and
the public show." *Ib.* 1774

By the waters of Babylon we sit down and weep,
when we think of thee, O America! *Ib.* 1775

The wisest prophets make sure of the event
first. *Ib.* 1785

Walpole, Sir Robert 1676-1745

All those men have their price. *Attrib.*

Madam, there are fifty thousand men slain this
year in Europe, and not one Englishman. *Remark
to the Queen*, 1734

The balance of power. *Speech, House of Commons*, 1741

Walton, Izaak   1593-1683

As no man is born an artist, so no man is born an angler. *Compleat Angler. Epistle to the Reader*

An excellent angler, and now with God. *Ib.* 4

We may say of angling as Dr. Boteler said of strawberries: "Doubtless God could have made a better berry, but doubtless God never did"; and so (if I might be judge) God never did make a more calm, quiet, innocent recreation than angling. *Ib.*

Ward Artemus (Charles Farrar Browne)   1834-1867

He [Brigham Young] is dreadfully married. He's the most married man I ever saw in my life. *Artemus Ward's Lecture*

Let us all be happy, and live within our means, even if we have to borrer the money to do it with. *Ib.*

Washington, George   1732-1799

Few men have virtue to withstand the highest bidder. *Moral Maxims*

To persevere in one's duty and be silent is the best answer to calumny. *Ib.*

Labor to keep alive in your breast that little spark of celestial fire, called Conscience. *Ib.*

431

I hope I shall always possess firmness and virtue enough to maintain what I consider the most enviable of all titles, the character of an "Honest Man." *Ib.*

Influence is not government. *Political Maxims*

Associate yourself with men of good quality if you esteem your own reputation; for 'tis better to be alone than in bad company. *Rules of Civility*

It is not a custom with me to keep money to look at. *Letter,* 1780

Be courteous to all, but intimate with few, and let those few be well tried before you give them your confidence. True friendship is a plant of slow growth, and must undergo and withstand the shocks of adversity before it is entitled to the appellation. *Ib.* 1783

Mankind, when left to themselves, are unfit for their own government. *Ib.* 1786

Liberty, when it begins to take root, is a plant of rapid growth. *Ib.* 1788

The very idea of the power and the right of the People to establish Government, presupposes the duty of every individual to obey the established Government. *Farewell Address,* 1796

'Tis our true policy to steer clear of permanent alliances, with any portion of the foreign world. *Ib.*

Watson, Sir William   **1858-1936**

The staid conservative,   Came-over-with-the
Conqueror type of mind.   *A Study in Contrasts*

Weatherly, Frederic Edward   **1848-1929**

The gallant boys of the old brigade,
They sleep in old England's heart.
                                    The Old Brigade

Webster, Daniel   **1782-1852**

There is always room at the top. *Remark*

The people's government, made for the people,
made by the people, and answerable to the
people. *Speech*, 1830

I was born an American; I will live an American;
I shall die an American. *Ib.* 1850

Webster, John   **c. 1580-1625**

We are merely the stars' tennis-balls, struck and
  bandied,
Which way please them. *The Duchess of Malfi*, 5

Call for the robin redbreast and the wren,
Since o'er shady groves they hover,
And with leaves and flowers do cover
The friendless bodies of unburied men.
                                    The White Devil, 5

Glories, like glow-worms, afar off shine bright,
But, looked too near, have neither heat nor light.
                                    The White Devil, 5

Is not old wine wholesomest, old pippins tooth-
somest? Does not old wood burn brightest, old
linen wash whitest? Old soldiers, sweethearts, are
surest, and old lovers are soundest.
                                    Westward Hoe, 2

Prosperity doth bewitch men, seeming clear;
As seas do laugh, show white, when rocks are near
The White Devil, 5

I saw him even now going the way of all flesh.
Westward Hoe, 2

Wedgewood, Cicely Veronica   b. 1910

. . . truth can neither be apprehended nor com-
municated . . . history is an art like all other
sciences. *Truth and Opinion*

Wellington, Arthur Wellesley, Duke of   1769-1852

The battle of Waterloo was won in the playing
fields of Eton. *Attrib.*

Up guards and at 'em! *Attrib. remark during
Battle of Waterloo (but see below)*

What I must have said and possibly did say was,
Stand up, Guards! and then gave the commanding
officers the order to attack. *Letter to J. W. Croker*

Publish and be damned. *Attrib.*

Wells, Herbert George   1866-1946

Every time Europe looks across the Atlantic to
see the American eagle, it observes only the rear
end of an ostrich. *America*

How d'you like her? Puts old Velasquez in his
place. A young mistress is better than an old
master, eh? *Autocracy of Mr. Parham, 3*

434

They feared the " low " and they hated and despised the " stuck up " and so they " kept themselves to themselves," according to the English ideal. *Kipps 1, 1*

I tell you, we're in a blessed drain-pipe, and we've got to crawl along it till we die. *Ib.* 1, 2

There's no social differences—till women come in. *Ib.* 2, 4

I don't 'old with Wealth. What *is* Wealth? Labour robbed out of the poor. *Ib.*

[Of the British officer] He muffs his real job without a blush, and yet he would rather be shot than do his bootlaces up criss-cross. *Mr. Britling Sees It Through 2, 4*

Moral indignation is jealousy with a halo. *The Wife of Sir Isaac Harman,* 9

Wesker, Arnold   b. 1932

There will always be human beings and as long as there are, there will always be the idea of brotherhood. *Chicken Soup with Barley, 3*

Wesley, John   1703-1791

I look upon all the world as my parish. *Journal,* 1739

Though I am always in haste, I am never in a hurry. *Letter,* 1777

Whistler, James Abbott McNeil   1834-1903

I am not arguing with you—I am telling you. *Gentle Art of Making Enemies*

[Oscar Wilde: I wish I had said that.]
Whistler: You will, Oscar, you will.

Oscar Wilde, Ingleby

[To a lady who said that a landscape reminded her of his work] Yes, madam, Nature is creeping up. *Whistler Stories*, D. C. Seitz

You shouldn't say it is not good. You should say, you do not like it; and then, you know, you're perfectly safe. *Ib.*

White, William Allen   1868-1944

All dressed up, with nowhere to go. *Remark*, 1916

Whitman, Walt   1819-1892

Women sit or move to and fro, some old, some
    young.
The young are beautiful—but the old are more
    beautiful than the young. *Beautiful Women*

Silent and amazed even when a little boy,
I remember I heard the preacher every Sunday
    put God in his statements,
As contending against some being or influence.
A Child's Amaze

If anything is sacred the human body is sacred.
I Sing the Body Electric

O Captain! my Captain! our fearful trip is done.
O Captain! My Captain!

Where the populace rise at once against the
    never-ending audacity of elected persons.
Song of the Broad Axe, 5

Where women walk in public processions in the
  streets the same as the men,
Where they enter the public assembly and take
  places the same as the men;
Where the city of the faithfullest friends stands,
Where the city of the cleanliness of the sexes
  stands. . . .
. . . There the great city stands. *Ib.*

[Of Animals]
They do not sweat and whine about their condition,
They do not lie awake in the dark and weep for
  their sins,
They do not make me sick discussing their duty
  to God,
Not one is dissatisfied, not one is demented with
  the mania of owning things,
Not one kneels to another, nor to his kind that
  lived thousands of years ago. *Song of Myself*

Behold, I do not give lectures or a little charity,
When I give I give myself. *Ib.*

The earth, that is sufficient,
I do not want the constellations any nearer,
I know they are very well where they are,
I know they suffice for those who belong to them.
  Song of the Open Road

That shadow my likeness that goes to and fro
  seeking a livelihood, chattering, chaffering,
How often I find myself standing and looking at
  it where it flits,
How often I question and doubt whether that is
  really me. *That Shadow My Likeness*

437

Youth, large, lusty, loving—youth full of grace,
force, fascination,
Do you know that Old Age may come after
you with equal grace, force, fascination?
Youth, Day, Old Age and Night

I no doubt deserved my enemies, but I don't
believe I deserved my friends. *Biography and the
Human Heart*, Bradford

Whittier, John Greenleaf   1807-1892

" Shoot if you must, this old grey head,
But spare your country's flag," she said.
Barbara Frietchie

For all sad words of tongue or pen,
The saddest are these: " It might have been! "
Maud Muller

The Indian Summer of the heart! *Memories*

Wilcox, Ella Wheeler   1855-1919

Laugh and the world laughs with you;
Weep, and you weep alone;
For the sad old earth must borrow its mirth,
But has trouble enough of its own.   *Solitude*

So many gods, so many creeds,
So many paths that wind and wind.
The World's Need

Wilde, Oscar O'Flahertie Wills   1854-1900

At least
I have not made my heart a heart of stone,
Nor starved my boyhood of its goodly feast,
Nor walked where Beauty is a thing unknown.
Apologia

That little tent of blue
Which prisoners call the sky.
The Ballad of Reading Gaol, 1

Yet each man kills the thing he loves,
By each let this be heard,
Some do it with a bitter look,
Some with a flattering word.
The coward does it with a kiss,
The brave man with a sword! *Ib.*

For Man's grim Justice goes its way,
And will not swerve aside:
It slays the weak, it slays the strong,
It has a deadly stride. *Ib.* 3

For he who lives more lives than one
More deaths than one must die. *Ib.*

There is no chapel on the day
On which they hang a man. *Ib.* 4

I know not whether Laws be right,
Or whether Laws be wrong;
All that we know who lie in gaol
Is that the wall is strong;
And that each day is like a year,
A year whose days are long. *Ib.* 5

Each passion being loth
For love's own sake to leave the other's side
Yet killing love by staying. *The Burden of Itys*

Sing on! sing on! I would be drunk with life,
Drunk with the trampled vintage of my youth. *Ib.*

No, my Lord Cardinal, I weary of her!
Why, she is worse than ugly, she is good.
The Duchess of Padua, 2

439

Ay! without love

Life is no better than the unhewn stone
Which in the quarry lies, before the sculptor
Has set God within it. *Ib.*

We are each our own devil, and we make
This world our hell. *Ib.* 5

And down the long and silent street,
The dawn, with silver-sandalled feet,
Crept like a frightened girl. *The Harlot's House*

Ah! somehow life is bigger after all
Than any painted Angel. *Humanitad*

Wickedness is a myth invented by good people
to account for the curious attractiveness of others.
*Phrases and Philosophies for the Use of the
Young. Chameleon,* 1894

Religions die when they are proved to be true.
Science is the record of dead religions. *Ib.*

Nothing that actually occurs is of the smallest
importance. *Ib.*

If one tells the truth, one is sure, sooner or later,
to be found out. *Ib.*

It is only by not paying one's bills that one can
hope to live in the memory of the commercial
classes. *Ib.*

The only way to atone for being occasionally a
little over-dressed is by being always absolutely
over-educated. *Ib.*

In examinations the foolish ask questions that
the wise cannot answer. *Ib.*

The old believe everything: the middle-aged suspect everything: the young know everything. *Ib.*

To love oneself is the beginning of a lifelong romance. *Ib.* (cf. *An Ideal Husband*, p. 442)

As for modern journalism, it is not my business to defend it. It justifies its own existence by the great Darwinian principle of the survival of the vulgarest. *The Critic as Artist*, 1

To give an accurate description of what has never occurred is not merely the proper occupation of the historian, but the inalienable privilege of any man of parts and culture. *Ib.*

Education is an admirable thing, but it is well to remember from time to time that nothing that is worth knowing can be taught. *Ib.*

For there is no art where there is no style, and no style where there is no unity, and unity is of the individual. *Ib.*

Movement, that problem of the visible arts, can be truly realised by Literature alone. It is Literature that shows us the body in its swiftness and the soul in its unrest. *Ib.* 2

Ah! don't say that you agree with me. When people agree with me I always feel that I must be wrong. *Ib.*

As long as war is regarded as wicked, it will always have its fascination. When it is looked upon as vulgar, it will cease to be popular. The

change will, of course, be slow, and people will
not be conscious of it. *Ib.*

I became the spendthrift of my own genius and
to waste an eternal youth gave me a curious joy.
                                    De Profundis

Most people are other people. Their thoughts
are someone else's opinions, their lives a mimicry,
their passions a quotation. *Ib.*

Everybody who is incapable of learning has taken
to teaching. *The Decay of Lying*

The final revelation is that Lying, the telling of
beautiful untrue things, is the proper aim of Art.
                                                    Ib.

Those things which the English public never
forgives—youth, power, and enthusiasm.
                        Lecture. The English Renaissance

Men can be analysed, women . . . merely adored.
                                An Ideal Husband, 1

Questions are never indiscreet. Answers sometimes are. *Ib.*

Morality is simply the attitude we adopt
towards people whom we personally dislike. *Ib.* 2

To love oneself is the beginning of a lifelong
romance, Phipps. *Ib.* 3   (cf. p. 441)

Really, if the lower orders don't set us a good
example, what on earth is the use of them? They

seem, as a class, to have absolutely no sense of moral responsibility. *The Importance of Being Earnest*, 1

The truth is rarely pure and never simple. Modern life would be very tedious if it were either, and modern literature a complete impossibility. *Ib*.

You don't seem to realise, that in married life three is company and two is none. *Ib*.

CECILY: When I see a spade I call it a spade.
GWENDOLEN: I am glad to say that I have never seen a spade. It is obvious that our social spheres have been widely different. *Ib*. 2

On an occasion of this kind it becomes more than a moral duty to speak one's mind. It becomes a pleasure. *Ib*.

Three addresses always inspire confidence, even in tradesmen. *Ib*. 3

Never speak disrespectfully of Society, Algernon. Only people who can't get into it do that. *Ib*.

Untruthful! My nephew Algernon? Impossible! He is an Oxonian. *Ib*.

Please do not shoot the pianist. He is doing his best. *Impressions of America*, Leadville

It is absurd to divide people into good and bad. People are either charming or tedious. *Lady Windermere's Fan*, 1

I couldn't help it. I can resist everything except temptation. *Ib*.

He thinks like a Tory, and talks like a Radical, and that's so important nowadays. *Ib.* 2

CECIL GRAHAM: What is a cynic?
LORD DARLINGTON: A man who knows the price of everything and the value of nothing. *Ib.*

[Wilde was to be charged a large fee for an operation] " Ah, well, then," said Oscar, " I suppose that I shall have to die beyond my means." *Life of Oscar Wilde*, R. H. Sherard

[At the New York Customs] I have nothing to declare except my genius. *Oscar Wilde*, F. Harris

There is no such thing as a moral or an immoral book. Books are well written or badly written. *Picture of Dorian Gray*, preface

There is only one thing in the world worse than being talked about, and that is not being talked about. *Ib.*

The only way to get rid of a temptation is to yield to it. *Ib.* 2

A cigarette is the perfect type of a perfect pleasure. It is exquisite, and it leaves me unsatisfied. What more can one want? *Ib.* 6

And out of the bronze of the image of *The Sorrow that endureth for Ever* he fashioned an image of *The Pleasure that abideth for a Moment*. *Poems in Prose. The Artist*

A thing is not necessarily true because a man dies for it. *Sebastian Melmoth and Oscariana*

444

If property had simply pleasures, we could stand it; but its duties make it unbearable. In the interest of the rich we must get rid of it.
The Soul of Man under Socialism

We are often told that the poor are grateful for charity. Some of them are, no doubt, but the best amongst the poor are never grateful. They are ungrateful, discontented, disobedient, and rebellious. They are quite right to be so. *Ib.*

As for the virtuous poor, one can pity them, of course, but one cannot possibly admire them. They have made private terms with the enemy, and sold their birthright for very bad pottage. *Ib.*

Most personalities have been obliged to be rebels. *Ib.*

The Lords Temporal say nothing, the Lords Spiritual have nothing to say, and the House of Commons has nothing to say and says it. We are dominated by Journalism. *Ib.*

Let God or the Czar look to it. *Vera or The Nihilists*

Experience, the name men give to their mistakes. *Ib.*

It is not customary in England, Miss Worsley, for a young lady to speak with such enthusiasm of any person of the opposite sex. English women conceal their feelings till after they are married.
A Woman of No Importance, 1

It is the problem of slavery. And we are trying to solve it by amusing the slaves. *Ib.*

The English country gentleman galloping after a fox—the unspeakable in full pursuit of the uneatable. *Ib.*

Twenty years of romance make a woman look like a ruin; but twenty years of marriage make her something like a public building. *Ib.*

Children begin by loving their parents. After a time they judge them. Rarely, if ever, do they forgive them. *Ib.* (also in Act 3)

You should study the Peerage, Gerald. It is the one book a young man about town should know thoroughly, and it is the best thing in fiction the English have done. *Ib. 3*

Moderation is a fatal thing, Lady Hunstanton. Nothing succeeds like excess. *Ib.*

Williams, Tennessee   b. 1912

Knowledge—Zzzzzp! Money—Zzzzzzp!—Power! That's the cycle democracy is built on! *The Glass Menagerie*

Wilson, Thomas Woodrow   1856-1924

Law is the crystallisation of the habit and thought of society. *Lecture*, 1893

Generally young men are regarded as radicals. This is a popular misconception. The most conservative persons I ever met are college undergraduates. *Address*, 1905

America lives in the heart of every man everywhere who wishes to find a region where he will be free to work out his destiny as he chooses.
Speech, April, 1912

The history of liberty is a history of resistance.
Ib. Sept., 1912

I fancy that it is just as hard to do your duty when men are sneering at you as when they are shooting at you. *Ib. 1914*

No nation is fit to sit in judgement upon any other nation. *Address, April, 1915*

There is such a thing as a man being too proud to fight. *Ib. 10th May, 1915*

The lines of red are lines of blood, nobly and unselfishly shed by men who loved the liberty of their fellowmen more than they loved their own lifes and fortunes. *Ib. 17th May, 1915*

Character is a by-product; it is produced in the great manufacture of daily duty. *Ib. 31st May, 1915*

One cool judgement is worth a thousand hasty councils. *Speech, Jan., 1916*

There is a price which is too great to pay for peace, and that price can be put in one word. One cannot pay the price of self-respect. *Ib. Feb., 1916*

It must be a peace without victory.
Address, Jan., 1917

The world must be made safe for democracy. *Ib. April, 1917*

The right is more precious than peace. *Ib.*

Let it be your pride, therefore, to show all men everywhere not only what good soldiers you are, but also what good men you are. *Address to the National Army*, 1917

By a progressive I do not mean a man who is ready to move, but a man who knows where he is going when he moves. *Speech*, 1919

Wolfe, Charles   1791-1823

But he lay like a warrior taking his rest,
With his martial cloak around him.
    The Burial of Sir John Moore at Corunna

We carved not a line, and we raised not a stone—
But we left him alone in his glory. *Ib.*

Wolsey, Thomas, Cardinal   c. 1475-1530

Had I but served God as diligently as I have served the King, he would not have given me over in my gray hairs. *Attrib.*

Wordsworth, William   1770-1850

Suffering is permanent, obscure, and dark,
And shares the nature of infinity. *The Borderers*

I wandered lonely as a cloud
That floats on high o'er vales and hills,
When all at once I saw a crowd,
A host of golden daffodils. *Daffodils*

For oft when on my couch I lie
In vacant or in pensive mood,
They flash upon that inward eye
Which is the bliss of solitude;
And then my heart with pleasure fills,
And dances with the daffodils. *Ib.*

448

On Man, on Nature and on Human Life,
Musing in solitude. *The Excursion*, preface

Oh! many are the Poets that are sown
By Nature; men endowed with highest gifts,
The vision and the faculty divine;
Yet wanting the accomplishment of verse. *Ib.* 1

Wisdom is ofttimes nearer when we stoop
Than when we soar. *Ib.* 3

          The wiser mind
Mourns less for what age takes away
Than what it leaves behind. *The Fountain*

   Not in entire forgetfulness,
   And not in utter nakedness,
But trailing clouds of glory do we come
   From God, who is our home:
Heaven lies about us in our infancy!
Shades of the prison house begin to close
   Upon the growing boy.
          Intimations of Immortality

To me the meanest flower that blows can give
Thoughts that do often lie too deep for tears. *Ib.*

In that sweet mood when pleasant thoughts
Bring sad thoughts to the mind.
          Lines Written in Early Spring

The world is too much with us; late and soon,
Getting and spending, we lay waste our powers.
          Miscellaneous Sonnets 1, 33

Earth has not anything to show more fair. *Ib.* 36
(*Composed upon Westminster Bridge*)

The Child is father of the Man. *My Heart Leaps Up*

A primrose by a river's brim
A yellow primrose was to him
And it was nothing more. *Peter Bell*

A reasoning, self-sufficing thing,
An intellectual All-in all! *A Poet's Epitaph*

But who is He, with modest looks,
And clad in homely russet brown?
He murmurs near the running brooks
A music sweeter than their own. *Ib.*

There is a dark
Inscrutable workmanship that reconciles
Discordant elements, makes them cling together
In one society. *The Prelude*, 1

Bliss was it in that dawn to be alive,
But to be young was very heaven. *Ib.* 11

There is
One great society alone on earth:
The noble living and the noble dead. *Ib.*

Instruct them how the mind of man becomes
A thousand times more beautiful than the earth
On which he dwells. *Ib.* 14

Choice words, and measured phrase, above the reach
Of ordinary men; a stately speech;
Such as grave livers do in Scotland use.
Resolution and Independence

Some natural sorrow, loss, or pain
That has been, and may be again.
The Solitary Reaper

The music in my heart I bore,
Long after it was heard no more. *Ib.*

Wisdom doth live with children round her knees.
Sonnets Dedicated to Liberty, 4

Happy is he, who, caring not for Pope,
Consul, or King, can sound himself to know
The destiny of Man, and live in hope. *Ib.* 5

Men are we, and must grieve when even the Shade
Of that which once was great is pass'd away. *Ib.* 6

Milton! thou should'st be living at this hour:
England hath need of thee. *Ib.* 14

We must be free or die, who speak the tongue
That Shakespeare spake; the faith and morals
    hold
Which Milton held. *Ib.*

We shall exult, if They who rule the land
Be Men who hold its many blessings dear,
Wise, upright, valiant; not a venal Band,
Who are to judge of danger which they fear,
And honour which they do not understand. *Ib.* 26

Books! 'tis a dull and endless strife:
Come, hear the woodland linnet,
How sweet his music! on my life,
There's more of wisdom in it. *The Tables Turned*

Sweet is the lore which Nature brings;
Our meddling intellect

Misshapes the beauteous forms of things:
We murder to dissect. *Ib.*

Feelings too
Of unremembered pleasure; such perhaps,
As may have had no trivial influence
On that best portion of a good man's life;
His little nameless, unremembered acts
Of kindness and of love. *Tintern Abbey*

But hearing oftentimes
The still sad music of humanity. *Ib.*

Sweet childish days, that were as long
As twenty days are now. *To a Butterfly*

O cuckoo! Shall I call thee bird,
Or but a wandering voice? *To the Cuckoo*

Every great and original writer, in proportion as
he is great and original, must himself create the
taste by which he is to be relished. *Letter to
Lady Beaumont*

I have said that poetry is the spontaneous overflow
of powerful feelings: it takes its origin from
emotion recollected in tranquillity: the emotion
is contemplated till, by a species of reaction, the
tranquillity gradually disappears, and an emotion,
kindred to that which was before the subject of
contemplation, is gradually produced, and does
itself actually exist in the mind. *Preface to the
Lyrical Ballads*

Wotton, Sir Henry   1568-1639

He first deceased; she for a little tried
To live without him: liked it not, and died.
        Death of Sir Albertus Morton's Wife

You meaner Beauties of the Night,
That poorly satisfie our Eyes.
On his Mistris, the Queen of Bohemia

Legatus est vir bonus peregrare missus ad mentiendum rei publicae causae. An ambassador is an honest man sent to lie abroad for the good of the state. *Written in the Album of Christopher Fleckamore, 1604*

Wren, Sir Christopher   1632-1723

Si monumentum requiris, circumspice. If you would see his monument look around. *Inscription, St. Paul's Cathedral, London*

Wyntoun, Andrew   c. 1350-c. 1420

Quhen Alysandyr oure King wes dede
That Scotland led in luve and lé,
Away wes sons of Ale and Brede,
Of wyne and wax, of gamyn and glé,
Oure gold wes changyd into lede.
Chryst, born into Virgynyté,
Succour Scotland, and remede
That stad in perplexyté.
Oryginale Cronykille of Scotland

Yeats, William Butler   1865-1939

A line will take us hours may be;
Yet if it does not seem a moment's thought,
Our stitching and unstitching has been naught.
Adam's Curse

And God-appointed Berkeley that proved all things a dream. *Blood and the Moon*

That dolphin-torn, that gong-tormented sea.
Byzantium

The years like great black oxen tread the world,
And God the herdsman goads them on behind,
And I am broken by their passing feet.
The Countess Cathleen, 4

MacDonagh and MacBride
And Connolly and Pearse
Now and in time to be,
Wherever green is worn,
Are changed, changed utterly:
A terrible beauty is born. *Easter*, 1916

A king is but a foolish labourer
Who wastes his blood to be another's dream.
Fergus and the Druid

" Call down the hawk from the air;
Let him be hooded or caged
Till the yellow eye has grown mild." *The Hawk*

And God stands winding His lonely horn,
And time and the world are ever in flight.
Into the Twilight

Those that I fight I do not hate,
Those that I guard I do not love;
My country is Kiltartan Cross,
My countrymen Kiltartan's poor,
No likely end could bring them loss
Or leave them happier than before.
An Irish Airman Foresees his Death

The years to come seemed waste of breath,
A waste of breath the years behind
In balance with this life, this death. *Ib.*

I will arise and go now, and go to Innisfree,
And a small cabin build there, of clay and wattles
  made.   *The Lake Isle of Innisfree*

Of a land where even the old are fair,
And even the wise are merry of tongue.
                The Land of the Heart's Desire

The wrong of unshapely things is a wrong too
  great to be told.   *The Lover tells of the Rose in
his Heart*

When I was a boy with never a crack in my heart.
        The Meditation of the Old Fisherman

A statesman is an easy man,
He tells his lies by rote;
A journalist makes up his lies
And takes you by the throat;
So stay at home and drink your beer
And let the neighbours vote.
          Said the man in the golden breastplate
         Under the old stone Cross
                The Old Stone Cross

If Folly link with Elegance
No man knows which is which.   *Ib.*

I think it better that in times like these
A poet's mouth be silent, for in truth
We have no gift to set a statesman right;
He has had enough of meddling who can please
A young girl in the indolence of her youth,
Or an old man upon a winter's night.
          On being Asked for a War Poem

In courtesy I'd have her chiefly learned;
Hearts are not had as a gift but hearts are earned
By those that are not entirely beautiful.
A Prayer for My Daughter

Danger no refuge holds, and war no peace,
For him who hears love sing and never cease.
The Rose of Battle

An aged man is but a paltry thing,
A tattered coat upon a stick, unless
Soul clap its hands and sing.
Sailing to Byzantium

A woman of so shining loveliness
That men threshed corn at midnight by a tress.
The Secret Rose

Was it for this the wild geese spread
The grey wing upon every tide;
For this that all that blood was shed?
September, 1913

Romantic Ireland's dead and gone,
It's with O'Leary in the grave. *Ib.*

It is love that I am seeking for,
But of a beautiful unheard-of kind
That is not in the world.   *The Shadowy Waters*

      Do you not know
How great a wrong it is to let one's thought
Wander a moment when one is in love?   *Ib.*

A girl arose that had red mournful lips
And seemed the greatness of the world in tears.

Doomed like Odysseus and the labouring ships
And proud as Priam murdered with his peers.
                              The Sorrow of Love

Know, that I would accounted be
True brother of a company
That sang, to sweeten Ireland's wrong,
Ballad and story, rann and song.
                    To Ireland in the Coming Times

Come near; I would, before my time to go,
Sing of old Eire and the ancient ways:
Red Rose, proud Rose, sad Rose of all my days!
                To the Rose upon the Rood of Time

Irish poets, learn your trade,
Sing whatever is well made,
Scorn the sort now growing up
All out of shape from toe to top,
Their unremembering hearts and heads
Base-born products of base beds.
                              Under Ben Bulben

          Cast a cold eye
          On life, on death.
          Horsemen, pass by!

                    Ib. (Yeats epitaph)

To dream of women whose beauty was folded in
     dismay,
Even in an old story, is a burden not to be borne.
                              Under the Moon

They that have red cheeks will have pale cheeks
for my sake, and for all that, they will think they
are well paid. *Cathleen ni Houlihan*

Twelve pennies! What better reason for killing a man? *The Death of Cuchulain*

A good writer should be so simple that he has no faults, only sins. *The Death of Synge*

We have no longer in any country a literature as great as the literature of the old world, and that is because the newspapers, all kinds of second rate books, the preoccupation of men with all kinds of practical changes, have driven the living imagination out of this world. *Samhain*, 1904

Young, Edward   1683-1765

Procrastination is the thief of time.
         The Complaint. Night Thoughts, Night 1

Man wants but little; nor that little long. *Ib.* 4

A God all mercy, is a God unjust. *Ib.*

   Be wise with speed;
A fool at forty is a fool indeed. *Love of Fame*

Zangwill, Israel   1864-1926

Let us start a new religion with one commandment, " Enjoy thyself." *Children of the Ghetto*

Zola, Emile   1840-1902

J'accuse. I accuse. *Title of letter to the President of the Republic*, 1898 (On the Dreyfus Affair)

SUPPLEMENT OF SONGS

A LIFE ON THE OCEAN WAVE, Epes Sargent (1813–80)
AFTER THE BALL, Charles K. Harris (1865–1930)
ALEXANDER'S RAGTIME BAND, Irving Berlin (1888–)
ANNIE LAURIE, William Douglas (1672–1748) *adapted by* Lady John Scott (1810–1900)
AULD LANG SYNE, Robert Burns (1759–96)
BURLINGTON BERTIE, William Hargreaves (1846–1919)
CAMPTOWN RACES, Stephen Collins Foster (1826–64)
CHERRY RIPE, Robert Herrick (1591–1674)
CLEMENTINE, Percy Montrose (19th century)
COCKLES AND MUSSELS, *Oxford Song Book*
COME, COME, COME AND MAKE EYES AT ME DOWN AT THE OLD " BULL AND BUSH," Harry Tilzer (1878–1956); *sung by* Florrie Ford
COME, LANDLORD, FILL THE FLOWING BOWL, *Oxford Song Book*
DADDY WOULDN'T BUY ME A BOW-WOW, Joseph Tabrar (1857–1931); *sung by* Vesta Victoria
DAISY BELL, Harry Dacre (fl. 1892)
EARLY ONE MORNING, *Oxford Song Book*
FLOW GENTLY, SWEET AFTON, Robert Burns (1759–96)
FORTY YEARS ON, Harrow School Song, Edward Ernest Bowen (1836–1901)
GALWAY BAY, Dr. Arthur Colahan
GOD REST YOU MERRY, *Oxford Book of Carols*
GOOD KING WENCESLAS, John Mason Neale (1818–66)
GREEN GROW THE RASHES, Robert Burns (1759–96)
GREENSLEEVES, *A Handful of Pleasant Delites*, 1584
HAS ANYBODY HERE SEEN KELLY?, C. W. Murphy (19th century)
HEART OF OAK, David Garrick (1717–79)
HELLO, YOUNG LOVERS, *The King and I*, Oscar Hammerstein II (1895–1960)
HOME ON THE RANGE, Dr. Brewster Higley (19th century)
HOME, SWEET HOME, *Clari, the Maid of Milan*, John Howard Payne (1791–1852)
I COULD BE HAPPY WITH YOU, *The Boy Friend*, Sandy Wilson (1924–)

459

I Do Like To Be Beside the Seaside, John A. Glover-Kind (19th century)

I Dream of Jeanie with the Light Brown Hair, Stephen Collins Foster (1826–64)

I Love a Lassie, Sir Harry Lauder (1870–1950)

I Saw Three Ships, Oxford Book of Carols

I Wonder Who's Kissing Her Now, The Prince of To-night (1909), Frank R. Adams and Will M. Hough

If I Loved You, Carousel, Oscar Hammerstein II (1895–1960)

Indian Love Call, Rose Marie, Oscar Hammerstein II and Otto Harbach

It's a Long Way to Tipperary, Harry Williams (1874–1924) and Jack Judge (1878–1938)

John Brown's Body, Charles Sprague Hall (fl. 1860)

John Peel, John Woodcock Graves (1795–1886)

Just a Wee Deoch-an' Dorris, Sir Harry Lauder (1870–1950)

Just Like the Ivy, I'll Cling to You, A. J. Mills (19th century)

Keep Right on to the End of the Road, Sir Harry Lauder (1870–1950)

Keep the Home Fires Burning, Lena Guilbert Ford (1916?)

La Marseillaise, Claude Joseph Rouget de Lisle (1760–1836)

Land of Hope and Glory, A. C. Benson (1862–1925); song from Pomp and Circumstance, Edward Elgar

Love's Young Dream, Thomas Moore (1779–1852)

Mad Dogs and Englishmen, Noel Coward (1899–   )

Mademoiselle From Armentières, Red Rowley (20th century)

Marching Through Georgia, Henry Clay Work (1832–84)

Mary of Argyle, Charles Jefferys (1807–65)

Maryland! My Maryland!, James Ryder Randall (1839–1908)

Men of Harlech, William Duthie

My Love is like a Red, Red Rose, R. Burns (1759–96)

My Old Dutch, Albert Chevalier (1861–1923)

My Old Kentucky Home, Stephen Collins Foster (1826–64)

O No John! No John! No John! No!, Oxford Song Book

OFT IN THE STILLY NIGHT, Thomas Moore (1779–1852)

OH, DEAR! WHAT CAN THE MATTER BE?, Anon.

OH WHAT A BEAUTIFUL MORNING, *Oklahoma*, Oscar Hammerstein II (1895–1960)

OL' MAN RIVER, *Show Boat*, Oscar Hammerstein II

OLD FOLKS AT HOME, Stephen Collins Foster (1826–64)

OLD SOLDIERS NEVER DIE, *Song of World War I*

OVER THE RAINBOW, *The Wizard of Oz*, E. Y. Harburg

PACK UP YOUR TROUBLES IN YOUR OLD KIT-BAG, George Asaf [George H. Powell] (1880–1951)

POOR OLD JOE, Stephen Collins Foster (1826–64)

POP GOES THE WEASEL, W. R. Mandale (19th century)

RULE, BRITANNIA, *Alfred: A Masque*, James Thomson (1700–48)

SHENANDOAH, *Sea Shanty*

SILVER THREADS AMONG THE GOLD, Eben Rexford (1848–1916)

SISTER SUSIE'S SEWING SHIRTS FOR SOLDIERS, R. P. Weston (1914); *sung by* Al Jolson

SOME ENCHANTED EVENING, *South Pacific*, Oscar Hammerstein II (1895–1960)

SWING LOW, SWEET CHARIOT, *American Negro Spiritual*, c. 1850

TA-RA-RA-BOOM-DE-AY!, Henry J. Sayers (1855–1932)

THE BLUE BELLS OF SCOTLAND, Dorothea Jordan (1762–1816)

THE BONNIE BANKS O' LOCH LOMON', *Songs of the North*

THE BRITISH GRENADIERS, Anon.

THE CAMPBELLS ARE COMIN', Anon (c. 1715)

THE COBBLER'S SONG, *Chu Chin Chow*, Frederick Norton

THE DESERT SONG, *The Desert Song*, Oscar Hammerstein II *and* Otto Harbach

THE GIRL I LEFT BEHIND ME, Anon., c. 1759, *Oxford Song Book*

THE HOLLY AND THE IVY, *Oxford Book of Carols*

THE HONEY-SUCKLE AND THE BEE, Albert H. Fitz

THE LAIRD O' COCKPEN, Carolina, Lady Nairne (1766–1845)

THE LAST TIME I SAW PARIS, Oscar Hammerstein II (1895–1960)

THE LINCOLNSHIRE POACHER, *Oxford Song Book*

THE LITTLE BROWN JUG, *Oxford Song Book*

THE MAN ON THE FLYING TRAPEZE, George Leybourne (d. 1884)

461

THE MAN WHO BROKE THE BANK AT MONTE CARLO,
Fred Gilbert (1850–1903)

THE MINSTREL BOY, Thomas Moore (1779–1852)

THE NOBLE DUKE OF YORK, Anon. First printed in
Mother Goose (1913), A. Rackham

THE STAR-SPANGLED BANNER, Francis Scott Key (1779–
1843)

THE VICAR OF BRAY, *British Musical Miscellany*, 1734

THE WEARIN' O' THE GREEN, *Irish Street*

THERE IS A LADY, SWEET AND KIND, Thomas Ford
(c. 1580–1648)

THERE IS A TAVERN IN THE TOWN, *Oxford Song Book*

THERE'LL ALWAYS BE AN ENGLAND, Ross Parker (1914–)
and Hughie Charles (1907–)

THERE'S NAE LUCK ABOOT THE HOOSE, *The Mariner's Wife*

THERE'S NO BUSINESS LIKE SHOW BUSINESS, *Annie Get
Your Gun*, Irving Berlin (1888–)

THIS IS MY LOVELY DAY, *Bless the Bride*, A. P. Herbert
(1890–)

'TIS THE LAST ROSE, Thomas Moore (1779–1852)

TWO LOVELY BLACK EYES, Charles Coborn [C. W.
McCallum] (1852–1945)

WAITING AT THE CHURCH, Fred W. Leigh (20th century);
sung by Vesta Victoria

WALTZING MATILDA, Andrew Paterson (1864–1941)

WE'LL GATHER LILACS, *Perchance to Dream*, Ivor Novello
(1893–1951)

WHAT SHALL WE DO WITH THE DRUNKEN SAILOR?, *Sea
Shanty*

WHEN JOHNNY COMES MARCHING HOME AGAIN, *Oxford
Song Book*

WHERE DID YOU GET THAT HAT?, James Rolmaz (19th
century)

WIDDICOMBE FAIR, *Oxford Book of Ballads*

WILL YE NO COME BACK AGAIN? (Bonnie Charlie's
Noo Awa'), Carolina, Lady Nairne (1766–1845)

YANKEE DOODLE, Edward Bangs (fl. 1775)

YE BANKS AND BRAES O' BONNIE DOON, Robert Burns
(1759–96)

YE MARINERS OF ENGLAND, Thomas Campbell (1777–
1844)

YES, WE HAVE NO BANANAS, Frank Silver *and* Irving
Cohn (20th century)

SUPPLEMENT OF HYMNS

A LITTLE CHILD THE SAVIOUR CAME William Robertson (1820–64)

A SAFE STRONGHOLD OUR GOD IS STILL, Martin Luther (1483–1546); *tr. by* Thomas Carlyle (1795–1881)

ABIDE WITH ME, Henry Francis Lyte (1793–1847)

ALL CREATURES OF OUR GOD AND KING, St. Francis of Assisi (1182–1226); *tr. by* William Henry Draper (1855–1933)

ALL HAIL, THE POWER OF JESUS' NAME, Edward Perronet (1726–92)

ALL PEOPLE THAT ON EARTH DO DWELL, William Kethe, c. 1593

ALL THINGS BRIGHT AND BEAUTIFUL, Cecil Frances Alexander (1823–95)

AND DID THOSE FEET IN ANCIENT TIMES, William Blake (1757–1827)

AS WITH GLADNESS MEN OF OLD, William Chatterton Dix (1837–98)

AWAY IN A MANGER, NO CRIB FOR A BED, Anon.

BE THOU MY VISION, O LORD OF MY HEART, Ancient Irish, *tr. by* Mary Byrne (1880–1931); *versified by* Eleanor Hull (1860–1935)

BRIGHTEST AND BEST OF THE SONS OF THE MORNING, Reginald Heber (1783–1826)

BY COOL SILOAM'S SHADY RILL, Reginald Heber (1783–1826)

CHILD IN THE MANGER, Mary Macdonald (1817–c. 1890); *tr. by* Lachlan Macbean (1853–1931)

CHRISTIANS, AWAKE, SALUTE THE HAPPY MORN, John Byrom (1691–1763)

COME, CHILDREN, JOIN TO SING, Christian Henry Bateman (1813–89)

COME, HOLY GHOST, OUR SOULS INSPIRE, 9th century; *tr. by* John Cosin (1594–1672)

COURAGE, BROTHER! DO NOT STUMBLE, Norman MacLeod (1812–72)

CROWN HIM WITH MANY CROWNS, Matthew Bridges (1800–94) and Godfrey Thring (1823–1903)

DEAR LORD AND FATHER OF MANKIND, John Greenleaf Whittier (1807–92)

ETERNAL FATHER, STRONG TO SAVE, William Whiting (1825–78)

FAR ROUND THE WORLD THY CHILDREN SING THEIR SONG, Basil Joseph Mathews (1879–1951)

FATHER, LEAD ME, DAY BY DAY, John Page Hopps (1834–1912)

FIGHT THE GOOD FIGHT, John Samuel Bewley Monsell (1811–75)

FOR THE BEAUTY OF THE EARTH, Folliott Sandford Pierpoint (1835–1917)

FROM GREENLAND'S ICY MOUNTAINS, Reginald Heber (1783–1826)

GLORIOUS THINGS OF THEE ARE SPOKEN, John Newton (1725–1807)

GOD MOVES IN A MYSTERIOUS WAY, William Cowper (1731–1800)

GOD OF OUR FATHERS, KNOWN OF OLD, Rudyard Kipling (1865–1936)

GOD, WHO MADE THE EARTH, Sarah Rhodes (1829–1904)

GOLDEN HARPS ARE SOUNDING, Frances Ridley Havergal (1836–79)

GOOD CHRISTIAN MEN, REJOICE, John Mason Neale (1818–66)

GRACIOUS SPIRIT, HOLY GHOST, Christopher Wordsworth (1807–85)

HARK THE GLAD SOUND! THE SAVIOUR COMES, Philip Doddridge (1702–51)

HARK! THE HERALD ANGELS SING, Charles Wesley (1707–82)

HOLY FATHER, THOU HAST GIVEN, William Bruce (1812–82)

HOLY, HOLY, HOLY, LORD GOD ALMIGHTY, Reginald Heber (1783–1826)

HOLY SPIRIT, HEAR US, William Henry Parker (1845–1929)

HOSANNA, LOUD HOSANNA, Jennette Threlfall (1821–80)

HUSHED WAS THE EVENING HYMN, James Drummond Burns (1823–64)

I LOVE TO HEAR THE STORY, Emily Huntington Miller (1833–1913)

I THINK, WHEN I READ THAT SWEET STORY OF OLD, Jemima Luke (1813–1906)

464

IF I COME TO JESUS, Frances Jane van Alstyne (1820–1915)

IMMORTAL, INVISIBLE, GOD ONLY WISE, Walter Chalmers Smith (1824–1908)

IN THE BLEAK MID-WINTER, Christina Georgina Rossetti (1830–94)

IN THE FIELDS WITH THEIR FLOCKS ABIDING, Frederic William Farrar (1831–1903)

IT CAME UPON THE MIDNIGHT CLEAR, Edmund Hamilton Sears (1810–76)

JERUSALEM THE GOLDEN, Bernard of Cluny (12th century); *tr.* by John Mason Neale (1818–66)

JESUS CALLS US! O'ER THE TUMULT, Cecil Frances Alexander (1823–95)

JESUS CHRIST IS RISEN TO-DAY, *Lyra Davidica*, 1708

JESUS, FRIEND OF LITTLE CHILDREN, Walter John Mathams (1853–1931)

JESUS LOVES ME! THIS I KNOW, Anna Bartlett Warner (1820–1915)

JUST AS I AM, THINE OWN TO BE, Marianne Farningham (1834–1936)

LAND OF OUR BIRTH, WE PLEDGE TO THEE, Rudyard Kipling (1865–1936)

LEAD US, HEAVENLY FATHER, LEAD US, James Edmeston (1791–1867)

LEAD US, O FATHER, IN THE PATHS OF PEACE, William Henry Burleigh (1812–71)

LET US WITH A GLADSOME MIND, John Milton (1608–74)

LORD, IN THE FULNESS OF MY MIGHT, Thomas Hornblower Gill (1819–1906)

LORD OF ALL BEING, THRONED AFAR, Oliver Wendell Holmes (1809–94)

LORD, THY WORD ABIDETH, Henry Williams Baker (1821–77)

LOVE CAME DOWN AT CHRISTMAS, Christina Georgina Rossetti (1830–94)

LOVE DIVINE, ALL LOVES EXCELLING, Charles Wesley (1707–88)

MINE EYES HAVE SEEN THE GLORY, Julia Ward Howe (1819–1910) and others

MY GOD, HOW WONDERFUL THOU ART, Frederick William Faber (1814–63)

NEARER, MY GOD, TO THEE, Sarah Flower Adams (1805–48)

NOW THANK WE ALL OUR GOD, Martin Rinkart (1586–1649); *tr. by* Catherine Winkworth (1829–78)

NOW THE DAY IS OVER, Sabine Baring-Gould (1834–1924)

O COME, ALL YE FAITHFUL, 18th century; *tr. by* (i) Frederick Oakeley (1802–80), (ii) William Mercer (1811–73)

O FOR A CLOSER WALK WITH GOD, William Cowper (1731–1800)

O GOD, OUR HELP IN AGES PAST, Isaac Watts (1674–1748)

O LITTLE TOWN OF BETHLEHEM, Phillips Brooks (1835–93)

O LOVE THAT WILT NOT LET ME GO, George Matheson (1842–93)

O PERFECT LOVE, Dorothy Frances Gurney (1858–1932)

O WHAT CAN LITTLE HANDS DO, Anon.

O WORSHIP THE KING ALL-GLORIOUS ABOVE, Robert Grant (1779–1838)

ONCE IN ROYAL DAVID'S CITY, Cecil Frances Alexander (1823–95)

ONWARD! CHRISTIAN SOLDIERS, Sabine Baring-Gould (1834–1924)

PLEASANT ARE THY COURTS ABOVE, Henry Francis Lyte (1793–1847)

PRAISE, MY SOUL, THE KING OF HEAVEN, Henry Francis Lyte (1793–1847)

PRAISE TO THE LORD, THE ALMIGHTY, THE KING OF CREATION, Joachim Neander (1650–80)

REJOICE, THE LORD IS KING, Charles Wesley (1707–88)

RIDE ON! RIDE ON IN MAJESTY, Henry Hart Milman (1791–1868)

ROCK OF AGES, CLEFT FOR ME, Augustus Montague Toplady (1740–78)

SAVIOUR, TEACH ME, DAY BY DAY, Jane Eliza Leeson (1807–82)

SEE! IN YONDER MANGER LOW, Edward Caswall (1814–78)

SOLDIERS OF CHRIST! ARISE, Charles Wesley (1707–88)

SPIRIT DIVINE, ATTEND OUR PRAYERS, Andrew Reed (1787–1862)

STAND UP! STAND UP FOR JESUS, George Duffield (1818–88)

STILL THE NIGHT, HOLY THE NIGHT, Joseph Mohr (1792–1848)

SUMMER SUNS ARE GLOWING, William Walsham How (1823–97)

TELL ME THE OLD, OLD STORY, Kate Hankey (1834–1911)

THE CHURCH'S ONE FOUNDATION, Samuel John Stone (1839–1900)

THE FIELDS ARE ALL WHITE, *The Book of Praise for Children*, 1881

THE FIRST NOWELL THE ANGEL DID SAY, *Trad. Carol*

THE KING OF LOVE MY SHEPHERD IS, Henry Williams Baker (1821–77)

THERE IS A GREEN HILL FAR AWAY, Cecil Frances Alexander (1823–95)

THROUGH THE NIGHT OF DOUBT AND SORROW, Bernhardt Severin Ingemann (1789–1862); *tr. by* Sabine Baring-Gould (1834–1924)

THY HAND, O GOD, HAS GUIDED, Edward Hayes Plumptre (1821–91)

WE PLOUGH THE FIELDS, AND SCATTER, Matthias Claudius (1740–1815); *tr. by* Jane Montgomery Campbell (1817–78)

WHAT A FRIEND WE HAVE IN JESUS, Joseph Scriven (1820–86)

WHEN HE COMETH, WHEN HE COMETH, William Orcutt Cushing (1823–1903)

WHEN I SURVEY THE WONDROUS CROSS, Isaac Watts (1674–1748)

WHILE HUMBLE SHEPHERDS WATCHED THEIR FLOCKS, Nahum Tate (1652–1715)

WHO IS HE, IN YONDER STALL, Benjamin Russell Hanby (1833–67)

WHO WOULD TRUE VALOUR SEE, John Bunyan (1628–88)

WORSHIP THE LORD IN THE BEAUTY OF HOLINESS, John Samuel Bewley Monsell (1811–75)

YE FAIR GREEN HILLS OF GALILEE, Eustace Rogers Conder (1820–92)

YE SERVANTS OF GOD, YOUR MASTER PROCLAIM, Charles Wesley (1707–88)

YIELD NOT TO TEMPTATION, FOR YIELDING IS SIN, Horatio Richmond Palmer (1834–1907)

INDEX TO ENGLISH QUOTATIONS

A

Abed: lie a. and rest 236

Abilities: from each according to his a. 291

Ability: a. grows in peace 215

Abomination: a. unto the Lord 18

Abou: A. Ben Adhem (may his tribe increase) 238

Abraham: the God of A. 192

Abroad: no more I will a. 228

set our young men a. 99

Absalom: A., my son 355

Absence: a. is to love 88

a. makes the heart 46

a. of body 341

fit of a. of mind 360

love . . . cannot admit a. 168

Absolutism: a. moderated by assassination 19

Abstinence: a. is as easy 249

Abundance: God give . . . of all virtue a. 177

Abused: so much a. as this sentence 360

Abyss: dark unbottom'd infinite A. 306

Accuse: I a. 458

Achieve: a. in time 211

those who a. something 239

Achilles: what name A. assumed 66

Acquaintance: a. may be a

long 'un 159

lost, in which I do not make a new a. 251

to have a visiting a. with 389

Acquainted: a. with grief 243

Acquisition: a. of knowledge . . . tedious as . . . a. of wealth 275

Act: a. is all 214

A. of God was defined 227

Englishmen a. better than Frenchmen 50

free to a. 25

Acting: a. without design 269

Action: a. and passion 105

a. . . . coarsened thought 17

prefer thought to a. 43

Actions: we are taught by great a. 189

Activity: power of sustained practical a. 411

Actors: a. speak of things imaginary 52

of what scene the a. 380

Adam: flower of A.'s bastards 94

when A. delved 23, 38

when A. dalfe 220

Adamantine: God put His a. fate 64

Adder: brings forth the a. 365

Addresses: three a. always inspire confidence 443

Adhere: a. to your own act 186

468

Adieu: bid an eternal a. 86

Administer'd: best a. is best 332

Admiral: to kill an a. 428

Admire: a. the momuments 183

Adonais: what A. is 381

Adored: women . . . merely a. 442

Adultery: and gods a. 95
do not a. commit 126
not quite a. 97
shalt not commit a. 193

Advance: a. or die 93
if you wish . . . to a. 213

Advantage: a. both of Eyes and Voice 290
a. rarely comes of it 126

Adventure: a. . . . held in delicate fingers 175

Adversity: A. doth best discover Virtue 33
A. is not without comforts 33
sweet are the uses of a. 362

Advertisement: one effective a. 238

Advice: a. is seldom welcome 118
to ask a. 132

Advise: a. if this be worth attempting 306

Aesthetics: long-haired a. 212

Affection: a. beaming in one eye 158

Afraid: be not a. 254
what you are a. to do 187

Africa: something new out of A. 329

Again: all's to do a. 236

Against: not with me is a. me 280, 295
who can be a. us 346

Age: a. cannot wither her 362
a., disease, or sorrows 126
a. of great men 17
a. shall not weary them 53
careworn a. 20
crabbed a. and youth 374
fetch the a. of gold 304
golden a. never . . . present a. 202
good old a. 122
green and smiling a. 406
grey with a. 355
hath not forgotten my a. 397
if only a. had the strength 192
lady of a " certain a." 96
let a. approve of youth 74
looks forward to, . . . old a. 155
may dawn an a. 26
old a. is no such uncomfortable thing 430
Old A. may come after you 438
old a. should burn 419
think, at your a. 108
what a. takes away 449
what an a. 126
woes that wait on A. 92
worth an a. without a name 314

Aged: a. man is but a paltry thing 456
object to an a. parent 157

A-gley: gang aft A. 85

Agnostic: appropriate title of " a." 240

Agony: conquers a. 94

Agree: when people a. with me 141

Agreed: a. to none of it in private 29

469

Aid: a. they yield to all 144

Ail: what can a. thee 255

Aim: it is all a. 272
two things to a. at 392

Airy: up the a. mountain 17

Alarms: used to war's a. 232

Albion: A.'s sins are crimson-dyed 55

Aldermanic: full many an A. nose 44

Ale: spicy Nut-brown A. 302

Alexander: A. wept 329

Algebra: hour o' th' day . . . by a. 88

Alien: in tears amid the a. corn 259

Alive: a. for evermore 344
officiously to keep a. 127

All: a. for one 176
a. is not lost 304
a. that a man hath 247

Alley: she lives in our a. 104

Alliances: steer clear of permanent a. 432

Almighty: A.'s orders to perform 13
Him the A. Power hurl'd headlong. 304

Alone: a., most strangely 64
a. on a wide, wide sea 129
a. on earth 92
fastest who travels a. 266
never less a. 210
may be placed a. 242
soul . . . content and cheerful a. 187
to be let a. 151

Alp: sit upon an A. 260

Alpha: I am A. 344

Alpheus: return A. 303

Am: return I a. 155

Amaryllis: sport with A. 303

Amaze: vainly men themselves a. 290

Ambassador: a. is an honest man sent to lie 453

Ambition: a. is the growth 55
a.'s honoured fools 91
good luck to your young a. 427
lowliness is 'young [a.'s ladder 365
only vaulting a. 370

Ambitions: a. are lawful 139
deceives with whispering a. 182

Ambitious: a. of doing the world some good 262

America: A. is a land where boys refuse to grow up 285
A. lives in the heart 446
A. . . . where law and custom alike 352
owe to the discovery of A. 224
think of thee, O A. 430
young man, there is A. 78

American: essence . . . of the A. Declaration of Independence 189
huge A. rattle of gold 245
I was born an A. 433

Americanism: hundred per cent A. 349

Americans: A. have little faith 189

Amiability: gained in a. 89

Amiable: a. are thy tabernacles 339

Ammunition: pass the a. 200

Amorous: a. as this lovely green 290
a. but chaste 98

Amphibious: a., ill-born mob 152

Amused: we are not a. 426

470

Amusement: I write for the general a. 359

Analysed: men can be a. 442

Anarchy: a. and competition, the laws of death 351

Anatomise: life is good when . . . we do not a. it 190

Ancestors: a. are very good kind of folks 389

glory belongs to our a. 330

Ancestry: I can trace my a. back 211

Ancients: a. without idolatry 118

learn what unsuspected a. say 175

Andrew: A. that tumbles for sport 83

Ands: if ifs and a. 326

Anecdotage: fell into his a. 162

Angel: a. is nobody 379

a. is the English child 57

a. of the Lord came upon them 280

beautiful and ineffectual a. 28

bigger . . . than any painted A. 440

ministering a. shall my sister be 364

woman yet think him an a. 417

Angels: A. affect us oft 163

a. and ministers of grace 363

a. came and ministered 293

A. fear to tread 332

behold the a. of God ascending 209

men would be a. 332

side of the a. 163

tears such as A. weep 305

they were called A. 218

Anger: mistress some rich a. shows 258

Angler: excellent a. 431

no man is born an a. 431

Angling: innocent recreation than a. 431

Angry: a. man always thinks he can do more 16

be ye a. 191

I was a. with my friend 57

when a. count four 424

Animal: this a. is very wicked 19

Animals: a. are equal 321

wild a. never kill for sport 204

Animation: constitutional a. 128

Anna: here thou, great A. 334

Annabel Lee: I and my A. 330

Annals: a. of the poor 218

Annan: A.'s water's wading deep 38

Annihilating: a. all that's made 291

Annihilation: doomed to complete a. 149

Annuity: a. is a very serious business 31

Anointest: a. my head 339

Answer: a. a fool 338

waitin' for aa. 156

Ant: a. herself cannot philosophise 240

epoch of the a.-hill 17

Anti-Caledonian: intellects . . . is essentially a. 267

Anti-Everythings: lean, hungry, savage a. 231

Antipodes: sheer opposite, a. 257

Antiquity: rejected all respect for a. 162

Anvil: England's on the a. 264

my heart is as an a. unto sorrow 286

Anxiety: nothing . . . is worthy of great a. 329

Anybody: is there a. there 153

Ape: how like us is the a. 191

is man an a. 163

Apology: a. for the Devil 90

Apostle: rank as an a. 212

Apostles: A. would have done as they did 95

Apostolic: a. blows and knocks 88

Apparition: as if I had seen an a. 153

Appearance: man looketh on the outward a. 354

Appetite: a. comes with eating 343

a. may sicken 375

Applause: greater and nobler a. 196

April: A., June and November 320

A., June, and September 217

A.'s in the west winds 292

A. with his shoures 113

now that A.'s there 70

Aquavitae: great god of A. 195

Arabia: perfumes of A. 371

Arabs: fold their tents, like the A. 277

Arbitrate: who shall a. 73

Arcadian: trod th' A. plain 395

Archimedes: your A.'s lever 139

Arguing: not a. with you 435

Argument: staple of his a. 369

Arguments: a. . . . are meant for their hearers 299

a. out of a pretty mouth 15

a. which influenced my opinion 195

Ariadne: A. was a vintager 256

Arise: I will a. and go 455

Aristocracy: a. means government 122

a. of the Money bag 106

our a. the most democratic 282

Arithmetic: life be without a. 393

Ark: walked straight out of the A. 393

Arm: a. clothed in white samite 413

a. of the Lord revealed 243

Armchair: loving that old a. 139

Armed: a. prophets were victorious 284

Armour: whole a. of God 191

Arms: foreign a. could never quell 395

laid down his a. 232

Army: a. marches on its stomach 18

A-Roving: go no more a. 99

Arrow: I shot an a. into the air 276

Art: almost lost in A. 133

a. . . . follows nature 148

a. had once worshipped 239

a. has its fanatics 238

a. is a jealous mistress 186

a. is either a plagiarist 206

472

a. is not a handicraft 422
a. is science 128
artists must be sacrificed
to their a. 188
A. most cherishes 72
a. must be parochial 313
A. must then give way 356
A. remains the one way 72
a. so long to learn 230
a. that is interested in
itself 355
excellence of every a. 261
glory and good of A. 72
history of a. 89
is it A. 265
living is an a. 239
must learn the hateful a.
263
no a. where there is no
style 441
people start on all this A.
227
produces great a. by a
deliberate attempt 181
proper aim of A. 442
Artist: a. will let his wife
starve 377
a. writes his own auto-
biography 185
to be a good a. in life 406
what an a. dies with me
316
Artists: a. must be sacrificed
to their art 188
Arts: cooks are spoiled by
. . . a. 206
fashion's brightest a. decoy
216
no a.; no letters 230
One of the Fine A. 155
ten thousand baneful a.
combined 216
Ascends: a. to mountain
tops 93
Ashes: a. of his fathers 281

Asia: jades of A. 289
Ask: a., and it shall be given
you 295
Asked: women are glad to
have been a. 323
Asker: love 's the great A.
270
Aspires: wh e man a. 214
Aspiring: a. to set himself
in Glory 304
teach us all to have a.
minds 288
Ass: A. goes free 241
a. spread terror 199
Assassination: absolutism
moderated by a. 19
Assyrian: A. came down
like the wolf 95
Astonished: I stand a. 126
Astonishment: your a.'s odd
19
Astuter: a. than another 270
Asunder: let no man put a.
136
Atahualpa: who strangled
A. 282
Ate: a. and drank, your fill
333
Atheism: inclineth Man's
Minde to A. 34
Athens: A. arose 383
Maid of A. 98
Athirst: give unto him that
is a. 345
Atomic: primordial a. glob-
ule 211
Atoms: a. . . . into ruin
hurl'd 332
Attacked: a. it defends itself
19
Attainment: disenchanting
as a. 405
Attempted: something a. 278
Attention: A. a stretching-to
106

Attic: keep his little brain a. stocked 170

Aunts: a. . . . knew that it was modern 181

Austen: Miss A. . . . husband-hunting butter-fly 311

Author: a. and giver 135
a. by experience finds it true 173
ruin half an a.'s graces 314
where is any a. in the world 369

Authors: a. whom they never read 122
praise of ancient a. 230

Autobiography: artist writes his own a. 185

Autumnall: one A. face 164

Avarice: a., the spur of industry 238
while A., and Rapine 310

Avenge: a., O Lord, thy slaughtered Saints 309

Avernus: are gone down to A. 336

Avilion: island-valley of A. 413

Avon: Swan of A. 253

Aweary: I am a. 415

Awful: this is an a. place 356

Axiom: a. of mine 170

Azure: sea's a. floor 382

B

Babes: b. reduced to misery 57

Babies: bit the b. 72

Baboon: bred out into b. 375

Baby: Bye, B. Bunting 18
when the first b. laughed 45

where did you come from, b. dear 284

Babylon: by the waters of B. 430

Bachelor: b.'s fare 408

Bachelors: all reformers are b. 313
reasons for b. to go out 181

Back: and yet not turn your b. 277
I sit on a man's b. 422
never turned him b. 74
those before cried "B." 281
will ye no come b. again 231

Backs: upon their b. to bite 'em 315

Bad: b. in the best of us 230
good and b. are but names 187
if we believe a thing to be b. 300
when she was b. 277

Badge: B. of Men 150

Ballads: b., songs and snatches 211
better than all the b. 277
permitted to make all the b. 199
she sang b. olden 420

Balm: b. upon the world 257

Banditti: to hedge us frae that black b. 195

Bang: b., whang, whang goes the drum 75
if the big b. does come 322

Bank: b. was greed 176
I know a b. 373

Bankrupt: penurious b. age 104

Banner: b. with a strange device 277

474

Banners: confusion on thy b. wait 217

Banquet: b. that is eloquent 290

Barabbas: always save B. 128

Barbara: her name was B. Allen 38

Barbarian: certainly a B. exercise 79

Barbarism: blame the b. of wars 412

Barbarous: Rime. . . Invention of a b. Age 304

Bard: he was the wisest b. 49

Bargain: bad is our b. 70
never was a better b. 391

Bargains: rule, for b. 158

Barley: a-shearing at her b. 40
taste the b.-bree 86

Baronet: B.'s rank is exceedingly nice 213

Baronets: b. are bad 213

Barrel: handful of meal in a b. 263

Barren: leave this b. spot to me 102

Barrenest: b. of all mortals 104

Barricade: at some disputed b. 360

Bars: look out through the same b. 269
nor Iron b. a Cage 278

Base: all that is b. hall dies 75

Basnet: b. a widow's curch 40

Bastard: satire . . . sort of b. humour 272

Bathtub: b. lined with white porcelain 335

Baton: French marshal's b. 59

Batter: b. my heart 165

Battering: b. the gates of heaven 416

Battle: b. of Britain is about to begin 124

Battle-cry: b. out of being ordinary 271

Battles: in field great B. win 308

Bauble: what shall we do with the b. 146

Bayonets: throne of b. 241

Be: b. what you like 316
to b., or not to b. 364

Beacçes: fight on the b. 124

Bear: B. of Very Little Brain 300
oft outwatch the B. 301

Beard: thy long grey b. 128

Beast: b., but a just b. 18
making the b. 374

Beat: b. my people to pieces 242

Beaten: some have been b. 88

Beauties: b. . . . eyes may roll 335
b., which we so justly admire 119
meaner B. of the Night 453

Beautiful: all that is b. shall abide 75
b. is as useful 237
good is the b. 328
old are more b. than the young 436
own that thou art b. 382
thousand times more b. 450

Beatitude: ninth b. 335

Beauty: B. and Truth 76

b. . . . in the eye of the beholder 429
b. is nature's coin 301
b. is something wonderful 297
b. is that pearl 421
b. is the child of love 185
b. is the lover's gift 138
B. is truth 258
b. of face is a frail ornament 312
being in close relationship with b. 261
everything has its b. 137
first in b. . . . first in might 258
mighty abstract idea I have of b. 262
perfect b. is its own sole end 421
simple b. and nought else 70
Spirit of B. 383
teaches such b. as a woman's eye 369
terrible b. is born 454
there is no Excellent B. 35
thing of b. is a joy 256
where B. is a thing unknown 438

Became: nothing in his life b. him 369

Becks: b. our ready minds 256
gold and silver b. me 368

Become: why fear we to b. 381

Becomes: hardly b. any of us 230

Bed: and so to b. 326
take up thy b. 248

Bedfellows: acquaints a man with strange b. 375

Beechen: spare the b. tree 102

Beef: roast b. of England 196

Been: only what might have b. 267

Beer: life isn't all b. 237
they who drink b. will think b. 242

Bees: artists . . . like b., must put their lives 188

Beethoven: music of the mighty B. 420

Before: I have been here b. 350

Begin: b. at the beginning 108

Beginning: b. of the end 411
in the b. God created 208

Begot: when they b. me 401

Begotten: b. by despair 290

Beguile: lady to b. 41

Behold: to b. was pleasns 169

Being: we move, and have our b. 13

Beings: always be human b. 435

Belial: B. with words 306
Sons of B., flown 305

Belief: b. in a brute Fate 189
b. is not true 18
if once we choose b. 68

Believe: b. your own thought 187
men will b. more 175

Believed: b. our report 243

Believers: b. in the world 37

Bell: b., book, and candle 368
for whom the b. tolls 164
I shall b. the cat 169
surly sullen b. 376

Bells: b. were ringing the Old Year out 214
liked the ringing of church b. 117
ring out, wild b. 414

Belly: Jonah was in the b. 252

Beloved: this is my b. Son 293

Ben Battle: B. Battle was a Soldier 232

Bend: b. and do not break 199

Bends: though she b. him 278

Benefit-Club: b.-c. for mutual flattery 131

Benevolence: b. of mankind 37

Berkeley: God-appointed B. 453

Berries: pluck your B. 302

Berry: brown as a b. 207
God could have made a better b. 431

Besieged: learning is like bread in a b. town 251

Bess: infernal B. Tudor 87

Best: all is for the b. in the b. of possible worlds 428
always to be b. 232
b. is yet to be 73
b. of times 160
ten thousand times I've done my b. 236
we will do our b. 124

Better: b. done . . . to sport 303
b. what we can 303
far b. thing that I do 160
for b., for worse 136
I am getting b. and b. 141

Beware: b., for the time may be short 125

Beweep: b. my outcast state 376

Bible: English B. . . . would alone suffice 282
starless and b.-black 419

Bibles: novels are as useful as B. 186

Bidder: withstand the highest b. 431

Bidding: thousands at his b. speed 310

Bills: by not paying one's b. 440

Biography: art of B. 51

Bird: B. of Time has but a little way 197
forgets the dying b. 324
no b. soars too high 56
rare b. upon the earth 254
song of the little brown b. 420

Birds: and no b. sing 255
God was very merciful to the b. 23

Birk: there sprang a b. 41

Birnam: B. wood do come 371

Birth: b. of that most significant word 120
my Love is of a b. 290
of sudden and portentous b. 358

Birthright: b. for very bad pottage 445
sold his b. unto Jacob 208

Bishop: how can a b. marry 393
no b., no king 244

Bitch-goddess: b., Success 239

Bitterness: no . . . b. towards anyone 111

Black: hoist the b. flag 297
I am b. 57
take them down in b. 91

Blackbirds: full of b. than of cherries 14

Bleed: do we not b. 372

Bleeding: b. brow of labor 75

Bless: b. our human ears 304
  b. the Lord, O my soul 340
  God b. us all 91
  Lord b. thee and keep thee
    318

Blessed: b. are they that
    dwell in thy house 340
  b. is he who has found his
    work 106
  b. is the man who expects
    nothing 335
  call her b. 338

Blest: Man . . . always to be
    b. 332

Blind: among the b. the
    one-eyed man is king
    191
  b. from sheer supremacy
    257
  b. mouths 303
  I have a right to be b. 316
  I was eyes to the b. 247

Bliss: b. was it in that dawn
    450
  deprived of everlasting b.
    286
  mutual and partak'n b.
    301
  sum of earthly b. 307

Blockhead: no man but a
    b. ever wrote 251

Blocks: you b., you stones
    364

Blood: b. is thicker than
    water 411
  b. of patriots 245
  b. that she has spilt 142
  brand sae drap with b. 39
  done by b. and iron 53
  flesh and b. so cheap 232
  for this that all that b. was
    shed 456
  I have nothing to offer but
    b. 123
  I smell the b. 368

in b. and battles was my
    youth 72
  innocent of the b. of this
    just person 296
  let there be b. 97
  lines of red are lines of b.
    447
  our country . . . reaped in
    b. 56
  sanction to the trade of b.
    386
  so much b. in him 371
  wash his b. clean from
    my hand 370

Bloody: b., but unbowed
    224
  not b. likely 379

Bloom: sort of b. on a
    woman 45

Blot: I will not b. out his
    name 344

Blotted: would that he had
    b. a thousand 253

Bludgeonings: under the b.
    of chance 224

Blunder: frae monie a b.
    free us 85

Blunders: escaped making the
    b. 224
  Nature's agreeable b. 142

Blush: b. is beautiful 215
  b. is no language 180
  b. to the cheek of a young
    person 159
  born to b. unseen 218
  rather see a young man b.
    110

Blushing: b. to the very
    whites of his eyes 160

Board: there wasn't any B.
    227

Boats: messing about in b.
    217

Body: b. did contain a
    spirit 366

478

b. gets its sop 67
b. is his booke 165
b. is the ready servant of his will 240
b. of a weak and feeble woman 184
commit his b. to the deep 136
commit his b. to the ground 136
pray for a . . . healthy b. 255

Boiling: with b. oil in it 212
Bold: hath made me b. 370
Boldest: b. measures are the safest 276
Boldness: b., and more b. 149
Bondage: whole eternity in b. 14
Bonds: think their girdles and garters to be b. 33
Bondsmen: hereditary B. 92
b. lie scattered on the Alpine mountains 309
ye dry b. 194
Bonfire: way to the everlasting b. 370
Bon-mots: by plucking b. from their places 314
Bonnets: b. of Bonny Dundee 357
Book: able to write a b. 107
b. is worth reading 351
B.'s a B. 97
do not throw this b. 49
kiss the b.'s outside 143
never read a b. before reviewing it 394
no such thing as a moral or an immoral b. 444
out of the b. of life 344
what is the use of a b. 107
when a new b. comes his way 76

Books: b. think for me 267
b.! 'tis a dull and endless strife 451
b. were sweet . . . companions 216
b. which are no b. 268
few friends, and many b. 142
his b. were read 49
house full of b. 269
many are engaged in writing b. 184
no furniture so charming as b. 393
of making many b. there is is no end 178
of writing many b. 66
out of olde b. 116
some B. are to be Tasted 36
stranger commodity . . . than b. 272
study of mankind is b. 238
this b. can do 144
Bootlaces: do his b. up 435
Boots: b.-b.-b.-b. 264
Bo-peep: Little B. 319
Borealis: like the B. race 84
Boredom: b. is a sign of satisfied ignorance 61
Bores: tribes, the B. and Bored 97
Born: b. out of my due time 315
never was b. 407
taken the trouble to be b. 47
they can't be b. 156
unto us a child is b. 242
Boroughs: bright b. 234
Borrow: go and try to b. some 203
men who b. 267
Borrower: neither a b. 363

479

Borrowing: b. only lingers 367

Bottle: b. of salvation 343
expect thy dog, thy b. 333

Bought: b., will stay b. 102

Bountiful: my Lady B. 194

Bourgeoisie: British B. is not born 391

Bourn: from whose b. no traveller returns 364

Bow : as unto the b. the cord 278
b. of burning gold 55
thou shalt not b. down 193

Bowels: in the b. of Christ 146

Bowl: B. they call the Sky 198

Boxe: to no B. his being owes 145

Boy: b. playing on the sea-shore 316
b. stood on the burning deck 224
b.'s will is the wind's will 277
Little B. Blue 319
when I was a b. 455

Boyhood: starved my b. of its goodly feast 438

Boys: b. will be b. 233
b. when I was a boy 50
old b. have their playthings 203
What Are Little B. Made of 321

Brace: therefore b. ourselves 124

Bradshaw: vocabulary of B. 171

Brag: one went to b. 145

Braided: b. her yellow hair 42

Brain: Bear of Very Little B. 300

has glean'd my teeming b. 261
heat-oppressèd b. 370
more b., O Lord 297
noise turns up my giddy b. 286
possess a poet's b. 172
thoughts of a dry b. 182
trade's unfeeling b. 215

Brains: b. out of a brass knob 158

Brass: b. knob with nothing in it 158
horns are tipped with b. 179

Brave: b. towards God 33
by defying it that the b. escapes 429
how sleep the b. 132
none but the b. 173
passing b. to be a King 288
refuse to be b. 271

Braver: I count him b. 25

Bravest: not to seem the b. 16

Breach: once more unto the b. 367

Bread: b. should be so dear 232
cast thy b. upon the waters 178
learning is like b. 251
man doth not live by b. alone 155
man shall not live by b. alone 293
one half-pennyworth of b. 366
our daily b. 294
troubled long for . . . b. 255

Break: b., b., b. 412
b., . . . shatter the vase 314
I bend and do not b. 199

Breast: soothe a savage b. 138

Breath: b. of her false mouth 382

b. of kings 81

waste of b. the years behind 454

Breathe: as tho' to b. were life 416

Breathed: Shakespeare . . . b. upon dead bodies 188

Breathes: b. there the man 358

Breed: happy b. of men 369

Breeze: fair b. blew 129

Brethren: we be b. 208

Brevity: b. is the soul of wit 363

its body b. 130

Brews: many a peer of England b. 236

Brick: found it b. 101

Bricks: throw b. at your father 48

Bride: barren B. 333

can ser' him for a b. 283

unravish'd b. of quietness 258

Bridge: keep the b. with me 281

Brigade: gallant boys of the old b. 433

Brightness: beauty of face . . . momentary b. 312

Brillig: 'twas b. 109

Brimstone: from his b. bed 130

Britain: B. a fit country for heroes 276

hail, happy B. 396

British: B. public . . . periodical fits of morality 282

B. public, ye who like me not 74

Briton: my-lorded him as only a free-born B. 418

Broken: b. by their passing feet 454

Bromides: b. and sulphites 77

Brood: b. of folly 301

b. of glory excellent 399

Brook: b. was full of breamis 176

Bronze: monument more lasting than b. 235

Brothels: b. with bricks of Religion 56

Brother: am I my b.'s keeper 208

love God, and hateth his b. 249

true b. of a company 457

you'll miss me b. 229

Brotherhood: always be the idea of b. 435

Brothers: all men will be b. 355

shall b. be 83

we band of b. 367

Brow: manly b. consents to death 94

Brown: b. as a berry 207

Brows: with scalled b. blake 114

Brutus: you too, B. 101

Brynhild: with the waking of B. 79

Bubble: b. winked at me 229

now a b. burst 332

world's a b. 36

Bubbles: b. winking at the brine 259

Buckingham: changing guard at B. Palace 300

Buds: darling b. of May 376

Bug: snug as a b. in a rug 201

Bugles: blow out, you b. 64

Bugs: b. that bite secretly at the eloquent 23

Build: Lord b. the house 341

Built: castles . . . b. with air 253

Bull: peculiarity of the Irish b. 179

Bullets: better pointed b. 53

Burden: b. of responsibility 179

increasing the b. of labour 315

White Man's B. 266

Bureaucracy: populace cannot understand the b. 379

Buried: b. in so sweet a place 380

Burn: I b. 207

Burned: b. is Apollo's laurel bough 287

Burning: boy stood on the b. deck 224

b. for b. 194

Burnt-out: b. ends of smoky days 183

Burrs: stick to them like b. 204

Bury: b. for nothing 158

Bush: b. burned with fire 192

common b. afire with God 67

Business: b. was his aversion 178

Men, some to B. 334

true b. precept 158

your b. is to paint the souls 70

Bustle: not formed for the b. of the busy 86

Busy: English are b. 313

nowher so b. a man 114

But: there is always a " b." 62

Butlers: we have friends and no b. 336

Butter: b. will only make us fat 214

like a little bit of b. 300

Butterfly: husband-hunting b. 311

Buy: do not b. what you want 111

Buying: b. and the selling 75

C

Cabbages: c.—and kings 109

Cabin: small c. build there 455

Cabined: I am c., cribb'd, confin'd 71

Cackling: c. save the monarchy of Tories 331

Caesar: all is C.'s 145

C. had his Brutus 225

C.'s self is God's 145

I come to bury C. 365

not that I loved C. less 365

that C. might be great 103

what C. did 167

where some buried C. bled 197

Cake: let them eat c. 286

plum-c. was a compensation 418

Cakes: hear, Land o' C. 84

Calais: " C. " lying in my heart 292

Calculation: c. shining out 158

Caledonia: C! stern and wild 358

Caledonian: erect the C. stood 232

Calf: fatted c. 280

Call: prophet ill sustains his holy c. 314

482

Called: many are c. 296
same thing as you wad be c. 344

Calling: c. of selling houses 272
how to live is all my c. 312

Calm: c. of mind all passion spent 309
c. the rage of thundering Jupiter 289
in the still c. we find 332

Calumny: best answer to c. 431

Calvin: land of C. 393

Cambridge: C. people rarely smile 64
C. science and a sausage 22
to C. books 66, 423

Came: C.-over-with-the-Conqueror type 433
c. wi' a lass 244
tell them that I c. 153

Camel: c. . . . through the eye of a needle 286

Camp: in the weakest c. 121

Can: he who c., does 379

Candle: c. throws his beams 373
lights a c. to the sun 198
we shall this day light such a c. 270

Candle-light: colours seen by c. 67

Candles: night's c. are burnt out 375

Candy: c. is dandy 316

Cannakin: why clink the c. 70

Cannon: c. ball took off his legs 232

Canoe: paddle his own c. 289

Canterbury: illusion . . . Archbishop of C. 394

Cantie: c. wi' mair 80

Capability: Negative C. 261
world of c. 69

Capacity: c. for taking pains 234
deprived . . . c. for love 103

Caparisons: c. don't become a young woman 389

Cape: nobly C. St. Vincent 71

Capernoity: we're sometimes c. 195

Capital: C., where kingly Death 380

Capitol: musing amidst the ruins of the C. 209

Captain: c. of my soul 225
o C.! my C. 436

Captains: C. and the Kings depart 266
c. of industry 106

Captivity: bring away c. thence captive 398

Care: ofttimes cumis c. 226
wrinkled C. derides 302

Career: might damage his C. 45

Cares: c. that infest the day 277

Cargo: c. of ivory 292

Carnage: c. and his conquests cease 91

Carolings: cause for c. 220

Carpenter: c. and workmaster 24
you may scold a c. 250

Cart: drive your c. 55

Carthage: C. should be destroyed 380

Carthaginian: C. faith 354

Carved: c. not a line 448

Casca: envious C. 366

Case: c. is still before the courts 234

483

nothing to do with the c. 212

Casement: c. ope at night 259

on this c. shone the wintry moon 256

Cash: c. payment is not the sole nexus 106

rhyme . . . for needfu' c. 81

Cassius: C. has a lean and hungry look 365

Cast: c. thy bread 178

Castle: house . . . is to him as his c. 128

Castlereagh: mask like C. 384

Castles: c. . . . are built with air 253

Casual: daughters ride away on c. pillions 183

Casuists: think with . . . c. . . . marriage is rather permitted 249

Cat: c. may look at a king 108

endow . . . a C. 334

I shall bell the c. 169

more ways of killing a c. 264

room to swing a c. 156

Catechisms: know but C. 167

Catiline: concerning C.'s conspiracy 249

Cats: c. in a red-hot iron cage 69

Cause: c. that perishes 126

for what high c. 291

Causes: aren't any good, brave c. left 322

from am'rous c. springs 334

home of lost c. 27

Cavalier: c. who loves honour 357

Cavaliers: former were called c. 196

Caverns: c. measureless to man 131

Caviare: c. to the general 363

Cease: c. I must hate and death return 383

fears that I may c. to be 261

thou should'st c. to be 388

Cell: each in his narrow c. 218

Cellar: born in a c. 200

Cenotaph: laugh at my own c. 381

Centaur: timorous wench from a c. 337

Censure: c. freely who have written well 331

Centuries: forty c. look down 59

Cerberus: of C., and blackest midnight born 302

Cerebration: well of unconscious c. 245

Certain: nothing . . . c., except death 201

Certainties: begin with c. 31

Certainty: in day-to-day work, was c. 103

Cesspool: London, that great c. 171

Chain: flesh to feel the c. 63

Chains: everywhere he is in c. 350

Chair: rack of a too easy c. 331

Cham: C. of literature 395

Chambers: consists of four c. 61

Chance: await no gifts from C. 26

c. . . . God's pseudonym 201

c. what we can 404
comes from art, not c. 331
God give to thee ane
blissed c. 177
under the bludgeonings of
c. 224
you haven't a c. 213
Change: ever-whirling wheel
of C. 399
ringing grooves of c. 415
the more things c. 255
things do not c.; we c.
421
Changed: we have c. all that
312
Changing: times are c., and
we are c. 22, 323
Chaos: fashions out of the
c. 297
Chapel: no c. on the day
439
Character: c. dead at every
word 390
c. . . . determination of
incident 245
c. (grows) in the current
of affairs 215
c. is a by-product 447
c. is like a tree 274
irreclaimable weakness of
c. 61
mind and c. slumber 189
Characters: c. . . . result of
conduct 25
man has three c. 255
Characteristics: universal c.
119
Charge: take thou in c. 281
Charity: c. suffereth long
139
have not c., I am nothing
139
poor are grateful for c.
445
with c. for all 274

Charity-boy: as the c. said
159
Charles I: C. (had) his
Cromwell 225
Charlie: C. is my darling
231
easier to lo'e Prince C. 283
Charmed: c. life 371
Charmer: other dear c.
away 207
Charms: c. strike the sight
335
Chariot: Time's wingèd C.
291
Chassis: terr . . . ible state
o' . . . c. 321
Chaste: c. to her Husband
333
Chastity: give me c. 28
Chatter: leave the world to
c. 148
Chaucer: Dan C., well of
English undefiled 399
Cheat: Fame is . . . unper-
forming c. 334
life . . . all a c. 173
Cheating: forbids the c. of
our friends 123
Check: dreadful is the c. 63
Cheek: c. that doth not fade
257
c. where growes 145
Cheeks: crack your c. 368
they that have red c. 457
Cheer: be of good c. 295
could scarce forbear to c.
281
Hell raised a . . . c. 151
Cheerfully: c. he seems to
grin 107
Cheerfulness: c. was always
breaking in 179
Cheering: cause of c. us all
up 50
Cheese: dreamed of c. 405

Chequer-board: C. of Nights 198

Chequer'd: dancing in the C. shade 302

Cherries: full of blackbirds than of c. 14

Cherry: c-ripe, . . . I cry 229
"C. ripe" themselves do cry 103
c. was her cheek 38

Chess-board: called the c. white 68

Chestnut: c. casts his flambeaux 236
spreading c. tree 278

Chevalier: young C. 231

Chicken: some c. 125

Chiel: vera clever c. 60

Chield: c.'s amang you 84

Child: beauty is the c. 185
c. imposes on the man 174
c. ought to be of the party 31
Monday's c. is fair 21
train up a c. 338

Childhood: c. shews the man 308

Childish: sweet c. days 452

Children: c. begin by loving their parents 446
c., tossed to and fro 191
her c. arise up 338
men are but c. 173
stars through the window pane are my c. 262
suffer the little c. 286
they shall be called the c. of God 293

Chill: bitter c. it was 256

Chimney-sweeps: as c. come to dust 362

Chivalry: he loved c. 113
save fallen C. 91

Choice: takes your c. 23

Chore: c. done by the gods 190

Chosen: few are c. 296

Christ: C., . . . became man 110
C. cannot save thy soul 286
C.'s loore . . . he taught 114
must then a C. perish 380
through C. which strengtheneth 327

Christendom: wisest fool in C. 225

Christian: forgive them as a C. 31
form C. men, for C. boys I can scarcely hope to make 28

Christians: call themselves C. 135
C. have burnt each other 95

Christianity: local cult called C. 221
loving C. better than Truth 131

Christmas: C. comes but once a year 423
C. is coming 19

Christopher: C. Robin is saying his prayers 300
C. Robin went down with Alice 300

Church: figure in a country c. 408
I like the silent c. 187
I will build my c. 295
nearer the C. 18
no salvation outside the C. 28

Churches: c. built to please the priest 83

Cicero: C. . . . never have alter'd the vote 101
what C. said 167

486

Cigar: good c. is a Smoke 264

Cigarette: c. is the perfect type 444

Cimabue: C. showed that art 239

Circle: draw a c. premature 70

Circumstance: clutch of c. 224

Circumstances: c. beyond my individual control 157

trust . . . not in c. 189

Citadels: circle-c. there 234

Cities: c. of many men 232

Citizen: c. of the world 161, 180

humblest c. 75

I am a Roman c. 126

requisite of a good c. 349

City: C. is of Night 419

day in the c. square 75

dull and witless c. 61

except the Lord keep the c. 341

first c. Cain 142

he so improved the c. 101

long in c. pent 260

there the great c. stands 437

City-builder: envy not him whom they name the C. 107

Civilisation: c. degrades the many 16

c. is paralysis 206

elements of modern c. 105

progressive advancement of c. 206

resources of c. 213

whole history of c. 37

Civilised: force another to be c. 299

Clad: c. in the beauty of . . . stars 287

Clamour: c. of the crowded street 277

Clanging: c. from the Severn 264

Claret: his c. good 232

Clarion: sound the c. 314

Classes: back the masses against the c. 213

extinction of all privileged c. 139

Clay: c.-cauld were her rosy lips 38

Cleopatra: C. strikes me as the epitome 100

Clergyman: c. with a one-story intellect 231

once a c. always a c. 21

Clerks: been noght the wysest man 115

c. preise wommen 115

olde c. saw 115

Clever: c., but is it Art 265

let who will be c. 263

like all very c. people, could not 95

Clock: open with a c. 389

Closet: back in the C. lays 198

Clothes: loves but their oldest c. 168

Cloud: lonely as a c. 448

Clownage: conceits as c. keeps 288

Cloy: women c. the appetites 362

Coals: heap c. of fire 338

Coat: c. of many colours 209

Cobbler: c. should not judge beyond his last 329

Cobwebs: laws were like c. 32

Cock: C. a Doodle Doo 318

487

C. and a Bull 403
c. who thought the sun 180
C. with lively din 302
Who Killed C. Robin 321
Coffee: measured out my life with c. spoons 182
Cognisance: c. of men and things 69
Coign: c. of the cliff 409
Cold: called a c. a c. 50
I was . . . c. in blood 362
Cole: Old King C. 319
Coleridge: not set up Wordsworth, C. 95
Coliseum: while stands the C. 94
College: endow a C. 334
Colossus: bestride the narrow world like a C. 364
Colour: he who c. loves 168
Colours: seen by candlelight 67
Combat: c. deepens 102
treaties . . . of the brain 174
Comedies: c. of manners . . . obsolete 141
Comeliness: no form nor c. 243
Comely: how c. it is 309
Comfort: a' the c. we're to get 85
be of good c. 270
cherishes the love of c. 137
c. cruel men 120
c.'s a cripple 171
speak not of c. 420
Comfortable: baith grand and c. 45
Comforted: they shall be c. 293
Command: learn to c. 328

Commandments: keep the c. of God 110
Commands: I gave c. 71
Commemorative: cold c. eyes 350
Commend: I c. my spirit 280
Commendation: c. of a painter 196
Commendeth: discommendeth . . . obliquely c. himself 66
Comment: c. is free 356
Commerce: c. . . . attracts the envy 78
c. its god 275
c. long prevails 216
eager c. of her eyes 421
Commons: House of C. has nothing to say 445
Communicating: c. of a Man's Selfe 35
Communion: lost c. with God 110
Community: c. . . . force another to be civilised 299
good of the c. 107
Company: ah, proud c. 148
better . . . alone than in bad c. 432
good c. improves a woman 194
Companion: poor, earthborn c. 85
Comparisons: c. are odorous 373
Competition: c. and mutual envy 230
Complexion: c. of the modern world 185
putting on a false c. 195
Compliment: live . . . on a good c. 423
Compositions: read over your c. 251

Comprehend: nor c. the heav'n. 332

Compromise: idea of a c. 237

Conceits: c. . . . greatest liars 171

Conceived: c. by the power of the Holy Ghost 110

Concentrates: c. his mind 251

Concerts: c. in England 378

Conclusion: but spot a c. 315

Conclusions: drawing sufficient c. 89

Concord: lover of c. 134

Condemn: censure or c. another 66

Conduct: rules of c. 298

Confidence: success is c. 186

Conflict: c. of opinions 249

Conformers: c. to commonplace 299

Confusion: c. on thy banners 217

c. worse confounded 307

Congratulate: c. yourself if you have not yet a. done something strange 186

Congregation: face of this c. 135

latter has the largest c. 152

Conquer: c. without danger 140

Conquered: I came, I saw, I c. 101

perpetually to be c. 78

we have not yet c. one 330

Conquering: so sharp the c. 116

Conqueror: hugged a C.'s chain 91

pity him whom they name C. 107

Conquest: subdue by C. 308

to joy in c. 269

Conscience: save free C. 310

spark of celestial fire, called C. 431

Conscientious: c. man 315

Consent: I will ne'er c. 95

Consequences: damn the c. 300

in nature . . . there are c. 242

Consequentially: acted c. 119

Conservation: means of its c. 79

Conservatism: C. discards Prescription 161

Conservative: called C., party 145

C. government . . . hypocrisy 163

make me c. when old 204

most c. persons 446

sound C. government 162

Consider: c. it warlie 169

Consistency: c. . . . hobgoblin of little minds 187

Conspiracy: society . . . in c. 187

Conspire: with Fate c. 198

Constancy: c. to a bad, ugly woman 99

Constant: c. as the northern star 365

c. in happiness 137

Constellations: I do not want the c. 437

Constitution: every country has its own c. 18

only right . . . after my own c. 187

principle of the English c. 53

principles of a free c. 210

right of election is . . . essence of the c. 254

Construe: c. things after

489

their own fashion 365

Consuls: let the c. see to it 19

Contagion: c. of the world's slow stain 381

Contemporaries: all of us be c. 15

Content: eneuch that is c. 177

Contented: c. wi' little 80

Contests: mighty c. rise 334

Continence: give me . . . c. 28

Continent: C. will not suffer England 162

Contradictions: bundle of c. 133

Contrariwise: "c.", continued Tweedledee 109

Control: beyond my individual c. 157

Conveniencies: c. of common life 250

Convention: c. is the dwarf-fish demon 91

Conventionality: c. is not morality 62

Conversation: best of life is c. 186

pleasures in life is c. 392

Conversing: with thee c. I forget 307

Converting: an' in c. public trusts 279

Converts: women can true c. make 194

Convicted: c. of sickness 394

Conviction: cherished a profound c. 157

Convictions: comforting c. 352

Comrade: where his c. stood 359

Cook: c. was a good c. 353

Cookery: c. do 298

Cooks: excellent c. are spoiled 206

Cool'd: draught of vintage . . . c. 259

Cooling: c. of our chivalrous passion 335

Copper: trust . . common c. 106

Coquettish: c. to the last 100

Coral: of his bones are c. made 375

Corbies: twa c. 43

Corn: amid the alien c. 259

make two ears of c. . . . to grow 408

Corner: c. of a foreign field 65

Cornishmen: twenty thousand C. 222

Coronets: kind hearts are more than c. 414

Corpse: c. which is man 410

make a lovely c. 158

Correct: all present and c. 18

Corruption: fatten on its c. 386

Corrupts: absolute power c. 13

Cortez: like stout C. 260

Cosmopolitan: c. in the end 313

Couch: on my c. I lie 448

Counsel: dost sometimes c. take 334

high c. . . . to a young person 187

Counsels: better c. might erect 307

Countenance: Knight of the Sorrowful C. 111

Lord lift up his c. 318

Counterpane: land of c. 403

Countries: to over-run large C. 308

Country: behalf of their c. 354

born . . . for his c. 328

die for one's c. 235

fit c. for heroes 276

God made the c. 143

God's own c. 20

I have no relish for the c. 393

I tremble for my c. 246

I vow to thee, my c. 400

leave his c. as good 127

my c., right or wrong 121

my soul, there is a c. 425

our c., right or wrong 152

unborrowed from my c. 131

Countryside: smiling and beautiful c. 170

Coupled: my c. contemporaries 100

Courage: be . . . of a good c. 254

c. never to submit 305

my c. (I give) to him 77

screw your c. 370

two o'clock in the morning c. 59

want of c. 138

Course: forgot his c. 198

Courted: better be c. and jilted 102

Courteous: be c. to all 432

Courtesy: be rude to him was c. 148

c. . . . found in lowly sheds 301

in c. . . . learned 456

Courts: c. for cowards 83

Courtship: c. to marriage 138

Covet: not c. thy neighbour's house 193

we do not c. anything 124

Cow: c. is kept for every three acres 300

I never saw a Purple C. 77

Coward: c. flies in vain 429

c. to the backbone 378

c. towards Men 33

flattery to name a c. 422

no c. soul is mine 63

Cowards: c. die many times 365

Coy: Fame . . . will still be c. 260

Crab: cannot make a c. walk straight 25

Cradle: hand that rocks the c. 430

who hast been my c. 381

Craft: c. so long to lerne 116

their desire is in their c. 24

Crafticant: written by C. 255

Craftiness: carried . . . by . . . cunning c. 191

Cream: choking her with c. 264

c. of others' books 314

Create: my business is to C. 55

Created: all men are c. free 273

Creation: facts of c. 205

Creations: acts his own c. 72

Creatures: meanest of his c. 72

Credit: an't much c. in that 158

Creditors: c. have better memories 203

Credulities: c. of mankind 139

Creed: every man will make himself a c. 175

I do not mean here the church c. 105

passions . . . got the better of his c. 402

wealthy man of my c. 224

Creeds: civilisation is strewn with c. 37

dust of c. outworn 385

so many c. 438

vain are the thousand c. 63

Crew: set the c. laughing 198

Crime: commonplace a c. 170

c. of being a young man 328

fear follows c. 429

no c.'s so great 122

punishment fit the c. 211

united by c. 429

Crimes: cancel private c. 172

Criminal: c. class I am of it 152

no child is born a c. 394

Crispian: feast of C. 367

Criterion: c. of goodness 86

c. of wisdom 79

Critic: c. and whipper-snapper 67

found it necessary to become . . . a c. 272

good c. is one who recounts 201

Criticism: definition of c. 27

people ask you for c. 296

Critics: lot of c. 313

they turn c. 132

turn'd C. next 331

who the c. are 162

Crooked: set the c. straight 315

Crocodile: C. . . . sheddeth tender tears 399

Cromwell: see C., damn'd 333

Crow: blak c. thinkis 169

Crowd: midst the c., the hum 92

will she pass in a c. 408

Crown: c. of our life 409

head that wears a c. 367

I count the glory of my c. 184

Crowns: c. are empty things 152

Crucified: choose who will be c. 128

c. 'twixt a smile 385

Crucify: not help c. mankind 75

would not even c. him 106

Cruel: c. he looks 385

c., only to be kind 364

Cruelty: fear is the parent of c. 204

Cruse: oil in a c. 263

Crusoe: poor Robin C. 153

Cry: heard my c. 339

I c. unto thee 341

Crystal: ring out ye C. spheres 304

Cuckoo: c.! Shall I call thee bird 452

lhude sing c. 22

merry c., messenger of Spring 398

Cult: c. called Christianity 221

c. of cheeriness 322

Culture: great aim of c. 27

men of c. . . . apostles 27

Cup: come, fill the C. 197

let this c. pass from me 296

Life's enchanted c. 92

my c. runneth over 339

Cupid: C. painted blind 373

Curate: sit upon the c.'s knee 120

Cure: sad c. 306

Curfew: c. tolls the knell 218

Curiouser: c. and c. 107

Curly: C. Locks 318

492

Curse: bless them that c. you 294
  c. God, and die 247
  c. upon them every one 83

Curses: c. which the Furies breathe 289
  fling the c. on his neighbours 64

Curtain: draw the c. 343
  Iron C. has descended 125

Custom: c. loathsome to the eye 244
  c. should corrupt the world 413
  what c. hath endeared 37

Customers: empire for . . . c. 392

Customs: what c. 126

Cut: c. is the branch 287

Cyclops: like the C. hammers 286

Cynic: what is a c. 444

Cynicism: c. is intellectual dandyism 298

Czar: C. look to it 445

D

D: big, big D. 212

Daemon: D. stole my pen 330

Daffodils: fair d., we weep 229
  host of golden d. 448

Daft: thinks the tither d. 359

Dagger: d. of the mind 370
  d. which I see 370

Dairy: nothing like a d. 181

Daisies: swiche as men callen d. 116

Daisy: " d.", or elles the " ye of day " 116

Dame: La belle D. 255

Damn: d. w1h faint praise 333

Damned: d. . . . first cries " Hold " 371
  one d. thing after another 237
  saved by being d. 233

Dance: d. more skilfully than an honest woman 354
  d. round in a ring 204

Dances: no sober man d. 126

Dancing: d. in the Chequer'd shade 302
  d. ? Oh, dreadful 79

Dandy: candy Is d. 316

Danger: bright face of d. 404
  d. no refuge holds 456
  d. past, both are alike ⁒ requited 254
  li e there is d. 190

Dangerous: such men are d. 365

Dangers: d. . . . of the old 165

Daniel: D. come to judgement 373

Dare: d. not put it to the touch 313
  d. do all 370

Darien: peak in D. 260

Daring: d. fellow is the jewel 410

Dark: at one stride comes the d. 129
  fear to go in the d. 33
  souls lost in the d. 70
  these are not d. days 124

Darkest: d. just before the day dawneth 206

Darkling: d. I listen 259

Darkness: d. was upon the face of the deep 208
  go out into the d. 222
  lighten our d. 134
  prince of d. 368

rear of d. 302
sit in d. here 306
Darling: Charlie is my d. 231
D. of the Gods 291
Darlings: curled d. of our
nation 374
Data: before one has d. 170
Daughter: D. of the Moon
278
marrying off your d. 352
Daughters: d. ride away 183
Dauntless: d. in war 358
Dawn: d., with silver-
sandalled feet 440
Dawneth: darkest . . . before
the day d. 206
Dawning: dewy d.'s cold
grey air 419
Day: brycht dawing of d.
169
d. after d. . . . waste 381
d. is a miniature eternity
188
D.'s harbinger 309
d. to dyrkyn 169
every d., in every way 141
every d. is the best d. 190
every d. to be lost 251
keeps . . . everlasting d. 163
life is but a d. 259
rare as a d. in June 279
weary d. have end 398
Daylight: it doesn't do a
man any good, d. 205
live-long d. fail 302
Days: as long as twenty d.
452
D. steal on us 98
happy those early d. 425
live laborious d. 303
these are great d. 124
thirty d. hath November
217
Dead: among the d. men 177
by the incurious d. 155

d. man win a fight 39
d. shall not have died in
vain 274
drive . . . over the bones
of the d. 55
for an' I war d. 40
I would that I were d. 415
never know that he is d.
89
over the rich D. 64
unto the d. gois la Estatis
177
when I am d. 350
when I am d. and opened
292
y'er a lang time d. 19
Deal: new d. for the
American people 347
Dear: d. at the price 213
Dearth: d. of noble natures
256
Death: angel of d. has been
abroad 61
any man's d. diminishes
164
cry'd out D. 307
d. after life does greatly
please 399
D. and his brother Sleep
381
d.-bill . . . passed off-hand
99
d. does not surprise 199
D. in the front 92
d. is slumber 384
d. is the privilege 351
d. is the veil 386
d. reveals the eminent
379
d.'s like . . . anchor 395
d.! the Jewel 425
D., thou shalt die 165
D. tramples it 98
D. who comes at last 358
how wonderful is D. 381

494

I have a rendezvous with
    D. 360
improved by d. 353
into the valley of D. 412
kingly D. keeps 380
laws of d. 351
make one in love with d.
    380
Men fear D. 33
no d., no change 387
not . . . afraid of d. 66
nothing . . . certain except
    d. 201
on him does d. lie 361
Pale D. with impartial foot
    235
Revenge triumphs over D.
    33
shapes of human d. 385
to every man . . . d.
    cometh 281
will d. . . . be a farewell 43
worst friend . . . is but D.
    65
Deathless: dead d. hour 350
Deaths: more d. than one
    439
Debt: National D. is a very
    Good Thing 361
women hate a d. 71
Debtors: better memories
    than d. 203
Debts: d. of . . . bankrupt
    age 104
forgive us our d. 294
Shakespeare is charged
    with d. 188
Decay: all human . . . sub-
    ject to d. 174
flavour of that d. 231
Deceased: he first d. 452
Deceit: men favour the d.
    173
Deceits: d. of the world 134
Deceive: d. one's self 154

practise to d. 358
Deceived: d. by what one
    loves 312
Decencies: dwell in D. 333
Decency: D. is Indecency's
    Conspiracy 379
Decent: family called d. 326
Declare: d. except my
    genius 444
Decline: idea of writing the
    d. 210
Decorous: monotony of a d.
    age 186
Dedicated: d. to the great
    task 273
Deed: good d. in a naughty
    world 373
I may do the d. 259
Deeds: all your better d. 47
d., not words 47
Deep: body to the d. 136
Defeat: in ourselves, are
    triumph and d. 277
possibilities of d. 426
Defend: d. our island 124
ministers of grace d. us 363
Defender: Faith's D. 91
Deficiency: symptom of
    mental d. 37
Deform: d. the human race
    54
Degenerate: d. from the ape
    238
Delaying: by d. saved 191
Deliberate: d., the love is
    slight 287
Delight: day rose with d. 263
my last d. 382
turned d. into a sacrifice
    228
very temple of D. 258
Deliver: d. us from evil 294
with thee . . . to d. thee 246
Deliverer: ask for this great
    D. 308

495

Democracies: d. against despots 154

Democracy: cycle d. is built on 446

d. in a republic 324

d. means government 122

d. . . . most aristocratic 282

to establish d. 122

world . . . safe for d. 447

Demon: wailing for her d. lover 131

Den: Seven Sleepers d. 165

Denied: d. none of it aloud 29

Denmark: rotten in . . . D. 363

Depart: not d. from it 338

Depravity: proof of . . . d. 250

Descended: desirable to be well d. 330

Descent: d. of birth 309

Description: d. of what has never occurred 441

Desert: d. and reward 345

d. of brick 421

d. where no life 233

sweetness on the d. air 218

Deserts: d. are small 313

Desire: d. of knowledge 402

nearer to the Heart's D. 198

tasted of d. 204

when vain d. at last 350

Desires: overcomes his d. 25

Desist: d. from the experiment 267

Desk: d. to write upon 88

Despair: Giant D. had a wife 76

life in our d. 93

Despaired: nothing need be d. under Teucer 235

Desperation: lives of quiet d. 421

Despised: d. and rejected 243

d. as well as served 90

Despiseth: who d. all 16

Despotism: whatever crushes individuality is d. 299

Destiny: belief in . . D. 189

D. with Men for Pieces plays 198

know the d. of Man 451

work out his d. 446

Destruction: D. in the rear 92

d. of our world 149

Detail: corroborative d. 212

Detection: labours to escape d. 195

Detest: d. at leisure 97

Detriment: d. to their estimation 299

Device: d. for avoiding thought 224

Devices: d. for cheapening labour 315

Devil: Cleopatra strikes me as . . . the d. 100

. D. always builds a chapel 152

d. can cite Scripture 372

D. did grin 130

D. sa deavit was 176

d. should have all the good tunes 230

d. was sick 315

D. whoops 265

d. will come 287

D. with D. damn'd 306

do the d.'s work for nothing 196

man is but a d. 404

mischievous d. Love is 90

we are each our own d. 440

who cleft the D.'s foot 167

496

Devilish: d. when respectable 67

Devourers: become so great d. 314

Dew: d. of yon . . . hill 363
d. on the mountain 357

Dewdrop: d. on its . . . way 259

Diamond: better a d. with a flaw 138
more of rough than of polished d. 119

Diapason: roll'd its loud d. 44

Dickens: d. his name is 373

Dictionary: walking d. 113

Did: d. was done with so much ease 172

Die: can't d., along the coast 156
d. before they sing 130
d. for one's country 235
d. in the lost, lost fight 126
d. is cast 101
d., . . . last thing I shall do 324
I d. as . . . I goe 166
if I should d. 65
lives to d. another day 236
not so difficult to d. 99
those about to d. 408
to d. . . . adventure 45
to-morrow we shall d. 243
who would wish to d. 60
you asked this man to d. 28

Died: liked it not, and d. 452
would have God I had d. 355

Diet: d. was accordant 116

Dieted: d. with praise 258

Different: show you something d. 184

Difficulties: in grave d. 276

Diffidence: name was D. 76

Digest: d. it in company 119

Digestion: d. . . . secret of life 393

Dignity: d. to starve 394

Digressions: d., . . . are the sunshine 401

Dim: d., as the borrowed beams 174

Dimensions: d. of this mercy 146

Dine: I shall d. late 268
we gang and d. 43

Ding: D., Dong, Bell 318

Dining: d.-room will be well lighted 268

Dinner: good d. enough 250
good d. upon his table 249
tocsin of the soul— the d.-bell 96
why people who want d. 37
would ask him to d. 106

Diogenes: D. struck the father 88

Diplomat: d. . . . a headwaiter 425

Directness: d. there must be 272

Disagree: men only d. 306

Disagreeables: making all d. evaporate 261

Disappointed: never be d. 335

Disapprove: d. of what you say 427

Disapproves: condemns whatever he d. 79

Disbelief: suspension of d. 132

Discipline: dull provincial d. 275
Kind of D. of Humanity 33

Discord: harmony in d. 234

Discount: life at a d. 205

Discourse: provision for d. 31

some in their D. 35

Discoverers: ill d. 31

Discretion: in taking suld. be 177

philosophy is . . . d. 361

Discuss: d. the late events 183

Disease: d. of modern life 27

Disgrace: in d. with Fortune 376

Disguised: d. in liquor 154

Disliked: get ourselves rather d. 337

Dismayed: neither be thou d. 254

Disobedience: by man's d. lost 308

Man's First D. 304

Disorder: d. in the dresse 229

Disparity: d. as is twixt Aire 163

Displeaseth: who despiseth all, d. all 16

Disquietudes: d. of this weary life 86

Dissect: murder to d. 452

Dissemble: d. your love 52

Dissolve: d., and quite forget 259

Dissolved: Union to be d. 273

Distance: d. lends enchantment 102

Distinguished: d. above others 232

Ditch: environed with a great d. 146

Divide: d. and rule 214

Divided: d. by interests 429

in their death they were not d. 354

it will cease to be d. 273

Divine: d. in woman 385

when d. souls appear 188

Diviner: d. than a loveless god 69

Divinity: d. in us 66

Dizziness: love is like a d. 231

Do: d. all things through Christ 327

d. as we say 58

d. as you would be done by 118

d. not unto others 378

d. other men 158

d. . . . what you can d. 186

less one has to d. 119

ought remains to d. 346

theirs but to d. and die 412

Doasyouwouldbedoneby: Mrs D. 264

Docile: men who are d. 297

Doctrine: every wind of d. 191

prove their d. orthodox 88

what d. call you this 286

winds of d. 311

Doctrines: d. responsible . . . difficulties 272

makes all d. plain 89

Dodecaphonic: d. bonfire 284

Does: not what man d. 74

Dog: beware of the d. 326

d. bites a man 147

d. has his day 60

expect thy d. 333

I am called a d. 161

Dogmas: d. will be dead 237

Dogmatise: I d. 249

Dogs: go to the d. 227

habits of d. 336

lap-d. breathe their last 334

Doing: see what she's d. 342

498

what everyone is d. 227
Dollar: almighty d. 22, 242
  power of the d. 189
Dominion: man's d. has
  broken 85
  yield of his mind 92
Done: been and gone and d.
  210
  but what we have d. 262
  d. those things which we
  ought not to have d.
  134
  d. when 'tis d. 370
  surprised to find it d. 250
  to have thought, to have d.
  26
  well . . . thou good . . .
  servant 296
  what . . . hast d. 208
Don't: about to marry—
  " D. " 341
Doom: d. . . . unmitigated
  dearth 420
  stretch out to the crack of
  d. 371
Doomsday: day is D. 190
Door: I stand at the d. 344
Double-bed: d. of a world
  205
Doubt: faith in honest d.
  414
  I show you d. 68
  life of d. 68
  mair I am in d. 176
  no manner of d. 211
  troubled with religious d.
  120
  wherefore didst thou d.
  295
Doubted: he d.; but God
  said 150
Doubts: end in d. 31
  saucy d. and fears 371
Douglas: doughty D. 38
Down: he that is d. 77

I must go d. to the seas 292
Downhearted: are we d. 19
  we are not d. 112
Downwards: look no way
  but d. 76
Drain: blessed d.-pipe 435
Drake: Drake . . . would call
  the Enterprise 171
Dram: tak aff your d. 80
Drama: d.'s laws the d.'s
  patrons give 252
Dramatist: d. only wants
  more liberties 245
Draw: d. but twenty miles
  289
Drawers: d. of water 254
Drawing-rooms: taste for d.
  has spoiled more
  poets 48
Dream: d. of battled fields
  no more 357
  d. that I am home 198
  dream'd a dreary d. 39
  hope beyond the shadow
  of a d. 256
  if I d. I have you 164
  if you can d. 265
  old men shall d. dreams
  248
Dreamed: I've d. of cheese
  405
Dreamer: this d. cometh 209
  d. of dreams 155, 315
Dreams: one dark maze of
  d. 420
  stuff as d. are made 375
Dreary: my life is d. 415
Dress: d. can be seen 189
  language is the d. of
  of thought 251
  we don't bother much
  about d. 380
Dressed: all d. up 436
  being occasionally . . .
  over-d. 440

499

good temper when he's well d. 158
think him the best d. 186

Dresses: world . . . d. so very soberly 246

Drink: d. not the third glasse 228
d. to me only 253
d. our bocks 183
leeze me on d. 82
nor any drop to d. 129

Drinker: gracious to this d. 25

Drinking: d. is the soldier's pleasure 173

Drinks: oft-times he d. 217

Drowned: not afraid of the sea will soon be d. 410

Drums: beat the d. 314

Drunk: hath made them d. 370
I would be d. with life 439
winks at d. men 217

Drunkard: rolling English d. 120

Drunkenness: d. of things 285

Dryden: believe in Milton, D. 95

Dubious: d. flag-signal 180

Ducks: d. on a pond 17

Due: d. participation of office 246

Dull: d. in a new way 251
not only d. in himself 200

Dunfermline: king sits in D. town 42

Dungeon: is his own d. 301

Dust: d. defil'd wi' sin 82
d. to d. 136
d. whom England bore 65
from d. I sprung 99
quelled by throwing a little d. 427

Duties: d. as King 179

Duty: discussing their d. to God 437
do your d. in all 271
d., d. must be done 213
d. God requires 110
d. . . . sublimest word 271
England expects . . . do his d. 316
every man's d. 127
I have done my d. 316
just as hard to do your d. 447
my d. to my country 324
path of d. 416

Dwarf: d. sees further 132

Dwells: he d. not in his own 307

Dyke: fill the d. 423

E

Eagle: American e. 434

Ear: e. begins to hear 63
give e. unto my voice 341
oon en it herde 117

Early: e. to bed 203

Earn: little to e. 264

Ears: e. that should be tickled 421

Earth: cool'd . . . in the deep-delved e. 259
E. cannot shew so brave 290
e. is the Lord's 339
e. laughs in flowers 188
e.'s crammed with heaven 67
e., that is sufficient 437
e. to e. 136
e. was nigher heaven 73
e. was without form 208
I saw . . . a new e. 345
I will move the e. 24

500

let the e. rejoice 122
loves but half of E. 342
must have a touch of e.
413
nor e. two masters 16
though the e. be removed
339
Earthquake: after the wind
an e. 263
Lord was not in the e. 263
Ease: counsel'd ignoble e.
306
Easel: get thee to thy e. 181
Easiest: e. thing 154
East: E. is E. 264
she sought him e. 41
Eat: e. to live 311
e. up . . . men themselves
314
let us e. and drink 243
Eaters: e. . . . incapable of
doing anything 225
Eccentricities: e. of genius
160
Ecclefechan: kent that E.
stood 283
Ecclesiastic: e. tyranny's the
worst 152
Echo: e. of a London coffee-
house 408
Eclipse: E. without all hope
309
Economist: I am a strict e.
87
Economy: balanced island e.
217
e. is going without 233
Principles of Political E.
52
Ecstatic: such e. sound 220
Eden: this other E. 369
through E. took thir
solitarie way 308
when man was put in the
garden of E. 428

Edifice: E. too large 307
Educated: being always . . .
over-e. 440
Education: by e. most have
been misled 174
e. . . . has produced a vast
population 423
e. is an admirable thing
441
e. of its youth 161
e. to his ruination 75
path of . . . noble E. 311
roots of e. 25
that man . . . has a liberal
e. 240
to direct popular e. 325
Edward: why does your
brand sae drap with
bluid? E.! E. 39
Effecting: e. difficult things
269
Effort: written with e. 249
Egg: goodness of a good e.
147
you've got a bad e. 342
Eggs: partridge sitteth on e.
246
taught us . . . to dress e.
313
Egoist: e. does not tolerate
egoism 351
Eildon: by the E. tree 42
Eire: sing of old E. 457
Elected: audacity of e.
persons 436
Election: right of e. . . . is
constitution 254
Electric: touch was as e.
poison 382
Elegancies: e. . . . of common
life 250
Elementary: "e.," said he
170
Elements: made cunningly
of E. 165

501

Elephant: e. by the hind leg 274

Elephants: e. never forget 353

Eleven: second e. sort of chap 45

Eleventh: hostilities will cease . . . at the 11th hour 199

Elfland: horns of E. 416

Elginbrodde: here lie I, Martin E. 284

Ellicot: Miss Nancy E. smoked 181

Elocution: public demands e. 325

Eloquence: e. . . . gets thing done 276

Eloquent: banquet that is e. 290

Emancipate: proposal is made to e. 99

Embarrassment: E. of Riches 17

Embrace: none . . . do there e. 291

Emotions: to kill the e. 44

Emperor: e. or nothing 59

Empire: e. is . . . power in trust 173

Empires: e. of the future 125 hatching vain E. 306

Employment: man who gives me e. 209 pleasure of an e. 31

Emprison: e. her soft hand 258

Emptiness: little e. of love 65

Enchantment: distance lends e. 102

Encyclopaedia: I am a whole E. behind 267

Endeavour: disinterested e. to learn 27

Endow: e. a College 334

Enemies: deserved my e. 438 love your e. 294 make [my e. ridiculous 428

Enemy: e. faints not 127 found me, O mine e. 263 how goes the e. 345 last e. that shall be destroyed 140

Engine: two-handed e. 303

Engineer: e. is nobody 189

Engines: e. more keen 140

England: body of E.'s 65 born and bred in E. 207 don't bother much about dress . . . in E. 380 E. expects every man 316 E., farewell 381 E. has saved herself 328 E. hath need of thee 451 E. . . . hell for horses 88 E. . . . island of beef flesh 285 E. is not the jewelled isle 321 E. is the mother of Parliaments 61 E. . . . paradise for women 88 E.'s green and pleasant Land 55 E. to itself do rest 368 know of E. who only E. know 265 oh, to be in E. 70 roast beef of E. 196 stately homes of E. 224 hat is for ever E. 65

English: close the wall up with our E. dead 367 dominion of the E. 20 E. . . . a foul mouthed nation 223 E. are busy 313

E. are mentioned in the Bible 424

E. are perhaps the least ... philosophers 36

E. are very little indeed inferior 317

E. Bible 282

E. public never forgives 442

if he went among the E. 45

made our E. tongue 399

under an E. heaven 65

Englishman: E. added the shirt 186

E. does not travel to see Englishmen 401

E. never enjoys himself 227

E. think he is moral 378

fifty-thousand men slain ... not one E. 430

he remains an E. 212

ill-natur'd thing, an E. 152

ordinary young E. 27

stirred the heart of every E. 356

weet an E. to the skin 344

Englishmen: characteristic virtue of E. 411

E. act better 50

you will not find E. doing it 378

Enjoy: one commandment, "E. thyself" 458

Enjoyment: innocent e. 212

Enjoys: Englishman never e. himself 227

Enough: e. that is content 177

never know what is e. 56

Enrich'd: we on every side e. 288

Enslaved: without being e. 103

Enthusiasm: little ordinary human e. 322

Envied: I e. not the happiest swain 395

Envy: attracts the e. of the world 78

E. would kill Pleasure 387

Epigram: what is an E. 130

Epitome: e. of her sex 100

Epoch: juster e. has begun 412

one does not blame an e. 128

Equal: all men are created e. 23

all men are e. is a proposition 239

proposition that all men are created e. 273

some animals are more e. 321

who sees with e. eye 332

Equality: e. is fundamental 379

law, in its majestic e. 201

true apostles of e. 27

Err: I e. in company with Abraham Lincoln 349

most may e. as grossly 173

to e. is human 331

Erred: e. ... from thy ways 134

Error: hosts of e. 75

Errors: some female e. fall 334

Esau: E. selleth his birthright 20

Estate: fourth e. 282

I reckon not in high e. 309

man without an e. 14

my e. is time 215

Esteemed: if I e. you less 387

we e. him not 243

Eternal: e. wrath burnt 307

Eternity: day is a miniature e. 188

I saw E. 426

radiance of E. 381
thoughts that wander through e. 306

Etherised: e. upon a table 182

Ethiopian: E. change his skin 246

Eton: playing fields of E. 434

Etrurian: E. shades 305

Eugene: E. Aram, though a thief 102

Euridices: my luve E. 226

Euripides: a chorus-ending from E. 68

Europe: history of E. 216
save E. by her example 328

Eve: Adam delved, and E. span 23

Evening: e. is spread out against the sky 182
take his e.'s rest 56
winter e. settles down 183

Evenings: e. steep'd in honied indolence 258

Ever: I go on for e. 412

Everlasting: e. Father 242
to know is e. life 135

Everyone: what e. is doing 227
when e. is somebodee 211

Everything: to e. there is a season 178

Everywhere: out of the e. 284

Evil: e. often triumphs 351
e. on the ground of expediency 348
e. that men do lives 366
I will fear no e. 339
notorious e. liver 135
root of all e. 422
sufficient unto the day is the e. 294

Evils: make imaginary e. 216

Exact: greatness not to be e. 78

Exaggeration: report of my death was an e. 424

Examinations: e. are formidable 133
in e. the foolish ask questions 440

Example: e. to a' Thy flock 82
lower orders don't set us a good e. 442
save Europe by her e. 328

Excel: daring to e. 122
who themselves e. 331

Excellence: dispute each other's e. 200

Excellent: parts of it are e. 342

Excelsior: banner with a strange device, E. 277

Excess: succeeds like e. 446

Excuses: principles are only e. 285

Exercises: they need their pious e. less 297

Exile: I die in e. 218
whose e. hath emptied Heav'n 305

Existence: struggle for e. 149

Exit: e., pursued by a bear 376

Expectation: certain our e. 183

Expediency: evil on the ground of e. 348

Expenditure: annual e. nineteen 156

Experience: e. and history teach 223
e. from his folly 386
E. is the child 162
e. keeps a dear school 202
e., . . . their mistakes 443
our author by e. 173

504

Experiment: desist from the
e. 267

Explanation: explain his e.
95

Express'd: ne'er so well e.
331

Exterminate: e. the human
race 326

Extravagancies: undisgraced
by those e. 119

Exult: we shall e. 451

Eye: cast a cold e. 457
e. for e. 194
flash upon that inward e.
448
only one e. 316
with his glittering e. 128
yellow e. has grown mild
454

Eyeless: e. in Gaza 308

Eyes: cannot shut one's e.
314
e. are brighter 289
e. as wise 64
e. lips, and hands to misse
168
e. more bright than stars
174
e. of gold and bramble-
dew 403
e. sublime 67
e. to the blind 247
e. were dashed with tears
150
e. were with his heart 94
get thee glass e. 368
lift up mine e. 341
through thine eager e. 315
whites of their e. 342

Face: angel's f. . . . shined
399
before I knew thy f. 163
f. made up 145
f. that launch'd 287
I who saw the f. of God
286
look on her f. 334
loved its silly f. 344

Faces: change their f. wi'
their clo'es 195
old familiar f. 268

Facility: painstaking f. 327

Fact: here . . . whole f. 190

Faction: no strife . . . from
F. 305

Facts: F. alone are wanted
157
F. are chiels 81
f. are sacred 356
f. do not cease to exist 239

Faculty: f., both good and
bad 62
f. of reading 107

Fade: f. far away 259

Fail: probability that we
may f. 273
we'll not f. 370

Failure: sure to be f. 137

Faint: f., yet pursuing 254

Fair: anything to show more
f. 449
f. . . . as summer mornings
174
false because she's f. 164
fancy what were f. 68
God . . . is f. 270
many thousand f. 336
what's right and f. 237

Fairer: f. than the evening
air 287
f. than whitest snow 288
I can't say f. 213

Fairies: beginning of f. 45

F

Fables: f. . . . agreed upon
428

f. at the bottom 206
I don't believe in f. 45
Fairness: f. . . . fading flour 226
Fairy: f.-tale written by God's fingers 18
loveliest f. 264
old-time f. tale 223
Faith: bloody F. 383
break f. with us who die 283
decisive in our f. 68
f., hope, charity 140
f. in honest doubt 414
f. of the poor 121
f. shines equal 63
his f. . . . might be wrong 142
I have kept the f. 422
I have not found so great f. 295
life is a profession of f. 17
life without f. . . . arid 141
nor f., nor love 386
not alter in my f. of him 253
not the dying for a f. 417
prove that f. exists 68
savage f. works woe 151
simple f. than Norman blood 414
thou of little f. 295
Faithful: better to be f. 348
f. in love 358
wills of thy f. people 135
Faiths: both were f. 26
Fall: haughty spirit before a f. 338
False: f. because she's faire 164
f. dreams, f. hopes, f. masks 419
not bear f. witness 193
Falsehood: foundation to f. 217

Fame: damn'd to everlasting f. 333
f. . . . bears up the lighter things 101
f. is love disguised 382
f. is no plant 303
f. is not won 148
f. is the spur 303
F. is . . . unperforming cheat 334
f. of a conqueror 119
F.'s eternal beadroll 399
f. . . . still be coy 260
f. . . . grant an honest F. 335
I trust . . . to common f. 188
only pleasure of f. 100
passion for f. 78
thou exceedest the f. 122
Families: two f. in the world 112
Family: f. of ten children 30
it (England) resembles a f. 321
Famous: better to be faithful than f. 348
praise f. men 24
Fanatic: f. . . . over-compensates 239
Fanaticism: f. . . . redoubling your effort 355
Fanatics: art has its f. 238
f. have their dreams 257
Fancies: woman . . . full of f. 261
Fancy: f. from a flower-bell 68
let the F. roam 257
Shakespeare, f.'s child 302
young man's f. 414
Fantastic: light f. round 301
light f. toe 302
Fantasticall: joyes are but f. 164

506

Farce: f. is played 343
  pet-lamb in a sentimental
    f. 258
Farewell: what does f.
  mean 43
Farm: little f. the Earth 130
Farthing: dear at a f. 111
Fashion: f.'s brightest arts
  216
Fashioned: f. so slenderly
  232
Fastest: travels the f. . . .
  alone 266
Fasting: lives upon hope will
  die f. 203
Fat: f. of the land 209
  men about me that are f.
    365
Fate: as f. has willed 15
  belief in a brute F. 189
  F., which God made 167
  fears his f. too much 313
  have conquer'd F. 26
  I am the master of my f.
    225
  when f. summons 174
  will . . . over-rul'd by f. 287
Father: about my F.'s
  business 280
  cometh unto the F. 248
  f. of the Man 450
  F. which art in heaven 294
  f. with his child 214
  honour thy f. 193
  wise f. that knows his own
    child 372
Fathom: full f. five 375
Fatted: f. calf 280
Fatten: f. and sterve 164
Fault: all f. who hath no f.
  413
  hint a f. 333
Faultless: faultily f. 415
  f. to a fault 74
Faults: f. are such . . .

  one loves him 216
  her f. were mine 98
  never see such f. 366
  not for they f. 94
Faustus: F. must be damn'd
  287
Favours: f. to none 334
Fawn: I f. on those who give
  161
Fear: f. follows crime 429
  f. in a handful of dust 184
  f. is an instructor 186
  f. is the parent 204
  f. . . . of violent death 230
  scorn to f. the face 87
  so long as they f. 13
  therefore will not we f. 339
  they hate whom they f. 191
  universal passion: f. 378
Fears: f. may be liars 127
  f. that I may cease 261
Feather: lighter than a f. 207
February: excepting F. alone
  320
  F. hath twenty-eight 217
Feed: f. the brute 176
  He that doth me f. 229
Feeling: f. in my soul 131
Feelings: confident of your
  own fine f. 418
  English women conceal
    their f. 445
Feet: f. beneath her petti-
  coat 407
Fell: I do not love you, Dr.
  F. 65
Fellow: death of his f.-
  creatures 204
  f. eight years old 70
Fellowship: f. with essence
  256
Felon: f.'s not engaged 212
Female: anythin' under a f.
  markis 160

507

f. of the species 265

Ferlie: f. he spied 42

Feud: f. of rich 414

Fever: f. call'd "Living" 330

Few: so many to so f. 124
thair is richt f. 226
we happy f. 367

Fiction: best thing in f. 446
stranger than f. 97

Fie: F., foh, and fum 368

Field: f. of human conflict 124
upon some well-fought f. 27
what though the f. be lost 304

Fields: out of olde f. 116

Fiend: f. doth close behind him tread 130

Fiends: f. in upper air 359

Fig: train up a f.-tree 157

Fight: I give the f. up 72
I have fought a good f. 422
they shall i. against thee 246
those that I f. 454

Fighter: no a bonny f. 405

Fighting: worth f. for 224

Figure: despair of ever making a f. 86

Filled: for they shall be f. 293

Filth: f. of the mouth 267

Findeth: he that f. his life 295

Finger: better a f. aff 344
Moving F. writes 198

Finite: bury under the F. 107

Fire: f. and people . . ., both good servants 219
f.-folk sitting 234
heap coals of f. 338
world will end in f. 204
youk'n hide de f. 221

you play with f. openly 347

Firmness: f. in the right 274

First: evening and the morning were the f. day 208
loved not at f. sight 287
test of a f.-rate work 51

Fish: f. out of water 362
presented him with a f.-slice 433
weed instead of a f. 194

Fishers: f. of men 293

Five: eat of the loaves . . . about f. thousand 286

Flaccid: I contemplate my f. shape 238

Flag: blush . . . only a dubious f.-signal 180
room . . . for but one f. 348
spare your country's f. 438
we shall not f. 124

Flambeaux: chestnut casts his f. 236

Flame: f. . . . shone round him 224

Flanders: poppies grow in F. 283

Flatter: too coy to f. 394
we fondly f. our desires 171

Flattering: f. with delicacy 29

Flatters: what really f. a man 377

Flattery: benefit-club for mutual f. 131
f. of greatness 200
f. wearis ane furrit gown 176
sincerest form of f. 133
tout for f. 132

Flaw: absence of f. in beauty 185

Flea: f. in his ear 26, 47

Fleas: great f. have little f. 315

Flesh: f. and blood so cheap 232
f. is bruckle 177
f. is weak 296
going the way of all f. 434
gone the way of all f. 138
in this thy f. 167
my f. longeth for thee 339
solid f. would melt 363
'tis the way of all f. 361
we wrestle not against f. 191
world, the f. 134

Flies: gilded f. 386
one catches more f. 225

Flight: time and the world are ever in f. 454

Flirt: lean, and f. 385

Flirtation: merely innocent f. 97
most significant word, f. 120

Flock: feed his f. like a shepherd 243

Flood: after us the f. 330
which taken at the f. 366

Floodgates: f. of life 86

Flower: blast the human f. 387
engendred is the f. 113
f. fade away 251
f. is born to blush unseen 218
f. of a blameless life 412
f. that smiles to-day 229, 384
meanest f. that blows 449
you seize the f. 84

Flowers: earth laughs in f. 188
f. of the forest 185
f. that bloom 212
garden full of f. 269

he forgets the f. 51
of al the f. 116

Flung: he f. himself from the room 271

Fly: f. from, need not be to hate 93

Foe: my noble f. I greet 358

Foemen: f. worthy of their steel 357

Foes: kings and subjects, mutual f. 386

Fog: f. of the mind 267
yellow f. that rubs its back 182

Foiled: f. by woman's arts 56

Folk: f. live that hae riches 85

Folks: other f. have what some f. would be glad of 196
some f. rail 196

Followers: f. applaud you 289

Folly: according to his f. 338
F. link with Elegance 455
f. of the Great 199
brood of F. 301
love . . . f. of the wise 249
lovely woman stoops to f. 184
wilfulness in f. 200

Fonder: Absence makes the heart grow f. 46

Food: sincerer than the love of f. 377

Fool: answer a f. 338
busie old. f. 168
clever woman to manage a f. 266
f. and his money 423
f. and his words 389
f. at forty 458
f. . . . is sport 168
f. some of the people 273

greatest f. may ask 133
he's a muddled f. 112
plaid the F. 400
silent and be thought a f.
274
wisest f. in Christendom
225

Foolery: f. of scholarship
239

Foolish: all . . . equally f. 180
deemed to be f. 137
never said a f. thing 346
women are f. 180

Fools: flannelled f. 265
f. by heavenly compulsion
368
f. of time 98
F. rush in 332
f. will learn 202
let f. contest 332
prov'd plain f. 331
two f. . . . for loving 168
verray naturall f. 275
what f. these mortals 373
wise, are greatest f. 16

Foot: f. for f. 194
f. is on my native heath
360
not suffer thy f. to be
moved 341

Footprints: f. on the sands
of time 278

Force: f. is not a remedy 61
quhat is your f. 169
use of f. alone 78
who overcomes by f. 305

Forces: F. needs must be
undone 290

Forefathers: rude f. 218

Foreseen: f. may be unexpected 183

Foretell: f. for what high
cause 291

Forget: art, how to f. 263
better . . . you should f. 349

dissolve, and quite f. 259
f. because we must 26
f. so much 151
forgive if I f. 63
if thou wilt, f. 350
lest we f. 266

Forgetfulness: not in entire
f. 449

Forgetting: memory for f.
405
world f. 331

Forgive: and to f. 409
Father, f. them 280
f. them as a Christian 31
f. us our debts 294
to f., divine 331
wilt thou f. that sinne 166

Forgotten: danger past, . . .
God is f. 254
f. even by God 72

Formed: f., as notes o
music 382

Fornication: committed—f.
288

Fortress: Lord is . . . my f.
338

Fortune: arrows of outrageous f. 364
F. and hir false wheel 115
F. has put to sic distress
226
f. is a woman 285
possession of a good f. 30
sphere of f. 309
thus trails our f. 288
what's one woman's f. 221

Fortunes: F. . . . come
tumbling 32

Forty: at f., the judgement
202
fool at f. 458
from f. to fifty 328

Forward: cried " Forward "
281

Foster: f.-child of silence 258

Fou: f. o' love divine 82
  I wasna f. 81
  we are na f. 86
  whan f., we're sometimes
    capernoity 195
Fought: f. each other for 396
  f. for life 397
Foul: no object so f. 189
Foul-mouthed: English are
  rather a f. nation 223
Found: hast thou f. me 263
Foundation: f. of every state
  161
Fountain: f. moves without
  a wind 94
  f. of the water of life 345
Fountains: two faithful f. 144
Four: f. things greater 264
Fourteen: f. months at
  Magdalen College 209
Fox: F. suspected 241
  galloping after a f. 446
  he (Charles James F.)
    talked 249
Foxes: f. grow grey 202
Frailty: f., thy name 363
  noblest f. 361
France: conquer F. 247
  fair blows the wind for F.
    286
  fair stood the wind for F.
    172
Frankincense: presented unto him . . . f. 293
Freaks: nature is full of f.
  190
Free: always and never f. 420
  but they shall be f. 80
  f. as the road 228
  he that ay hass levyt f. 44
  man is born f. 350
  we must be f. or die 451
  who would be f. 92
Freedom: battle for f. 241
  bird . . . live in f. 244

fight, but for f. 20
f. and curteisie 113
f. and whisky 80
f. has a thousand charms
  143
f. is a noble thing 44
I gave my life for f. 192
infringement of human f.
  328
perfect f. is reserved for
  the man 132
what is f. 130
whose service is perfect f.
  134
French: every F. soldier 59
  F. of Parys 114
  having invented the F. 424
Frenchies: F. seek him
  everywhere 321
Frenchman: F. invented the
  ruffle 186
Frenchmen: fifty million F.
  219
Friars: barefooted f. were
  singing 209
Friend: f. . . . masterpiece
  of Nature 186
  philosopher, and f. 333
  what is a f. 25
Friendly: f. eye could never
  see 366
Friends: city of the faithfullest f. 437
  don't believe I deserved
    my f. 438
  few f. and many books
    142
  f. are all that matter 77
  f. are rare 351
  f. in youth 130
  f., Romans, countrymen
    365
  f. who set forth 26
  happiness . . . not in the
    multitude of f. 253

511

keep f. with himself 404
laughter and the love of f. 49
love . . . f. in the garrison 219
man lay down his life for his f. 248
of home and f. 40
to meet one's f. 79
Friendship: f. in constant repair 250
f. often ends in love 133
in f. false 172
swear eternal f. 393
true f. is a plant 432
wing of f. 159
Friuli: blue F.'s mountain 94
Frivolity: gay without f. 26
Frog: how public, like a f. 161
no p'ints about that f. 424
Fromage: I am the big f. 316
Frontier: f. boundaries will be dead 237
Frugal: she had a f. mind 143
Fruit: f. is bot unfructuous fantasy 169
F. of that Forbidden Tree 304
Fruitful: rich and f. land 57
Fruitfulness: season of . . . mellow f. 255
Fruits: f. of the Spirit 134
Fugitive: I cannot praise a f. 310
Fume: black, stinking f. 244
Fun: I thought *What Jolly F.* 344
people must not do things for f. 227
Furies: curses which the F. breathe 289
see the F. arise 173

Furnace: burning fiery f. 147
Furrow: f. followed free 129
Furrows: smite the sounding f. 416
Fury: blind F. with th' abhorred shears 303
Future: divine the f. 137
I never think of the f. 179
no preparation for the f. 162
warning for the f. 386

G

Gaels: G. of Ireland 120
Gain: all is not g. 402
g. the whole world 295
stands to g. 126
Gained: g. both the Wind and Sun 290
Gall: g. and wormwood to an enemy 93
Gallant: very g. gentleman 18
Gallantry: what men call g. 95
Galleon: moon was a ghostly g. 317
Gallery: g. in which the reporters sit 282
Galloped: we g. all three 71
Gambler: g., by the state licensed 54
Game: time to win this g. 171
Games: bread and g. 255
Gang: g. wi' a lass 244
Gaol: who lie in g. 439
Garden: come into the g., Maud 415
fairies at the bottom of our g. 206
g. full of flowers 269
g. in her face 103

512

g. is a lovesome thing 65
Glory of the G. 265
God . . . planted a G. 35
God the first g. made 142
I value my g. more 14
look after our g. 428
while the happy G. sung
308
Gardens: in trim G. takes
his pleasures 301
Garland: immortal g. 310
Garment: g. of unsullied
snow 397
Garret: living in a g. 200
Garrison: love . . . hath
friends in the g. 219
Gate: burst the Iron G. 64
g. of the year 222
Gates: open the temple g.
398
Gather: g. ye rose-buds 229
Gathered: two or three are
g. together 296
Gaul: G. is divided 101
Gave: Lord g. 247
Gaveston: frantic for my G.
286
Gaza: eyeless in G. 308
Gazing: everybody was g.
at him 160
Geese: g. are getting fat 19
g. spread the grey wing 456
Gem: full many a g. 218
Generals: at the age of four
. . . all G. 425
Russia has two g. . . . G.
Janvier and Février
317
Generation: g. of leaves
232
pride in this coming g.
347
Generations: thirty g. of
my corn 421
to see three g. 336

Genius: eccentricities of g.
160
g. for painting, poetry 186
g. found respectable 66
g. is one per cent inspiration 179
man of g. and his money
389
models destroy g. 222
nothing to declare except
my g. 444
talent . . . recognises g. 171
that is g. 187
unseen G. of the Wood
301
works of g. are the first
things 262
you think you are a great
g. 47
Gentle: do not go g. 419
his life was g. 366
Gentleman: first true g. 153
G. who held the patent 81
prince of darkness is a g.
368
talking about being a g.
408
Gentlemen: distinguish God's
g. 187
g. were not seamen 282
Geography: G. is about
Maps 51
Geometric: by g. scale 98
Geometry: no royal road to
g. 192
George: any good of G.
the Third 268
G.s ended 268
G. the First . . . reckoned
vile 268
viler G. the Second 268
Georgie: G. Porgie 318
German: wee G. lairdie 146
Gestures: bored with all the
noble g. 271

Ghost: g. of a garden 410
with some old lovers g.
166

Ghosts: g. glut the throat of
hell 54
wining the g 337

Gift: as men a g. 71
g. . . . capacity for taking
pains 234

Giftie: Power the g. gie us
85

Gifts: presented unto him g.
293

Gigadibs: G. the literary
man 68

Gingerbread: piece of g. 418

Giotto: G. . . . showed that
art 239

Gipsy: g. by Reynolds 282

Girdle: g. round about the
earth 373

Girdles: g. and garters 33

Girl: all love a pretty g. 52
find some g. perhaps 64

Girls: dear to g. hearts 323
g. like . . . beauty praised
323
hockey-legged g. 418
prevent g. from being g.
233

Give: more blessed to give
13
when I g. I g. myself 437

Glad: g. when they said 341

Gladness: without g. availis
no tresour 176

Glass: mouths in a g. 368

Gleams: g. of a remoter
world 384

Gleaned: pen has g. my
teeming brain 261

Globule: primordial atomic
g. 211

Glorify: chief end is to g.
God 110

Glory: alone in his g. 448
declare his g. 340
g. belongs to our ancestors
330
g. gives me strength 337
g. is departed 75
g. of great men . . .
measured 270
G. of the Garden 265
G. of the Lord . . . revealed
243
g. of the Lord shone
round 280
g. of the world passes 262
g. . . . revealed 135
g. that was Greece 330
g. to God in the highest
280
greater g. of God 18
no road of flowers leads
to g. 199
path of duty . . . way to g.
416
paths of g. 218
set himself in G. 304
trailing clouds of g. 449

Glotoun: g. of wordes 269

Glove: wi' g. an' ring 39

Gloves: through the fields in
g. 140

Gluttons: in taverns with g.
148

Go: never g. down to the
end of the town 300

Goal: approaching the g.
161

God: adoration of the G.
in nature 131
before G. . . . all equally
wise 180
before the g. of Love was
borne 166
curse G., and die 247
distinguish G.'s gentlemen
187

514

feeble G. has stabb'd me 207

G. all mercy, is a G. unjust 458

G. and my right 345

G. and soldier we alike adore 254

G. be in my head 20

G. be thanked 72

G. erects a house of prayer 152

G. has written all the books 90

G., if there be a G. 21

G. is an unutterable Sigh 185

G. is in heaven 178

G. is just 246

G. is love 248

G. is Love, I dare say 90

G. is the perfect poet 72

G. made the country 143

G. of Love my Shepherd is 229

G. of nature and benevolence 386

G. or the Czar 445

G.'s in his heaven 73

G. so loved the world 248

G., thou art my G. 339

G. who loveth us 130

honest G. 90, 241

I found G. there 69

I maun face G. mysel' 283

if G. be for us 346

if G. did not exist 428

man whose g. is in the skies 378

nature of G. is a circle 22

nor G. alone 332

not-incurious in G.'s handiwork 69

once a man who said "G." 266

question then why . . . go into the house of G. 205

shall be called . . . mighty G. 242

stamps G.'s own name 143

think there is a G. 126

three person'd G. 165

thy G. my G. 352

trust G.: see all 73

ye cannot serve G. and mammon 294

Goddam: sing: G. 335

Godless: decent, g. people 183

Gods: G. of his Wives 308

g. they had tried 172

g.; they kill us for their sport 368

I thank whatever g. may be 224

most high g. may not 336

no other g. before me 192

twa g. guides me 60

whether there are g. 161

whom the g. love 96

Going: endure their g. hence 369

Gold: American rattle of g. 245

fetch the age of gold 304

gild refined g. 368

g. wes changyd into lede 453

man's the g. 82

Golden: g. age never . . . present age 202

Love in a g. bowl 54

Golf: g. its anodyne 275

monument . . . lost g. balls 183

Gone: been and g. and done 210

thou art g. 357

515

Good: all men are born g. 136

be g., sweet maid 263

better one want for a common good 288

do g. to them 294

go about doing g. 145

God make thee g. 413

God saw that it was g. 208

g. and bad are but names 187

g. as you be 189

g., but not religious g. 221

g. in the worst of us 230

g. is oft interred 366

g. is the beautiful 328

g.-night? ah¹ no 383

g. people's wery scarce 160

g. to be out on the road 292

g. want power 385

greatest g. 125

loves what he is g. at 362

music, the greatest g. 14

na g. in thine 176

no' for ony g. 82

no g. for which to strive 305

shouldn't say it is not g. 436

sovereign g. of human nature 32

to the public g. private respects mus yield 309

up and doing . . . up to no g. 205

what g. came of it 396

what is g. for them 146

when she was g. 277

whether a man is G. 55

worse than ugly. she is g. 439

Goodlier: g. than your gain 410

Goodness: g. and mercy 339

g. in removing it 196

true g. springs 136

Goose: g. a swan 264

every g. can 329

Goosey: G. G. Gander 318

Gorgonised: g. me 415

Gorgon Zola: myself as the G.Z. 316

Gormed: I'm G. 157

Gospel: g. of spilt milk 348

Gossip: known more than the g. 205

Gothic: G. ignorance 197

Gout: enemy the g. 232

Governed: many are g. by the few 238

not so well g. as they ought 233

Government: erected into a system of g. 213

Forms of G. let fools contest 332

g. a necessary evil 324

g. and co-operation are . . . the laws of life 351

g. by the uneducated 122

g. cannot endure . . half-slave 273

g. of the people 274

G. of the United States 139

g. shall be upon his shoulder 242

no G. can be long secure 161

oppressive g. is more to be feared 136

Republican form of G. 397

sister is given to g. 157

Governments: g. have never learned 223

Gown: g. of glory 343

wearing a black g. 118

Grace: g. of ease was perfect . . . not . . . g. of

516

uncertainty 245
g. of our Lord Jesus Christ
345
g. . . . to persevere 177
Graces: G. do not seem to
be natives of Great
Britain 119
half mile g. 86
Gracious: be g. unto thee
318
Grammar: g., that grounde
is of all 269
Grammarians: tribe of g. 23
Gramophone: record on the
g. 184
Grandchild: art . . . God's g.
148
Grandeur: g. he derived from
Heaven 174
g. of God 233
g. that was Rome 330
Grandfather: who my g. was
274
Grandson: concerned . . .
what his g. will be 274
Grape: G. that can with
Logic 197
Grapes: eaten sour g. 194
Grapeshot: whiff of g. 106
Grasp: exceed his g. 67
Grass: g. beyond the door
350
g. comes again 236
Grateful: g. . . . for a little
thing 415
Grave: dark inn, the g. 358
descend to th' g. 142
eat . . . honey on the g. 297
g. hides all things beautiful 385
g. is not its goal 278
G.'s a fine and private
place 291
if I were a g.-digger 247
in the cold g. 233

paths of glory lead but to
the g. 218
peace is in the g. 385
to glory, or the g. 102
kind of healthy g. 393
little g., an obscure g. 369
never be my dungeon or
my g. 381
Graven: g. image 192
Gravity: alters the centre of
g. 107
g. is only the bark 137
Gravy: person who disliked
g. 393
Great: cannot perform g.
things 430
folly of the G. 199
he was g., ere Fortune
made him so 174
Shade . . . once was g. 451
some are born g. 375
those who were truly g.
397
Great Britain: I lived in G.B.
272
Greater: four things g.
than all 264
Greatness: g. consists in
bringing all manner
of mischief 196
g. thrust upon them 375
nature of all g. 78
Greece: glory that was G.
330
G. might still be free 96
occupied G. subdued 234
Greek: a G. in pity and
mournful awe 26
I understand G. 205
it was G. to me 365
legal matters . . . G. to me
205
when his wife talks G.
249
Greeks: I fear the G. 426

517

which came first, the G. 162

Green: g. in judgement 362
g. Thought in a g. Shade 291
tree of life is g. 214
wherever g. is worn 454

Greyhounds: g. in the slips 367

Grief: G. brought to numbers 168
g. is . . . med'cine 142
g. never mended no broken bones 160
g. with heart's blood 420
my distracting g. 231
patch g. with proverbs 373
woman's g. is like a summer storm 37

Griefs: cutteth G. in halves 35
he hath borne our g. 243

Grieve: men are we, and must g. 451

Grind: g. the faces of the poor 242
mills of God g. slow 276
one demd horrid g. 158

Groan: hear each other g. 259

Grovelled: g. before him 418

Grow'd: I 'spect I g. 407

Growing: g. up into a pretty woman 29

Grub: old ones, g. 376

Grubby: John G. . . . was short 120

Grundy: Solomon G. 320

Guard: changing g. at Buckingham Palace 300
those that I g. 454

Guards: up g. and at 'em 434

Guests: g. (will be) few 268

Guide: thou wert my g. 333

Guile: packed with g. 64

Guilt: free from g. 235

Guilty: g. of our disasters 368

Guinea: g.'s stamp 82

Gules: g. on Madeline's fair breast 256

Guns: g. will make us powerful 214
loaded g. with boys 144

Gutters: taste for g. 48

H

Habit: creature of h. 379
h. . . . all the test 144

Habits: h. of man 336
h. that carry them 137

Hacked: h. him in pieces 40

Hair: h. of a woman 236

Halcyon: h. days 367

Half: h.-a-dozen of the other 289
h. was not told me 263
longest h. of your life 397
loves but h. enough 342

Hallelujah: H! I'm alive 322

Hallowed: h. be thy name 294

Hals: h.-ribbon of ruth 225

Halt: h., and the blind 280
how long h. ye 263

Hammers: hear the h. ring 264

Hand: bringing me up by h. 157
h. for h. 194
h. into the h. of God 222
h. that rules the world 430
not sweeten this little h. 371
seen her wave her h. 414
stand on either h. 281
thy h. findeth to do 178

518

wander h. in h. with love 317

Handicraftsmen: thousand h. wore 259

Handiwork: God's h. 69

Handkerchiefs: and moral pocket h. 159

Hands: into thy h. I commend 280
knit h., and beat 301
let not your h. be weak 122
not without men's h. 181
trust to their h. 24

Handsaw: hawk from a h. 363

Hang: day on which they h. a man 439
either go or h. 52

Hanged: he was h. 60
knows he is to be h. 251

Hanging: h. is too good 76
nane the waur o' a h. 60
no satisfaction in h. a man 378

Hangman: if I were . . . a h. 247

Happen: Can't H. Here 272
let it h. 342

Happened: nothing has ever h. 181

Happiness: consume h. without producing 377
divided and minute domestic h. 262
domestic h. 144
h. destroyed by preparation 29
h. in marriage 30
h. of the greatest number 51
h. of the whole 329
lifetime of h. 377
perfect h. . . . is not common 29
result h. 156

spectacle of human h. 393
true h. consists not 253
wherein lies h. 256

Happy: accounted yourselves h. 146
ask yourself whether you are h. 298
duty of being h. 406
every lot is h. 58
h. as a king 207
h. is he 451
h. the man 175
h. while we are young 20
how h. could I be 207
misfortune . . . to have been h. 58
one is never so h. 270
one thing to keep me h. 223
virtuous, and you will be h. 202
we want to see them h. 206

Hard: h. is the way up 148

Harm: fear we'll come to h. 42
no people do so much h. 145

Harmony: h. in discord 234
h. . . . of man 387

Harp: h. of Orpheus 311
heart and h. have lost a string 92

Harvest: h. is past 246

Haste: always in h. 435

Hasten: h. slowly 407

Hat: got his h. back 326
h. suld be of fair-having 225

Hate: behind in h. 306
enough religion to make us h. 409
if h. killed men 74
let them h. 13
men will not h. you 183

not in our power to . . . h. 287

they h. whom they fear 191

Hateless: h. thing as me 384

Haters: where the h. meet 70

Hating: h. . . . is an art 316

Hatred: h. . . . longest pleasure 97

h. will be dead 237

yet live in h. 306

Haunted: St. Andrews . . . is a h. town 269

Have: never to h. too much 417

to h. and to hold 136

Haves: H. and the Have-nots 112

Havoc: cry, " H." 365

Hawk: call down the h. 454

I know a h. 363

Hazard: you have won this h. 410

Head: h. was balled 114

if you can keep your h. 265

my h. is bloody 224

never bows its h. 149

off with his h. 108

old h. on young shoulders 190

small h. could carry all he knew 215

you incessantly stand on your h. 108

Headache: h. called thought 419

Headlong: h. themselves they threw 307

Headpiece: h. filled with straw 182

Heads: h. I win 145

Heal: physician, h. 280

Health: this h. deny 177

no h. in us 134

Healthy: h. mind in a h. body 255

Hear: h. the other side 28

h. them, read 135

Heard: h. it, but he heeded not 94

h. melodies are sweet 258

Hearers: shall never want . . . h. 233

Heart: because my h. is pure 416

have the h. . . . of a king 184

h. a h. of stone 438

h. aboon them a' 85

h. ay's the part 81

h. be still as loving 99

h. beating under four-score winters 190

h. distrusting asks 216

h. has its reasons 325

h. is as an anvil 286

h. is in their boots 120

H. of Man . . . is deceitful 61

h. was one of those 91

h. with pleasure fills 448

human h. is like Indian rubber 62

Lord looketh on the h. 354

man after his own h. 354

my h. aches 258

my h. . . . is clogged 151

my h. upon my sleeve 150

my sullen h. 64

my true love hath my h. 391

noble h., that harbours 399

not to get your h.'s desire 378

open my h. 69

re-mould it nearer to the H.'s Desire 198

send me back my h. 407

tell the most h.-easing things 260

520

write it on your h. 190
your h. be also 294

Hearts: h. are earned 456
heroic h., made weak 417
kind h. are more than
coronets 414
leave the sick h. 65
our h. are young 269
Queen of H. 108

Heathen: glory among the
h. 340

Heaven: can make a H. of
Hell 305
down from the verge of H.
307
gates of h. 76
H.-borne childe 304
H. cannot brook two suns
16
H. has no rage 138
H. in a Wild Flower 53
h. in hell's despair 56
h. is love 357
h. lies about us 449
H.'s light 381
H.'s peculiar care 396
H. thought otherwise 426
H. views it with delight 290
I saw a new h. 345
in h., a crime to love 331
is he in h. 321
Lord made h. 193
one H., one Hell 382
open face of h. 260
or what's a h. for 67
sends ane to a h. 82
serve in H. 305
tasted the eternal joys of h.
286
what pleases H. 358

Heavens: h. to suit the tastes
314
justice . . . though the h.
fall 195
let the h. be glad 122

Heed: h. of a young wench
229

Helen: like another H. 173
like H., in the night 351
Sweet H., make me im-
mortal 287
where H. lies 39

Hell: better to reign in H.
305
deepest pot of h. 176
England . . . h. for horses:
Italy . . . h. for
women 88
gates of h. 295
go to h. like lambs 120
having harrow'd h. 398
H. is a city 385
H. of Heav'n 305
h. on earth 377
H. trembled 307
make a h. of this world 47
nor H. a fury 138
sends . . . ten to h. 82
there was a way to h. 76
way to H. is easy 427
which way I flie is H. 307
why this is h. 286

Help: h. cometh 341
h. in time of trouble 18

Herald: h. of all revolutions
186

Herd: lowing h. wind 218

Herdsman: God the h. 454

Here: h. or nowhere 190

Heresies: truths to begin as
h. 240

Heritage: our h. the sea 147

Hermand: if H. had made
the heavens 128

Hermitage: take that for an
h. 278

Hero: conquering h. 314
h. the Conqueror Worm
330
no man is a h. 141

521

sees . . . a h. perish 332

Herod: out-herods H. 364

Heroes: fit country for h. 276

Heroic: refuse to be h. 271

Heroine: h. goes mad 389

Hewers: h. of wood 254

Hey: H. Diddle Diddle 318

Hickory: H., Dickory, Dock 319

Hideous: how h. it is 336

Hierarchy: Olympus' faded h. 259

High: be yours to hold it h. 283

equal'd the most H. 304

I would be h. 241

Highbrow: h. . . . looks at a sausage 227

Highbrows: article denouncing " h." 322

Highlandman: braw John H. 83

Highlands: heart's in the H. 360

H. and ye Lawlands 39

Hilarity: flame of h. 159

Hill: H. will not come to Mahomet 34

huge h., cragged 167

Hills: h. and valleys . . . yields 288

strength of the h. 340

Himself: he speaks so much of H. 35

Hippocrene: blushful H. 259

Hiss: universal h. 307

Historian: h. . . . wants more documents 245

occupation of the h. 441

tell me the acts, O h. 53

Historical: find the h. fact 183

History: h. has many cunning passages 182

h. in all men's lives 367

h. . . . is adaptable 425

h. is an art 434

h. is bunk 200

h. is past politics 360

H. is Philosophy 58

h. of Europe 216

H. of the Great Men 105

h. . . . register of the crimes 210

h. teaches wise men 189

h. teems with . . . truth 299

h. warns us 240

never learned . . . from h. 223

takes a great deal of h. 245

Universal H. 105

world's h. is the world's judgement 356

Hit: never h. soft 348

Hitch: h. his wagon to a star 190

Hitler: H. has missed the bus 113

Hobgoblin: h. of little minds 187

Hog: go the whole h. 289

Hole: knows of a better h. 38

Holidays: year were playing h. 366

Holiness: holiness of the heart's affections 261

lost in h. 89

put off H. 55

Holland: H. . . . lies so low 233

Hollow: we are the h. men 182

Hollows: h. crown'd with summer sea 413

Holyday: Sunshine H. 302

Homage: owes no h. unto the sun 66

522

Home: blest by the suns of h. 65

difficult is it to bring it h. 170

dream that I am h. 198

h. in my ain countree 146

h. is the sailor 403

h. . . . where . . . they have to take you in 203

Homer: H. sometimes sleeps 96

not read H. 37

when worthy H. nods 234

Homes: stately h. of England 224

Homesickness: h. for the gutter 28

Honest: character of an "H. Man" 432

dance more skilfully than an h. woman 354

good to be h. 21

h. God . . . noblest work 241

h. Man's the noblest work 333

made h. by an act 253

'tis well to be h. 296

to be h., to be kind 404

whatsoever things are h. 327

Honey: eat our pot of h. 297

flowing with milk and h. 192

on h.-dew hath fed 131

spoonful of h. 225

Honour: h. his memory 253

h. pricks me on 366

h. sinks where commerce 216

h. thy father 193

if I give thee h. due 302

lov'd I not H. more 278

no point of h. 228

sin to covet h. 367

think we h. merit 331

titles do not reflect h. 284

to h. lost 84

Honoured: these h. dead 273

Honours: H. . . . give an ideal and local value 403

Hook: draw out Leviathan with an h. 248

Hoot: h. about posterity 141

Hooter: because the h. hoots 120

Hope: abandon h. 147

fooled with h. 173

he that lives upon h. 203

h. beyond the shadow of a dream 256

h. deferred 338

h. is a good breakfast 32

h. of death 148

h. springs eternal 332

live in h. 451

some blessed H. 220

tea there's h. 327

Hoped: he who has never h. 376

Hopes: fifty h. and fears 68

h. of all men 95

h. which obscure 63

if h. were dupes 127

Horace: H.; whom I hated 94

we learn from H. 96

Horizontal: best life is led h. 205

Horn: h. invites thee 396

Horse: for want of a h. 203

like a pawing h. 129

my kingdom for a h. 369

secret . . . between a rider and his h. 408

where's the bloody h. 102

Horseman: h., pass by 457

Horses: Women and H. 264

Hospitals: rot in h. 396

523

Hostages: H. to Fortune 33
Hostilities: h. will cease 199
Houghmagandie: end in h. 82
Hound: sleping h. to wake 117
Hour: h. is come 359
h. is ill which severs 383
h. of glorious life 314
one far fierce h. 120
one h. was sunlit 336
their finest h. 124
Hours: chase the glowing H. 92
h. will take care of themselves 118
Lovers h. be full eternity 166
six h. in sleep 128
House: all-night sitting in the H. of Commons 380
dwell in the h. of the Lord 339
erects a h. of prayer 152
go into the h. of the Lord 341
hold my h. in the high wood 50
h. . . . his castle 128
H. of Have and the H. of Want 209
H. of Peers . . . did nothing 211
in my Father's h. 248
man builds a fine h. 190
set thine h. in order 243
them that join h. to h. 242
Housed: third of a nation ill-h. 348
Household: study h. good 307
Housemaids: damp souls of h. 182

Houses: calling of selling h. 272
Housewife: h. that's thrifty 390
Hovel: prefer . . . a h. 101
Howling: flee, h. in terror 337
Hubbard: Old Mother H. 319
Hum: h. of human cities 93
Human: all that is h. must retrograde 210
h. bodies are sic fools 85
h. kind cannot bear . . . reality 183
h. race, to which so many of my readers belong 122
h. species . . . two distinct races 267
nothing h. indifferent 417
this is h. life 256
to step aside is h. 80
work of h. hearts 385
wrought by h. hands 385
Humanity: rival portions of h. 200
still sad music of h. 452
Humble: to God be hummill 176
we are so very h. 156
Humbleness: no man in h. 115
Humdrum: spliced in the h. way 63
Humour: phrase " unconscious h." 90
Hump: without an absolute h. may marry 418
Humpty: H. Dumpty 319
Hundred: his h.'s soon hit 70
same a h. years hence 158
Hunger: best sauce . . . is h. 112

blessed are they which do
h. 293
make h. thy sauce 423

Hungry: h. as a hunter
268
she makes h. 362

Hunter: hungry as a h. 268
h. home from the hill
403
H. of the East 197
man is the h. 416

Hunting: ever to call h. one
of them 249

Hurry: I am never in a h.
435
old man in a h. 123

Husband: being a h. is a
whole-time job 51
he makes a bad h. 186
h.-hunting butterfly 311

Husbands: h. at chirche dore
114
reasons for h. to stay 181
when h. . . . breathe their
last 334

Hynde: H. Horn fair 40

Hyphenated: h. Americans
349

Hypocrisy: love is taught h.
95
organised h. 163

I

I: here am I 242

Ice: world will end . . . in i.
204

Ichabod: I., the glory is
departed 75

Idea: fight for an i. 378
pain of a new i. 37

Ideas: invasion of i. 237
trust in i. 189

Identity: sleep without i. 63

Ides: beware the I. of March
364

Idiot: i. race 84

Idleness: day in i. 111
i. is only the refuge 119

Idling: impossible to enjoy
i. 246

Idolatries: bowed to its i. 93

Idols: worship national i.
379

If: i. you can keep your head
265

Ifs: if i. and ands 326

Ignominy: i. of our natures
66

Ignorance: blind and naked
I. 413
exchange of i. 98
Gothic i. 197
names to hide its i. 387
no sin but i. 287
oppress'd with i. 167
putting us to i. 69
your i, cramps my con-
versation 233

Ill: i. men . . . spake worse
252

Illegitimacy: stain of i. 29

Illiberal: nothing so i. 118

Ills: nae real i. perplex 85

Illusion: only one i. left 394

Illusions: don't part with
your i. 424

Image: make man in our i.
208

Imaginary: speak of things i.
52

Imagination: driven the
living i. out 458
heart is . . . his i. 377
i. is more impact 180
of i. all compact 373
save those that have no i.
380
truth of i. 261

Imitation: i. is the sincerest form 133

Immensities: probing their i. 463

Imminent: war seem i. 270

Immorality: nurseries of ... i. 196

Immortal: everyone is an i. 89
i. with a kiss 287
know thyself first i. 117

Immortality: crown'd with i. 256
i. of the human soul 149

Imparadis'd: i. in one another's arms 307

Impediments: i. to great enterprises 33

Imperfect: say not Man's i. 332

Implacable: i. in hate 172

Importance: nothing ... is of the smallest i. 440

Important most i. thing 417

Impossibility: swore ... fond i. 279

Impossible: eliminated the i. 171
one *can't* believe i. things 109
with men this is i. 296

Impotence: i. of mind 308

Improbable: whatever remains, *however* i. 171

Improvement: schemes of political i. 250

Improving: corner ... certain of i. 240

Inaccuracy: I hate i. 90

Incapacity: old maid courted by i. 56

Incarnadine: multitudinous seas i. 370

Incident: character ...

Income: annual i. twenty pounds 156
live beyond its i. 89

Inconstant: i., childish, proud 261

Inconvenient: i. to be poor 142

Incorruptible: sea-green I. 106

Increment: unearned i. 300

Independence: first of earthly blessings, i. 210
i. of solitude 188
my boasted i. 87

Independent: poor and i. 127

Index: mere i. hunter 395

Indian: go, like the I. 333
good I. is a dead I. 389

Indictment: i. against a whole people 78

Indignation: moral i. is jealousy 435

Indiscreet: questions are never i. 442

Indiscretion: green i. 200

Individual: duty of every i. 432

Individualism: rugged i. 233

Individuality: ceases to possess i. 299
whatever crushes i. 299

Indolence: honied i. 258

Industry: captains of i. 106
i. ... of no avail 239
spur of i. 238

Inexactitude: terminological i. 123

Infamous: wipe out the i. 428

Infancy: shin'd in my Angel-i. 425

Infant: i. crying for the light 414

determination of i. 245

Inferior: been in anything i. 62

Infest: cares that i. the day 277

Infinite: I. in him 107
though i. can never meet 290

Infinity: I. in the palm 53
Reason reach I. 174

Infirmity: last i. of Noble mind 303

Inflicted: by man on man i. 131

Influence: i. is not government 432

Influenza: no i. in my young days 50

Infortune: worst kinde of i. 117

Inglorious: not i. son 27

Ingratitude: unkind as man's i. 362

Inherit: i. the earth 293

Inheritance: time is my i. 215

Inhumanity: man's i. to man 84

Iniquity: hated i. 218
i. of the fathers 193
i. of us all 244

Injuries: insult to i. 313

Injury: i. . . . sooner forgotten 118
repaying i. with kindness 269

Injustice: i. of it is almost perfect 322

Inn: no room for them in the i. 279

Innisfree: go to I. 455

Innocence: itself has many a wile 95

Innocent: of the blood 296
i. are worried . . . by their looks 323
Minds i. and quiet 278

Insolence: flown with i. 305

Inspiration: genius is one per cent i. 179

Instinct: healthy i. for it 90

Instrument: i. of ten strings 340
tune the I. 166

Insult: i. to injuries 313
one more i. to God 71
sooner forgotten than an i. 118

Insulted: allows himself to be i. 140

Intellect: i. is ready like a steam engine 240
meddling i. misshapes 451
one-story i. 231
put on I. 55

Intellects: imperfect i. 267

Intellectual: being i. 102
more i. our pleasure 100
self-sufficing thing, an i. 450

Intercourse: i. with foreign nations 152

Interest: I du in i. 279

Interesting: novel . . . that it be i. 245

Interruptions: interrupt my i. 181

Intimate: i. with few 432

Intoxicate: draughts i. the brain 331

Intoxication: best of life is but i. 95

Invasion: i. of armies 237

Invention: happy i. 22
reasonable is an i. 205

Inventions: effective i. 429

Invents: best thing God i. 70

Ireland: romantic I.'s dead 456
sweeten I.'s wrong 457

Irish: I. poets, learn your trade 457

527

Irishman: I.'s heart 377
Irks: i. care the crop-full bird 73
Irony: i. is the essence 43
Isaac: God of I. 192
Iser: flow of I. 102
Island: no man is an *I.* 164
Islander: prejudices of an i. 99
Israelite: call him an I. 224
Italy: Creator made I. from designs 424
graved inside of it, " I." 69
I. . . . hell for women 88
I. . . . paradise for horses 88
Itch: i. of literature 279
Ivy: with I. never-sere 302

J

Jack: J. and Jill 319
J. Spratt 319
Little J. Horner 319
Jackdaw: J. sat on the Cardinal's chair 44
Jackson: J. standing like a stone wall 48
Jacob: God of J. 192
Jads: I like the j. 83
Jam: never j. to-day 109
Jargon: j. o' your schools 81
Jaws: gently smiling j. 107
Jealous: art is a j. mistress 186
I . . . am a j. God 193
I'm not a j. woman 227
Jealousy: beware . . . of j. 374
j. with a halo 435
Jerkin: man's body . . . like a j. 402

Jerks: bring me up by j. 157
Jerusalem: till we have built J. 55
Jesus: if J. Christ were to come 106
J. wept 238
shove J. and Judas 187
thou shalt call his name J. 292
Jew: Germany will declare that I am a J. 180
hath not a J. eyes 372
they call him a J. 224
Jewel: j. in his head 362
J. of the Just 425
Jilted: better be courted and j. 102
Job: doing one's j. well 103
muffs his real j. 435
we will finish the j. 124
Jocund: j. day stands tiptoe 375
John: Honest J. 76
Johnny: J. was as brave 40
Johnson: as Dr. J. never said 45
Dr. J. condemns 79
Joined: whom God hath j. 136
Joke: j. well into a Scotch understanding 393
Jokes: accomplished at seeing my j. 360
for every ten j. 401
Jonah: J. was in the belly 252
lot fell upon J. 252
Jonson: J. knew the critic's part 133
Jostling: not done by j. 54
Journalism: as for modern j. 441
dominated by J. 445
Journalist: j. makes up his lies 455

528

Journalists: j. say a thing 51

Jove: lovelier than the love of J. 288

Joy: efter j. oftimes cumis care 226
headlong j. is ever on the wing 309
heart . . . asks if this be j. 216
j., lovely gift of the Gods 355
j. of joys 82
j. . . . over one sinner 280
let j. be unconfined 92
pure and complete j. 422
to j. in conquest 269
world of capability for j. 69

Joys: hence vain, deluding j. 301
it redoubleth J. 35
j. bene bot jangling 169
j. of all his life 256
j. to this are folly 87
rich man's j. increase 216

Judas: J. Iscariot was a sad dog 87
shove Jesus and J. 187

Judge: j. not 295
sober as a j. 196
'tis yours to j. 216
to j. great and lofty matters 312
who made thee a . . . j. 192

Judgement: at forty, the j. 202
history is the world's j. 356
J. in discerning what is true 35
j. of the world 28
nor is the people's always true 173
one cool j. 447
rawness of j. 200
time and God give j. 410
when the day of j. comes 262

Judgements: 'tis with our j. 331

June: April, J., and November 320
April, J., and September 217
rare as a day in J. 279

Juno: J. when she walks 253

Just: actions of the j. 390
cause we believe to be j. 273
path of the j. 338
sleep of the j. 343
whatsoever things are j. 327

Justice: I have loved j. 218
J. hath heaved a sword 55
j. to those who can 430
let j. be done 195
Man's grim J. 439
price of j. 51
sword of j. first lay down 152
Thwackum was for doing j. 197
to put j. till execution 275
we love j. greatly 351

Justify: j. God's ways 236

K

Kalends: at the Greek K. 101
K. are begun 244

Keats: whether . . . K . . . likes them or not 261
who killed John K. 98

Keel: no k. . . . ploughed 382

Keeper: my brother's k. 208

Kew: K. in lilac-time 317

Keys: two massy K. he bore 303

Kick: k. against the pricks 13

why did you k. me downstairs 52

Kiddie: k. in school 316

Kill: animals never k. for sport 204

men are prepared to k. 377

shalt not k. 193

shalt not k.; but need'st not strive 127

Killed: k. by frowns 385

Killing: more ways of k. a cat 264

Kills: k. the thing he loves 439

Kilmeny: K. had been she knew not where 231

Kiltartan: my country is K. Cross 454

Kindles: k. . . . a wantonnesse 229

Kindness: any k. that I can show 219

human k. 104

kill a wife with k. 375

passion of k. 187

shew forth thy loving k. 340

unremembered acts of k. 452

King: born K. of the Jews 293

cat may look at a k. 108

country guidit by . . . prudent k. 275

despised, and dying k. 387

distinguish a true k. 140

God save our gracious k. 104

God save the k. 354

happy as a k. 207

heart . . . of a king of England 184

here lies a K. 104

kind of k. for me 211

k. can do no wrong 53

k. is but a foolish labourer 454

k. of shreds and patches 364

k. springs from . . . slaves 329

no bishop, no k. 244

Old K. Cole 319

unjust and wicked k. 361

wal enough agin a k. 279

Kingdom: k. of heaven is like to a grain 295

k. . . . too small 366

rich man to enter into the k. 286

such is the k. of God 286

their's is the k. of heaven 293

thine is the k. 294

thy k. come 294

what vails your k. 275

Kingdoms: many . . . k. seen 260

Kings: sport of k. 396

towers of k. 235

Kirk: buried in Marie's k. 41

Kirkconnell: K. lea 39

Kirtle: kilted her green k. 42

Kiss: coward does it with a k. 439

each k. a heart-quake 96

k. but in the cup 253

k. me, Hardy 316

k. till the cow comes home 47

last lamenting k. 165

let us k. and part 172

never k. the girls 70

Kissed: k. her cow 408

Kisses: bread and cheese, and k. 408

give me a thousand k. 111

Kissing: k. don't last 298

when the k. had to stop 74

Kitchens: plates in the basement k. 182

Knave: honest man a k. 153

Knee: bend the supple k. 307

human k. is a joint 220

Kneeling: k. ne'er spoil'd silk stocking 228

Kneels: Little Boy k. 300

Knees: religion . . . not in the k. 247

woo her with too slavish k. 260

Knell: all-softening, over-powering k. 96

curfew tolls the k. 218

Knew: k. only this . . . k. nothing yet 49

Knife: k. under the cloke 115

Knight: K.-at-arms 255

K. of the Sorrowful Countenance 111

k. without fear 19

verray, parfit gentil k. 114

Knock: k., and it shall be opened 295

stand at the door, and k. 344

Knocking: k. on the moonlit door 153

Know: k. . . . he nothing knew 308

k. not what they do 280

k. then thyself 332

they k. enough 13

Knowing: misfortune of k. anything 30

Knowledge: activity . . . road to k. 379

desire of k. 402

excelled in ornamental k. 250

imagination is more important than k. 180

(k is) a rich storehouse 31

k. is not happiness 98

k. is of two kinds 251

K. is, ourselves to know 333

k. itself is power 36

k. . . . like the great flood 388

k. of nothing 160

k. of the world . . . acquired 118

k. of what is excellent 16

k. . . . vanish away 140

my k. is but vain 16

no k. that is not power 190

pangs us fou o' k. 82

road to k. 379

scientific acquisition of k. 275

want of true k. 402

what is all k. 105

Known: hath ye not k. 243

Knows: no man truly k. 66

Knuckle: k.-end of England 393

Knucklebones: harmless art of k. 404

Kubla Khan: in Xanadu did K.K. 131

L

Labour: anyone who votes L. 313

devices for cheapening l. 315

l. for the one 94

l. in vain 341

l. is in vaine 226

not cease to l. 404

we l. soon 85

Laden: I l. will returne 279

Ladies: old l. of both sexes 158

out of the l. company 362

531

Lady: but-not-altogether-satisfactory l. 335
l. in the case 210
L. would be Queen for life 334
lang will his L. 39
My L. Bountiful 194

Ladylike: too l. in love 227

Laird: L. o' Drum is a-wooing 40

Lairdie: wee German l. 146

Lakes: light shakes across the l. 416

Lamb: l. in a sentimental farce 258
Little L., who made thee 57

Lambs: gather the l. 243

Lame: feet . . . to the l. 247

Lammas: L. tide 38

Lamp: L. at midnight hour 301
l. in her hand 284
thy word is a l. 341

Lamps: l. are going out all over Europe 219
light the l. 403
old l. for new 24

Land: between a splendid and a happy l. 216
house and l. are gone 200
l. flowing with milk 192
l. is cultivated . . . by the spade 300
l. no one can define 79
l. of lobelias 183
L. of our birth 265
l. of such dear souls 369
l. that has taught us 313
l. . . . where wealth accumulates 215

Lands: comes from the west l. 292
l. where the Jumblies live 271

Language: best chosen l. 30
consenting l. of the heart 207
l. all nations understand 49
l. is the dress of thought 251
l. was not powerful enough 158
no. l. but a cry 414
room for but one l. 348
when any l. is lost 252

Languages: l. are the pedigree 252

Lards: l. the lean earth 366

Large: l. as life 109

Lark: hark! hark! the l. 362
l., messeger of day 115
l. shall sing me hame 146
l.'s on the wing 15

Lass: cam' wi' a l. 244
lover and his l. 362

Last: l. thing I shall do 324

Latin: L.-bred woman 229

Latium: introduced the arts to rustic L. 234

Laud: your famous l. 226

Laugh: I make myself l. 46
know when to l. 323
l. and the world laughs 438
l. at any mortal thing 96
l. broke into . . . pieces 45
l. that spoke the vacant mind 215

Laughable: political improvement . . . l. 250

Laughing: you also, l. one 155

Laughs: earth l. 188
he who l. on Friday 343
man who l. at anyone . . . afraid 311
when he l., it adds 401

Laughter: ill-bred, as audible l. 118

l. and the love of friends 49

L. holding both his sides 302

l., learnt of friends 65

l. with some pain is fraught 388

Laundry: l. trade of the mainland 217

Laura: if L. had been Petrarch's wife 96

Laurel: burned is Apollo's l. bough 287

Laurels: l. all are cut 236

yet once more, O ye L. 302

Lave: whistle owre the l. 83

Law: I'll find them l. 61

judgements of the English l. 410

l. . . . forbids the rich 201

l. is a ass 159

l. is the crystallisation 446

no l. can be sacred 187

Laws: l. of a nation 199

l. . . . made to keep fair play 54

l. were like cobwebs 32

l. were made to be broken 317

whether L. be right 439

Lawyers: l. too powerful 133

Lays: constructing tribal l. 265

Lead: l. those that are with young 243

Leaf: thou cursed l. 83

Leak: one l. will sink a ship 77

Leap: great l. in the dark 230

l. into the dark 65

Learn: gladly wolde he l. 114

know how to l. 13

l. by doing 25

l. men from books 162

we l. so little 151

Learned: l. to love all beauty 240

opinion with the l. 138

Learning: a' the l. I desire 81

l. is a dangerous thing 331

l. is but an adjunct 369

l. is like bread in a besieged town 251

l. is most excellent 200

l. . . . makes a silly man 14

l. was painfully beaten 433

l. without thought 137

mad with much l. 327

of such deep l. 398

picker up of l.'s crumbs 69

same age saw L. fall 332

swallow all your l. 119

wear your l. 118

whence is thy l. 207

Leave: l. it alone 342

l. to come unto my love 398

Leaves: l. dead . . . like ghosts 384

l. on the trees 236

L. that strow the Brooks 305

Leavings: sacrifice to God of the devil's l. 409

Leer: assent with civil l. 333

Leerie: L., I'll go round 403

Leg: standing long upon one l. 329

Legal: l. matters . . . Greek to me 205

Legions: all these puissant L. 305

Legislators: ancient l. thought 199

Legs: cannon-ball took off his l. 232

Leisure: add to these retired L. 301

Lemons: Oranges and L. 320

Lend: *men who l.* 267

533

Leopard: l. follows his nature 418

l. shall lie down 242

or the l. his spots 246

Lesbia: L., let us live 111

Less: l. one has to do 119

l. the greater comprehend 174

Lesson: jolly good l. 265

well koude he rede a l. 115

Lethe: go not to L. 258

tedious shores of L. 267

Letter: made this l. longer 325

Letters: man of l. 327

no arts: no l. 230

Leviathan: draw out L. 248

Liar: perfect l. 50

Liberties: never give up their l. 78

Liberty: calls them L. 76

cause of a single life, is L. 33

establish our own true l. 312

God hath given l. to man 147

history of l. 447

hour of virtuous l. 14

lamp of l. 273

l. began to increase 54

l. . . . don't agree with niggers 279

L.! Equality! Brotherhood 21

l. means responsibility 379

l. of their fellowmen 447

l. . . . plant of rapid growth 432

l.'s a glorious feast 83

l. was born in England 429

l.! what crimes 346

light! take l. L. 383

man, and lackith l. 244

nation conceived in l. 273

preferring hard l. 306

revel on the grave of L. 382

seek Power and lose L. 34

tree of l. must be refreshed 245

when they cry l. 309

Library: lumber-room of his l. 170

no gentleman's l. should be without 268

Licence: l. they mean 309

Licker: l. talks mighty loud 221

Lie: l. for the good of the State 328

l. just made 143

l. . . . that doth the hurt 33

what is a l. 97

Lies: cursed be the social l. 415

great l. about his wooden horse 198

Lieth: say that a man l. 33

Life: ane mirrie l. 275

best l . . . horizontal 205

best of l. is conversation 186

count l. just a stuff 71

crowded hour of glorious l. 314

dost thou love l. 202

each loved one blotted from L.'s page 92

every man's l. is a fairy-tale 18

fraile l. 150

have everlasting l. 248

he that findeth his l. 295

his L . . . . in the right 142

I gave my l. for freedom 192

I have lived my l. 413

if l. was bitter 409

laws of l. 351

lay down his l. 248

534

l. . . . a poem 105
l. and death is cat and dog 205
l. for l. 194
l. has crept so long 415
l. is bigger 440
l. is but a day 259
l. is but a dream 419
l. is good only when it is magical 190
l. is just one damned thing 237
l. is more like l. 321
l. isn't all beer 237
l. is one dark maze 420
l. is real! L. is earnest 278
l. is short 396
l. is sweet 69
l. is the art 89
l. is the thing 392
l. levels all men 379
l., like a dome 381
l. lived for others . . . l. worthwhile 179
l. . . . not a dream 62
l. of man . . . brutish and short 230
l. of man less than a span 36
l.'s enchanted cup 92
l.'s more amusing 269
l. so fast doth fly 151
l. so short, the art so long 230
l. so short, the craft so long 116
l. that will be envied 410
l. there is danger 190
L., 'tis all a cheat 173
l. . . . understood backwards 263
l. without faith . . . arid 141
loathing our l. 98

man's l. was spacious 180
measured out my l. 182
not so much l. as on a summer's day 257
righteous and sober l. 134
sells us l. at a discount 205
slits the thin-spun l. 303
this is human l. 256
to lengthen thy l. 202
tree of l. is green 214
value of l. is not the end of it 312
way, the truth, and the l. 248
what is this l. 151
where L. was slain 121
Light: as the shining l. 338
dim religious l. 301
give me a l. 222
into the world of l. 425
let there be l. 97, 208
l. begouth to quynkill 169
l. . . . first of painters 189
l. such a candle 270
my l. is spent 310
Like: doing as they l. 299
I know what I l. 48
look upon his l. again 363
say, you do not l. it 436
who l. me not 74
Liked: how I like to be l. 268
Likewise: go, and do thou l. 280
Lilac: Kew in l.-time 317
Lillabullero: whistling . . . L. 401
Lily: paint the l. 368
Limousine: all we want is a l. 285
Linden: on L., when the sun 102
Line: l. will take us hours 453
not a l. . . . written 188

535

Lines: l. and life are free 228

Lingered: l l. round them 64

Lingering: l., with boiling oil 212

sit l. here 425

Linnet: hear the woodland l. 451

Lion: dressed in the l.'s skin 199

l. is the beast 342

Lips: l., where all Day 145

l. with laughter shook 150

red mournful l. 456

Liquor: drynke l. of the vyne 116

l. Is quicker 316

livelier l. 236

when the l.'s out 70

List: I've got a little l. 211

Listen: darkling I l. 259

Lit: l. again in our lifetime 219

Literature: contribution . . . to the current l. 90

failed in l. and art 162

itch of l. 279

l. clear, cold, pure 272

l. flourishes best 241

l. has truly told 188

l. of the old world 458

L. that shows us the body 441

lover of l. is never fastidious 397

Literary: l. attempt was more unfortunate 238

those l. cooks 314

Little: l. things . . . most important 170

man wants but l. 458

so l. done 345

so l. done, such things 414

very l. one 289

Live: all would l. long 202

come l. with me 163, 288

eat to l., not l. to eat 311

in him we l. 13

know how to l. 312

learn to l. well 333

l. and love 111

l. not in myself 93

l. with her, and l. with thee 302

to l. is like love 90

whom you l. with 118

Livelihood: earned a precarious l. 217

Liverpool: folk that live in L. 120

Lives: l. of those who ceased to live 220

Liveth: I am he that l. 344

Living: be happy while y'er l. 19

crieth out for the l. God 339

fever call'd " L." 330

l. blood and a passion for kindness 187

l. is an art 239

their l. to earn 175

Livingstone: L., I presume 400

Loaf: L. of Bread beneath the Bough 197

Loaves: did eat of the l. 286

Lochinvar: young L. 358

Lodgers: Queer street is full of l. 159

Log: l. was burning brightly 214

Logic: L. absolute 197

projected lines of l. 204

that's l. 109

Loitered: l. my life away 223

Loitering: alone and palely l. 255

London: city much like L. 385

L! Pompus Ignorance sits enthroned 61
L., that great cesspool 171
L., that great sea 384
nails can reach . . . L. 359
people of L. . . . say 124
vilest alleys of L. 170
Loneliest: strongest creatures . . . l. 323
Long: desires to live l. 409
how l., O Lord 380
Longitude: l. with no platitude 205
Look: l. before you 89
Looked: she should never have l. 69
Looks: l. canst clear the darken'd sky 289
l. commercing with the skies 301
l. went everywhere 71
Looms: passage through these l. 425
Loose: l. as the winde 222
Lord: glorious L. of life 398
L. be with thee 354
L. gave, and the L. hath taken 247
L. God of your fathers 192
L. was not in the wind 263
surely the L. is in this place 209
there liv'd a l. 41
Lords: women . . . who love their l. 231
Lordship: L. says he will turn it over 52
Lose: l. his own soul 295
Losers: in war . . . all are l. 112
Loseth: he that l. his life 295
Lost: all is not l. 304
nothing is l. 150

Lot: l. fell upon Jonah 252
wish to ease his l. 422
Loungers: l. of the Empire 171
Love: all for l. 399
be my l. 288, 343
can l. like a fool 316
cannot but admit L. 34
come . . . be my l. 288
crime to l. too well 331
enough to make us l. 409
fallen was in l.'s dance 244
for l.'s sake only 67
God is l. 248
greater l. hath no man 248
he excludeth L. 228
him who hears l. sing 456
hold your tongue and let me l. 163
I could not l. thee 278
I l. it, I l. it 139
if a man say, I l. God 249
killing l. by staying 439
let the warm L. in 259
l. a place the less for having suffered 30
l. according to the gospel 28
l. all burningly golden 420
l., and beauty 387
l. and do what you like 29
l. and to be wise 78
l. . . . best sweetners of tea 196
l. built on beauty 164
l. ceases to be a pleasure 49
l., cherish and to obey 136
l. conquers all 427
L.! Could you and I 198
l. . . . improves a woman 194
l. in friendship 133
L. in her Sunny Eyes 142
L. is a greater law 58, 115

l. is ane fervent fire 356
l. . . . is exactly like war 402
l. is heaven 357
L. is like a dizziness 231
l. is like the measles 246
l. is more cruel 409
l. is only chatter 77
l. is the great Asker 270
l. is the lesson 398
l. is the wisdom of the fool 249
l. looks not with the eyes 373
l. must have some future 103
l. . . . no season knowes 168
l. . . . object of l. 195
l. of God 346
l. rules the court 357
l. seeketh not itself to please 56
l.'s not so pure 166
l., so much refin'd 168
l. sought is good 376
l. . . . spoke the consenting language 207
l. that I am seeking 456
l. that makes the sport 407
l. that makes the world go round 108
L., thou art Absolute 144
l. thy neighbour 296
l. which was more than l. 330
l. wi' a scunner 284
l. . . . would contemplate 166
man moot nedes l. 115
marriage without l. 202
men l. in haste 97
money . . . sinews of l. 194
my L. is of a birth 290
never had a l. affair 270
not in our power to l.

off with the old l. 21, 296
our l. hath no decay 163
our l. might take no end 228
should not l. her 69
sigh my hot l.'s folly 241
sighed for the l. 213
sweet L. of youth 63
ten men l. what I hate 73
tests of generous l. 86
thought wander . . . when one is in l. 456
true L. in this differs 382
'twixt womens l. 163
two parties to a l. transaction 418
unholy mantrap of l. 205
way to l. each other 263
when l. for you died 64
with l. and wine at once oppressed 173
without l. life is no better 440
Loved: better l. ye canna be 231
better to have l. and lost 90, 414
l. not wisely, but too well 374
l. three whole days 407
never l. . . . never liv'd 207
some we l., the loveliest 197
till we l. 165
to have l. 26
whoever l. that l. not at first sight 287
Lovelier: nothing l. . . . in woman 307
Loveliness: its l. increases 256
l. within hath found 168
woman of so shining l. 456
Lovely: l. in a lonely place 153

538

whatsoever things are l.
327
Lover: l. and his lass 362
l.'s quarrel with the world
204
Lovers: dull sublunary l.
168
give a law to l. 58
Loves: chang'd l. . . .
chang'd sorts of meat
164
deceived by what one l.
312
Lovesome: garden is a l.
thing 65
Loveth: he that l. not 248
Loving: l. himself better 131
l. the land that has
taught 313
privilege of l. longest 30
Low: feared the " l." 435
Lower: l. class, I am in it
152
Lowliness: l. . . . ambition's
ladder 365
Loyalty: room for but one l.
348
Luck: good l. to your young
ambition 427
Luke: L., the beloved
physician 133
Lullaby: dreamy l. 211
Lunatic: l. fringe 348
l., the lover, and the poet
373
Lust: fashed wi' fleshly l.
82
more cruel than l. 409
Luxury: pamper l. 216
Lying: I do not mind l. 90
L. . . . is the proper aim
of Art 442
privilege of l. 328
Lyric: include me among the
l. poets 234

M

Macduff: lay on, M. 371
Macgregor: my name is M.
360
Machiavel: world think M.
is dead 287
Machine: m. unmakes the
man 189
Machinery: m. has greatly
increased . . . idlers
291
Machines: m. are worshipped 352
Mad: m. with much learning
327
men that God made m.
120
Madding: m. crowd's
ignoble strife 218
Madmen: m. . . . made men
mad 93
Madness: m. . . . possess a
a poet's brain 172
money is our m. 270
though this be m. 363
wits . . . to m. near allied
172
Madonna: vein o'er the
M.'s breast 68
Magdalen: fourteen months
at M. 209
Maggots: m. half-form'd in
rhyme 330
Magical: life is good only
when it is m. 190
Magnificent: m., but it is not
war 60
Mahomet: M. will go to the
Hill 34
Maid: be good, sweet m. 263
where's the m. 257

539

Maiden: m. of bashful fifteen 390
m. with white fire laden 381

Majesty: infinite M. 134
m. that from man's soul 315
rounded them with m. 220

Majority: liberal m. 241
m. . . . no more right to tyrannise 348

Malice: m. toward none 274

Malt: m. does more than Milton 236
wha hes gud m. 23

Mammon: ye cannot serve God and m. 294

Man: be a m. before your mother 143
great m. . . . keeps . . . independence of solitude 188
he was a m. 363
let him pass for a m. 372
let us make m. in our image 208
life of even the meanest m. 105
m. . . . a political animal 26
m. bites a dog 147
M. is a lumpe 168
m. is a tool-using animal 106
m. . . . is a wicked creature 312
m. is all symmetrie 228
m. is as old as he's feeling 132
m. is . . . better pleased 249
m. is something to be surpassed 317
m. is the greatest (marvel) 396

m. is the superior animal 336
m. must be tempted 297
m. . . . must get drunk 95
m. of many thoughts 98
m. of wealth and pride 216
M.'s chief end 110
m. shall not live by bread alone 293
m. to m. the world o'er 83
m. was not born for himself 328
m. . . . will be a far more perfect creature 149
m. will live 237
m. with all his noble qualities 149
no mere m. since the fall 110
piece of work is a m. 363
play is the tragedy, " M." 330
sabbath was made for m. 286
this was a m. 366
what a m. may do 417
whoso would be a m. 187
unholy m. trap of love 205

Manacles: mind-forged m. 57

Manage: silliest woman can m. a clever man 266

Mane: runs with all his m. 342

Manger: dog in the m. 423
in the rude m. lies 304

Manhood: conspiracy against the m. 187

Mania: m. of owning things 437

Mankind: advantages of looking at m. 99
improvements in the lot of m. 298
involved in M. 164

540

m. by their fall 110
m. minus one 299
m. . . . unfi' for their own government 432
need not be to hate m. 93
study of his is Man 332
Manly: m. part is to do . . . what you can 186
Manner: m. rude and wild 49
Manners: as a nation . . . we've no m. 380
comedies of m. 141
good m. are made up 189
m. of a Marquis 212
M. take a tincture 333
no longer any m. 141
poets have . . . m. of their own 221
reform the m. of any city 199
Manoa: M. left his fields 56
Mansions: are many m. 248
Mantle: twitch'd his M. blue 303
Manure: its natural m. 245
Manuscripts: brown Greek m. 68
Many: m. still must labour 94
owed by so m. 124
wretched M. 131
Marathon: mountains look on M. 96
Marble: left it m. 101
m of great sculpture 239
m. to retain 91
March: droughte of M. 113
Margin: meadow of m. 390
Marie: thought mair o' M. Hamilton 41
Maries: Queen had four M. 41
Mariner: an ancient M. 128
M. hath his will 128

Marksmen: you are all m 342
Marlow: Neat M., bathed 172
Marquis: manners of a M. 212
Marriage: care . . . more for a m. 36
happiness in m. . . . matter of chance 30
in m. hree is company 443
m. in the vulgar, weak sense 62
m. is like life 405
m. . . . is not a joke 312
m. is popular 378
m. is rather permitted 249
m. is the greatest earthly happiness 162
m. of true minds 376
m. without love, . . . love without m. 202
sweet bird's m. hymns 181
twenty years of m. 446
Marriages: m. . . . selling one's soul 285
Married: ashamed of not being m. 31
if ever we had been m. 207
m., but I'd have no wife 144
m. to a single life 144
most married man I ever saw 431
once . . . m., . . . nothing left 406
pity the m. 336
strange as if . . . m. a great while 138
thankfu' ye're no m. 60
well-bred as if . . . not m. 138
when you're a m. man 159

541

Marries: changed with him who m. 406

Marry: advice to persons about to m. 341
m. is to domesticate 406
m. . . . to an indigent man 14
men that women m. 277

Martyrs: noble army of m. 134

Mary: M., Quite Contrary 319

Masquerade: miss a m. 334

Mass: Paris is well worth a m. 225

Massachusetts: M. Bill of Rights 189

Masses: I will back the m. 213

Master: I am the m. of my fate 225
that man is my m. 209

Masterpiece: friend . . . m. of Nature 186

Masterpieces: adventures of his soul among m. 201

Masters: ill m. be 219
people are the m. 78

Mate: artificer made him my m. 403

Mathematical: m. fact 107

Matrimonial difference in m. affairs 31

Matrimony: barrier against m. 262
improved by m. 100
in m. . . . begin with a little aversion 389
m., . . . origin of change 29
take m. at its lowest 405

Matter: heart of the m. 234
m. . . . lies subjected and plastic 387

Matthew: M., Mark, Luke and John 15

Maturer: work of m. years 262

Maw: m.-crammed beast 73 whose Gospel is their m. 310

Maxim: m. with Foxey 159 that grounded m. 309

May: leads with her the Flow'ry M. 309
weel-far'd M. 40

Mazes: walks the pleasant M. 142

Meal: handful of m. 263

Meals: lessen thy m. 202

Mean: what I choose it to m. 109

Means: die beyond my m. 444
glory . . . measured by the m. 270
live within our m. 431

Measure: m. of iniquity 87 m. of our torment 265

Measured: m. out my life 182

Meddle: wha daur m. 21

Meddling: had enough of m. 455

Mediæval: lily in your m. hand 212

Medicine: grief . . . a m. 142 use in m. for poison 186

Medicines: worthlessness of . . . m. 202

Meek: blessed are the m. 293

Melancholy: affect an holy m. 241
hence, loathèd M. 302
m. as a sick monkey 289
most m. of human reflections 37
naught so sweet as M. 87

542

veil'd M. has her sovran
    shrine 258
Mellow: not old, but m. 327
Melodies: heard m. are
    sweet 258
Melt: I m., I burn 207
Members: m. one of another
    191
Memoirs: fam'd m. of a
    thousand years 255
Memorable: days m. in the
    history 253
Memorial: M. from the
    Soul's eternity 350
    which have no m. 24
Memories: I have more m.
    46
    m.: a heap of tumbling
      stones 155
Memory: I . . . honour his
    m. 253
    inequalities of m. 29
Men: all m. are created free
    273
    de m.s, dey does de
      walkin' 221
    for m. must work 264
    m. are but children 173
    m. decay 215
    m. may come 412
    m., my brothers, m. the
      workers 415
    M. who hold its many
      blessings 451
    more I see of m. 100
    titles do not reflect honour
      on m. 284
    we are the hollow m. 182
    what good m. you are 448
    when m. and mountains
      meet 54
    when m. were first a nation
      54
    women . . . to match the
      m. 180

Mene: M., Tekel, Upharsin
    147
Mental: padlock of silence
    on m. wealth 62
Merci: belle Dame sans M.
    255
Merciful: blessed are the m.
    293
Mercy: crowning m. 146
    hae m. o' my soul 284
    leaving m. to Heaven 197
    m. is the surest sign 140
    m. upon us . . . sinners
      134
    murdered both his parents
      . . . pleaded for m. 274
    quality of m. 372
    when m. seasons justice
      372
Merit: indigent man of m.
    14
    m. wins the soul 335
Merits: m. you're bound to
    enhance 213
Merriment: ill-manag'd M.
    301
Merry: be m., man 176
    good to be m. 21
    m., dancing, . . time 175
    'tis well to be m. 296
Merrygoround: it's no go
    the m. 285
Messing: m. about in boats
    217
Method: m. in it 363
Methodist: morals of a M.
    212
Methods: by different m. 123
    you know my m. 171
Metropolis: m. of the empire
    127
Mice: feet . . . like little m.
    407
    schemes o' m. an' men 85
    Three Blind M. 320

Michelangelo: talking of M. 182

Mickle: mony a m. 112

Middle: die ere m. age 98
m.-aged suspect everything 441

Midnight: budding morrow in m. 260
threshed corn at m. 456

Midst: there am I in the m. 296

Might: invincible m. to quell 309
m. half slumb'ring 260

Mighty: how are the m. fallen 355

Mildest: m. manner'd man 96

Mile: compel thee to go a m. 294

Milk: crying over spilt m. 297
flowing with m. and honey 192
gospel of spilt m. 348
m. . . . likely to be watered 90
m. of human kindness 370

Mill: John Stuart M. 51

Million: aiming at a m. 70

Millions: what m. died 103

Mills: m. of God grind slow 276

Milo: I may be found a M. 94

Milton: believe in M. 95
M.! thou shouldst be living 451
morals hold which M. held 451

Mimicry: lives a m. 442

Mimsy: m. were the borogoves 109

Mind: he . . . knew their m. 232

inter-assured of the m. 168
man's m. is the man himself 126
m. and character slumber 189
m. is its own place 305
m. of man . . . beautiful 450
m., that very fiery particle 97 . .
M. . . . withdraws into its happiness 291
out of m. 127
pleased to call his m. 52
pray for a healthy m. 255
save with my m. 238
spoke the vacant m. 215
steam-wheels of the m. 383
who teach the m. 276
woman's m. is like wind 344

Minds: lose myself in other men's m. 267
m. like ours . . . above national prejudices 317
m. . . . shrunken things 32

Mine: while He is m. 229

Minerva: M. when she talks 253

Minister: wisdom of a great m. 254

Ministries: *The Times* has made many m. 36

Ministry: merit of a m. 254
more for a marriage than a m. 36

Minority: m. is always right 241
right to tyrannise over a m. 348

Minstrel: M. was infirm 357
wandering m. I 211

Minute: every m. dies a man 20

544

Minutes: five m. too late 142
take care of the m. 118
Mirror: hold the faithful m.
up to man 276
m. reflects all 137
Mirth: earth must borrow
its m. 438
fence against . . . ill health
. . . by m. 401
M., admit me 302
m. of cracker-barrel men
50
now leiff thi m. 57
Miserable: nothing is m. 58
Misery: m. acquaints a man
375
result m. 156
Misfortune: cruellest kind
of m. 58
Misfortunes: m. great and
sma' 86
Misquote: enough of learning to m. 97
Missed: never would be m.
211
Mist: Scots m. will weet 344
Mistake: blue and gold m.
161
Mistaken: you may be m.
146
Mistakes: name men give to
their m. 445
Mistress: art is a jealous
m. 186
M. moderately fair 142
m. some rich anger shows
253
no M. but ther Muse 166
select . . . a m. 382
teeming M. 333
young m. is better 434
Mistresses: m. with . . .
marbly limbs 68
one wife and hardly
any m. 353

Wives are young men's M.
33
Mists: season of m. 255
Misunderstood: admired
through being m. 128
Misunderstand: m. a lot 201
Mite: inspect a m. 332
Mob: governors, the m. 430
Mobs: suppose there are
two m. 159
Mock: m. on, Voltaire 55
Moderation: astonished at
my own m. 126
m. is a fatal thing 446
Modern: disease of m. life
27
Moderns: speak of the m.
118
Modesty: consequent m. 325
true m. . . . abound 213
Moment: every m. dies a
man 417
m. may with bliss 103
Moments: m. big as years
257
Monarch: m. of all I survey
143
nature rejects the m. 386
Monarchs: m. must obey
174
Monarchy: M. of wit 104
Monday: M. is a parson's
holiday 408
M's child is fair 21
Money: Aristocracy of the
M. bag 106
care how hard m. is 279
keep m. to look at 432
know the value of m. 203
M. is like Muck 34
m. is our madness 270
m. . . . root of all evil 422
m. . . . sinews of love
194
m. speaks sense 49

545

ever wrote, except for m. 251

time is m. 201

what m. will do 326

you pays your m. 23

Monk: devil a m. would be 315

Monkey: melancholy as a sick m. 289

Monomaniacs: art has its . . . m. 238

Monotony: bleats articulate m. 400

ever-flowing m. 336

m. of a decorous age 186

Monster: green-ey'd m. 374

Montezuma: who imprisoned M. 282

Monument: m. more lasting than bronze 235

only m. the asphalt road 183

see his m. look around 453

Mood: pairt o' an eternal m. 283

Moon: I saw the new m. 42

M. is up 94

m. was a ghostly galleon 317

mortals call the M. 381

shone the wintry m. 256

silently, now the m. 154

Moonlight: sweet the m. sleeps 373

Moral: Englishman thinks he is m. 378

m. of the Scilly Islanders 217

persons attempting to find a m. 424

Moralist: cursed the canting m. 151

Scotchman must be a very sturdy m. 250

Morality: goodbye, m. 227

m. . . . attitude we adopt 442

people talk of m. 178

periodical fits of m. 282

Moralize: loves shall m. my song 398

Morals: foundation of m. 51

m. of a Methodist 212

poets have m. . . . of their own 221

Morn: it is already M. 279

m., in russet mantle 363

Morning: lucid m.'s fragrant breath 419

M. in the Bowl of Night 197

m. shews the day 308

Moron: see the happy m. 22

Morrow: budding m. in midnight 260

no thought for the m. 294

Morsel: no deyntee m. passed 116

Mortal: m., and may err 390

m. taste brought Death 304

Mortals: greatest good that m. know 14

m. love the letters 73

most that m. are permitted 16

what fools these m. be 373

Moth: desire of the m. 388

Mother: little did my m. ken 41

m. will be there 227

my m., drunk or sober 121

veins of rhyming m.-wits 288

Motherland: M. we pledge 265

Motion: God order'd m. 425

546

Motive: mercenary, and the prudent m. 31

persons attempting to find a m. 424

Motor-cycle: son would have his m. 183

Moulds: distan your m. 40

Mountain: m. . . . made low 243

Mountains: m. be carried into the . . . sea 339

m., waves, and skies 93

when men and m. meet 54

Mourn: blessed are they that m. 293

no longer m. for me 376

Mourns: wiser mind m. less 449

Mouse: leave room for the m. 353

Move: does not m. 206

Movement: M., that problem of the visible arts 441

Moving: M. Finger writes 198

Much: so m. to do 345

Muchness: much of a m. 425

Mud: one sees the m. 269

Munch: m. on, crunch on 73

Murder: I met M. 384

M. . . . One of the Fine Arts 155

m. will out 138

what is slavery? . . . M. 337

Murdered: m. both his parents 274

Murray: slain the Earl of M. 39

Music: don't know . . . about m. 48

formed, as notes of m. 382

how potent cheap m. is 141

if m. be the food of love 375

like classical m. 378

m. alone with sudden charms 138

m. has charms 138

m. in my heart 451

m. of the spheres 150

m. sweeter than their own 450

m., the greatest good 14

m.. . . . vibrates in the memory 388

never merry when I hear sweet m. 373

sounds of m. creep in our ears 373

Musical: life is good only when . . . m. 190

Musing: m. in solitude 449

Mustard: grain of m. seed 295

Muttering: m. grew to a grumbling 73

Mutton: old was his m. 232

Myriads: united voice of m. 217

Myrtle: m. mixed in my path 72

Myrtles: ye M. brown 302

Myself: m. am Hell 307

Mysteries: Loves m. in soules 165

Mystery: m. will lead millions 58

N

Nail: for want of a n. 203

hit the n. on the head 329

Naked: n. and ye clothed me 296

n. as a worm was she 117

Name: filches . . . my good n. 374

n. of the Lord thy God 193

what's in a n. 374

Nameless: image of a n. dread 420

Napoleon: N.'s armies . . . march on their stomachs 361

Narrative: unconvincing n. 212

Nation: n. grieve 173

n. is not governed 78

n. . . . shall have a new birth 274

n. shall not lift up sword against n. 242

new n. conceived in liberty 273

no n. is fit to sit in judgement 447

no n. . . . ruined by trade 203

Nations: formed Two N. 162

Native: my own, my n. land 358

Natural: twice as n. 109

Nature: God and N. link'd the gen'ral frame 333

good-n. and good-sense 331

highest type of human n. 397

his n. to advance 93

honest N. made you fools 81

in n. . . . neither rewards 242

it can't be N. 123

lore which N. brings 451

muse on N. 103

N. impartial in munificence 387

N. is creeping up 436

N. is full of freaks 190

N. is often hidden 35

N. . . . . lost in Art 133

N. made her what she is 80

N. might stand up 366

N. rejects the monarch 386

N.'s social union 85

n.'s white hand sets ope 145

N. that framed us 288

rest on N. fix 128

spark o' N.'s fire 81

then n. rul'd 207

when N. conquers 356

yet do I fear thy n. 370

Natures: dearth of noble n. 256

men's n. are alike 137

strife of little n. 75

Naughty: good deed in a n. world 373

Navy: n. of Charles the Second 282

Necessity: curst n. compels 87

n. hath no law 146, 411

n. is the plea 328

n. makes an honest man 153

n. never made a good bargain 202

no virtue like n. 369

thy n. is greater 391

vertu of n. 115

Neck: n. wrung like a chicken 125

Necklace: lose her . . . n. at a ball 334

Necks: submit your n. 307

Needle: eye of a n. 286

sharp as a n. 207

Needlework: brave with the n. 68

Needs: to each according to his n. 291

Negation: n. of God 213

Negative: N. Capability 261

Neglect: n. breed mischief 203

Negroes: providing the infant n. 159

Negroid: God was all n. 270

Neighbour: covet . . . anything that is thy n.'s 194

fain wad gar ilk n. think 195

love thy n. as thyself 296

n.'s name to lash 81

policy of a good n. 347

Neighbours: happening to our n. 112

with thy n. glaidly len' 176

Nelly: let not poor N. starve 113

Nelson: death of N. . . . public calamity 397

Nest: n. of singing birds 250

News: ill n. hath wings 171

man bites a dog that is n. 147

Newspaper: n. is . . . monopoly 356

n. . . . may be compared to a stage coach 196

Newspapers: n. . . . driven the living imagination out 458

Never: n. do to-day 342

Nexus: sole n. of man 106

Nigger: call me a damned n. 289

Night: black bat, n., has flown 415

moonless n. in the small town 419

n. come and all thing levand seisst 169

n. seems termless hell 420

n. that should banish all sin 214

Nights: passed the n. of years 98

Noah: God remembered N. 208

N. . . . said to his wife 121

Nobility: all were noble, save N. 91

Noble: do n. things 263

except for a n. purpose 227

n. living and the n. dead 450

work of n. note 416

Nobler: n. in the mind to suffer 364

Noblest: amongst the n. of mankind 102

n. work of God 333

n. work of man 90, 241

Nocht: will n. when he may 226

Nod: Wynken, Blynken, and N. 321

Noisy: n. man is always in the right 143

Nokomis: Daughter of the Moon, N. 278

Nonconformist: man, must be a n. 187

Noodledom: needlework of N. 68

Nook: privacy, an obscure n. 72

Noon: amid the blaze of n. 309

to N. he fell, from N. to dewy Eve 305

North: this was in the N. 151

Nose: Cleopatra's n. had been shorter 325

n. and chin they threaten 86

549

Note: said to the fi' pun n. 159

Notes: chield's amang you taking n. 84

Nothing: blessed is the man who expects n. 335

did n. in particular 211

do the devil's work for n. 196

n. done while aught remains 346

n. is ever done 377

n. to say, say n. 133

speaks an infinite deal of n. 371

to whom n. is given 196

we are n. 267

Nothingness: never pass into n. 256

Nouns: n. of number 127

render into n. 190

Novel: given away by a n. 261

n. . . . that it be interesting 245

only a n. 30

Novelists: n. should never . . . weary 62

Novels: n. . . . useful as Bibles 186

November: April, June, and N. 320

thirty days hath N. 217

Nuisance: " Progress " . . . exchange of one n. 185

Null: splendidly n. 415

Number: care of n. one 289

Numbness: n. pains my sense 258

Nuncheon: take your n. 73

Nurse: dear n. of arts 367

Nursed: n. upon the selfsame hill 302

Nurses: old men's N. 33

Nut-tree: I Had a Little N. 319

Nymph: Poesie! thou n. reserv'd 84

O

Oak: hollow o. our palace 147

Oaks: strokes fell great o. 202

tall o. 257

Oaths: o. are but words 89

Obadiah: O. Bind-their-kings-in-chains 281

Obedience: through o. learn to command 328

Object: o. all sublime 211

Oblivion: commend to cold o. 382

Observation: development of its powers of o. 325

Obstinacy: o. in a bad (cause) 401

Occupying: o. oneself without making a business 269

Ocean: Mind, that O. 291

O. Queen, the free Britannia 92

Oceans: compendious o. 144

Odd: think it exceedingly o. 266

Odds: facing fearful o. 281

Odysseus: doomed like O. 457

Odysseys: last of all our O. 49

Offence: o. from am'rous causes 334

Offend: o. and make up 346

Offender: notorious o. 394

Offenders: list of society o. 211

Offertory: song an o. 115
Office: by o. boys 353
  due participation of o. 246
  suited for o. if only 411
Official: o. . . . . grossly
  overpaid 227
  o. is incontestable 205
Oil: midnight o. 207
  o. in a cruise 263
Old: balance of the O. 104
  grow o. along with me 73
  grow o. with a good grace
  400
  I am too o. 113
  love everything that's o.
  216
  man is as o. . . . . woman
  as o. 132
  may be O. in hours 35
  no man would be o. 409
  none would be o. 202
  not o., but mellow 327
  o. are fair 455
  o. are more beautiful 436
  o. believe everything 441
  o. boys have their playthings 203
  o. in their youth 98
  season for the o. to learn
  15
  they shall grow not o. 52
  when you are very o. 347
  world must be getting o.
  246
Oliver: O. Twist has asked
  159
Olympic: spectators of the
  O. games 94
Olympus: O.' faded hier-
  archy 259
Omega: Alpha and O. 344
Omnibuses: ridden more in
  o. 224
Omnipotent: o. but friendless 386

Omniscience: specialism is
  o. 170
One: all for o. 175
  o.-eyed man is king 191
Opinion: ask no o. 326
  justifies that ill o. 85
  live after the world's o. 188
  mankind . . . of one o. 299
  o. of His Majesty's
  Government 123
  o. of the sex 100
Opinions: between two o.
  263
  man of common o. 36
  out of men's minds, vaine
  o. 32
  public buys its o. 90
  so many o. 417
  wish to punish o. 37
Opium: o. of the people
  291
  subtle, and mighty o. 155
Opportunity: must make his
  o. 31
  O. makes a thief 36
Opposition: duty of an O.
  123
  without a formidable o.
  161
Oppression: by O.'s woes 80
  great men for . . . o. 177
  O. stretches his rod 56
Optics: were finer o. giv'n
  332
Optimism: as agreeable as
  o. 51
Oranges: O. and Lemons
  320
Orator: o. . . . says what he
  thinks 75
Ordained: o. for uses 307
Order: old o. changeth 413
  o. of mortals on the earth
  98
  o. of your going 371

Ordered: all things there are o. 46

Orders: lower o. don't set us a good example 442

Ore: load . . . subject with o. 262

Original: more o. than his originals 188

Ornament: deceived with o. 372

Oscar: you will, O., you will 436

Ostrich: rear end of an o. 434

Other: can do no o. 281
passed by on the o. side 280

Otherwise: and some are o. 395

Ourselves: in o., are triumph 277

Overcomes: who o. by force 305

Overtopped: o. in anything else 86

Owed: so much o. by so many 124

Owl: O. and the Pussy-cat 271
o. . . . was a-cold 256
sadder than o.-songs 97

Owner: like the o. of the look 127

Ox: o. goeth to the slaughter 338

Oxen: hundred pair of o. 236

Oxford: O. gave the world marmalade 22
to O. sent a troop 66, 423

Oxonian: He is an O. 443

Oyster: the world's mine o. 373

P

Paces: two p. of the vilest earth 366

Pacific: he star'd at the P. 260

Paddle: p. his own canoe 289

Padlock: p. of silence on mental wealth 62

Pain: deserve such p. 69
p. of a new idea 37
show for all my p. 236
unnumbered hours of p. 103

Paint: as fresh as p. 391
p. the souls of men 70

Painted: idle as a p. ship 129

Painter: vast commendation of a p. 196

Painters: light . . . first of p. 189
p. imitate nature 112

Palace: p. and a prison 93

Pale: why so p. and wan 407

Palm: win the p. 290

Palms: p. before my feet 120

Pamphleteer: become a p. to defend 272

Panaceas: beyond all their p. 87

Pangs: p. are in vain 258

Parachute: moth in his brother's p. 391

Paradise: bliss of P. that has survived 144
drunk the milk of P. 131
England is a p. for women 88
enjoy in the next 47
Italy a p. for horses 88
Joy . . . daughter of P. 355
keys of P. 155

now sing recover'd P. 308
p. for a sect 257
P. for the snob 61
P. Lost . . . P. found 185
Paradox: man is an em-
bodied p. 133
Parallel: ours so truly P. 290
Paralysis: civilisation is p.
206
Parchment: black upon
white p. 336
Parent: p. who could see
his boy as he really is
271
Parents: begin by loving
their p. 446
Paris: P. . . . worth a mass
225
Parish: all the world as my
p. 435
Parliament: Impression of
P. 100
P. is nothing less 36
Parliaments: England is the
mother of P. 61
Parlour: will you walk into
my p. 237
Parochial: art must be p.
313
Parpaglion: published by P.
255
Parsee: there lived a P. 266
Parsons: p. are very like
other men 118
p. too lazy 133
Part: kiss and p. 172
p. good friends 289
Partaker: first p. of the
fruits 422
Parthenophil: P. is lost 200
Participation: due p. of
office 246
Particle: very fiery p. 97
Parties: there were particu-
larly two p. 196

Parting: p. is such sweet
sorrow 374
Partner: p. in the pro-
gressive advancement
206
Parts: p. of it are excellent
342
Pass: I shall not p. this way
again 219
they shall not p. 326
things have come to a
pretty p. 297
Passage: p. to the intellectual world 402
Passages: p. that strike your
mind 90
Passed: p. by on the othe
side 280
so he p. over 77
Passion: all p. spent 309
each p. being loth 439
keep the p. fresh 298
man that is not p.'s slave
364
one universal p. 378
p. for fame 78
p. too much indulged 249
ruling P. conquers Reason
334
tender p. . . . overrated 175
young days of p. 92
Passions: discoloured thro'
our P. shown 333
martyrdom of our p. 44
Men subdue their P. 400
p. as . . . fire and water 272
their p. a quotation 442
two p., vanity and love 119
Women dissemble their P.
400
Past: I know the p. 386
study the p. 137
world is weary of the past
383
Pastures: p. new 303

Patches: thing of shreds and p. 211

Patelat: her p. of gude pansing 225

Patent: p. for his honours 81

Path: downhill p. is easy 349

light unto my p. 341

make not my p. offensive 15

p. of the just 338

Pathetic: "p.", he said 300

Paths: all her p. are peace 338, 400

many p. that wind 438

p. of glory lead 218

trodden p. of men 380

Patience: p. is now at an end 230

Patiently: waited p. for the Lord 339

Patriot: P. King 59

Patriotism: p. is not enough 111

P. is of no party 395

Pea-green: beautiful p. boat 271

Peace: all her paths are p. 338, 400

and give thee p. 318

arts of p. are great 55

author of p. 134

blessed are the p.makers 293

calls it—p. 91

choose between p. 348

deep dream of p. 238

defences of p. 22

desolation, and call it p. 411

forever hold his p. 136

if p. cannot be maintained 352

keep the p. 374

laughing heart's long p. 63

make p. in Europe 50

never . . . a bad p. 201

on earth p. 280

p. does nothing to relieve 143

p. for our time 112

p. hath her victories 310

p. in our time 134

p. is in the grave 385

P. is poor reading 221

p. . . . kept by force 180

p. of God 135, 327

p. . . . with honour 163

p. without victory 447

p. . . . world cannot give 134

poor, and mangled P. 367

right is more precious than p. 447

too great to pay for p. 447

who desires p. 426

Peaceful: grown p. as old age 67

Peacocks: proud as p. 361

Peaks: p. most wrapt 93

Pearls: p. before swine 295

Peasantry: bold p., their country's pride 215

Pebble: casting of this p. 107

p. them wi stanes 359

smoother p. 316

Pedant: p. colleges and cells 174

Pedants: plague take all your p. 74

Pedigree: p. of nations 252

Peer: many a p. of England 236

Peerage: study the P. 446

Peerless: deep upon her p. eyes 258

Peers: House of P. . . . did nothing 211

554

Pelican: wonderful bird is the p. 298

Pelting: p. each other 143

Pen: ask my p. 402
more cruel the p. 87
p. has glean'd my teeming brain 261

Pencil: sharpens his p. 76

Pendulum: vibration of a p. 254

Pennies: twelve p. 458

Penny: p. in the old man's hat 19
p. in the way of trade 143

Pennyworths: ruined by . . . . p. 202

Pension: labourer to take his p. 351
man in higher rank to take his p. 351

People: condition of the p. 254
divide p. into good 443
fool some of the p. 273
for our own p. 206
government of the p. 274
most p. are other p. 442
new p. takes the land 121
ne'er forget the P. 81
p. are either charming 443
p. are the masters 78
p. . . . may be progressive 299
p. never give up 78
p. of England, that never have spoken 121
p.'s government . . . answerable to the p. 433
power and right of the P. 432
Privileged and the P. 162
thy p. shall be my p. 352
voice of the p. 16
will p. accept . . . songs 337

wrong p. going hungry 322

Peoples: p. and governments 223

Percy: old song of P. 391

Perdition: bottomless p. 304

Perfect: be ye therefore p. 294
machine is so p. 189
Man's as p. 332

Perfection: ascertain what p. is 27
attain to the divine p. 277
heart contains p.'s germ 387
let us speak of p. 337

Perhaps: seek a great p. 343

Perils: defend us from all p. 134

Peripatetic: p. flock 326

Peripatetics: p. of long-haired aesthetics 212

Perish: free us for we p. 336
let me p. young 99
many p. for a private man 288

Persecution: truth put down by p. 299

Perseverance: p. in a good cause 401

Personalities: p. have been . . . rebels 445

Personality: attempt to express his own p. 181

Persons: no respector of p. 13

Perspiration: genius . . . ninety per cent. p. 179

Persuaded: p., that neither death, nor life 346

Persuading: p. others, we convince ourselves 254

Pessimism: p. . . . agreeable as optimism 51

Peter: P. Piper 320

Saint P. sat by the celestial gate 99
thou art P. 295

Petticoat: turned out of the Realm in my p. 184

Petty: we p. men walk under 364

Pharisee: mask from the face of the P. 62
self-righteous p. 63

Phenomenon: describe the infant p. 158

Philistines: P. may jostle 212

Philosopher: same time a profound p. 132
tried too ... to be a p. 179

Philosophers: nation of pure p. 36
p. beheld mankind 94

Philosophie: ant herself cannot p. 240

Philosophy: dreamt of in your p. 363
fountains of divine p. 381
high-rife with old P. 258
I have brought p. out of closets 14
innate p. 93
p. . . . discretion 361
P. inclineth Man's Minde to Atheism 34
Socrates . . . brought p. down 14

Physician: beloved p. 133
he's the best p. 202
p., heal thyself 280
Time is the great p. 162

Physicians: p. too mercenary 133
words are the p. 15

Pianist: do not shoot the p. 443

Picasso: thinks of P. 227

Piccadilly: walk down P. with a poppy 212

Picket: p.'s off duty 48

Picture: I mean by a p. 79
paint my p. freely 146

Pictures: without p. or conversations 107

Pieces: p. of eight 405

Pierian: taste not the P. spring 331

Piety: nor all thy P. 198

Pigs: p. have wings 109

Pilate: jesting P. 32

Pilgrimage: I'll make my p. 343

Pillar: p. o' Thy temple 82

Pilot: P. of the Galilean lake 303

Pimpernel: demmed, elusive P. 321

Pimples: p., and everything 146

Pin: not p. pricks 150

Pine: p. for what is not 388

Pioneering: p. does not pay 107

Pipe: put that in your p. 44

Pipes: P. of wretched straw 303

Pity: love, nor p. knew 104
p. is but one remove from love 345
p. never ceases to be shown 173
p. of it, Iago 374
p. those who are better off 336

Place: comen swiftly to that p. 117
give me a p. to stand 24
Lord is in this p. 209
never the time and the p. 72
p. for everything 392
till there be no p. 242

Plagiarist: art is either a p. 206

556

Plague: p. had deprived us 103

Plagues: p. with which mankind are curst 152

Planet: p. swings into his ken 260

Plans: felonious little p. 212

Plant: fame is no p. 303
p. nothing else 157

Plates: breakfast p. in the basement kitchens 182

Platitude: longitude with no p. 205

Platitudes: mere p. 139

Play: do you come to the p. 79
judge not the p. 151
no time to read p.-bills 79
p. is the tragedy, " Man " 330
p. . . . pleased not the million 363
p.'s the thing 363
p. the man 270

Played: you've p. and lov'd 333

Players: men and women merely p. 362

Plays: write three p. 379

Playthings: love p. well 406
old boys have their p. 203

Pleasance: p. . . . vain glory 177

Pleasantness: ways of p. 338

Please: live to p., must p. to live 252
more hard to p. 173
say what they p. . . . do what I p. 203
yeven hym to p. 113

Pleasing: art of p. 222

Pleasure: gave p. to the spectators 282

image of *The P. that abideth* 444

no such p. in life 75

on p. . . . bent 143

P. at the helm 218

p. never is at home 257

p. was his business 178

read without p. 249

seize the p. at once 29

Pleasures: all the p. prove 288
indulge in . . . usual p. 103
paucity of human p. 249
p. are ever in our hands 332
p. are like poppies 84
purest of human P. 35
schooling in the p. 297
some new p. prove 163
understand the p. of the other 29
unreproved p. free 302

Pledge: p. to thee head 265

Plod: to p. on 298

Plot: attempting to find a p. 424

Ploughman: p. homeward plods 218

Plowshares: swords into p. 242

Pluck: p. your Berries 302

Plumage: pities the p. 324

Plunder: p. from a bleeding land 92

Plurality: p. of loves 165

Pocket: scruple to pick a p. 154

Poem: life of man . . . a p. 105
married to a p. 261
p. may be worked over 204

Poems: p. . . . for the love of Man 419
ye are living p. 277

557

Poesie: hail, P. 84
Poesy: beginning in p. 96
overwhelm . . . in p. 259
shower of light is p. 260
wore the mask of P. 259
Poet: accounted p. kings 260
God is the perfect p. 72
good p.'s made 253
honour the greatest p. 148
lover, and the p. 373
p. and the dreamer 257
p.'s mouth be silent 455
with a p.'s eye 103
without the help of a lyric
. . . p. 199
worst tragedy for a p. 128
yet a great p. 132
Poetic: constitutes p. faith
132
learn to crawl upon p. feet
330
nurse for a p. child 358
Poetry: cradled into p. 383
in whining P. 168
p. . . . by a fine excess 262
p., for those who know 350
p. . . . in the world 188
p. nocht tane 169
p. of earth is never dead
260
p. . . . record of the best
389
p. sinks and swoons 268
p. is the spontaneous
overflow 452
reach . . . a summit in P.
262
read a little p. sometimes
233
she that with p. is won 88
what is p. 100
Poets: giddie fantastique P.
167
passion . . . overrated by
the p. 175

p. . . . (get knowledge)
cavalierly 204
p. have morals 221
P. painful vigils keep 330
P. . . . sown by Nature 449
p. . . . unacknowledged
legislators 388
p. utter . . . wise things 328
subtract from many mod-
ern p. 133
Poison: drank the p. 232
use in medicine for p. 186
Policeman: p.'s lot 212
Polite: time to be p. 313
Political: man . . . p.
animal 26
not a good p. adviser 180
schemes of p. improve-
ment 250
Politician: honest p. . . .
will stay bought 102
like a scurvy p. 368
Politicians: race of p. 408
Politics: mistaken zeal in p.
254
p. . . . no preparation is
thought necessary 405
p. present history 360
softer, saner, p. 220
these are my p. 404
Polly: P. Flinders 319
Polygamy: p. was made a sin
172
Pomp: yoke of servile P. 306
Pompey: knew you not P.
364
Poor: as for the virtuous p.
445
blessed are the p. 293
dare to be p. 207
grind the faces of the p.
242
inconvenient to be p. 142
p. and independent 127
p., and the maimed 280

p. are never grateful 445

p.-folk maun be wretches 85

p. man surrounded by riches 235

p. wot gets the blame 21

space that many p. supplied 216

Pope: believe in Milton, Dryden, P. 95

better to err with P. 98

Poppies: like p. spread 84

p. grow in Flanders 283

Porpoise: p. close behind us 108

Port: let him drink p. 232

Portable: hold of p. property 157

Portentous: phrase, "I told you so " 97

Portrait: two styles of p. painting 158

Position: every p. must be held 219

Possible: if it be p. 296

with God all . . . p. 296

Posterity: don't give a hoot about p. 141

Potage: mess of p. 20

Potomac: quiet along the P. 48, 283

Pots: p. and pans 326

Pound: p. notes is the best religion 48

Pounds: two hundred p. a year 89

Poverty: crime so shameful as p. 194

in honoured p. thy voice 388

p. al aloon 117

p. is an anomaly 37

p. is no disgrace 393

Power: balance of p. 431

desire to seek P. 34

earthly p. . . . likest God's 372

extent of my p. 16

legislative p. is nominated 210

lies not in our p. 287

no knowledge that is not p. 190

P. and War 264

p. dwells apart 384

p. tends to corrupt 13

shadow of some unseen P. 383

wad some P. 85

Powerful: p. goodness want 385

Powers: wrestle . . . against p. 191

Practice: selfish . . . in p. 31

Praise: damn with faint p. 333

dieted with p. 258

dispraised, is the most perfect p. 252

if there be any p. 327

p. a fugitive 310

p. is the best diet 394

p. ourselves in other men 331

p. the Lord and pass 200

p. ye the Lord 341

wretched lust of p. 335

Praising: be still p. 340

Pray: p. for them which spitefully use you 294

p. without ceasing 418

two went to p. 145

Prayer: four spend in p. 128

made but one p. to God 428

with storms of p. 416

Prayers: Christopher Robin is saying his p. 300

three mile p. 86

Prayeth: he p. best 130

559

Preacher: I heard the p. 436
p. . . . attempted to collect
money 326

Preachers: p. . . . speak of
things real 52

Preaching: better than any
p. 187
woman's p. is like a dog's
walking 250

Precept: by p. and example
98

Precepts: we love the p. 194

Precipice: p. in front 191

Preferment: knocking at P.'s
door 27

Prejudice: full of vulgar p.
75
Scottish p. in my veins 86

Prejudices: above national
p. 317
p. of an islander 99
strengthen their own p.
175

Premier: tumbler, ca'd the
P. 83

Premises: insufficient p. 89

Preparation: no p. . . .
necessary 405

Prepare: p. ye the way of
the Lord 243, 293

Presbyter: New P. . . . Old
Priest 310

Presence: come before his
p. 340
dark P. watching by my
bed 420
p. of mind in a railway
accident 341

Present: all p. and correct 18
no redress for the p. 162
this p. were the worlds 165

Presents: P. . . . endear
Absents 267

Preserve: Lord shall p. thee
341

Lord shall p. thy going out
341

President: rather be right
than be P. 126

Press: *dead-born from the p.*
238

Pretender: God bless . . . the
P. 91

Pretexts: tyrants seldom
want p. 79

Pre-war: p. mentality 50

Preying: p. till one bursts
279

Priam: proud as P. murdered 457

Price: men have their p.
430

Pricks: kick against the p.
13

Pride: family p. . . . inconceivable 211
fear . . . no p. 77
human p. is skilful to
invent 387
lacks a proper p. 283
p. goeth before destruction
338
p. of the rich 121
p. that apes humility 130
whare was then the p. of
man 220

Priest: Old P. writ Large 310
turbulent p. 225

Priests: p. are only men 74
p. dare babble 387

Primordial: p. atomic
globule 211

Primrose: p. way to the
everlasting bonfire
370
yellow p. was to him 450

Prince: I the P. of Love
beheld 56
p. and a judge over us 192
P. of Peace 242

560

Princes: put not your trust in p. 341

Principal: *don't* believe in p. 279

Principle: called this p. 149
does everything on p. 378

Principles: die for our p. is heroic 347
p. are only excuses 285
p. of a free constitution 210
p. of freedom 324
test . . . by reference to p. 412
win for our p. 347

Print: one's name in p. 97
p. of a man's naked foot 153

Printed: p. by people who don't understand 272

Prison: I was in p. 296
shades of the p. house 449
Stone walls do not a P. make 278

Prisoners: bring me p. 61

Prisons: p. are built 56

Privilege: p. I claim 30

Privileged: certain p. classes 139
P. and the People 162

Prize: p. worth wrestling for 94
so rich a p. 289

Problem: common p. 68
three-pipe p. 170

Problematical: undercuts the p. world 205

Processions: women walk in public p. 437

Procrastination: p. is the thief 458

Products: base-born p. 457

Profane: far . . . let all p. ones be 427

Profession: p. and assertion 105

Professions: of the p. it may be said 133

Professors: American p. like their literature 272

Profit: p. by his errors 386
quick returns of p. 70

Profited: what is a man p. 295

Progress: calls each fresh link P. 76
disavows P. 161
p. is based upon 89
p. is not real 209
"P." is the exchange of one nuisance 185
p. of a deathlesse soule 167

Progressive: by a p. I do not mean 448
people . . . may be p. 299

Prologue: p. to a very dull Play 138

Promiscuous: exhaust . . . in p. living 353

Promises: p. and pie-crust 408

Promoted: p. everybody 211

Propaganda: p. makes war seem imminent 270

Property: if p. had . . . pleasures 445
little snug p. 178
poor have no right to the p. 351
universe is the p. 189
what is p. 337
young 'ooman o' large p. 160

Prophecies: whether there be p. 140

Prophecy: urn of bitter p. 383

Prophesy: sons . . . daughters shall p. 248

Prophet: p. ill sustains 314

Prophetess: p. . . . pretty young woman 180

Prophets: p. make sure 430

Proportion: strangeness in the p. 35

Prose: p. . . . bear . . . poetry 268
p. is verse 98
speaking p. without knowing 311
unattempted yet in P. 304

Prospect: p. which a Scotchman ever sees 250

Prosperity: man to have ben in p. 117
P. . . . discover Vice 33
P. is not without many fears 33

Prostitution: p. Selling one's body 285

Protection: p. . . . against the tyranny of the magistrate 298

Protest: lady doth p. too much 364

Proud: kaught is p. 117
too p. to fight 447
too p. to serve 394

Prove: cannot p. a lover 369

Proverb: fynd this p. perfyte 169
Spanish p. 118

Proverbs: patch grief with p. 373
p. are art 139

Providence: assert Eternal P. 304
character of P. 43
P. their guide 308

Prudence: ounce of p. 395
p. . . . ugly, old maid 56

Prudent: stocked with p. men 174

Prunes: p. and prism 158

Psalmist: p. of Israel 355

Pseudonym: God's p. 201

Public: for the p. good 143
p. buys its opinions 90
p. demands elocution 325

Publish: p. and be damned 434

Puff: p. of vapour . . . man's soul 69

Pulse: feeling a woman's p. 401

Pun: vile a p. 154

Punishment: p. fit the crime 211

Pure: blessed are the p. 293
whatsoever things are p. 327
within Himself make p. 413

Purgatory: no other p. but a woman 47

Puritan: P. hated bear-baiting 282

Purity: Aire and Angells p. 163

Purpose: clean from the p. 365

Purse: consumption of the p. 367
who steals my p. 374

Pussy-Cat: Owl and the P. 271
P., Where Have you Been 320

Pye: shine with P. 98

Pyramids: summit of these p. 59

Q

Quad: always about in the Q. 19

Qualities: endued with such q. 184

562

q. that you lacked 183

Quarrel: hath his q. just 367
lover's q. with the world 204
q. with my bread 409
q. with the foe 283

Quarrels: Liberty . . . from the q. of tyrants 429
q. of lovers . . . renewal of love 417

Queen: every lass a q. 264
flaunting extravagant q. 390
God will save the Q. 236
I am your anointed Q. 184
Lady would be Q. 334
Q. of Hearts 108
Q. was in a furious passion 108

Queer: Q. Street is full 159

Quell: q. the mighty 309

Quest: shuttle, to whose winding q. 425

Question: Ball no q. makes 198
that is the q. 364

Questions: asks no q. 266

Quiet: Men, some to Q. 334

Quietness: unravish'd bride of q. 258

Quinquireme: Q. of Nineveh 292

Quire: Q. of Saints 166

Quires: Q. . . . where they sing 134

Quote: kill you if you q. 77

R

Race: I wish I loved the Human R. 344
ill-fated, impious r. 259
r. that binds its body 76
steady wins the r. 276

Rack: r. of a too easy chair 331

Radical: dared be r. 204
talks like a R. 444

Radicals: young men are regarded as r. 446

Radio: gospel of the r.-phonograph 28

Rage: cold r. seizes 419
I r. 207
instead of r. 305

Rags: no scandal like r. 194
r. of time 168

Rail: folks r. against other folks 196

Railway: better . . . in a r. accident 341

Rain: droppeth as the gentle r. 372
morning r. foretells 62

Rainbow: r. in the morning 18
r.'s lovely form 84

Rake: r. among scholars 282

Randal: hunting Lord R. 41

Rank: r. . . . guinea's stamp 82

Rapine: R. share the land 310

Rapture: first fine careless r. 71

Raptures: r. were all air 172

Rare: r. as a day in June 279

Rascals: r. use me 154

Rationalist: he was a r. 117

Rats: r.! they fought the dogs 72

Reach: man's r. should exceed his grasp 67

Read: able to r. but unable to distinguish 423
asked what we have r. 262
I can r. anything 268
if I could always r. 100

some r. to think 133
Readers: r. to become more indolent 216
Reading: faculty of r. 107
I prefer r. 392
my early . . . love of r. 210
not walking, I am r. 267
r. . . . an ingenious device 224
r. is to the mind 400
soul of r. 401
Reality: human kind cannot bear . . . r. 183
Realms: travell'd in the r. of gold 260
Reap: you are like to r. 89
Rear: r. of darkness 302
Reason: dim . . . is R. to the soul 174
elocution rather than r. 325
finite R. reach Infinity 174
gloomy Englishman . . . wants to r. 429
I will not R. 55
know the r. why 222
men r. to strengthen their own prejudices 175
Passion conquers R. still 334
their's not to r. why 412
worse appear the better r. 306
Reasonable: more r. in France 429
r. is an invention of man 205
what is r. is true 223
Reasoning: away with your r. 53
r. and belief 105
truth by consecutive r. 261
Reasons: heart has its r. 325
r. are as two grains of wheat 371

r. for husbands to stay at home 181
Rebel: your r. sex 104
Rebellion: r. . . . a good thing 245
Receive: more blessed to give than to r. 13
Receiver: r. . . . bad as the thief 118
Recognise: not r. me by my face 423
Recommendation: other r. than their own weight 403
Rectitude: unctuous r. of my countrymen 345
Redeemer: I know that my r. liveth 247
Redress: r. to all mankind 414
Reef: time is the r. 141
Reference: no r. to fun in any Act 227
Reflection: prefer . . . r. 43
Reform: lunatic fringe in all r. 348
Reformers: all r. are bachelors 313
Refreshment: accept r. at any hands 211
Refuge: God is our r. 339
r. of weak minds 119
Refusal: great r. 148
Regiment: led his r. from behind 210
Regret: desire . . . and vain r. go 350
I r. a little 67
Reign: Chief's unwholesome r. 91
friendless is to r. 386
to r. is worth ambition 305
Rejects: r., but never once offends 334

564

Rejoice: amazed to find it could r. 151

r. with them that do r. 347

Relativity: theory of r. . . . successful 179

Religion: best r. in the world 48

enough r. to . . . hate 409

grey with age becomes r. 355

let us start a new r. 458

man's r. is the chief fact 105

man talks loudly against r. 402

mistaken zeal . . . in r. 254

one r. is as true 88

r. but a childish toy 287

r. is allowed to invade 297

R. is the opium 291

r.'s in the heart 247

r.'s iron age 387

r. teaches us content 174

there is only one r. 379

Religions: r. die when . . . proved true 440

Remedies: not apply New R. 34

Remedy: r. to all diseases 87

Remember: if thou wilt, r. 350

like to something I r. 200

little note nor long r. 273

r. and be sad 349

r. me when I am gone 349

r. with tears 17

things will be pleasant to r. 426

we will r. them 53

Remembering: r. him like anything 121

Remembrance: and appear almost as a r. 262

drive away r. 261

thirtieth with the poynt of r. 113

Reminiscences: r. make one feel . . . aged 377

Renowned: no less r. than war 310

Repay: I will r. 347

Repentance: cool r. came 359

decline to buy r. 154

just persons, which need no r. 280

r. is the hire 356

sinners to r. 295

Winter Garment of R. fling 197

Repented: r. but of three things 111

r. . . . his former naughty life 135

Report: whatsoever things are of good r. 327

Reporters: gallery in which the r. sit 282

Reports: read nothing but the race r. 184

Reproach: burns toward heaven with fierce r. 386

Republican: an acrimonious and surly r. 252

Reputation: esteem your own r. 432

r. like its shadow 274

r. nothing 214

r. of a woman 79

Resemble: when I r. her to thee 430

Resistance: r. against her is vain 290

Resolution: native hue of r. 364

Resolve: change my r. 94

his r. is not to seem the bravest 16

565

Resource: man of infinite-r. 266

Resources: r. of civilisation 213

Respect: covet . . . their r. 124

Man hath any R. for her 400

r. others as himself 240

Respectable: most devilish when r. 67

r. means rich 326

Respecter: no r. of persons 13

Respects: private r. must yield 309

Responsibility: heavy burden of r. 179

no sense of moral r. 443

Rest: better r. that I go to 160

crept silently to R. 197

man was not born for r. 428

Restraint: r. with which they write 102

Resurrection: hope of the R. 136

Retire: r. from the world 162

Retirement: must be no r. 219

Revenge: R. triumphs over Death 33

shall we not r. 372

study of r. 305

Revered: loved at home, r. abroad 80

Reversion: r. . . . to the unity 43

Reviewers: r. are usually people 132

Reviewing: never read a book before r. 394

Revivals: history of r. 89

Revolts: r. me, but I do it 211

Revolution: r. . . . to establish a democracy 122

Revolutionist: art is . . . a r. 206

Revolutions: r. are not about trifles 25

women hate r. 297

Reward: desert and r. 345

nothing for r. 399

Rewarded: be plenteously r. 135

Reynolds: prefer a gipsy by R. 282

Rhodope: brighter than is the silver R. 288

Rhyme: I r. for fun 81

maggots half-form'd in r. 330

R. being no necessary Adjunct 304

r. the rudder is 88

unattempted yet in . . . R. 304

Rib: r. . . . made he a woman 208

Riband: r. to stick in his coat 71

Rich: he wished all men as r. 211

I would be r. 241

in the interest of the r. 445

r. have butlers 336

r. man to enter into the kingdom 286

r. wot gets the pleasure 21

Riches: Embarrassment of R. 17

he that getteth r. 246

poor man surrounded by r. 235

r. are needless 308

R. . . . no real use 35

Rides: who r. so late 214

566

Ridiculous: sublime and the r. . . . related 324

sublime to the r. 59

Rift: load every r. . . . with ore 262

Right: exclusively in the r. 239

life is in the r. 332

makes us r. or wrang 81

measures r. and wrong 151

mind conscious of the r. 426

only r. is what is after my own constitution 187

r. deed for the wrong reason 183

r. is more precious 447

R. or Left, as strikes the Player goes 198

r. than be President 126

though r. were worsted 74

to do a great r. 372

to see what is r. 138

to set things r. 67

what's r. and fair 237

your r. to say it 427

Righteous: not come to call the r. 295

r. man turneth away 89

Righteousness: I choose r. 348

leadeth me in the paths of r. 339

that is the path of r. 42

Rights: certain unalienable r. 23

maintaining . . . r. of the people 139

Ring: r. out ye Crystal spheres 304

Riot: sound of R. 301

Ripeness: r. is all 369

Rise: r. on stepping-stones 413

Rising: r. to Great Place 34

Road: good to be out on the r. 292

high r. . . . to England 250

like one, that on a lonesome r. 129

no r. of flowers leads to glory 199

no royal r. to geometry 192

r. is hard to climb 337

r. lies long . . . to the grave 406

rolling English r. 120

simple Entepfuhl r. 106

Robbing: forbids the r. of a foe 123

Rock: lord is my r. 338

upon this R. I will build 295

Rocket: he rose like a r. 324

Rocks: throw r. at seabirds 315

Rod: spareth his r. 328

Roderick: I am R. Dhu 357

Rogues: world cannot move without r. 186

Roland: child R. to the dark tower 368

Roman: noblest R. of them all 366

R. came to Rye 120

R. holiday 94

R.'s life . . . take thou in charge 281

Romance: beginning of a life-long r. 441, 442

r. make a woman . . . a ruin 446

Rome: grandeur that was R. 330

I loved R. more 365

if you are in R. 17

Learning fall, and R. 332

R. has spoken 29

R. shall perish 142

when R. falls 94

567

you cruel men of R. 364

Ronald: Lord R. said nothing 271

Room: coming to that Holy r. 166
little to have chang'd our r. 167
no r. . . . in the inn 279

Rope: r. of sands 228

Rose: boy . . . saw a wild r. 214
gather ye r.-buds 229
go, lovely R. 430
never blows so red the R. 197
red R., proud R., sad R. 457
r. by any other name 374
under the r. 52

Roses: r., all the way 72
r. and white lillies grow 103
r. have thorns 376
scent of the r. will hang 314

Rotten: r. in the state 363

Round: light fantastic r. 301

Roundabouts: lost upon the r. 112

Rowing: r. against the stream 359
r. home to haven 292

Royalty: R. will be strong 36

Rubber: human heart is like Indian r. 62

Rudder: r. is of verses 88

Rude: to be r. to him 148

Rue: naught shall make us r. 368
ne will r. up-on woman 44

Ruffle: Frenchman invented the r. 186

Ruin: brink of r. 254
r. seize thee 217

Ruined: r. by buying good pennyworths 202

Rule: golden r. . . . no golden rules 379
r. applies to everyone 213

Rules: r. and models destroy 222

Rum: yo-ho-ho, and a bottle of r. 405

Rumbling: grew to a mighty r. 73

Run: elephant . . . trying to r. away 274
r. . . . twice as fast 106
r. with all your might 342

Runic: some fallen R. stone 26

Running: all the r. you can do 109
r. in the stadium 161

Runs: man that r. away 236

Rushy: down the r. glen 17

Russet: clad in homely r. brown 450

Russia: R. has two generals 317

Russian: an intelligent R. once remarked 18

Rust: thrown aside to r. 396

Rustum: R., my father 27

Rusty: his keys were r. 99

Ruth: through the sad heart of R. 259

S

Sabbath: born on the S. day 21
remember the s. 193
s. was made for man 286

Sabine: exchange my S. valley 235

Sacred: human body is s. 436

568

Sacrifice: no s. . . . more
        acceptable 361
    s. . . . of the devil's leavings
        409
Sacrificed: artists must be
        s. 188
Sacrifices: manners are
        made up of petty s.
        189
Sad: s. as widdercock 226
    why I am so s. 223
Saddens: s. while it soothes
        72
Sadder: s. and a wiser 130
Saddest: s. are these: "It
        might have been" 438
    s. when I sing 46
Safeguard: one s. . . . —
        suspicion 154
Safest: boldest measures
        are the s. 276
    when we are s. 68
Sagacity: man of infinite-
        resource-and-s. 266
Sages: s. have seen 143
Sahib: young S. shot
        divinely 23
Said: as well s., as if I had
        s. it myself 409
    so very little s. 123
Sail: white and rustling s.
        147
St. Agnes': St. A. Eve 256
St. Andrews: St. A. by the
        Northern Sea 269
St. Ives: going to St. I. 318
Saints: in church with s. 148
    ready to receive Thy s.
        380
    thy slaughtered S. 309
Salad: my s. days 362
Sally: none like pretty S.
        104
    to s. forth . . . more than
        heroic 347

Salt: how s. is the taste 14
    pillar of s. 208
Salute: those about to die s.
        thee 408
Salvation: no s. outside the
        church 28
Samaritan: ready enough
        to do the S. 394
Same: more they are the s.
        255
    we must all say the s. 297
Sample: I am here, a chosen
        s. 82
Samson: S., the strongest o
        the children 56
Sand: name upon the s. 398
    s. against the wind 55
    World in a Grain of S. 53
Sands: s. of time 278
Sane: in your s. hour 188
Satan: Auld Hornie, S. 80
    get thee behind me, S. 295
Satire: purpose of s. . . .
        aggression 272
Satyr: stoic or a s. 328
Sauce: best s. in the world
        112
Saul: S. and Jonathan were
        lovely 354
Savage: s. . . . guesses at
        Heaven 257
Save: God S. the King 81
    God will is her 236
    s. your world 28
Say: careful indeed wha we
        s. 137
    not much matter which we
        s. 297
    right to s. it 427
Says: s. what he thinks 75
Scaffold: s. will be dead 237
Scallop-shell: my s. of quiet
        343

Scan: s. your brother man 80

Scandal: in s., as in robbery 118

no s. like rags 194

s. . . . best sweeteners of tea 196

Scarlet: in S. town 38

sins were s. 49

Scent: s. of the roses 314

Scepter'd: this s. isle 369

Sceptre: to gain a S. 308

Scheme: sorry S. of Things entire 198

Schemes: of kings 221

best laid s. 85

Scholar: humour of a S. 35

s. among rakes 282

s. who cherishes 137

Scholars: dispute 234

s. get theirs (knowledge) 204

Scholarship: s. for s.'s sake 239

School: experience keeps a dear s. 202

in the strongest s. 121

sent . . . to a public s. 433

Schoolboy: every s. knows it 412

every s. knows who imprisoned 282

s.'s tale 92

Schools: public s. . . . nurseries of all vice 196

Science: art is s. 128

cometh al this newe s. 116

eel of s. by the tail 395

everything that relates to s. 267

magnificent applied s. 179

s. . . . exchange of ignorance 98

s. is for those who learn 350

s. is organised knowledge 397

s. is the record of dead religions 440

s. struck the thrones 386

ultimate destiny of s. 326

Sciences: in s. untaught 98

S. may be learned by rote 402

Scorn: s. delights 303

s. the guilty bays 335

s. the sort now growing up 457

sound of public s. 307

think foul s. 184

Scorn'd: like a woman s. 138

Scorning: s. the base degrees 365

Scot: na S. have comforting 275

Scotch: inferior to the S. 317

Scotch'd: s. the snake 370

Scotchman: much may be made of a S. 251

noblest prospect . . . S. ever sees 250

S. . . . sturdy moralist 250

Scotchmen: trying . . . to like S. 267

Scotia: old S.'s grandeur 80

Scotland: Chryst . . . succour S. 453

for poor auld S.'s sake 85

grave livers do in S. 450

ha'e S. to my eye 283

love S. better than truth 250

S. led in luve 453

seeing S., Madam 251

stands S. where it did 371

swordless S. 275

Scots: peculiar to the S. 250

S. wha hae 80

570

Scotsman: any S. without charm 45
moral attribute of a S. 45
S. of your ability 45
S. on the make 46

Scoundrel: every man over forty is a s. 379

Scoundrels: ane o' thae daamned s. 60

Scratching: s. of a pen 279

Scrimp: s. my glass 83

Scripture: cite s. for his purpose 372

Scriptures: S. principally teach 110

Sculptor: s. has set God 440

Scum: equal to the s. 337

Scunner: love wi' a s. in't 284

Scuttled: that ever s. ship 96

Sea: all the s. were inke 21
burst into that silent s. 129
gong-tormented s. 454
s. hath no king 350
s. is boiling hot 109
s. is his 340
s. shall give up her dead 136
see nothing but s. 31
there was no more s. 345
under the deep, deep s. 233
went by s. 111

Seafaring: s. man may have a sweetheart 395

Seamen: s. in the navy of Charles II 282
s. were not gentlemen 282

Search: not worth the s. 372

Seas: I must go down to the s. 292
s. but join the regions 335
tossed upon cloudy s. 317
up and down the salt s. 264

Season: s. of mists 255

to everything there is a s. 178

Seasons: interested in the changing s. 355

Secret: no s. so close 408
S. sits in the middle 204
three may keep a s. 202
trusted a woman with a s. 111

Secrets: s. in all families 194
s. with girls 144

Sect: I never was attached to that great s. 382

Sects: founders of s. 93
jarring S. confute 197
whence arise diversity of s. 398

Sedge: s. has wither'd 255

See: did not s., or would not 95
s. oursels as others s. us 85

Seek: s., and ye shall find 295
s. ye first the kingdom of God 294
s. ye the Lord 244
we s. him here 321

Seeketh: s. thou great things 246

Seen: loveth not his brother whom he hath s. 249

Sees: I can't see what he s. in her 227

Seeth: Lord s. not as man s. 354

Selection: term of Natural S. 149

Self: improving . . . your own s. 240

Selfish: s. being all my life 31

Self-knowledge: leading it to s. 325

Self-love: S. and Social be the same 333

571

Self-protection: sole end . . . is s. 299

Self-reproach: bitter s. 154

Self-respect: cannot pay the price of s. 447 compelled by their own s. 188

Self-righteousness: s. is not religion 62

Sell: I'll s. him 271

Selling: lives by s. something 404

Selves: dead s. to higher things 413

Senators: green-rob'd s. 257

Send: whom shall I s. . . . s. me 242

Sense: all that glads the s. 131

betray'd me into common s. 330

good-nature and good-s. must ever join 331

it is not s. 123

swerv'd frae Common S. 84

take care of the s. 108

Senseless: you worse than s. things 364

Senses: my s. five 283

Sentimentalist: barrenest of all mortals is the s. 104

Sentimentality: piece of idle s. 299

Sentinel: s. stars set their watch 103

Sentry: where stands a winged s. 425

September: April, June, and S. 217

thirty days hath S. 320

Seraphs: s. and saints 150

Serious: s. and the smirk 158

Sermon: honest and painful s. 326

s. . . . will suit any text 402 who a s. flies 228

Sermons: s. and soda water 95

Serpent: sharper than a s.'s tooth 368

Servant: s. depart in peace 280

s. of a tender conscience 240

thou good and faithful s. 296

Servants: both good s. 219

good s. but bad masters 272

Men in Great Place are thrice S. 34

Serve: let mee not s. 164

s. thee with a quiet mind 135

they also s. who only stand 310

Served: had I but s. God as diligently 448

Serves: s. us jolly well right 265

Service: done the public any s. 317

hewn with constant s. 396

Servility: s. of mankind 298

Servitude: s. is at once the consequence 147

Sesame: open S. 24

Seven: s. years were come 42

Seventh: s. day is the sabbath 193

Seventies: man gets well into his s. 406

Sex: formed for the ruin of our s. 395

speak . . . of the opposite s. 445

572

women are a s. by themselves 48

Sexes: city of the cleanliness of the s. 437

old ladies of both s. 158

there are three s. 394

Sexton: s. toll'd the bell 232

Shade: sit under the s. 157

Shades: s. of night were falling 277

Shadow: s. at morning . . . s. at evening 184

s. has fallen 125

that s. my likeness 437

Shadows: half sick of s. 414

Shakespeare: all that may be found in S. 133

fed with S.'s flame 121

S. fancy's child 302

S. is charged with debts 188

S. . . . never blotted out 253

S., on whose forehead 67

S.'s genius . . . cultivated 119

tongue that S. spake 451

we all talk S. 30

Shalott: Lady of S. 414

Shame: all a blooming s. 21

coward a s. distain 84

s. to men 306

Sharp: s. as a needle 207

Sharper: s. once played 145

Shears: Fury with th' abhorred s. 303

Sheep: Baa, Black S. 318

hold a S.-hook 303

hungry S. look up 303

like s. have gone astray 244

return to our s. 22

s. . . . become so great devourers 314

Sheet: wet s. and a flowing sea 147

Shell: fling away the s. 164

Shelley: peace in S.'s mind 388

Shepherd: feed his flock like a s. 243

good s. giveth his life 248

Lord is my s. 339

truth in every s.'s tongue 343

Shield: trusty s. 281

Shine: his face s. upon thee 318

Ship: s. is floating in the harbour 382

Ships: s. that pass 278

wrong with our bloody s. 46

Shirt: Englishman added the s. 186

Shiver: s. in the air 46

Shock: s. them and keep them up to date 377

Shoe: for want of a s. 203

One, Two, Buckle My S. 319

Shoes: of s.—and ships 109

Shoon: in her silver s. 154

Shoot: s. if you must, this old grey head 438

s. the way you shout 349

Shoots: who s. at the mid-day sun 391

Shop: keep a little back s. 312

Shopkeepers: nation of s. 59, 392

Shore: native s. fades 91

Shores: s. of Gitche Gumee 278

Short: s. and long of it 373

Shoulder: giant's s. to mount 132

573

Shout: shoot the way you s. 349

s. to him golden shouts 298

s. with the largest 159

Shouting: s. dies 266

Shouts: s. and plaudits 277

Shove: s. Jesus and Judas 187

Show: books . . . s. to subjects, what they s. to kings 144

Shower: s. of light 260

Shows: outward s. be least 372

Shriek: solitary s. 95

Shrieks: s. to pitying heaven 334

Shun: s. what I follow 73

Shuttered: in s. rooms 150

Shuttle: man is the s. 425

Sick: maketh the heart s. 338

s. and ye visited me 296

Side: hear the other s. 28

one s. of the case 90

Sides: much . . . said on both s. 14

Sighing: s. sound 350

Sighs: on the Bridge of S. 93

Sight: in the s. of God 135

out of s. 127

Signal: do not see the s. 316

Silence: flashes of s. 394

rest is s. 364

s. is as full of potential wisdom 239

s. more musical 349

s. . . . virtue of fools 32

s. where hath been no sound 233

Silencing: no more justified in s. 299

Silent: better to remain s. 274

gone . . . into the s. land 349

impossible to be s. 78

Silver: for a handful of s. 71

Simon: Simple S. 320

Sin: born of her, yet without s. 110

dreadful record of s. 170

forgive that s. 166

he that is without s. 248

his darling s. 130

night . . . banish all s. 214

no s. but ignorance 287

one s. will destroy 77

s. against the strength of youth 415

s. will find you out 318

Sincerity: test of your s. 51

Sing: let us s. unto the Lord 340

s. a sang at least 85

s. *God save the King* 81

swans s. before they die 130

Singing: nest of s. birds 250

Sinner: one s. that repenteth 280

Sinners: us miserable s. 134

Sins: save his people from their s. 292

writer . . . no faults, only s. 458

Sip: s. is the most . . . permitted 16

Sipped: who s. no sup 213

Sire: their s., butcher'd 94

Sirens: song the S. sang 66

Sires: happy were our S. 165

Sister: confound this surly s. 411

Sisters: twa s. lived in a bower 39

Sit: though I s. down 162

574

Six: s. days shalt thou labour 193
s. o'clock. The burnt-out ends of smoky days 183
s. of one 289

Sixpence: bang—went s. 342
Sing a Song of S. 320

Sixty: s. years are told 190

Skelp: I gie them a s. 80

Skies: look up at the s. 234

Skill: s. comes so slow 151
'tis God gives s. 181

Skinny: fear thy s. hand 129

Skipper: where will I get a gude s. 42

Sky: blue which prisoners call the s. 439
Bowl they call the S. 198
dwynis the even s. away 169
under the wide and starry s. 403

Slander: angry at a s. 252

Slaughter: goeth to the s. 338

Slave: design'd yon lordling's s. 84
government . . . half-s. and half-free 273
s. has had kings 329

Slavery: classified as s. 123
s. of being waited upon 285
what is s. 337

Slaves: necessity . . . creed of s. 328
s., howe'er contented, never know 143
solve it by amusing the s. 445

Slays: Justice . . . s. the weak 439

Sleep: Death and his brother S. 381
give their readers s. 330
I met . . . Prince of S. 153
life is rounded with a s. 375
one short s. past 165
power of s.'s fine alchemy 420
profund swoch of s. 169
quiet s. and a sweet dream 292
sent gentle s. from Heaven 129
s. after toil 399
s.; and if life was bitter 409
s. is not for the weary brain 420
s. it is a gentle thing 129
s. like a top 150
s. may I nocht 176
s. of the just 343
s. to wake 74
time when I shall s. 63
we shall not s. 283

Sleeping: growing . . . when ye're s. 359
s. hound to wake 117

Sleepless: s. with cold commemorative eyes 350

Sloth: cares and woes of s. 386

Slow: s. and steady wins 276

Slumber: he that keepeth thee will not s. 341

Slumbers: golden s. kiss your eyes 153
unquiet s. for the sleepers 64

Small: is it so s. a thing 26
S. have suffered 199
this s.-talking world 205
what the s. man seeks 137

Smattering: s. of everything 160

575

Smile: better . . . forget and s. 349

s. at us, pay us 121

s. must be of the right kind 323

Smiler: s. with the knyf 115

Smiles: all s. stopped 71

s. awake you 153

to all she s. extends 334

Smithy: village s. stands 278

Smoke: do wid de s. 221

no woman should marry . . . . a man who does not s. 405

smoorit them with s. 176

Smoking: what a blessing this s. is 224

Smug: generation of the thoroughly s. 337

Snaffle: s. and the curb 102

Snake: s. lurks in the grass 427

Snakes: s. that they rear 173

Snarling: silver, s. trumpets 256

Sneer: poorest way to face life . . . with a s. 348

teach the rest to s. 333

Sneered: I have never s. 379

Sneering: hard to do your duty when men are s. 447

s. doesn't become either the human face 379

Sneers: ten thousand s. 154

Snob: who . . . admires mean things is a S. 417

Snow: I never shall love the s. again 61

s. on Scythian Hills 288

Snows: s. have scattered 236

s. of yesteryear 426

Snuffed: s. out by an article 97

Snug: s. as a bug 201

Soars: no bird s. too high 56

Sober: no s. man dances 126

s. as a judge 196

walk s. off 333

Sobriety: disguised by s. 154

Social: cursed be the s. wants 415

no s. differences 435

our s. spheres . . . different 443

Self-love and S. be the same 333

Socialists: rattled-brained S. 275

Society: bloodless veins of desolate s. 387

feel the want of s. 100

never speak disrespectfully of S. 443

no arts . . . no s. 230

no s. . . . . flourishing 392

one great s. alone 450

s. for providing the infant negroes 159

s. . . . in conspiracy 187

s. . . . one polish'd horde 97

Socrates: S. . . . . brought philosophy 14

S. realises that his wisdom is worthless 328

Softening: s. in the presence of a woman 100

Solace: no s. mycht his sobbing cease 226

Soldier: boastful s. 329

British s. can stand up to anything 377

old s. by . . . his holsters 376

our s. slighted 254

s. armed with sword 53

s., rest! thy warfare o'er 357

576

Soldiers: show . . . what good s. 447

s. are becoming too popular 133

Solitude: delighted in s. 34

I love tranquil s. 387

independence of s. 188

inward eye . . . bliss of s. 448

makes a s. 91

s.! where are the charms 143

Solomon: heart of wisest S. 308

S. Grundy 320

S. his son reigned 122

Solstice: in Wintry s. 309

Somebody: dreary to be s. 161

spoke a brisk little s. 67

Something: time for a little s. 300

Son: bring forth a s. 292

every s. would have his motorcycle 183

only begotten S. 248

s. of his old age 209

spareth his rod hateth his s. 338

this is my beloved S. 293

unto us a s. is given 242

Song: sing unto the Lord a new s. 340

s. of a merryman 213

S. . . . of such hard matter 381

s. that found a path 259

s. that nerves 412

Songs: best of all trades, to make s. 50

everything ends in s. 47

lean and flashy s. 303

sing no sad s. for me 350

s. are sad 120

s. consecrate to truth 388

s. of Spring 255

sweetest s. . . . tell of saddest thoughts 388

Sonnet: S. is a moment's monument 350

Sonnets: ten passably effective s. 238

written s. all his life 96

Sons: S. of Belial 305

s. your fathers got 236

three stout and stalwart s. 43

Sophistries: old s. of June 161

Sorrow: anvil unto s. 286

image of The S. that endureth 444

natural s., loss or pain 451

pure and complete s. 422

put away s. like a shoe 410

s. and sighing 243

s. for angels 71

wi' S. and Care 80

Sorrowing: goes a s. 203

Sorrows: man of s. 243

Sorts: and conditions 135

Soul: adventures of his s. 201

boasts two s.-sides 72

Christ cannot save thy s. 286

hae mercy o' my s. 284

let the s. be assured 186

man must have such a s. 312

my s. in agony 129

my s. is white 57

my s. that flashed 151

my unconquerable s. 224

part of me and of my S. 93

progresse of a deathlesse s. 167

save my s., if I have a s. 21

single S. does fence 290

s. completes the triumph of the face 252
s. has ... decreed 259
s. has simply nothing to do 187
s. in prison 152
s. of man-like unextinguished fire 386
s. spits lies 228
s.-stirrings ... quelled 427
s. that knew not fear 150
three books on the s. 69
unless s. clap its hands 456
vapour from his mouth, man's s. 69
what of s. was left 74
whose s. is not a clod 257
Souls: divine s. appear 188
God help all poor s. 70
people sell their s. 392
s. of the brave 126
s. to weary and s. to hope 157
Sounding: s. through the toun 39
Sounds: s. will take care of themselves 108
Source: s. of a' my woe 83
Southern: in the s. wild 57
Southey: Wordsworth, Coleridge, S. 95
Sovereign: here lies our S. Lord 346
Sovereignty: top of s. 257
Sow: as you s. 89
Space: s. may produce New Worlds 305
Spade: call it a s. 443
cultivated ... by the s. 300
Span: life of man less than a s. 36
strength ... for a s. 409
Spaniards: thrash the S. 171
Spanish: whether a shoe be S. 88

Spare: s. the beechen tree 102
Spark: s. o' Nature's fire 81
Sparks: s. fly upwards 247
Sparrer-grass: look lak s. 221
Sparrow: s. hath found an house 339
Sparrows: two s. sold 295
Speak: difficult to s. 78
let him now s. 136
moral duty to s. 443
s., Lord; for thy servant heareth 354
s. out and remove 274
Speakers: not formidable as s. 100
Spearmen: stubborn s. 359
Spears: ten thousand s. 56
Specialists: other men are s. 170
Spectacle: no s. so ridiculous 282
Spectatress: s. of the mischief 351
Speech: common and continuous s. 37
s. created thought 386
s. ... sweet harmony 289
stately s. such as grave livers ... use 450
Speeches: all the easy s. 120
Speechless: fair s. messages 372
Speed: be wise with s. 458
spirit ... teach me s. 368
Speiring: gey an' easy s. 405
Spendthrift: s. of my own genius 442
Spice: s. of life 143
Spider: s. to a fly 237
Spilling: forces ... bent on s. 297
Spinsters: dreams of s. 352
Spirit: hail ... blithe S. 388

578

holy s. of man 409
I commend my s. 280
pour out my s. 248
s. indeed is willing 296
S. of God moved 208
Spirits: good s. and good
    temper 158
s. of great events 130
Spiritual: s. wickedness 191
Splendour: s. falls 416
Spliced: s. in the humdrum
    way 63
Spoiler: worst dull s. 92
Spoils: carried off the finest
    s. 185
s. of meaner Beauties 279
Spoke: s. among your
    wheels 47
Spoons: played with s. 68
Sport: animals never kill for
    s. 204
s. . . . Care derides 302
what sort of s. 23
Spot: tip me the black s. 405
Spright: Angelike s. 165
Spring: can S. be far behind
    384
in love with s. 384
in the S. a young man's
    fancy 414
liv'd light in the s. 26
messenger of S. 398
no S. nor Summer Beauty
    164
s. still makes s. 190
where are the songs of S.
    255
Spur: Fame is the s. 303
no s. to prick the sides
    370
Square: never make a s. 217
Squires: last sad s. ride 121
Staff: s. of faith 343
Stag: s. at eve had drunk
    357

Stage: all the world's a s.
    362
shoves you from the s. 333
s. but echoes 252
Stagecoach: outside of a s.
    222
Stain: s. her honour 334
Stakes: s. are vice and
    misery 386
Stale: nor custom s. her
    infinite variety 362
Stamp: s. of his lowly origin
    149
Stand: no time to s. 151
Star: catche a falling s. 167
hitch his wagon to a s. 190
morning S., Day's har-
    binger 309
seen his s. in the east 293
Stars: beauty of a thousand
    s. 287
catch the s. 51
eyes more bright than s.
    174
I shall touch the s. 234
look at the s. 234
one (sees) the s. 269
permitted us fixed s. 128
puts the S. to Flight 197
s. more still 287
s. through the window
    pane 262
way to the s. 427
Starve: s. with nothing 372
State: I am the S. 278
lie for the good of the S.
    328
no harm come to the s.
    19
our object in the con-
    struction of the s. 329
resolved . . . to rule the s.
    172
s. without the means of
    some change 79

579

Statesman: constitutional s. 36

gift to set a s. right 455

s. is an easy man 455

Statue: why I have no s. 111

Steaks: smell of s. in passageways 183

Steal: thou shalt not s. 193

Steamers: all you Big S. 264

Steer: s. two points nearer 46

Step: with even s. 301

Stick: fell like the s. 324

s. to nothing deliberately 204

Still: beside the s. waters 339

Stinking: stinking'st of the s. kind 267

Stir: no s. of life 257

s. up . . . O Lord 135

Stirrup: I sprang to the s. 71

Stitching: s. and unstitching has been naught 453

Stocking: kneeling ne're spoil'd silk s. 228

Stoic: s. or a satyr 328

Stolen: better, had I s. the whole 403

s. waters are sweet 338

Stomach: army marches on its s. 18

empty s. is not a good political adviser 180

pride of s. 87

Stomachs: lazy fokes' s. 221

Napoleon's armies . . . march on their s. 361

Stone: first cast a s. 248

written of me on my s. 204

Stones: never throw s. at your mother 48

Stooped: never s. so low 166

Stop: s. and consider 259

s. everyone from doing it 227

Store: oft amid thy s. 255

Storehouse: (knowledge is) a rich s. 31

Storm: mounts the s. 332

Storms: s. the strongest breake 165

Story: it is an ancient s. 223

s. always old 74

Strain: s. of man's bred out 375

Strand: far northern s. 26

Stranger: I was a s. 296

s. in a strange land 192

Street: city's horrible s. 70

trampled edges of the s. 182

Strength: deem'd equal in s. 306

grew from s. to s. through centuries 180

s. is as the s. of ten 416

s. itselfe by confidence growes weake 165

try the soul's s. 71

what is s. 308

Strengtheneth: through Christ which s. 327

Strenuous: doctrine of the s. life 349

Stretched: things which he s. 424

Strife: let there be no s. 208

no s. can grow up there 305

not cease from Mental S. 55

s. of little natures 75

Strings: like untun'd golden s. 287

s. . . . in the human heart 156

Stripe: s. for s. 194

Strive: not s. officiously 127

why should I s. 315

Strokes: little s. fell great
oaks 202

Strong: be ye s. 122

Stronghold: safe s. our God
281

Strove: little still she s. 95

Struggle: s. for existence 149
s. naught availeth 127

Stuck up: despised the " s "
435

Studies: Crafty Men contemn S. 35
too much Time in S. 35

Study: proper s. of Mankind
238, 332
s. is the weariness of the
flesh 178
s. of real life 62
we that did nothing s.
263

Stung: s. by the splendour
69

Stupidity: proof of s. 250

Style: no art . . . no s. 441

Subject: we know a s. 251

Subjects: good of s. is the
end of kings 152

Sublime: s. and the ridiculous 324
s. to the ridiculous 59

Substantial: one vast s.
smile 156

Succeed: if at first you don't
s. 230

Success: criterion of wisdom
. . . s. 79
greatest s. is confidence
186
not in mortals to com-
mand s. 13
road to s. is filled with
women 155
S. . . . demands strange
sacrifices 239

s. depends upon previous
preparation 137
s. is banished 404
true s. is to labour 406

Succubus: perfidious S. . . .
Queen Elizabeth 87

Sucker: s. born every
minute 45

Suffer: better one s. 173
s. the little children 286

Sufferer: best of men . . . a
s. 153

Suffering: learn in s. what
they teach in song 383
nothing but s. 30
s. is permanent, obscure
448

Sufficient: s. unto the day
294
whom shall we find s. 306

Sultry: where the climate's
s. 95

Summer: come, S., come 244
compare thee to a s.'s day
376
Indian S. of the heart 438
made glorious by . . .
York 369
s. is ended 246
s. is icumen in 22
s.'s lease . . . too short 376
welcome, s., oure gov-
ernour 116

Summits: climb to the
highest s. 377

Sun: assisted the s. materially 421
busie old foole, unruly S.
168
enjoy'd the s. 26
heat o' the s. 362
I will sing of the s. 335
let the s. in, mind it wipes
its shoes 419
lights a candle to the s. 198

581

s. go down upon your wrath 191

s. has gone in 392

s. is coming down 298

S.'s rim dips 129

Sunday: S. papers make *you* feel ignorant 322

Sunset: s. divides the sky 94

there's a s.-touch 68

Sunshine: s. in the shady place 399

Supererogation: Works of S. 136

Superior: what the s. man seeks 137

Superman: I teach you the s. 317

Superstitions: truths . . . end as s. 240

Support: s. of a cause we believe to be just 273

Supremacy: blind from sheer s. 257

Surfeit: as sick that s. 372

Surpassed: man . . . to be s. 317

Surpasses: s. or subdues mankind 93

Surprise: taking myself by s. 424

Surrender: shall never s. 124

Survival: s. of the fittest 149, 397

Suspect: always s. everybody 159

Suspicion: one safeguard . . . s. 154

Swan: like a black s. 254

sweet S. of Avon 253

Swans: s. sing before they die 130

Swear: when very angry s. 424

Sweet: melodies are s. 258

Sweetheart: s. of the nation 285

Sweetness: keeps with perfect s. . . . solitude 188

Sweets: stolen s. are best 125

Swimmer: cry of some strong s. 95

Swine: pearls before s. 295

Swing: room to s. a cat 156

Swings: pulls up on the s. 112

Switzerland: S. . . . inferior sort of Scotland 393

Sword: brave man with a s. 439

but vain the s. 54

lighted down my s. 40

my s., I give 77

nor a good s. 229

strokes of the s. 150

s. of sorowe 113

Swords: beat their s. into plowshares 242

country is ploughed with s. 56

Swore: when the son s. 88

Symmetry: frame thy fearful s. 57

man is all s. 228

Sympathy: founded on complete s. 52

System: I must Create a S. 54

T

Tabernacles: amiable are thy t. 339

Table: preparest a t. before me 339

you cannot make a t. 250

Tails: t. you lose 145

Taking: in t., suld discretioun be 177

582

Tale: t. to tell of the hardihood 356
thereby hangs a t. 375

Talent: no substitute for t.
239
t. . . . recognises genius 171
T. which is death to hide
310

Talents: t. increase in the
using 62

Tales: t. of grim old men 111

Talk: t. about the rest of us
230

Talked: he t. on for ever 222
so much they t. 123
worse than being t. about
444

Tames: t. it, that fetters it
168

Tamper: t. with the minds
of men 99

Tankard: he grips the t. 217

Tao: method of T. 269

Taper: my little t. 97

Tar-baby: T. ain't sayin'
nothin' 221

Target: satire has a great
big blaring t. 272

Tartarly: so savage and T.
98

Task: t. for all that a man
has 404
t. for life 190
what is our t. 276

Taste: inch-rule of t. 13
matter o' t. 159
t. by which he is to be
relished 452

Tastes: t. may not be the
same 378

Taught: nothing that is
worth knowing can
be t. 441

Tavern: resolved to die in a
t. 25

Taverns: he knew the t. we¦
114

Tax: to t. and to please 78

Taxes: as true . . . as t. is 156
nothing . . . certain except
death and t. 201

Tea: counsel take — and
sometimes T. 334
t. and scandal 138
we'll have t. and toast 384
while there's t. 327

Teach: t. others who themselves excel 331

Teaches: he who cannot, t.
379

Teaching: incapable of
learning has taken to
t. 442

Teacup: Storm in a T. 52

Tears: events have t. 426
greatness of the world in
t. 456
t. and laughters for all
time 67
t. and sweat 123
t. are in my eyes 292
t. such as Angels weep 305
T. wash out a Word 198
too deep for t. 449
wrought with t. 150

Tedious: sport would be as
t. 366

Teeth: children's t. are set
on edge 194
set my t. in rascals 161

Teetotaller: no woman
should marry a t. 405

Temperance: t. would be
difficult 249

Temple: t. half as old as
time 346

Tempt: not t. the Lord 293

Temptation: last t. is the
greatest treason 183
lead us not into t. 294

583

marriage . . . maximum of t. 378

resist everything except t. 443

way to get rid of a t. 444

Temptations: in spite of all t. 212

Tempted: one thing to be t. 371

t. . . . hoist the black flag 297

Ten: 1066 And All That 361

Tenderness: want of t. 250

Tennis: we are merely the stars' t.-balls 434

Tent: t. of blue . . . the sky 439

t. of war 288

Tern: no t. unstoned 315

Terse: t. but limited 171

Teucer: under T.'s leadership 235

Text: excellency of this t. 402

rivulet of t. 390

Thames: sweet T. 399

Thankless: t. child 368

Thanks: give t. unto the Lord 340

to give t. is good 409

Theatre: all-night sitting in a t. 380

Theft: " what is property"? . . . " T." 337

Theme: my t. is alwey oon 116

Themselves: kept t. to t. 435

Theorise: mistake to t. 170

Theory: t. . . . is grey 214

Thespian: bathed in the T. springs 172

Thief: opportunity makes a t. 36

t. of youth 309

Things: as t. have been they remain 127

beareth all t., believeth all t. 140

more t. in heaven 363

t. are where t. are 15

t. both great and small 130

t. shall be added 294

Think: I t., therefore I am 155

make me believe that I t. 429

t. on these things 327

to t. is to see 43

we t. as we do 89

we t. so because other people t. so 390

Thinking: never thought of t. for myself 212

t. . . . greatest fatigue 425

t. makes it so 363

Thinks: he t. too much 365

Third: drink not the t. glasse 228

Thirst: t. for goodness 195

Thirty: t. days hath September 320

Thomas: T. lay on Huntly bank 42

Thorns: no t. go as deep as a rose's 409

Thought: constitution of their modes of t. 298

due to patient t. 317

harbours virtuous t. 399

holy and good t. 24

language . . . dress of t. 251

no t. for the morrow 294

pale cast of t. 364

prefer t. to action 43

t. came like a . . . rose 256

T. . . . child of Action 705

t. wander . . . in love 456

t. which saddens 72

t. without learning 137

to believe your own t. 187

Thoughts: pettie t. have
made 228
pleasant t. bring sad t. 449
thinking Thy t. 263
t. of a dry brain 182
t. of youth . . . long t. 277
t. . . . too deep for tears
449
t. vagrant as the wind 200
thousand t. lying within
a man 418
wording of his own highest
t. 262

Thousands: countless t.
mourn 84
t. . . . kiss the book's
outside 143

Thraldom: cowpyt to foule
t. 44

Thrall: hath thee in t. 255

Three: tell you t. times 110

Thrice: t. is he arm'd 367

Thrive: wive an' t. 344

Throne: light which beats
upon a t. 412
mounts the t. for beauty 73
royal t. of kings 369
t. of bayonets 241

Thrush: that's the wise t. 71

Thunder: steal my t. 154

Thwackum: T. was for
doing justice 197

Tiber: T.I father T. 281

Ticket: t. for the peep show
285

Tickled: t. not with straws
421

Tide: out with the t. 156
t. in the affairs of men 366
t. in the affairs of women
96

Tiger: t.! burning bright 57

Time: Bird of T. has but a
little way 197

do not squander t. 202
foster-child of . . . t. 258
gude t. coming 359
half as old as t. 346
how T. is slipping 197
last syllable of recorded t.
371
laughing . . . unthinking t.
175
my t. is filched 151
never-resting thing called
T. 106
never the t. and the place
72
no t. to stand and stare 151
O aching t. 257
sweetest t. . . . allotted 56
thief of t. 458
T. and Fate of all their
Vintage prest 197
t. brings everything 328
t. consecrates 355
T. is the greatest Innovator
34
t. . . . great physician 162
t. has come 109
t. is money 201
t. is my inheritance 215
T. is still a-flying 229
t. is the reef 141
t. meanwhile flies 427
t. runs 287
T.'s winged Charriot 291
t., that may not sojourne
117
t. the devourer of all things
323
T., the subtle thief of
youth 309
t. to make it shorter 325
t. will come 162
t. will run back 304
where T. stands still 151
you have all there is (t.)
189

585

Times: it was the best of t.
160

my t. be in Thy hand 73
The T. has made many
ministries 36

Timing: perfect t. and
consent 190

Tincture: Manners take a t.
333

t. in the blood 152

Tinkers: no work for the t.
326

Title: persons require to
possess a t. 299

t. from a better man I stole
403

t.'s uncommonly dear 213

whatever t. suit thee 80

Titles: enviable of all t. 432

t. are shadows 152

t. distinguish the mediocre
379

t. do not reflect honour on
men 379

Toad: like a t., ugly 362

Toads: t. in a poisoned tank
69

Tobacco: superexcellent t.
87

take air, in a t. trance 183

Tocsin: t. of the soul 96

To-day: call t. his own 175

if T. be sweet 197

snatch at t. 235

we are here t. 49

Toe: gout had taken him in t.
232

light fantastic t. 302

Toil: faint with t. 386

with great t. all that I can
attain 16

Told: half was not t. me 263

have it not been t. you
243

" I t. you so " 97

Tom: T., the Piper's Son
320

Tomb: our living T. 167

Tombs: read the several
dates of the t. 15

To-morrow: already walks t.
130

here today, and gone t.
49

put off till t. 342

t., and t., and t. 371

t. do thy worst 175

t. to fresh Woods 303

t. will be dying 229

trust as little . . . in t. 235

unborn T. 197

Tom Thumb: thought about
T.T. 249

Tongue: falser t., that utter'd
all 164

his T. dropt Manna 306

hold your t., and let me
love 163

man keip weil ane t. 274

rank t. blossom 68

t. could utter the thoughts
412

t. . . . wery good thing 159

wise are merry of t. 455

Tongues: innumerable t. 307

whether there be t. 140

whispering t. can poison
truth 130

Tools: give us the t. 124

Top: room at the t. 433

sleep like a t. 150

Torch: we throw the t. 283

Tories: angels all are T. 99

monarchy of T. 331

ossified T. 244

T. own no argument 66

Torment: measure of our t.
265

Tormented: t. with ten
thousand hells 286

586

Tormenting: most t. are
black Eyes 290

Torrent: t. of darkness 317

Tory: he thinks like a T. 444
T. men and Whig measures
162
t. rory ranter boys 196
what is called the T. 145

Tosser: t. of balls in the sun
155

Tower: be as a strong t. 149
some high lonely T. 301

Towers: topless t. of Ilium
287

Town: down to the end of
the t. 300
man made the t. 143

Trade: literature . . . half a
t. 241
no nation was ever ruined
by t. 203
not your t. to make tables
250
now there isn't any t. 227
t.'s unfeeling train 215

Trades: best of all t. 50
t. on a bottom 195

Tradesmen: inspire con-
fidence, even in t. 443

Tragedies: two t. in life 378

Tragedy: worst t. for a poet
128

Trail: pull out, on the Long
T. 266

Train: t. up a child 338

Traitors: on strang t. mak
punitioun 275

Tranquillity: emotion recollected in t. 452

Transaction: two parties to
a love t. 418

Trash: t. will remain 133

Travel: t. for t.'s sake 405
t. hopefully is a better
thing 406

T. . . . part of Education
34

Travelled: t. in the realms
of gold 260

Travels: go again to my t.
113
t. the fastest who t. alone
266

Tray: tea t. in the sky 108

Treason: greatest t. 183
if *this* is t. 225

Treasure: preserve it as your
chiefest t. 49
where your t. is 294

Treasures: lay not up . . . t.
upon earth 294

Treaties: t. are but the
combat of the brain
174

Treatise: T. of Human
Nature 238

Tree: old t. with shoots 336
she gave me of the t. 208
to the top of every t. 211
t. continues to be 266
why the t. will continue to
be 19
ye may be ay sticking in
a t. 359

Trees: all the t. are green
264
all the t. were bread 21
among the gusty t. 317
infant t. fill out 181

Trelawney: shall T. die 222

Triangle: eternal t. 22

Tribe: T. is all 421

Tribes: two mighty t. 97

Tricks: t. an' craft hae put
me daft 83

Trifles: snapper-up of unconsidered t. 376

Trimmer: innocent word
" T." 219

Trinket: haggled for a t. 421

587

Trip: come and t. it 302
  our fearful t. is done 436

Triumph: in ourselves are t.
    and defeat 277
  one more devils'-t. 71
  t. in the dreadful strife 420
  t. of the female soul 252
  t. without glory 140

Trivial: contests rise from t.
    things 334

Troth: plight thee my t. 136

Trouble: little t. had been
    given 99
  man is born unto t. 247
  present help in t. 339
  t. efter great prosperitie
    226

Troubled: calm the t. mind
    138

Troubles: take arms against
    a sea of t. 364

Trouncings: receives his
    private t. 391

Trousers: never put on one's
    best t. 241

Trowel: lays it on with a t.
    138

Troy: cornfield where T.
    once was 323
  fired another T. 173
  plains of windy T. 416

True: as t. . . . as taxes is
    156
  if it is not t. 22
  not necessarily t. because
    a man dies 444
  saying it long enough it
    will be t. 51
  t. for you . . . is t. for all
    187
  what is t. is reasonable 223
  whatsoever things are t.
    327

Trumpet: blow your own t.
    213

heart moved more than
  with a t. 391

Trumpets: silver snarling t.
    256
  sound the t. 314
  t. sounded for him 77

Trust: his t. was with th'
    Eternal 306
  put not your t. in princes
    341
  t. in ideas 189

Trusted: he t. to have
    equal'd the most High
    304

Trustees: T. of Posterity
    162

Trusts: convartin' public t.
    279

Trusty: t., dusky, vivid 403

Truth: all the test of t. 144
  battle for freedom and t.
    241
  beauty is t. 258
  bitter old and wrinkled t.
    419
  great ocean of t. 317
  her tepat of t. 225
  history teems with in-
    stances of t. 299
  how any thing can be
    known for t. 261
  if one tells the t. 440
  in thee was t. 58
  inquiry of T. 32
  kept thy t. so pure 310
  mainly he told the t. 424
  must be the t. 171
  plain t. will influence 58
  rejoiceth in t. 140
  telling the disreputable t.
    50
  T. be in the field 311
  t. can neither be appre-
    hended 434
  t. can never be told 56

588

t. . . . has an inherent power 299
t. in masquerade 97
T. is a naked and open daylight 32
t. is always strange 97
t. is rarely pure 443
t. is within ourselves 72
t. never hurts the teller 70
t. of imagination 261
t. sits upon the lips 27
T. stands 167
t. that peeps over the edge 67
t. that's told with bad intent 53
t. universally acknowledged 30
T. was slandered 121
T. . . . worthy to be sought 76
way, the, 248
we grope for T. 150
what is T. 32
ye friends to t. 216
Truths: new t. to begin as heresies 240
Try: t., t. again 230
Tumult: t. and the shouting dies 266
Tunes: devil should have all the good t. 230
Tuscany: ranks of T. 281
Twain: never the t. shall meet 264
Twelvemonth: t. with the undergraduates 222
Twentieth: t. century, war will be dead 237
Twenty: at t. . . . will reigns 202
Twice: gives t. who gives soon 411
t. or thrice had I loved 163
Twinkle: t., little bat 108

T., Little Star 320
Tyrannies: t., despaire . . . hath slaine 165
Tyranny: t. of the prevailing opinion 298
Tyrant: became a t. 54
hated thee, fallen t. 382
Tyrants: all men would be t. 152
argument of t. 328
t. seldom want pretexts 79

U

Ugliest: u. of trades have their moments of pleasures 247
Ugly: worse than u. 439
Ulster: U. will fight 123
Ultimate: welfare of the people is the u. law 125
Unarmed: u. perished 284
Unattempted: things u. yet 304
Unbelief: gained then by our u. 68
Unblemished: u. let me live 335
Unbowed: bloody, but u. 224
Unbuild: arise and u. it 381
Unburnished: how dull . . . to rust u. 416
Uncomfortable: generation of the . . . u. 337
Unconscionable: u. time dying 113
Undergraduates: most conservative . . . college u. 446
twelvemonth with the u. 222
Understand: better to u. little 201

printed by people who don't u. 272

Understanding: peace . . . achieved by u. 180
peace of God which passeth all u. 135, 327

Undiscover'd: u. country from whose bourn 364

Uneasy: u. lies the head 367

Unfettered: u. use of all the powers 130

Unforgetful: teach the u. to forget 350

Unfortunate: u. need no introduction 394

Unhappiness: Man's u. . . . comes of his greatness 107

Unhappy: instinct for being u. 353
till his death be called u. 66

Unimportance: u. of events 181

Unintelligent: u. . . . as an ordinary young Englishman 27

Unite: u. and lead 214

United States: I believe in the U.S. 324

Unity: no style where there is no u. 441
u. which is God 43

Universe: corner of the u. . . . certain of improving 240
u. is the property 189

Universities: state of both his u. 422

Unknown: tread safely into the u. 222

Unmetaphorical: u. style 106

Unprepared: courage of the u. 59

Unremembered: feelings too of u. pleasure 452

Unremembering: u. hearts and heads 457

Unseen: u. before by Gods 257

Unsought: love . . . giv'n u. is better 376

Unspeakable: u. in full pursuit 465

Upper: u. room at midnight 28

Upright: man of u. life 235

Use: u. we make of it 312

Used: u. to be so 312

Useful: beautiful is as u. as the u. 237

Useless: lodg'd with me u. 310
u. each without 278

Uses: to what base u. we may return 364

Usher's: wife at U. Well 43

Usurous: fed with . . . u. hand 57

Usurp: u. the land 215

V

Vacancies: how are v. to be obtained 246

Vain: v. is now the burning 258

Vainly: v. men themselves amaze 290

Valet: hero to his v. 141

Valiant: v. never taste of death 365

Vallambrosa: Brooks in V. 305

Valley: every v. shall be exalted 243
v. of the shadow of death 339

590

Valour: better part of v. 366
deliberate v. breath'd 305
in vain doth V. bleed 310
my v. is certainly going 389
v. true is found 213
who would true v. see 77
Valuations: false v. 32
Value: v. of life is not the end 312
Vanities: guides us by v. 182
Vanity: name of V.-Fair 76
speckl'd v. will sicken 304
v. of vanities 177
Vanquished: v. . . . carried off the greatest spoils 185
woe to the V. 276
Variable: v. as the shade 359
Variety: v.'s the very spice of life 143
Vase: shatter the v. 314
Vein: blue as a v. 68
Veins: drain our dearest v. 80
v. of rhyming mother-wits 434
Velasquez: puts old V. in his place 434
Venerable: beautiful city! so v. 27
Vengeance: hand of v. found the bed 54
v. is mine 347
Venice: I stood in V. 93
Ventricle: four ∗chambers, the right v. 61
Venus: V. when she smiles 253
Verbosity: thread of his v. 369
Verisimilitude: give artistic v. 212
Verse: fetters it in v. 168

of all my v., like not a single line 403
v. is merely prose 98
v. is not a crown 228
v. may finde him 228
wanting the accomplishment of v. 449
Verses: murmur my v. 347
Vessel: gilded v. goes 218
Vexes: other v. it 257
Vice: nurseries of all v. 196
Vices: hym that my v. telleth me 115
Vicious: can't expect a boy to be v. 353
Victor: vanquished v. sunk 173
Victories: peace hath her v. 310
Victory: 'twas a famous v. 396
v. and triumph will never do't 157
Westminster Abbey or v. 316
Vigilance: condition . . . God hath given liberty . . . eternal v. 147
Vigils: Poets painful v. keep 330
Vile: vilest thing must be less v. 420
Villain: determined to prove a v. 369
Villains: v. by necessity 368
Villainy: no v. ne sayde 114
Vinegar: twenty casks of v. 225
Vintage: O for a draught of v. 259
trampled v. of my youth 439
Vintager: since Ariadne was a v. 256
591

Vintners: what the V. buy 198

Violet: perfume on the v. 368

Violins: could not make Antonio Stradivari's v. 181

Virginians: rally behind the V. 48

Virtue: cannot praise . . . cloistered v. 310

household v., most uncommon 99

if there be any v. 327

in moral v. was his speche 114

in thee was v. 58

maken v. of necessitee 115

mysterious v. of wax 78

na v. may be of price 44

V. owns a more eternal foe 383

v. she finds too painful 333

v. . . . . to admire 166

Virtues: all the v. but one 176

v. were her own 98

Virtuous: be in general v. 202

grow v. in their old age 409

v. person with a mean mind 37

Visage: of his v. children were aferd 114

Vision: latest born and loveliest v. 259

V. of the world 415

Visions: every man . . . hath v. 257

young men shall see v. 248

Visits: ceremony of receiving . . . v. 395

Vitality: v. of poison 93

Vocabulary: one-horse v. 231

v. of Bradshaw is nervous 171

Voice: melting v. through mazes 302

still small v. 263

v. I hear this passing night 259

v. of him that crieth in the wilderness 243

v. of one crying in the wilderness 293

v. of the kingdom 408

v. of the people is the v. of God 16

Voices: two v. are there 400

where airy v. lead 256

Volcano: dancing on a v. 354

Voltaire: mock on, V. 55

V. smiled 238

Volumes: Earth's v. carry 113

v. which " no gentleman's library should be without " 268

Vote: let the neighbours v. 455

never have alter'd the v. 101

one which influenced my v. 195

though we cannot out-v. them 251

Voted: v. at my party's call 212

Votes: anyone who v. Labour 313

Vow: v. to thee, my country 400

Vows: v. can't change nature 74

592

Voyage: all the v. of their life 366

take my last v. 230

Vulgar: worse than wicked ... it's v. 342

Vulgarest: survival of the v. 441

W

Wages: w. of sin is death 346

Waited: slavery of being w. upon 285

Waldo: W. is one of those people 353

Walk: w. a little faster 108

where'er you w. 334

Walking: craves wary w. 365

Wall: backs to the w. 219

Wallace: story of W. 86

wha hae wi' W. bled 80

Walls: Stone W. do not a Prison make 278

Want: House of W. 209

not what they w. 146

to get what you w. 392

w. for a common good 288

Wanting: w. that have wanted everything 223

Wanton: flies to w. boys 368

Wantonness: kindles in cloathes a w. 229

sing of cleanly-w. 229

Wants: everything that he w. 237

War: all whom w. ... hath slain 165

easy to begin a w. 354

except the British W. Office 377

first invented w. 288

god of w. is drunk 54

I should be much for open W. 306

image of w. 396

in many a w. it has been the vanquished 185

let slip the dogs of w. 365

magnificent but it is not w. 60

neither shall they learn w. 242

never was a good w. 201

no less glorious than ... w. 55

Power and W. 264

prepare for w. 426

tell us all about the w. 396

W. but endless w. still breed 310

w. ... is all hell 390

w. is regarded as wicked 441

w. is sweet to those who do not fight 192

w. lays a burden 143

W. makes rattling good history 221

w. will be dead 237

work w.'s overthrow 54

Warm: be w. but pure 98

Warrior: lay like a w. taking his rest 448

Warriors: stern joy which w. feel 357

Wars: levy cruel w. 306

w. are merry 120

w. begin in the minds of men 22

Washed: often have I w. 236

w. his hands 296

Washing: taking in one another's w. 217

Waste: lay w. our powers 449

Watched: w. that hour as it passed 336

593

Watcher: like some w. of the skies 260

Watches: w., starves, freeses 167

   with our judgements as our w. 331

Watchman: w. waketh but in vain 341

Water: don't care where the w. goes 121

   shall be in w. writ 47

   w. clears us of this deed 370

   w. that doun renneth ay 117

   w., w., everywhere 129

Waterloo: meets his W. 327

   W. was won on the playing fields 434

Waters: cast thy bread upon the w. 178

Wax: virtue of w. 78

   w. to receive 91

Way: homeward plods his weary w. 218

   I am the w. 248

   woman has her w. 231

Ways: justify the w. of God 304

   w. are w. of gentleness 400

   w. are w. of pleasantness 338

Weak: w. alone repent 94

Weaklings: w., fools and knaves 275

Wealth: routine acquisition of w. 275

   surplus w. is a sacred trust 107

   w. accumulates, and men decay 215

   w. that brings more troubles 235

   w. of nations 387

   w. . . . . progress brings 209

what is W. 435

Weapon: shield and w. 281

Weapons: w. of war perished 355

Weariness: study is the w. of the flesh 178

   the w., the fever 259

Web: tangled w. we weave 358

Wedding-Guest: W. stood still 128

Wedlock: in holy w. 136

Weed: w. instead of a fish . . . pull up 194

Weeds: worthless as withered w. 63

Weep: that I may not w. 96

   w., and you w. alone 438

   w. on Sunday 343

   w. with them that w. 347

Weight: willing to pull his w. 349

Weighty: lets the w. sink 101

Welfare: w. of the people 125

Well: do all things w. 123

   ofter of the w. 115

   w. of unconscious cerebration 245

Wench: joly w. in every toun 116

   take heed of a young w. 229

   w. is dead 288

Wept: Alexander w. 329

West: go w., young man 396

   W. is W. 264

Western: wonders of the w. world 410

Westminster: W. Abbey or victory 316

Wether: tainted w. of the flock 372

Wheels: spoke among your w. 47

Whence: w. are we 380
Where: fixed the w. and
  when 222
Whiff: w. of grapeshot 106
Whig: Tory men and W.
  measures 162
Whigs: W. admit no force
  66
Whim: w., envy, or resent-
  ment 122
Whimper: bang but a w. 182
Whine: do not sweat and w.
  437
Whirlwind: rides in the w. 13
Whisky: freedom and w.
  gang thegither 80
Whisper: hush! W. who
  dares 300
Whistle: w. owre the lave 83
White: no w. nor red 290
  w. as an angel 57
  W. Man's Burden 266
  w. shall not neutralise 74
Whites: w. of their eyes 342
Whither: w. thou goest 352
Whole: w. is equal to the
  scum 337
Whore: w. and gambler 54
Wicked: 'cause I's w.—I is
  407
  through w. language 226
  w. to deserve such pain 69
  worse than a w. 342
Wickedness: path of w. 42
  spiritual w. in high places
  191
  w. is a myth 440
Widow: here's to the w. 390
Wife: he that hath W. and
  Children 33
  in another life expect . . .
  thy w. 333
  kill a w. with kindness 375
  seafaring man . . . steer
  clear of a w. 395

Western custom of one w.
  353
W. and Children are a
  Kind of Discipline 33
w. talks Greek 249
w. wol laste 116
wind is my w. 262
Wigwam: w. of Nokomis
  278
Wilderness: voice . . . crieth
  in the w. 243
  voice . . . crying in the w.
  293
  W. is Paradise enow 197
Will: at twenty . . . w.
  reigns 202
  boy's w. is the wind's w.
  277
  man has his w. 231
  man's fantastic w. 70
  not my w., but thine 280
  Thy w. be done in earth
  294
  unconquerable W. 304
  what w. be, shall be 286
  w. in us is over-rul'd by
  fate 287
William: old, Father W. 108
Willing: Barkis is w. 156
  spirit indeed is w. 296
Win: w. or lose it all 313
  w. the Palm, the Oke 290
Wind: fair blows the w. 286
  fair stood the w. 172
  Lord was not in the w.
  263
  never hear the west w. 292
  walks upon the w. 332
  wild West W. 384
  w. and running water 111
  w. is my wife 262
  w. is to fire 88
  w.'s like a whetted knife
  292
  w. that follows fast 147

w. was a torrent of dark-
ness 317
woman's mind is like w.
344
Winds: blow, w., and crack
your cheeks 368
Windows: storied W. richly
dight 301
through w., and through
curtaines 168
Windward: w. of the law 123
Wine: come to drink the w.
39
Flask of W., a Book of
Verse 197
flown with insolence and
w. 305
mellow, like good w. 327
not look for w. 253
pass the rosy w. 159
red sweet w. of youth 64
truth in w. 329
w. and women 95
wolf's-bane . . . poisonous
w. 258
Wings: beating of his w. 61
shade of your soft w. 355
Winkie: Wee Willie W. 321
Winners: there are no w. 112
Winning: worth the wear of
w. 49
Winter: blow, thou w. wind
362
English w.—ending in July
97
if W. comes 384
it was the W. wild 304
w. is icummen in 335
w. of our discontent 369
Wisdom: bark of w.'s tree
137
bettre than w. 116
criterion of w. 79
double share of w. 308
full of potential w. 239

learn w. even from a foe 25
learned by rote, but W.
not 402
love . . . w. of the fool 249
one half . . . of thy w. 122
W. be put in a silver rod
54
w. doth live with children
451
w. is being wise in time 349
w. is oft times nearer when
we stoop 449
w. is worthless 328
W. makes him an Arke 168
w. of a great minister 254
w. of a man 190
Wise: all equally w. 180
deemed to be w. 137
he must needs be a w.
man 35
heart of the w. 137
history teaches w. men 189
I would be w. 241
some folks are w. 395
w. men from the East 293
w. want love 385
wisest of the w. may err
15
Wisest: w. man can answer
133
w. of them all profess'd
308
Wish: I w. I loved the
Human Race 344
Wishes: what a man w. 154
Wit: at thirty, the w. 202
Commendation of W. 35
in thee was w. 58
soul of w. 363
true W. is Nature to
advantage dress'd 331
w. . . . is laughing im-
moderately 393
.w. its soul 130
W.'s a feather 333

596

w.'s the noblest frailty 361
With: he that is not w. me 280
Wits: W. then Poets past 331
w. . . . to madness near 172
Witty: I am too w. 345
Wive: canna w. an' thrive 344
Wives: w. are on hand from bridal night 353
W. are young men's Mistresses 33
Woe: hideous notes of w. 97
w. unto them that join house 242
w. to the vanquished 276
Woes: w. that curse our race 210
w. that wait on Age 371
Wolf: w. also shall dwell with the lamb 242
w. on the fold 95
Wolf's-bane: neither twist w. 258
Wolves: w. behind 191
W. teare out his heart 164
Woman: bettre than a good w. 116
body of . . . feeble w. 184
dear, deluding W. 82
delicate as the reputation of a w. 79
every W. . . . a Rake 334
fat white w. 140
growing up into a pretty w. 29
love . . . improves a w. 194
man that lays his hand upon a w. 422
never yet fair w. 368
nothing lovelier can be found in w. 307
nowhere lives a w. true 167

Old W. Who Lived in a Shoe 320
she is a w. 343
she was a wonderful w. 162
silliest w. can manage a clever man 266
so unto the man is w. 278
softening in the presence of a w. 100
thy name is w. 363
what is w. 142
when it an't a w.'s 159
w. as a beautiful, romantic animal 15
w. governs America 285
w. has her way 231
w. as old as she looks 132
w. is only a w. 264
w. . . . . misfortune of knowing anything 30
w.'s preaching is like a dog's walking 220
w., therefore . . . be won 367, 375
W. . . . . uncertain, coy 359
w. wailing for her demon lover 131
W.! when I behold thee 261
w. who runs 175
w. whom thou gavest 208
worthy W. al hir lyve 114
Womanhood: I sall excuse . . . thy w. 226
Womankind: think better of w. 261
thinks the worst . . . of w. 231
Women: as w. wish to be 231
de w., dey does de talkin' 221
dream of w. whose beauty 457

597

English w. conceal their feelings 445
experience of w. 170
like untun'd golden strings all w. are 287
nonsense of the old w. 402
old w. sit, stiffly 155
opinion I have . . . of w. 262
proper function of w. 181
sung w. in three cities 335
w. and elephants never forget 353
W. and Horses 264
w. are foolish 180
w. are glad to have been asked 323
W. are like the Arts 164
w. . . . beguil'd the heart of wisest Solomon 308
w. can true converts make 194
w. come and go 182
w. desiren have sovereynetee 115
w. . . . like each other 119
w. . . . like to be married to a poem 261
w. must weep 242
w. . . . only children 119
w. pushing their husbands 155
w. sit or move 436
w. walk in public processions 437
w. who have never had a love affair 270
Wonder: I w. by my troth 165
still the w. grew 216
w. of an hour 92
Wonderful: name shall be called W. 242
Wonderland: love in summer's w. 317

Wonders: w. will never cease 175
Woo: w. her with too slavish knees 260
Wooden: lies about his w. horse 198
Woods: to the w. no more 236
to-morrow to fresh W. 303
w. shall to me answer 398
Wooed: beautiful and therefore to be w. 367
woman, therefore may be w. 375
Word: dry bones, hear the w. 194
duty . . . sublimest w. 271
every w. that proceedeth 155
I kept my w. 153
thy w. is a lamp 341
when I use a w. 109
W. was God 248
Words: choice w. . . . above the reach 450
deeds, not w. 47
glotoun of w. 269
good w. for the lips 158
let thy w. be few 178
long w. Bother me 300
woman's w. to an eager lover 111
w. are the physicians 15
w. but wind 89
w. cloth'd in reason's garb 306
w. like Nature, half reveal 413
Wordsworth: W., both are thine 400
W., Coleridge, Southey 95
W. sometimes wakes 96
Work: blessed is he who has found his w. 106
counsel—w., w., w. 53

598

day's w. is a day's w. 380
I like w. 247
lives by his own w. 132
measure not the w. 66
sympathy because he has
　to w. 349
till God's w. is unmade
　157
unless one has plenty of w.
　246
wery of w. 169
w. conquers all 427
w. hard at w. worth doing
　349
w. is prayer 21
w. shall be rewarded 122
w. without question 428
wrought at one great w.
　150
Workers: w. have nothing
　to lose but their
　chains 291
w. of the world, unite 291
Workmanship: inscrutable
　w. 450
Works: fruit of good w. 135
good w. in her Husband
　to promote 307
look on my w. 385
w. done least rapidly 72
Workshop: w. of the world
　162
World: all's right with the
　w. 73
brave new w. 375
days in this dark w. 310
fals w. is but transitory 177
glory of the w. passes 262
God so loved the w. 248
half forget what w. or
　worldling meant 260
half of the w. cannot
　understand 29
half of the w. thinks the
　tither daft 359

have a w. to win 291
I am a little w. 165
I called the New W. 104
I will move the w. 139
if all the w. were paper 21
justice . . . though the w.
　perish 195
knowledge of the w. 118
lead you to the end of the
　w. 106
leaves the w. to darkness
　218
life was spacious in the
　early w. 180
live after the w.'s opinion
　188
make this w. our hell 440
makes the w. go round 108
morning of the w. 73
new w. may be safer 165
not loved the W. 93
not too late to seek a
　newer w. 416
O blynde w. 117
pass through this w. but
　once 219
send in search of this new
　w. 306
there is no other w. 190
these laid the w. away 64
this is a puzzling w. 181
way the w. ends 182
when all the w. is young
　264
w. as made for me 395
w. forgetting 331
w. is a fine place 224
w. is an old woman 106
w. is made up . . . of fools
　76
w. is too much with us 449
w. may end to-night 71
w. passed by with lofty
　look 150
W. was all before them 308

w. will end in fire 204
w. will . . . follow only those 90
w. will little note 273
Worlds: infinite number of w. 329
so many w. 414
space may produce new W. 305
wandering between two w. 26
Worm: Hero the Conqueror W. 330
loving w. within its clod 69
w. beneath the sod 382, 388
Worship: if ye w. not 147
various modes of w. 210
Worshipped: w. Stocks and Stones 310
Worships: everybody w. me 141
Worst: do your w. 124
his w. is better than . . . best 222
Wound: willing to w. 333
Wrath: eternal w. burnt 307
I told my w. 57
sun go down upon your w. 191
Wrecks: vomits its w. 384
Wrestle: w. not against flesh 191
Wretch: w. that dares not die 84
Wrinkle: stamps the w. deeper 92
Write: I w. of youth 229
masters may conceivably w. 284
restraint with which they w. 102
takes up his pen to w. 418

Writer: good w. should be so simple 458
original w. . . . must create the taste 452
Writers: w. become more numerous 216
Writes: Moving Finger w. 198
Writing: man is tired of w. 46
true ease in w. 331
w. . . . pleased me best 223
w. that was written 147
Written: w. by people who don't understand 273
w. without effort 249
Wrong: does, not suffers w. 385
Englishman in the w. 378
w. of unshapely things 455
w. what is against it 187
Wrongs: multitude of W. 131
people's w. his own 173
Wrote: no man but a blockhead ever w. 251
Wynken: W., Blynken 321

Y

Yard: maketh oft a y. 117
Yarn: all I ask is a merry y. 292
Yarrow: bonny banks o' Y. 39
found him drown'd in Y. 42
Year: bells were ringing the Old Y. out 214
each day is like a y. 439
hansel of . . . new y. 177
y. is dying in the night 414

Years: first twenty y. are the
  longest 397
  fleeting y. are slipping 235
  O for ten y. 259
  y. like great black oxen 454
  y. steal fire 92
  y. to come seemed waste
    of breath 454
Yell: such a y. was there 358
Yelp: y. at those who refuse
  161
Yesterday: dead Y. 197
Yield: to find, and not to y.
  417
Yo: y.-ho-ho, and a bottle
  of rum 405
Yoke: cast off this Y. 307
Young: crime of being a y.
  man 328
  embarrassing y. 206
  friendly to the y. 285
  if he be caught y. 251
  Man that is y. in yeares
    35
  must they fall? the y. 91
  not so y. as she has been
    345
  to be y. was very heaven
    450
  what it was like to feel y.
    322
  when . . . world is y. 264
  world and love were y. 343
  y. and old come forth 302
  y. and so fair 232
  y. as they are painted 48
  y. can do for the old 377
  y. know everything 441

Youth: adventurous and
  honourable y. 406
  after carefree y. 20
  done it from my y. 144
  I write of y. 229
  in the days of my y. 397
  measure of our y. 265
  now leiff thi y. 57
  O y., be glad 226
  thoughts of y. are long 277
  to y. . . . three words 53
  waste an eternal y. 442
  Y. and Pleasure meet 92
  y. had the knowledge 192
  y. is full of pleasance 374
  y., large, lusty, loving 438
  y. means love 74
  Y. of a Nation are the
    Trustees 162
  Y. on the prow 218
  y.'s a stuff will not endure
    375
  y. shows but half 73
  y. is the time to go
    flashing 406
  y. will be served 60
  y. will stand foremost 383

Z

Zeal: holy mistaken z. 254
Zealots: graceless z. fight
  332
Zenith: dropt from the Z.
  305
Zenocrate: Z., lovelier than
  the love of Jove 288

601

INDEX TO FOREIGN QUOTATIONS

FRENCH

Absence: a. est à l'amour 88

Accuse: j'a. 458

Action: préfère la pensée à l'a. 43

Adieu: que signifie a. 43

Aime: dupé par ce qu'on aime 312

Ame: faut une â. de même 312

Amiral: tuer de temps en temps un a. 428

Amour: absence est à l'a. 88
a. demande un peu d'avenir 103

Ane: de la peau de lion, l'â s'étant vêtu 199

Anglais: A. sont occupés 313
sombre A. 429

Animal: a. est très méchant 19

Appétit: a. vient en mangeant 343

Attaque: quand on l'a. 19

Audace: encore de l'a. 149

Bâton: b. de maréchal de France 59

Beau: b. aussi utile que l'utile 237

Beauté b. . . . frêle ornement 312

Boutique: réserver une arrière b. 312

Boutiquiers: nation de b. 59

Brave: b. l'évite 429

Brioche: qu'ils mangent de la b. 286

Certitude: là était la c. 103

Change: plus ça c. 255

Changé: c. tout cela 312

Chansons: tout finit par des c. 47

Chevalier: c. sans peur 19

Clémence: c. est la plus belle marque 140

Cléopâtre: nez de C. 325

Coeur: c. a ses raisons 325

Commencement: c. de la fin 411

Courage: quant au c. moral 59

Crainte: c. suit la crime 429

Crime: pour la c. unis 429

Critique: bon c. . . . raconte les aventures 201

Déluge: après nous le d. 330

Dieu: D. et mon droit 345
si D. n'existait pas 428

Dimanche: il pleurera 343

Dormeurs: d. sont incapables de rien 225

Eclat: é. d'un moment 312

Ecrire: homme est las d'é. 46

Embarras: E. de Richesse 17

Enfants: e. terribles 206

Epée: coups d'é. 150

Epingle: pas de coups d'é. 150

Esclave: sans en être l'e.103

Etat: E. c'est moi 278

Face: f. de la terre aurait changé 325

Farce: f. est jouée 343

Femme: en un mot, elle est f. 343

Fers: partout il est dans les f. 225

Fin: plus f. qu'un autre 270

Français: tout soldat f. 59

Frisson: air est plein du f. 46

Génie: vous vous croyez un grand g. 47

Gloire: aucun chemin de fleurs . . . à la g. 199
g. des grands hommes 270

Grands: sottises des G. 199

Guerre: ce n'est pas la g. 60

Hasard: h. . . . le pseudonyme de Dieu 201

Heureux: jamais si h. 269

Homme: h. . . . méchant animal 312

Idées: l'invasion des i. 237

Improviste: courage de l'i. 59

Infâme: écrasez l'i. 428

Intérêts: divisés d'i. 429

Invasion: résiste à l'i. des armées 237

Ironie: i. est le fond 43

Jardin: cultiver notre j. 428

Jeunesse: si j. savoit 192

Jours: tous les j. 141

Juger: j. des choses grandes 312

Lâche: l. fuit en vain 429

Laissez: l. faire, l. passer 342

Liberté: établissons notre vraie l. 312
L.! Egalité! Fraternité 21
L. est née en Angleterre 429
l.! que de crimes 346

Libre: homme est né l. 350

Lion: peau de l. 199

Longue: fait celle-ci plus l. 325

Magnifique: m. mais ce n'est pas la guerre 60

Manger: faut m. pour vivre 311

Mangeurs: grands m. . . . incapables 225

Mariage: m. . . . pas un badinage 312

Messe: Paris vaut bien une m. 225

Métier: bien faire son m. 103
mon m. . . . c'est vivre 312

Mieux: je vais de m. en m. 141
tout est pour le m. 428

Monarque: connaître un vrai m. 140

Mort: m. ne surprend point le sage 199
m. serait-elle un adieu 43

Moutons: revenons à nos m. 22

Moyens: m. . . . pour l'acquérir 270

Naître: peine de n. 47

Neiges: où sont les n. d'antan 426

Nostalgie: n. de la boue 28

Ordre: tout n'est qu'o. 46

Passeront: ils ne p. pas 326

Pensée: préfère la p. à l'action 43

Penser: p., c'est voir 43

Peste: p. avait enlevé 103

Petits: P. ont pâti 199

Peut-être: chercher un grand p. 343

Plaisirs: tous les p. normaux 103

Pleurer: être obligé d'en p. 46

Plie: je p. et ne romps pas 199

Polis: pas les temps d'être p. 313

Pouvoir: p. de l'amour 103

Prose: je dis de la p. 311

Providence: caractère de la P. 43

Pseudonyme: hasard . . . le p. de Dieu 201

Pyramides: du haut de ces
p. 59

Raisonnable: plus r. en
France 429

Retour: r. de toutes choses
43

Richesse: Embarras de R. 17

Rideau: tirez le r. 343

Ridicule: du sublime au r. 59

Rire: je me presse de r. 46

Rit: qui r. d'autrui 311
tel qui r. vendredi 343

Romps: je plie et ne r. pas
199

Ronsard: R. me célébrait
347

Siècles: quarante s. vous
contemplent 59

Sommeil: du s. des justes 343

Souvenirs: j'ai plus de s. 46]

Sublime: du s. au ridicule
59

Tendresse: c'est la t.
humaine 104

Tous: t. pour un, un pour t.
175

Unité: u. qui est Dieu 43

Utile: beau est aussi u. que
l'u. 237

Utilité: u. du vivre 312

Valet de chambre: grand
homme pour son v.
141

Vent: ce qu'est au feu le v.
88

Vieille: quand vous serez
bien v. 347

Vieillesse: si v. pouvoit 192

Vivre: faut manger pour v.
311

mon métier et mon art,
c'est v. 312

utilité de v. 312

Volcan: dansons sur un v.
354

GERMAN

Anders: ich kann nicht a.
281

Bedürfnissen: jedem nach
seinen B. 291

Blut: B. und Eisen 53

Burg: feste B. . . . Gott 281

Charakter: C. in dem Strom
der Welt 215

Enzwei': e. und gebiete 214

Erfahrung: E. aber and die
Geschichte 223

Fähigkeiten: jeder nach
seinen F. 291

Freude: F., schöner Götterfunken 355

Geschichte: alte G. 223
Erfahrung aber und die G.
223

Gottesmühlen: G. mahlen
langsam 276

Irrt: es i. der Mensch 214

Kunst: so muss die K.
entweichen 356

Lebens: grün des L. goldner
Baum 214

Märchen: M. aus alten
Zeiten 223

Mensch: M. . . . überwunden
werdensoll 317

Menschen: alle M. werden
Brüder 355

Natur: und siegt N. 356

Proletarier: P. aller Länder,
vereinigt euch 291

Religion: R. . . . das Opium
des Volkes 291

Röslein: sah ein Knab' ein
R. 214]

Ruhm: nicht der R. 214

Spitzkugeln: lieber S. 53

Strebt: so lang er s. 214

Talent: es bildet ein T. 215

Tat: die T. ist alles 214

Theorie: grau, . . . ist alle T. 214

Traurig: das ich so t. bin 223

Ubermenschen: ich lehre euch den U. 317

Vater: V. mit seinem Kind 214

Verein: v. und leite 214

Vernünftig: was v. ist, das ist wirklich 223

Welt: W. zu gewinnen 291

Weltgeschichte: W. ist das Weltgericht 356

Wirklich: was w. ist, das ist vernünftig 223

Zeit: Z. ist mein Vermächtniss 215

GREEK

Eureka: e. 24

Kosmopolites: K. 161

ITALIAN

Arte: a. vostra quella, quanto puote 148

Compagnia: ahi fiera c. 148

Cortesia: e c. fu in lui esser villano 148

Dio: arte a D. quasi è nipote 148

Dir: lascia d. le genti 148

Duro: com' è d. calle 148

Fama: in f. non si vien 148

Muove: e pur si m. 206

Poeta: on orate l'altissimo p. 148

Rifiuto: il gran r. 148

Rossore: bello è il r. 215

Sale: come sa di s. lo pane altrui 148

Santi: ma nella chiesa coi s. 148

Sera: che s., s. 286

Speranza: la sciate ogni s. 147

questi non hanno s. di morte 148

Taverna: in t. coi ghiottoni 148

Torre: sta come t. ferma 149

Trovato: è molto ben t. 22

Vero: se non è v. 22

Villano: e cortesia fu in lui esser v. 148

LATIN

Acu: tetigisti a. 329

Africa: ex A. semper aliquid novi 329

Alea: iacta a. est 101

Ama: a. et fac quod vis 29

Amantibus: legem dat a. 58

Amor: major lex a. est 58 omnia vincit A. 427

Angli: quod A. vocarentur 218

Anguis: latet a. in herba 427

Anni: fugaces . . . labuntur a. 235

Artifex: qualis a. pereo 316

Astra: itur ad a. 427

Audi: a. partem alteram 28

Averni: facilis descensus A. 427

Avis: rara a. in terris 254

Basia: da mi b. mille 111

Beata: b. sors omnis est 58

Bellum: dulce b. inexpertis 192

praeparet b. 426

Bono: cui b. 126

605

Bonum: summum b. 125
Brute: et tu , B. 101
Caecos: inter c. luscum regnare 191
Caesar: aut C. aut nihil 59
Calamus: c. saevior ense patet 87
Canem: cave c. 326
Carthaginem: C. esse delendam 110
Castas: delectant etiam c. 323
Castitatem: da mihi c. 28
Circenses: panem et c. 255
Cogito: c., ergo sum 155
Concordia: c. discors 234
Consules: caveant c. 19
Continentiam: da mihi castitatem et c. 28
Cordi: virginibus c. grataque 323
Corpore: in c. sano 255
Cunctando: c. restituit rem 191
Cycno: nigroque simillima c. 254
Danaos: timeo D. 426
Dat: bis d. qui cito d. 411
Desperandum: nil d. Teucro duce 235
Despicit: qui omnes d. 16
Diem: carpe d. 235
Dis: d. aliter visum 426
Diserta: cena d. tua est 289
Displicet: omnibus d. 16
Divites: quos odisse d. solent 327
Divitias: d. operosiores 235
Ecclesiam: salus extra e. non est 28
Exilio: propterea morior in e. 218
Fatum: te prae litteras f. esse 327

Felicem: fuisse f. 58
Felicitas: curiosa f. 327
Festina: f. lente 407
Forma: cordi grataque f. sua est 323
Formae: delectant etiam castas draeconia f. 323
Fortissima: f. quaeque consilia tutissima sunt 276
Fortunae: in omni adversitate f. 58
Gallia: G. est omnis divisa 101
Gaudeamus: g. igitur 20
Gloria: dat mihi g. vires 337
sic transit g. mundi 262
Gloriam: ad majorem Dei g. 18
Graecia: G. capta ferum victorem cepit 234
Gramina: redeunt iam g. campis 236
Grammatici: g. certant 234
Homerus: bonus dormitat H. 234
Homines: quot h. 417
Homo: h. sum 417
Humani: h. nil a me alienum puto 417
Ignotus: i. moritur sibi 361
Imperii: capax i. nisi imperasset 411
Impune: nemo me i. lacessit 21
Iniquitatem: odivi i. 218
Integer: i. vitae scelerisque purus 235
Irae: amantium i. amoris integratio 417
Iter: magnum i. ascendo 337
Justitia: fiat j. 195

606

Justitiam: dilexi j. 218
Juventutem: post jucundam
   j. 20
Kalendas: ad Graecas K.
   101
Labor: l. omnia vincit 427
Laborare: l. est orare 21
Lacessit: nemo me impune
   l. 21
Lacrimae: sunt l. rerum 426
Latericiam: l. accepisset 101
Legatus: l. est vir bonus 453
Lex: salus populi suprema
   est l. 125
Lis: sub iudice l. est 234
Litteras: te prae l. fatuum
   esse 327
Litteratum: l. esse 327
Lupi: a tergo l. 191
Luscum: inter caecos l.
   regnare 191
Lyricis: quodsi me l. vatibus
   inseres 234
Marmoream: m. se relin-
   quere 101
Meminisse: haec olim m.
   iuvabit 426
Mens: m. cuiusque is est
   quisque 126
   m. sana in corpore sano
   255
   m. sibi conscia recti 426
Metuant: oderint dum. m.
   13
Metuunt: quem m., oderunt
   191
Miles: m. gloriosus 329
Miserum: nihil est m. 58
Monumentum: exegi m. aere
   perennius 235
   si m. requiris 453
Mores: O m. 126
Mori: pro patria, m. 235
Morituri: m. te salutant
   408

Mors: m. gravis incubat 361
   pallida M. 235
Mulier: m. cupido quod
   dicit amanti 111
Necessitas: n. non habet
   legem 411
Nimis: ut nequid n. 417
Nives: diffugere n. 236
Oderint: o. dum metuant
   13
Oderunt: quem metuunt, o.
   191
Opes: magnas inter o. inops
   235
Orare: laborare est o. 21
Pacem: p. appellant 411
   qui desiderat p. 426
Panem: p. et circenses 255
Patria: pro p. mori 235
   pro p., pro liberis 354
Postero: quam minimum
   credula p. 235
Potatori: deus sit propitius
   isti p. 25
Praecipitium: a fronte p. 191
Probae: quam necesse est p.
   354
Procul: p. este, profani 427
Pulveris: p. exigui iactu
   compressa 427
Punica: P. fide 354
Quasiveris: nec te q. extra
   326
Res: in medias r. 234
Rogatae: gaudent tamen
   esse r. 323
Romae: si fueris R. 17
Romanus: civis R. sum 126
Rumoresque: r. senum sever-
   iorum 111
Saltare: neminem s. sobrius
   126
   s. elegantius 354
Salus: s. extra ecclesiam
   non est 28

s. populi 125
Scientia: ipsa s. potestas est
36
Securus: s. indicat orbis
terrarum 28
Simia: s., quam similis turpis-
sima bestia 191
Sobrius: neminem saltare s.
126
Solitudinem: ubi s. faciunt
411
Sutor: ne supra crepidam
s. iudicaret 329
Taberna: in t. mori 24
Tempora: O t. 126
t. mutantur 22, 323
Tempus: fugit inreparabile t.
427
t. edax rerum 323
Timor: t. Mortis conturbat
me 177
Troia: ubi T. fuit 323
Urbem: u. . . . excoluit adeo
101
Vae: v. Victis 276
Vento: in v. . . . scribere
oportet 111
Vici: veni, vidi, v. 101

Vino: in v. veritas 329
Virtute: macte nova v. 427
Vivamus: v. . . . atque
amemus 111
Vox: v. populi, v. dei 16

SPANISH

Caballero: C. de la Triste
Figura 111
Figura: la Triste F. 111
Hambre: mejor salsa . . .
el h. 112
Intervalos: lleno de lúcido i.
112
Linages: dos l. sólos 112
Loco: es un entreverado l.
112
Mucho: hacen un m. 112
Pintores: buenos p. imitan
la naturaleza 112
Pucos: muchos p. hacen un
mucho 112
Salsa: mejor s. del mundo
112
Tenir: el t. y el no t. 112